THE GUINNESS
DRINKING
COMPANION

Leslie Dunkling

THE GUINNESS
DRINKING
COMPANION

◆

Leslie Dunkling

GUINNESS PUBLISHING

Editor: Beatrice Frei
Design and Layout: Stonecastle Graphics Ltd.
Picture Research: P. Alexander Goldberg and James
M. Clift

Typeset in Century Oldstyle, Futura and Optima by
Ace Filmsetting Ltd., Frome, Somerset.
Printed and bound in Great Britain by
The Bath Press, Bath

A catalogue record for this book is available from the
British Library.

ISBN 0-85112-988-9

ACKNOWLEDGEMENTS

Special thanks are due to Peter Mitchell, Kevin
Baker and Martin Cannon (Guinness), John Foley
and Gordon Wright. Beatrice Frei has, as usual,
meticulously edited the entire text. The author also
gratefully acknowledges the information generously
supplied by Sue Garland (Guinness), Nicholas Barritt
Redman (Whitbread), Sarah Carr (Home Brewery),
Jenny Thirsk (Theakston), Ken Thomas (Courage),
P.F. Smith (Ruddles), B.R. Hanks (Grand
Metropolitan), The Archivist (Joshua Tetley), Andrew
Sangster (CAMRA), The Brewers' Society.
Sources for tables on pp. 23, 114, 167 and 202 are
H.M. Customs and Excise and Office of Population
Censuses and Surveys.

PICTURE CREDITS

The Advertising Archives; The Bridgeman Art
Library; Cheltenham Art Gallery and Museums;
Christopher Wood Gallery, London; Explorer
Archives; Guinness Brewing Worldwide Limited;
The Hulton-Deutsch Collection; Image Select
International; Mary Evans Picture Library;
Picturepoint Limited; Royal Holloway and Bedford
New College, Surrey; Schuler Wine, Lukas Zihlmann;
Victoria Wine Company; Wolverhampton Art Gallery,
Staffs. Woodcuts from *1800 Woodcuts by Thomas
Bewick and his School*, Dover Publications, Inc., N.Y.

Contents

PREFACE

COMPARED to previous generations, most of us today are reasonably well-informed about what we eat. I doubt if that is true about what we drink. Recent studies by the Portman Group, Mori and an Edinburgh University alcohol research group, for example, have all shown that three out of four drinkers are unaware of the alcoholic strength of what they normally drink. Would such drinkers be able to explain, then, the difference between bitter, stout and lager, or describe the simple processes by which those beers are made? Could they say why some wines are 'drier' than others and what puts the sparkle into champagne? Could the more literate amongst them explain the 'sack' that Falstaff loves, or the 'purl' drunk in Dickensian pubs? And why was James Bond wrong to specify 'shaken and not stirred'?

I mention these last examples because we constantly come across other people's drinking in books and films as well as real life. Apart from any drinking we do ourselves, we are surrounded by drinks and drinkers, just as our ancestors were before us. Even if we have decided not to drink, we really should know something about the subject.

I hope that this book will interest the kind of drinker I have been most of my life – casual and rather indiscriminate. My drinking biography accurately reflects my life, as it does for all of us. I have lived in four countries and visited about thirty others, and you do not visit a country without sampling its drinks. In China, for instance, it was Maotai, but it was also the local beer. I drank it as I had a game of darts in The Bell, the pub which is inside the British Embassy compound in Beijing. It said 'Peking beer' on the label and came in a generous size of bottle. The beer was pleasant enough, but as usual I lost the game of darts.

As with most people, my memories of drinking tend to be of that kind – associated with pleasant social occasions. Moderate drinking in such circumstances is very definitely one of life's pleasures. This book is meant to add in some small way to the enjoyment of a modest tipple.

INTRODUCTION

SEVERAL thousand years ago our ancestors noticed an interesting phenomenon. In certain circumstances, when cereal grains became saturated with rain water, a liquid was produced which was stimulating to drink. Something similar happened with honey and the juice of fruits, especially the grape. Long before they understood how fermentation produced alcohol, our ancestors benefited from and appreciated its effects. It was a gift from the gods.

It was a gift that, in part, had to be returned. In most primitive religions, libations were offered to the ever-thirsty deities. The Greeks and Romans identified Dionysus, or Bacchus, as the god of wine and accorded him annual festivals.

All this may seem to belong to the remote past, but William Hone relates in his *Every-day Book* that within living memory English farmers would go to their orchards on Twelfth Night with a pitcher of cider. There they would circle one of the best trees, toasting it and wishing it prosperity. Whatever remained in the pitcher would then be 'given' to the tree, or to the hamadryad, the tree-god, that dwelt within it.

LIBATIONS TO THE GODS

John Steinbeck, in *To A God Unknown*, describes a scene in California: 'To start the fiesta Joseph did a ceremonial thing Old Juan had told him about, a thing so ancient and natural that Joseph seemed to remember it. He took a tin cup from the table and went to the wine cask. The red wine sang and sparkled into it. When it was full, he raised the cup level with his eyes and then poured it on the ground. Again he filled the cup, and this time drank it, in four thirsty gulps. Father Angelo nodded his head and smiled at the fine way in which the thing was done.

'When his ceremony was finished, Joseph walked to the tree and poured a little wine on its bark, and he heard the priest's voice speaking softly beside him: "This is not a good thing to do, my son." Joseph whirled on him: "What do you mean? There was a fly in the cup!" But Father Angelo smiled wisely and a little sadly at him. "Be careful of the groves, my son. Jesus is a better saviour than a hamadryad".'

But Christianity, too, has its vinous traditions. In *Monsignor Quixote*, Graham Greene has a Communist mayor and a priest share a bottle of wine. Greene says: 'It is strange how quickly a bottle can be emptied when one debates without rancour. The Major poured the last few drops upon the ground. "For the gods," he said. "Mind you, I say the gods not God. The gods drink deep, but your solitary God is, I'm sure, a tee-totaller."

"You are saying what you know to be wrong,

MEAD

Mead is one of the oldest alcoholic drinks, made by fermenting a mixture of honey and water. It is sometimes compared to a light Moselle wine. The classical form of the word is hydromel, 'water-honey'.

There are several variations of the drink. When herbs are added, the drink becomes metheglin. Apple juice has been used instead of water to produce a drink variously called cyser, cyster (the words are probably variants of 'cider'). Other fruit juices have also been substituted for water and the result is called melomel.

Sancho. You studied at Salamanca. You know very well that God, or so I believe, and perhaps you once believed, becomes wine every morning and every evening in the Mass."'

Apart from the use of wine in the chief Christian sacrament, Jesus's first miracle, at Cana in Galilee, was to turn water into wine for the wedding feast. It was a clear acceptance of the fact that drinking should accompany a celebration. In many other passages, the Bible refers to drinking as a normal part of life and even comments on its medicinal aspects, though it does not forget to warn of its dangers. The *Book of Genesis*, for instance, tells us that after the Flood, Noah planted a vineyard. It goes on to say that in due time he became rather shamefully drunk.

STARTING OUT

Noah, we may say, should have known better, but like most of us, he had to learn by experience. Even in these enlightened times, drinking is not one of those subjects we tend to discuss with our children. There are obvious parallels with sex education. In that area, too, we are dealing with one of life's natural pleasures which can, in certain circumstances, cause terrible problems. Talking about it, trying to instil a cautious attitude without setting up crippling inhibitions, is a difficult and delicate matter. There must be many parents who cross their fingers and hope, in matters of sex as well as drinking, that somehow their children will sort it all out for themselves.

They usually do, but not without a few adventures along the way. An anthology of early drinking experiences would probably make entertaining reading and arouse a few memories. In *Edens Lost*, for instance, Sumner Locke Elliott describes a 17-year-old boy drinking Medoc for the first time: 'He was slowing down, delightfully, into a state of rapture so that smiles kept bursting over his face for no reason, smile after smile burst from him like hiccups.' Alas, it is not smiles which burst from him later in the bathroom.

David Copperfield has a similar experience when he hosts his first dinner party. Charles Dickens was no doubt thinking of his own young manhood as he describes the wine circulating with ever-increasing speed. The reaction inevitably sets in as time passes: 'Somebody was leaning out of my bedroom window, refreshing his forehead against the cool stone of the parapet, and feeling the air upon his face. It was myself.'

Still later Copperfield remembers 'somebody, lying in my bed, at cross purposes, in a feverish dream all night – the bed a rocking sea, that was never still! How, as that somebody slowly settled down into myself, did I begin to parch, and feel as if my outer covering of skin were a hard board;

SERVING AS AN EXAMPLE

The Lacedaemons [Spartans] sometimes purposely caused their rustic servants to be made very drunk, and so to be brought in at their common dinners, to the intent that young men beholding the deformity and hasty fury of them that were drunkards should live the more soberly, and should eschew drunkenness as a thing foul and abominable.

Sir Thomas Elyot *The Book Named The Governor*

my tongue the bottom of an empty kettle, furred with long service, and burning up over a slow fire; the palms of my hands, hot plates of metal which no ice could cool!'

Other writers comment on the innocence of young drinkers: 'Perhaps a long drink'. He knew that was all right. Real drinkers scarcely ever drank long drinks.

Stanley Price *A World of Difference*

FLIRTATION WITH SIN

Tallulah Bankhead has a chapter in her autobiography, *Tallulah*, which is called 'Flirtation With Sin'. She talks of the beginning of her career, when she shared an apartment with Bijou Martin, another aspiring young actress. 'One afternoon Biji came home with a bottle of port and suggested we sample it . . . We had no wine glasses so we used our tooth-brush tumblers. Biji and I filled our mugs to the brim and tossed them off. I had no reaction. Disappointed, I said, "Let's try another." A third beaker, and the roof fell in. Both of us were so tight we couldn't walk. We had to crawl through the hall to our bedrooms on our hands and knees.

'The room was spinning like a top. In my agony I heard Biji moaning. I crawled back down the hall. Biji was trying to get into the bathtub. "I want to take a shower," she pleaded. I saw no flaw in this, though she was fully clothed. I put her hat on her head, she clambered into the vat, and I turned on the water. Then I crawled away to die . . .'

Drinking horn at Queen's College, Oxford.

'I'd like some Montrachet.' Magnus leaned forward eagerly. 'Would you really?' he asked. 'It's a magnificent wine: I had no idea you knew it. I thought your repertory consisted of Champagne and Liebfraumilch and Benedictine.' 'You don't know everything about me,' said Margaret crossly. Magnus's estimate of her knowledge of wine had been very nearly correct: she had overheard, in casual conversation, the name Montrachet . . .
Eric Linklater *Magnus Merriman*

'I'd like some gin and ginger ale, with very little gin.' 'That's a college girl's drink,' he said. 'You must still be in college.' 'Why, I am, as a matter of fact,' she said. 'Next year will be my second year at Vassar.'
John P. Marquand *Women and Thomas Harrow*

'Anything in it, Sylvia? Splash of something? Orange? Good Lord, I didn't think anyone over the age of sixteen drank gin and orange.'
Hilary Mantel *Every Day is Mother's Day*

HIT OR MISS

All of this speaks of the hit-or-miss nature of early drinking. Spirits are not really the right drink for beginners – however they are diluted – yet they are consumed in great quantities by the young. The drinks have names which are vaguely familiar amongst hundreds of others that are not. The choice, on that first exciting visit to a pub, is bewildering and asking for advice embarrassing.

Mary McCarthy, in *The Company She Keeps*, describes a rare act of confession, when a young man at a dinner party announces that he doesn't drink: 'This act of abstention was a challenge to everyone at the table, an insult to the host. "You don't *drink*?" said a woman at last in a loud, bewildered voice. "I drank a cocktail," he admitted. "It went to my head. If I took any more I might make a fool of myself." He twisted his head and looked up at Pflaumen with a disarming boyish grin. "You'll have to give me a course in the art of drinking."'

Somehow, thankfully, most young people muddle through without such a course, useful though it would be. For teenagers, it would have to begin

EMPTYING ONE'S GLASS

My grandfather, as a student at the regular university 'drunks', had a habit of pouring superfluous beer into his eighteen-fortyish riding-boots, when nobody was watching.

Robert Graves *Goodbye to all That*

It was terrible gin. It burned her throat till her eyes watered. Quickly, when the woman was not watching, she emptied the cup out into the sound hole of the guitar.

Truman Capote *A Tree of Night*

'The local wine's a bit too vigorous for me, although it's done wonders for that plant.' He pointed to a mauve chrysanthemum in a pot on the table. 'It was quite dead when I arrived.'

Jilly Cooper *Prudence*

with basics, not launch into the subtle differences between one wine and another as existing courses do. Something along the lines indicated in this scene from Godfrey Smith's *The Business of Loving* might be suitable: 'I can buy you a shandy.' 'What exactly is a shandy, Pop?' 'A shandy is a mixture of beer and ginger beer generally; sometimes beer and lemonade. A marvellous thirst-quencher. We used to drink it on route marches during the war.' 'But I can't drink *beer*, can I, Pop?' 'Why ever not? Got to start sooner or later.'

Margaret Powell, in *Below Stairs*, describes another kind of parental sheltering: 'I used to go into a pub on a Saturday night with my Mum and Dad. It would be crammed with people, you'd stand there holding your glass right up close to your chest, but you felt happy and it was lively, it was life. That's how I started drinking. I liked the life of the pubs, and I still do.'

CHOICE OF DRINK

A great many people who would echo those words drink in a haphazard manner and know very little about what they are drinking. Nor could they always adequately explain why they have chosen one drink rather than another. This book is meant to help in that direction, to say something about the drinks themselves and to provide at least a part-explanation of why we drink what we do. There are broad historical reasons why some drinks are more readily available to us than others, but we have to consider as well the sociology and psychology of drinking. A drink is chosen not just for its taste: fashion, convention, social aspiration or downright snobbery is likely to influence our choice.

There is nothing new in this. William Thackeray, in *Vanity Fair*, describes Miss Crawley's reaction when she learns that her nephew has been drinking gin: 'Had he drunk a dozen bottles of claret, the old spinster could have pardoned him. Mr Fox and Mr Sheridan drank claret. Gentlemen drank claret. But eighteen glasses of gin consumed among boxers in an ignoble pot-house – it was an odious crime, and not to be pardoned readily.'

A different way of recognising the social levels of different drinks is shown by A.J. Cronin, in *The Citadel*. His hero Andrew Manson is from a working-class background, but begins to be successful. Cronin records the drinks that mark his rise through the social ranks – his first cocktail, his first glass of Amontillado vintage sherry, his first bottle of vintage wine in an expensive restaurant. Manson's wife is quietly distressed that he should consider such things important. Ultimately he comes to share her view.

Henry James, in *The American*, delicately sneers: 'Mr Stanislas Kapp was the son and heir of a rich brewer of Strasbourg. Although he passed in a general way for a good fellow, he had already been observed to be quarrelsome after dinner. *"Que voulez-vous?"* said Valentin. "Brought up on beer, he can't stand Champagne".'

BLOODY DRUNK

The phrase 'bloody drunk' occurs fairly frequently in literature of the late 17th and early 18th centuries. It probably means 'as drunk as a blood', where 'blood' in turn refers to one of the young, aristocratic rowdies who were a nuisance at the time. They were young men of good blood, hence their name. 'Bloody drunk' was therefore the equivalent of 'as drunk as a lord', though the latter phrase was not recorded until much later.

It is likely that 'bloody' was soon re-interpreted in phrases like 'bloody drunk'. It was taken to be an intensifier, with a meaning like 'very'. Later, when any references to the distasteful subject of blood were banned from polite conversation, 'bloody' became the taboo word it remains today.

TYPING THE DRINKERS

To make judgements about people on the basis of what they normally drink is commonplace. We put the beer-drinkers and wine-drinkers into markedly different social categories. We probably think of gin-and-tonic people and whisky people as different types of personality. We instinctively categorise drinkers in another way as beginners, occasional or casual drinkers, interested drinkers, serious drinkers and alcoholics.

Most of us are probably occasional or casual drinkers, mildly lubricating friendly conversations in a pub or complementing our food in a restaurant. We drink to quench our thirst on a hot day and to relax at a party. Drinks are brought into the house when needed and when funds permit.

Interested drinkers are likely to be wine buffs who study vintage charts. They swirl their wine before nosing it and spend their vacations visiting châteaux. There they tramp through cool cellars which they try to recreate in miniature at home.

Serious drinkers automatically head for a bar in

the interludes that punctuate their days. They have been drinking hard for many years, often for what they perceive to be professional reasons, and have usually built up a resistance to alcohol so that they do not easily show its effects. They drink doubles because 'life is too short for singles' or, if beer-drinkers, drink two-thirds of their pint and have it topped up with a liberal 'half'. The home of a well-to-do serious drinker has a fully-stocked bar and is equipped with ice-container, cocktail-shaker, strainer and other tools of the trade.

Alcoholics are addicts who need expert help. There are those who see alcoholism as a psychological problem. Others believe it to be more a matter of individual biochemistry and would say that alcoholics are born, not made. Either way, the person concerned has a serious problem. As Captain Fellows remarks in Graham Greene's *The Power and the Glory*: 'My dear, when you are older you'll understand the difference between drinking a little brandy after dinner and – well, needing it.'

DRINKING IN THE PAST

In general terms, what we would now call heavy drinking was once normal. Dickens is talking about the end of the 18th century when he says, in *A Tale of Two Cities*: 'Those were drinking days, and most men drank hard. So very great is the improvement Time has brought about in such habits, that a moderate statement of the quantity of wine and punch which one man would swallow in the course of a night, without any detriment to his reputation as a perfect gentleman, would seem, in these days, a ridiculous exaggeration. The learned profession of the law was certainly not behind any other learned profession in its Bacchanalian propensities . . .'

There is plenty of evidence in literature, published diaries and the like, to support Dickens's statement. He talks about the improvement that has occurred, yet his own characters get through prodigious amounts of brandy and gin, and are constantly ordering pints of sherry or port. Sometimes they drink more than is good for them; sometimes they are not allowed to do so. 'George Jones,' says Miss Abbey Potterson to one of her customers in 'The Six Jolly Fellowship-Porters', 'your time's up! I told your wife you should be punctual.' Captain Joey, another customer, is refused a glass of gin-and-

water. 'You have had as much as will do you good,' says Miss Abbey, firmly.

ANOTHER DRINK?

'Would you care for another drink?'
'Never say another, just say a drink. My father often said that another drink means you're counting the drink before.'

Peter de Polnay *The Dog Days*

'She holds up her empty glass and twists it meditatively over the table cloth. Ro waves for the waiter. She smiles gratefully.'

John Dos Passos *The Great Days*

Trotter turned his glass upside down, by way of reminding his companion that he had nothing left wherewith to slake his thirst. Sam observed the hint; and feeling the delicate manner in which it was conveyed, ordered the pewter vessel to be re-filled.

Charles Dickens *The Pickwick Papers*

As R. W. delicately signified that his glass was empty by throwing back his head and standing the glass upside down on his nose and upper lip, it might have been charitable in Mrs. Wilfer to suggest replenishment. But that heroine briefly suggesting 'bedtime' instead, the bottles were put away, and the family retired.

Charles Dickens *Our Mutual Friend*

'Viola dear, are you trampling your own grapes?' cried a member of the Economics Department, entering the kitchen with an empty glass.

Malcolm Bradbury *Eating People is Wrong*

ETYMOLOGICAL DRINKING

The etymology of 'whisky' takes us to Irish *uisge bheatha* or Gaelic *usque baugh*, 'water of life'. How many of the following drinks can you recognise from the meanings of their names?

1. 'Golden drink' or (according to some authorities) 'the drink that satisfies'

2. 'Lawyer's drink'

3. 'Burnt wine'

4. 'Grape stalk'

5. 'Strong drink'

6. 'Glow wine'

7. 'Green wine'

8. 'Witch'

9. 'Bleeding'

10. 'Juice' or 'sweat'

ANSWERS

1. 'Yellow or golden drink' is the literal meaning of Gaelic *dram buidhe. An dram buidheach*, in the same language, is said to mean 'the drink that satisfies'. It is not clear which of these led to Drambuie, the proprietary name for the liqueur Scotch whisky which also contains heather, honey and herbs. It has been marketed commercially since the 1890s but claims to be much older. Bonnie Prince Charlie, according to legend, presented the recipe for it in 1745 to a Mackinnon of Strathaird after the latter had helped him escape.

2. This is Advocaat, the Dutch drink made of egg yolks, sugar and brandy. Its full name in Dutch is *advocaatenborrel*, 'lawyer's or advocate's drink'. Apparently lawyers were especially fond of it at one time. It has been known in Britain since the 1930s.

3. 'Burnt wine' is the literal translation of Dutch *brandewijn*, but the first part of the word was adapted into English as brandy. Brandy is obtained by distilling fermented fruit juice (usually that of the grape). The 'burnt' description refers to the distillation process, when the liquid is heated.

4. When grapes have been pressed to extract the juice for wine-making, a residue of skins, pips, stalks and the like remains. This residue is pressed again and the juice distilled to make a rough kind of brandy. In France the resulting drink is known as *marc*. In Italy it is grappa, literally 'grape-stalk'.

5. The Hebrew word *shekar*, 'strong, fermented drink', became Greek *sikera* in the earliest translation of the Old Testament. This in turn became medieval Latin *sicera*, Old French *cisdcre*. In France the word took on the more specialised meaning of a strong drink made from fermented apple-juice. The Normans then brought the word to England where it became our cider or cyder. In early English translations of the Bible, 'cider' is sometimes used in its original general sense of 'strong drink'.

6. This is wine that glows with heat – the mulled, spiced claret still popular in Germany and known there as *Glühwein*. It is an ideal drink on a cold winter's afternoon, as I discovered when attending a football match in Munich.

7. As in English, the Portuguese word for 'green' can mean 'immature'. *Vinho verde*, therefore, is not literally green – it can be white or red – but it is a young wine that contrasts with *vinho maduro*, 'mature wine'. It is a wine to drink as soon as possible after purchase.

8. A legend says that witches once held covens on the banks of the River Sabato in Benevento, north of Naples. There they

concocted a magic potion: lovers who drank it would remain in love for ever. Giuseppe Alberti of Benevento saw the possibility of exploiting such a tale. He used some 70 or so herbs to make a liqueur and named it *Strega*, Italian for 'witch'. The liqueur has been marketed successfully since the 19th century and is usually drunk after a meal.

9. Sangria is a punch based on red wine. Properly made it will have some brandy, fruit juice and soda water added, with perhaps some slices of fruit. Its blood-like appearance caused it to be named *sangria*, a derivative of Spanish *sangre* 'blood'.

10. Arrack is mainly found in the Middle and Far East. It is variously made by distilling rice, molasses, sugar-cane or dates, though the best type is said to be based on the fermented sap of the coconut palm. The ultimate source of the name is thought to be Arabic *'araq* 'juice, sweat'.

TOBY

The Toby jug became very popular in the 18th century. It is said that in the translation of a Latin poem (1761), Francis Fawkes used the name Toby Philpot. This was later applied to the jug. Toby had earlier been associated with drinking by Shakespeare, in the character of Sir Toby Belch. Sir Toby is last seen in *Twelfth Night* in a far from sober state.

(Right) A typical Toby jug.

In *Our Mutual Friend* Dickens writes with particular affection and humour of the Fellowship-Porters and its landlady. The pub stands beside the Thames. Its bar – one 'to soften the human breast' – is filled with 'corpulent little casks, and by cordial-bottles radiant with fictitious grapes in bunches, and by lemons in nets, and by biscuits in baskets, and by the polite beer-pulls that made low bows when customers were served with beer.' It has 'red curtains matching the noses of the regular customers'.

As for the landlady, 'being known on her own authority as Miss Abbey Potterson, some waterside heads which (like the water) were none of the clearest, harboured muddled notions that, because of her dignity and firmness, she was named after, or in some sort related to, the Abbey of Westminster. But Abbey was only short for Abigail . . .'

Dickens is much quoted – distilled as it were – in this book because he deserves to be. He was an appreciative drinker himself, as the 1870 auction-list of his Gad's Hill cellar makes clear. He was also a marvellous observer of other drinkers. Because they are subjects of importance to both individuals and society, most serious writers have something to say about drinks and drinking. None that I have yet discovered is as wide-ranging, tolerant, amusing and consistently interesting as Charles Dickens.

General glossary

(There are separate glosses for words related specifically to beer, wine, spirits and cocktails. Some words that are defined in the text are not entered in the glossaries. Please see index.)

Adulteration – the debasement of a drink by adding a weaker liquid, usually water. The word 'adultery' derives from the same source. Cyril Pearl, in his *Beer, Glorious Beer!*, reveals that the addition of water to beer by publicans has long been an Australian problem. Australians drink beer at such low temperatures that changes in taste are not noticed.

Alcohol – from the Arabic words *al-koh'l*. Kohl is a black powder used as eye make-up in eastern countries. The word was later applied to other fine chemical powders, then to essences. The present meaning of alcohol derives from the phrase 'alcohol of wine', referring to the spirit obtained by distillation or rectification. By 'alcohol' we normally mean ethyl alcohol (or ethanol), which is produced as a waste product as yeast digests sugar. Wine also contains other kinds of alcohol, such as methyl, isopropyl, propyl, isobutyl, butyl and amyl. These are known collectively as fusel oils. 'If it is true, as I surmise, that "alcohol" is a word of the Arabs, it is interesting to realise that our general word for the essence of wine and beer and such things comes from a people which has made particular war upon them.' G.K. Chesterton *Wine When It Is Red.*

Alcohol content – the amount of alcohol in a liquid, its strength, has traditionally been measured by different systems (with names like Gay Lussac, Windisch, Reichard, Tralles, Richter, Sykes, Tessa, Cartier) in different countries. In Europe there is now a general move towards the use of percentage of alcohol by volume. By this measure, normal beers are within the range 3%–6%. Table wines tend to be within the range 10%–12%. Fortified wines, vermouths and patent aperitifs are 15%–24%. Most spirits are 40% or more. It is impossible to obtain 100% pure alcohol – there would always be at least 5% water mixed with it. (See also below under Proof.)

Alcoholic – containing alcohol; addicted to the consumption of alcohol. In its 'addict' sense the word has given rise to neologisms such as 'workaholic'.

Alcoholics Anonymous – the highly-regarded voluntary organisation founded in 1947 to help alcoholics.

Alcoholiday – a word coined during the American Prohibition period, referring to a holiday in a country where drinks were freely available. (Quoted by Ernest Weekley in his *Etymological Dictionary of Modern English.*)

Alkee – also alkie, alky. US slang for alcohol. Alk is also possible – 'I always say have a drink an' get to know each other. There's nothin' like a spot of the old alk for making acquaintances into friends . . .' Peter Cheyney *You Can Call It A Day.*

Alkie – Australian slang for an alcoholic.

American gallon – 8 pt of 16 fl oz each.

Anker – a cask holding an anker (10 old wine gal, 8.5 imp gal) of beer. The word may be present in some pub names as 'Anchor'.

Anti-fogmatic – an American term recorded in 1790 for 'an alcoholic drink, jocosely reputed to be valuable for counteracting the bad effects of fog'.

Arm-twisting – persuading someone to do some further elbow-bending.

Balderdash – this word at first referred to frothy liquid, such as soapy water. By the 17th century it was used of any mixture of drinks that did not naturally blend, such as beer and wine, milk and beer. It was then used metaphorically of speech that did not make sense – nonsense. The ultimate origin of the word is unknown.

Barfly – a person who spends a great deal of time in a bar.

Barrel – a 36-gal cask. Loosely used of casks in general.

Barrelhouse – an American term for a cheap drinking and dancing establishment. Later associated with a jazz style.

Bat – slang: a drinking spree.

Beads – bubbles. Peter McCall says in his *Brewer's Dictionary* that 'bead' is used for the column of fine bubbles rising from the bottom or side of a glass of beer. John Keats made the phrase 'beaded bubbles' famous in his 'Ode To A Nightingale'.

Beaker – a large drinking cup with a wide mouth, a goblet.

Bender – slang: a drinking spree.

Bicker – a bowl-shaped wooden drinking vessel with two lugs or ears, used in Scotland in the 18th century.

Binder – slang expression for the last drink, the 'one for the road', according to the anonymous *Word for Word*, published by Whitbread.

Binge – a drinking bout. Wilfred Granville, in *A Dictionary of Sailors' Slang*, refers to the former naval expression 'binge (or bull) the cask'. Water was poured into an empty rum cask to rinse out any remaining liquor.

Bombard – also bumbard. A large leather jug for liquor used in the 17th century.

Bootlegger – a distiller and distributor of illicit whiskey in the USA, the name deriving from the flat bottles of liquor that were concealed in boot tops.

Booze – (to drink) any kind of alcohol. Derivatives include 'boozer', a drinking place or person, 'boozed' or 'boozy', drunk, 'booze-up', a drinking bout, 'booze-hoister', a heavy-drinker (railwaymen used to refer instead to a 'booze-shunter'). Earliest spellings were bouse and bowse. The origin of the word is unclear, though Dutch *buizen* 'to drink to excess' is often mentioned. German *bauschen* 'swell, inflate' appeals to some etymologists. Others quote an Egyptian *bouzah*, a kind of beer said to be named after a city, Bousiris. Bouzy is a village in the Champagne area of northern France. Chapman, in his *Dictionary of American Slang*, thinks that use of the word was influenced 'by the name of a 19th-century Philadelphia distiller, E.G. Booze'. People who bear this name (or Boosey, Boosie, Bousie, etc) derive it either from a *bos*, 'cattle-stall' or from Balhousie in Fife.

Bottom fermentation – used in the production of lager and wine. The yeast falls to the bottom of the fermenting vessel. Carried out at cooler temperatures than top fermentation, and a longer-lasting process.

Bracer – a drink taken as a stimulant.

Brewer's droop – temporary impotence caused by excess drinking of any alcohol.

Brewer's horse – formerly used in the slang phrase 'bit by the brewer's horse', i.e. addicted to drink.

Brown bagging – an American term for taking one's own alcohol to a club or restaurant that is otherwise 'dry'. 'I thought this was a dry town,' says Craig. 'Brown-bagging is legal,' the PR man says, producing a pint bottle of whiskey in a paper bag. 'The waitress will bring ice and setups.' (Robert Daley *Only A Game.*) The 'setups' would be glasses, ice, soda, etc.

Bung hole – the hole in a cask which is used to fill it. Closed with a shive.

Burn – as in 'to burn sherry'. To heat it, mull it. A common 19th-century term.

Bush – the symbol since Roman times of an inn. It gave rise to the proverb 'a good wine needs no bush', which can be used with a more general application. Graham Greene is talking of a brothel, for instance, when he writes in *The Honorary Consul*: 'There were no exterior signs to differentiate her establishment from the other houses in the respectable street. A good wine, Doctor Plarr thought, needs no bush.'

Butcher – a beer glass used in South Australia, formerly favoured by abattoir butchers.

Butt – a cask holding 108 gal of beer or sherry.

Can – a general word for a container of liquid, long before it came to mean more specifically a metal can. 'Two cans of beer' sounds a very modern phrase, but it occurs in Ben Jonson's play *Every Man In His Humour* (1598).

Carbonation – the artificial injection of carbon dioxide into beer or wine.

Carbon dioxide – a colourless, odourless gas given off by yeast during the fermentation of beer or wine. Some remains in beer and helps to condition it. It also gives sparkling wine its fizz. Often added to beer in the cask to protect it from exposure to air, but this sometimes makes the beer too gassy.

Carousal – a drinking revelry. To carouse is to drink freely and repeatedly.

Case-bottle – references to such bottles occur in 19th-century literature. Some were meant to fit into a case, and were therefore square. Others were protected by a case. 'The spirit being set before him in a huge case-bottle, which had originally come out of some ship's locker.' Charles Dickens *The Old Curiosity Shop*.

Cask – the general word for a container – traditionally made of oak – for storing and transporting beers, wines and spirits. Casks of different sizes are known as – butt (108 gal), puncheon (varies), hogshead (varies), barrel (36 gal), Kilderkin (18 gal), firkin (9 gal), pin (4.5 gal).

Cattie – also catty, kati, katti. Normally a Chinese measure of weight (the origin of our tea-*caddy*), but Han Suyin, in *A Many Splendoured Thing*, writes: 'We had my most excellent Maotai wine, and then hot yellow wine . . . We now called for another cattie of hot yellow wine to toast the moon . . .'

Chloe, drunk as – Australian slang – very drunk (in use since 1820s, still current).

Chopin – A traditional Scottish liquid measure. (See Gill.)

Coaster – a small tray or mat for a bottle or glass. Originally a small (silver) tray, often fitted with wheels, enabling a decanter to coast round the table after a meal.

Coffin varnish – an early American slang term for liquor.

Coggie – also cogie. A small cogue or cog, which was a round wooden drinking vessel made of staves and hoops. Used in Scotland.

Costrel – formerly known as a 'pilgrim's bottle'. A large bottle with ears which allowed it to be suspended from the waist; later applied to a small wooden keg, used for carrying wine, beer or other liquid, e.g. by farm-hands to take refreshment with them to distant fields.

Crack – drink, as in 'We'll crack a bottle or two'. Used since Shakespeare's time.

Crapulent – given to indulging in alcohol; drunk. Crapulence = drunkenness. The Greek word *kraipale* referred specifically to a drunken headache and nausea. It was adopted into Latin as *crapula*.

Deadhouse – Australian slang, a room attached to a hotel for drunks to sleep it off.

Dead marine – also dead soldier. Slang, an empty bottle, something which has done its duty.

Decoction – a liquor obtained by boiling down, an essence. 'And now,' began Mr Tristram, when they had tasted the decoction which he had caused to be served to them, 'now just give me an account of yourself'. Henry James *The American*.

Demijohn – a large bottle with a bulging body and narrow neck, cased in wicker-work and with one or two wicker-work handles. Traditionally of 5-gal capacity or more, but a 1-gal version is used for home-brewing and wine-making. Demijohn adapts the French *Dame Jeanne*, following the practice of giving personal names to pots and jugs.

Deoch-an-doris – also doch an dorris. Scottish and Irish, a drink taken at the door as one is about to leave. A stirrup-cup, or valedictory nip.

Dew-drink – a drink before breakfast, accorded to farm-labourers at harvest-time.

Dipsomania – an abnormal craving for alcohol. The word literally means 'thirst-mania'.

Doctor a drink – adulterate it.

Dodger – a dram of liquor. Also the glass which contains it.

Dram – a small drink. The word is now thought of as Scottish, the invitation to 'take a dram' usually referring to whisky. Dram formerly had a more general sense; 'You are not ill, I hope, cousin? Some water! a dram this instant!' Henry Fielding *Tom Jones*. In *Romeo and Juliet* occurs: 'Let me have a dram of poison.' The word is a form of 'drachma', the name of an ancient Greek weight and coin.

Drink with the flies – Australian slang, to drink alone in a pub.

Dry – wines and beers are said to be dry when all natural sugar has been converted by the yeast into alcohol.

Dutch courage – pot valour, induced by alcohol.

Ebriosity – habitual drunkenness.

Elbow-bending – drinking. 'The Stork stumbled into the train's club car. At the far end was a semi-circular bar and a convivial group of men bending their elbows.' Denison Hatch *The Stork*.

Eye-opener – a drink that makes the drinker become wide-awake.

Fermentation – the action of yeast as it converts sugar to alcohol and carbon dioxide. (See pp. 87–90.)

Finger – an alcoholic measure. '. . . washed them down with a finger of Four Roses.' Truman Capote *Shut A Final Door*.

Finings – products such as isinglass used to clarify wines and beers. (See p. 95.)

Firkin – a cask holding 9 gal.

Flagon – originally a large bottle for carrying wine or other liquids. Applied in the 19th century to a large, flattened wine bottle and later to a quart bottle for cider or beer.

Free house – British term for a pub that is not tied to a particular brewery. Offers a wide range of beers.

Fusel oils – the higher alcohols, other than ethanol, present in spirits. James Bond puts black pepper into his vodka because 'there's often quite a lot of fusel oil on the surface of this stuff – at least there used to be when it was badly distilled. Poisonous. In Russia,

where you get a lot of bath-tub liquor, it's an understood thing to sprinkle a little pepper in your glass. It takes the fusel oil to the bottom.'

Gallon – an imperial gallon represents the volume of 10 lb of distilled water; 8 imp pt of 20 fl oz, 4.5 l. (See also American gallon.)

Gelatine – frequently used as a fining.

Gill – a liquid measure, a quarter of a pint. The traditional Scottish gill was slightly less than the English gill. In the 18th century 4 Scottish (3 English) gills equalled a mutchkin. The other Scottish measures were: 2 mutchkins = 1 chopin; 2 chopins = 1 pt. The relationship between Scottish and English measures was as follows: 1 chopin = (English) 1 pt and two gills; 1 pt = (English) 3 pt; 1 gal = (English) 3 gal.

Go – a quantity of liquor supplied at one time, the exact quantity not being specified. 'Couple of glasses of bar mixture for these ladies, and a go of gin for myself.' Benjamin Disraeli *Sybil*.

God-forgive-me – 'Jacob stooped to the God-forgive-me, which was a two-handled tall mug. Such a class of mug is called a God-forgive-me in Weatherbury and its vicinity for uncertain reasons; probably because its size makes any given toper feel ashamed of himself when he sees its bottom in drinking it empty.' Thomas Hardy *Far From the Madding Crowd*.

Grace-cup – a cup passed round to the assembled guests after grace had been said. Similar to the loving-cup.

Grog – Australian slang, alcohol. Grog up = beer up.

Grog blossom – slang term for the red nose of a heavy drinker.

Grog on – Australian slang, to continue steady drinking. Howard Jacobson in his novel *Redback*, demonstrates the use of Australian drinking slang – 'Mine's [i.e. my throat's] as dry as a nun's nasty.' He embraces his old mate and carts him over to the sly grog shop on King's Parade. They grog on until they are as full as ticks, whereupon an altercation breaks out as to whose shout it is. Australian slang expressions are from G.A. Wilkes *A Dictionary of Australian Colloquialisms*.

Gum-tickler – a strong drink in undiluted form. In *Our Mutual Friend*, by Charles Dickens, Venus offers Wegg rum and invites him to mix it with water. Wegg replies: 'I think not, sir. On so auspicious an occasion, I prefer to take it in the form of a Gum-Tickler.'

Happy Hour – an hour in the early evening when double measures are served for the price of a single.

High – drunk, or slightly drunk. Originally rhyming slang, high as a kite = tight. '. . . still a little high from all those daiquiris at lunch.' John Dos Passos *The Great Days*.

Hob-nob – to drink with someone. Originally the phrase was to 'drink hob or nob', to drink to one another alternately, clinking glasses.

Hocus – there are several references to hocussing liquor in 19th-century literature. Charles Dickens explains, in *The Pickwick Papers* – 'The opposite party bribed the barmaid at the Town Arms, to hocus the brandy-and-water of fourteen unpolled electors as was a-stoppin' in the house.' 'What do you mean by "hocussing" brandy-and-water?' inquired Mr Pickwick. 'Puttin' laud'num in it,' replied Sam. 'Blessed if she didn't send 'em all to sleep till twelve hours arter the election was over.'

Hogs-head – a cask of varying capacity, according to what it contains, e.g. sherry, beer 54 gal, but otherwise ranging from 46–72 gal.

Hoist a few – an invitation to have a drink or two.

Hooch – strong drink, especially when inferior or obtained illegally. Said to derive from the liquor made by the Hoochinoo Indians of Alaska. In Edward Albee's *Who's Afraid of Virginia Woolf?* George says – 'I'll just hooch up Martha.' Edna O'Brien uses hooch to refer to wine in *Girl With Green Eyes*.

Host – the Shakespearean term for a publican. The British pub trade prefers the term to 'licensee'.

Imperial gallon – 8 pt of 20 fl oz each.

Inebriate – to make drunk, to intoxicate. It is also possible to describe a person as an inebriate – a habitual drunkard. Inebriation is a synonym for drunkenness, as in: 'First drunkenness is as much a rite of passage as loss of virginity, and ritual inebriation is often required on other occasions.' Ian Irvine *The Correspondent*.

Jigger – a measure of drinks, 1.5 fl. oz. 'People are so sensitive about colour around here that you can't even ask a barman for a jigger of rum. You have to ask for a jegro.' Ian Fleming *Diamonds Are Forever*.

Jolt – US slang, a drink. 'Sit down and have a jolt with us.' Sinclair Lewis *Elmer Gantry*.

Jorum – a large drinking bowl or vessel, especially one used for punch. Probably a use of the biblical name Joram, a variant of Jehoram. Other drinking vessels, bottles, etc., have been given such names. 'Here's Mistress Corney mixing me another jorum.' Mrs Gaskell *Sylvia's Lovers*.

Jungle juice – originally a beverage concocted by servicemen in tropics e.g. surgical spirit and fermented coconut milk. Applied later to any drink of doubtful quality. 'Give us a drink, darling. That lovely punch concoction.' Hewitt tipped the pitcher of thick yellow sludge towards her glass. 'Real jungle-juice, darling. Tastes as though there's dandelions in it.' Stanley Price *A World of Difference*.

Keystone – a wooden bung which has the centre partially bored to enable a tap to be driven into the cask.

Kilderkin – an 18-gal cask.

Lactose – a sugar that occurs in milk (Latin *lac/lactis* 'milk'). It is used to sweeten beers and wines because yeast is unable to convert this kind of sugar into alcohol.

Lamb down – Australian slang, to defraud a bushman by keeping him drunk until his money is spent.

Lees – the sediment at the bottom of a bottle or cask.

Leg-opener – Australian slang, wine or spirits used to make a woman more susceptible to sexual advances.

Long drink – a refreshing drink in a tall glass, usually a small amount of alcohol diluted with a carbonated soft drink.

Loving-cup – a large drinking vessel, usually made of silver, with handles,

passed from hand to hand amongst a group of people for each to drink from it. A 19th-century custom which brought a gathering to an end. The person drinking would stand up with his neighbour, who then took the cup and turned to his neighbour on the other side, who in turn would stand.

Malt – barley or other grain that has been steeped, partially germinated and roasted. Used for brewing and distilling. (See pp. 81–2.)

Mazer – a bowl or drinking cup, originally made of wood and ornamented with silver, gold, etc.

Methyl alcohol – also known as methanol. The primary alcohol present in methylated spirits. Highly toxic, and unlike ethanol not a by-product of fermentation.

Mock beers and wines – a term applied to ginger beer, gooseberry wine and the like.

Mug – a drinking vessel, usually applied to a beer glass with a handle. In the 18th century often decorated with a grotesque human face, so that 'mug' became a slang word for the face. The meaning of 'stupid person' came later, the idea being that you could pour anything into a mug. 'To mug' in the modern sense of demanding money with menaces in the street comes from the earlier notion of hunting for a mug, i.e. someone easy to rob.

Mull – to make wine or beer, usually to which spices and other ingredients have been added, into a hot drink. The word was first used in this sense in the 17th century and baffles the experts as to its origin. Possibly from French *mollir* 'to soften'. 'The landlord retired to draw the beer, and presently returning with it, applied himself to warm the same in a small tin vessel shaped funnel-wise, for the convenience of sticking it far down in the fire and getting at the best places. This was soon done, and he handed it over to Mr Codlin with that creamy froth upon the surface which is one of the happy circumstances attendant upon mulled malt.' Charles Dickens *The Old Curiosity Shop*.

Mutchkin – a Scottish liquid measure, three-quarters of an imperial pint, and a container of that capacity: 'He uncorked his mutchkin and drank it like water.' George Douglas *The*

House With the Green Shutters. (See Gill.)

Nightcap – an alcoholic drink taken at bedtime to help induce sleep.

Nip – an abbreviation of nipperkin. A nip is a vessel holding a liquid measure of half-a-pint or less. Also applied to any small quantity of the liquor itself. Specifically applied to a size of bottle that contains a third of a pint, used especially for barley-wines and other strong ales.

Noggin – originally the name of a small mug or cup. Later applied to a small quantity of liquor, usually a third of a pint. In ordinary colloquial use – an alcoholic drink of any kind. 'How about another noggin of the usual all round?' Len Deighton *Funeral In Berlin*. 'Whiskey, please.' 'A double, sir?' 'No, a quadruple.' 'A noggin?' 'Two noggins, for God's sake.' 'That will be eight altogether, sir?' asked the landlord, incredulously. 'If you please.' Henry Williamson *The Dream of Fair Women*.

Nose paint – an early American slang term for liquor.

Nuncheon – often as nuncheons: this useful word referred to a slight refreshment of liquor and perhaps a snack taken in the afternoon. Literally it means a 'noon-draught'. Luncheon originally referred to a light meal taken between breakfast and the mid-day meal. Nuncheon(s) was still being used dialectically in the 19th century but now appears to be obsolete.

Off it – synonymous with 'on the wagon'. 'Bob Babbitt was "off the stuff". Which means that he had "cut out the booze"; that he was "on the water wagon".' O. Henry *The Rubaiyat of a Scotch Highball*.

On it – Australian slang, drinking steadily and heavily.

Pasteurisation – sterilisation by flash heating. Named after the French scientist Louis Pasteur (1822–95).

Peg – one of the pegs or pins in an 18th-century drinking vessel, indicating the level to which each drinker was allowed to go. Typically, a tankard holding two quarts with pegs at half-pint intervals. Peg later became an Anglo-Indian slang term for a drink, usually of spirits. Popularly explained at that time as deriving from the fact that every drink was a peg or nail in one's coffin. 'We shall have a peg before we start – just one. There's the whisky, here's the syphon.' E.W. Hornung *Raffles.* 'Will ye be taking a peg o' something, Mr Forrester? The doctor brought us gin from Calcutta.' H.E. Bates *The Purple Plain.* Longfellow, in *The Golden Legend,* has – 'Come, old fellow, drink down to your peg, But do not drink any farther, I beg.'

Pick-me-up – a drink which acts as a tonic. 'He concocted a powerful mixture of gin, whisky, and French vermouth, a liberal dash of bitters and plenty of ice, a real blinder of a pick-me-up.' H.E. Bates *When the Green Woods Laugh.* The word also occurs in the form 'pickup'. 'Luke poured three fingers of bourbon into a glass, topped it with ice and water, and handed it to her. "Here, baby," he grinned; "have a little pickup." "I don't drink." "Time you was learning how." Timidly Fancy took the glass and tasted the drink. It burned like fire, going down.' Frank Yerby *A Woman Called Fancy.*

Pin – a cask containing 4.5 gal.

Pioneer drinker – one who is always willing to try a drink not previously sampled. 'I'm going to have a brandy and ginger ale on the rocks. What will you have?' 'Perhaps I could try what you're having. I've never had it.' 'A pioneer drinker: I like that.' Elizabeth Jane Howard *Getting It Right.*

Pipe – a cask of varying capacity, e.g. 115 gal of port.

Pledge someone – drink someone's health. It is sometimes said that the original idea was to guarantee someone's safety from attack while he was drinking.

Pocket pistol – an old slang term for a pocket liquor-flask. It was something carried for self-defence. 'Newman slowly brought forth from his desk one of those portable bottles currently known as pocket-pistols . . .' Charles Dickens *Nicholas Nickleby.*

Pony – in Britain a glass or a bottle, usually containing one-third of a pint. In the US a pony glass contains 2 fl oz, but a pony – as a liquid measure for cocktails – is one fluid ounce. 'I lay in a lounge chair swallowing pony upon pony of gin.' Vladimir Nabokov *Lolita.*

Posset – a drink made with hot milk curdled with ale, wine or other liquor, often with added sugar and spices. In Shakespeare's time it was thought to be a cold cure.

Pot valiant – made courageous by liquor. 'There's a saying, you know, pot-valiant. You'll have to beware the pot isn't empty by the time you reach home.' Compton Mackenzie *Whisky Galore.*

Proof – a traditional system of describing the alcoholic strength of spirits. In the United Kingdom proof spirit, at a temperature of 51 degrees Fahrenheit, weighed exactly twelve-thirteenths of a volume of distilled water equal to the volume of the spirit. In other words, proof spirit (100 degrees proof) was 57.1% alcohol and 42.9% water. Whisky was formerly described as '30 degrees under-proof', or '70 degrees proof'. It would now be described as 40% alcohol by volume. In the USA 100 degrees proof spirit is exactly 50/50 alcohol and water. Halving the degrees proof therefore gives the alcohol content by volume, e.g. 80 degree proof rye whiskey is 40%.

Public house – the term has been in use in England since the mid-17th century. The first recorded use of 'pub' is not until 1865. 'But don't say "public-house", milord; a "public-home", I like to call it.' 'Fudge! It's a boozery – a gin-pond – a grog-swamp – and you know it.' A.P. Herbert *Derby Day.* Other terms for drinking places in English-speaking countries have included: ale house, beer house, beer shop, boozer, dive, dram house, dram shop, gin palace (other drinks than gin were sold), gin shop, grog shop, honky-tonk, hostelry, hotel, inn, local, pot house, roadhouse, saloon, shebeen, speakeasy, tap house, tavern, toddy shop, wine vaults.

Puncheon – a cask of varying capacity, e.g. 120 gal of rum.

Punt – the hollow at the bottom of a wine bottle. The word is connected with the iron rod used in traditional glass-blowing, variously known as a punto, punty, ponty, pointel, pontil.

Quaff – to drink deeply. It is probably a mistake for quass, a Germanic word meaning to eat and drink immoderately.

Quaich – a kind of shallow drinking cup with two ears, or handles. Made of hooped wooden staves with a silver rim, or entirely of silver. Gaelic *cuach* 'bowl'.

Qualify a drink – weaken it with water. A common 19th-century expression. 'It's *rather* early. I should like to qualify it, if you have no objection.' Charles Dickens *The Pickwick Papers.*

Quick one, a – a drink. 'Jimmy Nunn and Mr. Morton Mitcham, having what they called "a quick one" with the manager.' J.B. Priestley *The Good Companions.*

Quist, to be Adrian – Australian slang, to be drunk (name of tennis-player, rhyming on 'pissed').

Rack – to draw off beer or wine so as to clear it of dregs or lees.

Rhyming slang – general expressions include tumble (= tumble down the sink = drink), pick and choose (booze). (See also River.) Many expressions rhyme on drunk or slang synonyms of that word. Examples are – elephants (= elephant's trunk; to cop an elephant = to get drunk. To jack-roll an elephant's trunk is to pick the pocket of a drunk); high (= high as a kite), fly-by-night (tight), Scotch mist, Brahms and Listz, earlier Mozart and Liszt (pissed). Pint pot, says Julian Franklyn, in his *Dictionary of Rhyming Slang,* is a sot, or drunkard.

River – British criminal rhyming slang, short for River Ouse – booze. It can lead to misunderstandings. Criminal to barrister – 'I was on the river all day.' Barrister to judge – 'My client was boating all day.' James Morton *Low Speak.*

Rosiner – Australian slang, a stiff drink.

Round – an order of drinks for two or more people, usually paid for by one person. A shout in Australia.

Rouse – a shortened form of carouse. A full glass, a bumper. Also a carousal or bout of drinking.

Rummer – a kind of large drinking glass, perhaps originally Roman.

School – Australian slang, a drinkers' group.

Schooner – in the USA and Australia a tall beer glass of different capacities – e.g. 15 oz in New South Wales, 9 oz in South Australia. In Britain a small glass used mainly for sherry.

Seltzer - originally the medicinal carbonated mineral water from Nieder-Selters in Germany, described in German as *Selterser Wasser*. Later it came to mean soda water, an artificial substitute for the original. 'Have another brandy and soda? Or would you like hock and seltzer? I always take hock and seltzer myself.' Oscar Wilde *The Picture of Dorian Gray*.

Session - slang, a period of steady drinking.

Set 'em up - colloquial American expression; to pay for drinks.

Shebeen - in Ireland, an unlicensed house selling alcohol.

Sheep dip - an early American slang term for liquor.

Shicker - Australian slang, liquor.

Shive - a circular wooden plug partly bored in the centre, hammered into the bush of a wooden cask when filled.

Shot - a drink of straight liquor. Mainly American. The earlier expression was shot in the neck, which became shot in the arm. 'In front of him is a shot glass of bourbon . . .' Robert Daley *Only A Game*. Ben Jonson refers to each man paying his shot, which meant paying for a round of drinks.

Shout - Australian slang, to buy drinks for others, stand treat, pay bill for all.

Shypoo - Australian slang, liquor of poor quality.

Skin beginning to crack - a phrase used by Australians to mean that they are extremely thirsty.

Slake one's thirst - the meaning is to slacken one's thirst, make it inactive.

Sleeve - a straight glass with no handle.

Slug - mainly American usage, a tot of liquor. 'He swallowed three slugs of bourbon . . .' Bernard Wolfe *The Late Risers*. There is a special Scottish use of the word - 'He was what the Scotch call a "slug for the drink." A slug for the drink is a man who soaks and never succumbs.' George Douglas *The House With the Green Shutters*.

Sly grog shop - Australian slang, place where liquor is sold without a licence (old fashioned, but still used).

Smile - a 19th-century euphemism for a drink, especially whisky. 'Harris proposed that we should go out and have a smile.' Jerome K. Jerome *Three Men In A Boat*.

Snake juice - Australian slang, an improvised alcoholic drink.

Snake medicine - an early American slang term for liquor.

Snifter - a small drink of alcohol. In the US it is the name of the balloon brandy glass. 'Here's an old friend back from barbarous places, and I haven't a sensation to offer him, not so much as a wee snifter.' Compton Mackenzie *Whisky Galore*. 'I took a stiff slug of what remained in my snifter and returned to the living room.' Peter de Vries *The Tunnel of Love*.

Snort - a drink, especially of strong spirits. From the sound made by the drinker. 'Have a snort? Don't be a fool; of course you will.' Sinclair Lewis *Cass Timberlane*. Also snorter. 'He poured himself a moderate drink and the Colonel a snorter.' David Walker *Digby*.

Soak - drink consistently, booze. Also a noun, used of a heavy drinker. 'A small queue of soaks were standing at the phone waiting their turn to call fellow-members of drinking syndicates.' Ian Jefferies *Thirteen Days*.

Sober - Latin *sobrius* 'sober' appears to be derived from Latin *ebrius* 'drunk' and mean 'not drunk', though logic would seem to demand that 'drunk' should mean 'not sober'.

Soda water - a weak solution of aerated sodium bicarbonate, used to dilute many drinks.

Sot - for at least six centuries, this word meant 'fool'. It was only at the beginning of the 17th century that it took on the meaning of a person who makes himself stupid by drinking too much.

Speakeasy - a cheap saloon, especially a place where it was possible to drink illegally, or a shop where illegally-distilled liquor could be purchased. The name derives from the idea of speaking about such a place quietly, keeping it hush-hush. The term first began to be used in the USA at the end of the 19th century.

Spiggot - the wooden or brass tap used to draw liquor from a cask.

Spike a drink - make a drink stronger by adding alcohol. 'Sono brought out a bottle and spiked his tea with cognac or Chivas Regal.' Saul Bellow *Herzog*.

Splice the mainbrace - this originally referred to a double tot of rum served to a ship's company on an occasion of celebration. It soon acquired the more general sense, in sailor's slang, of drinking freely. Authorities differ as to the origin of the expression. Professor Weekley pointed out that when the mainbrace on a sailing ship was spliced, it was strengthened. Liquor may have been looked on as something that strengthened the crews. Other writers have said that splicing the mainbrace was an especially difficult job and that its completion was worthy of celebration. The expression would now be used humorously to mean that serious drinking was in the offing.

Spot - a drink. 'Come on, let's have a spot.' Frederic Raphael *The Limits of Love*.

Stiff - used of a strong drink that stiffens the backbone and gives one courage. 'I poured myself a stiff drink.' Louis Auchincloss *The Book Class*. 'Do you have to give yourself a stiffener to tell me? Is there brandy in that champagne?' John Welcome *Stop at Nothing*.

Sting - Australian slang for a strong drink.

Stirrup cup - a drink handed to a departing guest when his feet were in the stirrups, i.e. when he had already mounted his horse and was preparing to leave. A parting drink, now associated with huntsmen about to begin the day. The expression has also been used of a drink offered immediately on arrival, before a guest has dismounted. The expression can also refer to the 'cup' itself, which traditionally should have no base. 'Mine host ran to fill the stirrup-cup (for which no charge was ever made) from a butt yet charier than that which he had pierced for the former stoup.' Sir Walter Scott *The Monastery*.

Straight - colloquial American, not diluted, neat.

Sundowner - an alcoholic drink taken at sunset. 'We lingered, long

after the hour of the "sundowner".'
Francis Brett Young *Marching on
Tanga*. 'He would get really drunk
several times a year, but between
these indulgences kept to his three
whiskies at sundown.' Doris Lessing
Five.

Sup – drink. Used especially in the
north of England. The original
meaning was to take soup or tea by
sips, or spoonfuls.

Sweeten a drink - top up the glass
or refill it, if empty. 'Would you like it
if I sweetened your drink a little?'
John P. Marquand *Women and Thomas
Harrow*. 'Let me get you a sweetener.'
David Walker *Digby*.

Swift one, a – also swifty. Variants of
a quick one, a drink which is
theoretically going to be drunk
quickly.

Swig – to drink eagerly and copiously.
Also used as a noun, as in have a swig
from a bottle – have a hefty drink
from it.

Swill – drink in a greedy way. Inferior
liquor of any kind can also be
described as swill.

Tanglefoot – an early American slang
term for liquor.

Tap – the tap of a cask, and by
extension, the liquor tapped from a
particular cask. 'What's your usual
tap?' was a 19th-century way of asking
'What do you usually drink?'
Derivatives include tap-room, tap-
house, tapster, tapstress.

Tappit Hen – a very large Scottish
drinking vessel having a lid with a
knob, resembling the crest or topknot
of a hen. Sir Walter Scott refers to it
in *Waverley* – 'A huge pewter
measuring-pot, containing at least
three English quarts, familiarly
denominated a tappit hen.' 'Tappit' is a
Scottish form of 'topped'.

Tapster – an old term for a man or
woman who tapped the cask in an inn
in order to serve customers. The -ster
ending is theoretically feminine, but
the word was later applied to both
sexes, causing tapstress to be used for
a woman.

Tee-total – the word is a reinforced
form of total, emphasising that the
person concerned abstains from all
alcoholic drinks. 'After marrying my
mother and turning teetotaller, he is

said to have lost something of his
playfulness.' Robert Graves *Goodbye
To All That*.

Tiddly – a British term meaning
'slightly drunk'. The original
expression was – 'Let's have a tiddly
wink = drink.' This led to the
meaning of tiddly 'affected by drink'.
'She was a woman who easily got
tiddly (which was the correct vulgar
word for it).' Michael Innes
Honeybath's Haven.

Tig – also tyg. An old drinking cup
with two or more handles.

Time, gentlemen, please – the
conventional announcement in British
pubs to signal the end of licensed
drinking time. The fact that there *is* a
conventional announcement is useful;
individual publicans might otherwise
use less polite expressions. 'Time,
ladies and gentlemen, please,' to
which he now occasionally added
'Bugger off with you!' David Brynley
Seth.

Tipple – to drink intoxicating liquor
regularly, usually in small amounts.
Also a noun referring to a strong
drink, drunk by a tippler.

Tope – drink alcohol to excess,
become a toper.

Trimmings – ice, garnishing, etc.
When ordering e.g. a Bloody Mary, the
barman's question 'with all the
trimmings?' means 'with a dash of
Worcester sauce, ice, slice of lemon?'

Tumbler – the glass of this name
originally had no base, so that its
contents had to be drained in a single
draught. It was then stood upside
down. Now made with a flat bottom
and the glass least likely to tumble.

Tun – a very large cask of varying
capacity.

Turps – Australian slang, liquor.

Two-pot screamer – Australian
slang, someone susceptible to alcohol.

Ullage – originally the amount of
wine or other liquor required to fill a
cask or bottle to the proper level,
some having been lost by leakage or
absorption. The 'ullage allowance'
given by a brewery to a pub or club
refers to waste beer, including spillage
and beer that has to remain in a cask
because of sediment.

Vintage – normally used of high-
quality wine made from the grapes of
a particular season. Applied also to
some beers such as blue-capped
Chimay, Courage's Imperial Russian
Stout and others which improve with
age.

Wagon, on the – originally, 'on the
water-wagon', not drinking any
alcohol.

Wassail bowl - a large bowl or
loving-cup, in which drink was
circulated to the company, especially
at New Year or Twelfth Night. Wassail
derives from an Old English
salutation, 'be of good health'.

Wet, have a – slang, have a drink.
'Wet one's whistle' is similar. 'To wet
the baby's head' is to have a drink to
celebrate the birth of a new-born
child.

When – in drinking language this
means 'Enough, thanks'. Many people
say the word after being asked to 'say
when'.

Whiskin – a shallow drinking-vessel
used in the 17th century. The word
was only used in northern dialects and
is of unknown origin.

Wino – slang, an alcoholic.

Woodser, Jimmy – Australian slang,
a person drinking alone, one who
never shouts.

Works, all the – same as 'all the
trimmings'. (See Trimmings.)

Yeast – the microscopic plant which
feeds on malt worts, grape juice or
other sources of carbohydrates,
producing alcohol as a by-product.
There are about 1000 varieties of
yeast. (See also pp. 87–90.)

UK CONSUMPTION OF ALCOHOLIC DRINKS
PER HEAD OF POPULATION AGED 15 AND OVER

Year	Pints per head		Litres per head			
	Beer	Cider	Beer	Cider	Wine	Spirits 100% alcohol
1960	196.9	3.7	111.9	2.1	3.0	1.0
1961	204.9	4.0	116.4	2.3	3.2	1.0
1962	203.1	3.6	115.4	2.0	3.3	1.0
1963	204.0	3.6	115.9	2.0	3.6	1.1
1964	212.8	3.7	120.9	2.1	4.1	1.1
1965	211.6	3.8	120.2	2.2	3.9	1.1
1966	216.2	4.3	122.9	2.4	4.1	1.1
1967	219.4	4.8	124.7	2.7	4.5	1.1
1968	224.2	4.9	127.4	2.8	5.0	1.1
1969	233.5	5.5	132.7	3.1	4.9	1.1
1970	239.8	6.0	136.3	3.4	5.0	1.2
1971	247.7	6.0	140.8	3.4	5.8	1.3
1972	250.9	6.0	142.6	3.4	6.7	1.5
1973	263.5	6.5	149.7	3.7	8.4	1.8
1974	267.9	6.5	152.2	3.7	8.7	2.0
1975	272.2	7.5	154.7	4.3	8.2	1.9
1976	275.6	8.8	156.6	5.0	8.5	2.1
1977	270.3	8.2	153.6	4.7	8.2	1.8
1978	273.6	8.3	155.5	4.7	9.5	2.2
1979	276.4	8.5	157.1	4.8	10.3	2.4
1980	263.7	8.4	149.8	4.8	10.2	2.2
1981	250.4	9.0	142.3	5.1	10.9	2.1
1982	242.1	10.7	137.6	6.1	10.9	2.0
1983	244.0	11.8	138.7	6.7	11.9	2.0
1984	242.3	11.7	137.7	6.7	13.0	2.0
1985	240.0	11.2	136.4	6.4	13.5	2.1
1986	238.5	11.6	135.5	6.6	14.0	2.1
1987	239.5	11.2	136.1	6.3	14.8	2.1
1988	240.5	10.7	136.6	6.1	15.3	2.2
1989	239.7	11.6	136.2	6.6	15.7	2.2
1990	239.2	12.8	135.9	7.3	15.8	2.1

Note: Includes low and no alcohol beers.

THE STAMP OF APPROVAL

In favour of drinking

DR HENRY Aldrich was an eminent scholar who became dean of Christ Church, Oxford, in 1647. He is mainly remembered today for a few lines in which he suggested some reasons for drinking:

> If all be true that I do think,
> There are five reasons we should drink:
> Good wine - a friend - or being dry -
> Or lest we should be by and by -
> Or any other reason why.

For those who need little persuasion that there are good reasons for drinking, that probably says it all. Non-drinkers will dismiss it as a piece of frivolity. It is worth considering what a number of writers have had to say about the subject. In this chapter those who agree with the dean will have their say - so look forward to a mini-anthology of positive references to drinking. The opponents of drinking will have the next chapter to themselves.

A RULE OF THREE

There is a rule to drink,
I think,
A rule of three
That you'll agree
With me
Cannot be beaten
And tends our lives to sweeten:
Drink ere you eat,
And while you eat,
And after you have eaten!

Wallace Rice

What is interesting about Dr Aldrich's little poem is his inclusion of the word 'should'. He does not explain, apologetically, why people drink. He says clearly that we *should* drink. In that, as it happens, he is immediately more positive than Ernest Hemingway. There is a passage in *Green Hills of Africa* where someone says to Hemingway: 'But drink. I do not understand about that. That has always seemed silly to me. I understand it as a weakness.' The only reply that Hemingway can muster - surprisingly for a man who was known to be so much in favour of drinking, is: 'It is a way of ending a day. It has great benefits.'

FALSTAFF AND HIS SACK

Other writers have been more specific. Shakespeare gives Falstaff, in *King Henry the Fourth, Part Two*, a long monologue in praise of 'sherris-sack'. Falstaff says that sack fills his brain 'full of nimble, fiery, and delectable shapes; which delivered o'er to the voice . . . becomes excellent wit'. Learning, he continues, is 'a mere hoard of gold kept by a devil till sack commences it and sets it in act and use'.

Dr Johnson later agreed with that view, remarking that wine 'animates a man and enables him to bring out what a dread of the company has repressed'. It has a thawing effect, he said, and 'puts in motion what has been locked up in frost'.

Needless to say, it is drink taken in moderate quantities that has such a beneficial effect. Drinking slightly too much, Thomas Love Peacock points out in *The Misfortunes of Elphin*, 'sets the tongue tripping, in the double sense of nimbleness and titubancy.' Len Deighton offers the thought, in *Funeral In Berlin*: 'If God had made the world for humans we would have alcohol that

PURE GENIUS

Let schoolmasters puzzle their brain,
With grammar, and nonsense, and
    learning,
Good liquor, I stoutly maintain,
Gives genius a better discerning.

Oliver Goldsmith *She Stoops to Conquer*

makes the head clearer instead of drowsy and the tongues of men more articulate instead of slurred. For it is when a man has consumed alcohol that he has the most important things to say.'

DRINKING PHILOSOPHIES

Samuel Johnson would have wanted to amend that statement. He himself gave up drinking wine because, as he frankly admitted, 'I found myself apt to go to excess in it.' He told James Boswell that not to drink wine was a great diminution of pleasure, but said that 'a man should cultivate his mind so as to have that confidence and readiness without wine, which wine gives'.

That last remark recalls a long passage in *The House With the Green Shutters*, by George Douglas, in which a young student who has recently taken to drinking whisky is at a philosophy lecture. The professor says: 'The mind, indeed, in its first blank outlook on life is terrified by the demoniac force of nature and the swarming misery of man . . . Phenomena, uninformed by thought, bewilder and depress.

'But the labyrinth cannot appal the man who has found a clue to its windings. A mind that has attained to thought lives in itself, and the world becomes its slave. The world no longer frightens, being understood. Its sinister features are accidents that will pass away, and they gradually cease to be observed. For real thinkers know the value of wise indifference. And that is why they are often the most genial men; unworried by the transient, they can smile and wait, sure of their

eternal aim. The man to whom the infinite beckons is not to be driven from his mystic quest by the ambush of a temporal fear; there is no fear – it has ceased to exist. That, gentlemen, is what thought can do for a man.'

We can be quite sure, Dr Johnson would heartily have approved of those sentiments. He would not have approved the interpretation that the student imposes on them: '"By Jove," thought Gourlay, "that's what whisky does for me!" And that, on a lower level, was what whisky did. In the increased vitality it gave, he was able to tread down the world. If he walked on a wretched day in a wretched street, when he happened to be sober, his mind was hither and yon in a thousand perceptions and a thousand fears, fastening to (and fastened to) each squalid thing around. But with whisky humming in his blood he paced on in a happy dream. The wretched puddles by the way, the frowning rookeries where misery squalled, the melancholy noises of the street, were passed unheeded by. His distracted powers rallied home; he was concentrate, his own man again, the hero of his musing mind. "Just imagine," he thought, "whisky doing for me what philosophy seems to do for Tam [the professor]. It's a wonderful thing the drink!"'

Gourlay, then, uses drink to escape from harsh reality. By contrast a character in Eric Linklater's *Magnus Merriman*, who describes himself as a 'philosophical drunkard', has this to say: 'I drink because I like drink, and I like the good fellowship that goes with drinking. But there's a more important reason. What was the social argument for classical drama? By rousing emotion it purged the mind of emotion. It was a cathartic. Well, drink is a better cathartic than anything that Aeschylus or Euripides ever wrote, and when I'm tired of poetry, weary with the loveliness and the height of poetic thought, drinking washes out the poetry and brings me back to the ordinary common world. I touch things with the common touch and relieve my overwrought senses. Drink does that for a man.'

STIFFENING THE BACKBONE

Falstaff, praising his sherris-sack, is also made to say that it warms the blood, 'which before, cold and settled, left the liver white and pale, which is the badge of pusillanimity and cowardice . . . Valour comes of sherris, . . . skill in the weapon is nothing without sack.'

This is a far more delicate point. Robert Graves, in *Goodbye To All That*, relates a youthful experience to do with cherry-whisky. Occasional swigs from a bottle that has been smuggled into the school enable him to thrash several opponents in the boxing-ring. The problem is that too many swigs could easily have led to pot valour, or Dutch courage, and a foolish, unjustified bravery, or to a slowing-down of physical and mental responses. The phrase 'Dutch courage', incidentally, did not necessarily come about as an inten-tional insult to the Dutch. It is said that English soldiers serving in the Netherlands induced it by drinking Dutch gin.

A certain amount of apprehension is now considered to be both normal and even desirable in many situations. An actor may *need* to experience stage-fright in order to stimulate natural adrenalin. Once on stage, his basic training and specific rehearsals will come to his aid. Sometimes, though, ordinary people are faced with abnormal situations and are afraid that they will not be able to cope. A drink may help. 'He's priming himself,' Osborne whispers to Dobbin, in Thackeray's *Vanity Fair*, as they watch the ludicrous Joseph Sedley downing glass after glass of claret. They

A 16th-century drinking scene.

know that he is thinking of proposing to Rebecca Sharp. Sedley over-does the priming, and the proposal is never made.

In *Bleak House*, Dickens shows Mr Guppy rapidly consuming several glasses of wine before proposing, in a ridiculous manner, to Esther Summerson. She turns him down. In real life many a young man, his emotions in a turmoil, must have downed a quick glass before uttering the fateful words.

Some would argue that the 'valour' claimed by Falstaff is little more than the 'confidence' mentioned by Johnson. When fear is present to a great degree, alcohol is unlikely to replace it with courage. Enough alcohol may merely act as a sedative, lowering one's emotional responses but not replacing something negative with something positive. Aircraft passengers who drink heavily are presumably sedating themselves, wanting to dull their thoughts of danger. They are using alcohol passively, but they are, after all, in a passive situation. Such usage does not deny the ability of alcohol to stiffen a person's resolve at a critical moment in a more positive way. As usual, everything depends on how much is drunk and on individual capacity to absorb it.

O. Henry comments in his usual idiosyncratic way on the temporary courage – 'bottle' as it is now significantly called in British slang – conveyed by alcohol. In his short story, *The Brief Debut of Tildy*, a diffident young man one day kisses Tildy, a waitress, because he has had a drink or two. A few days later he apologises: 'I was pretty well tanked up or I wouldn't of done it.'

Feminists will not be pleased to hear that Tildy is said to be very upset about the apology. Until now Tildy has never enjoyed the attentions lavished on her more attractive work-mate. The kissing incident has given her a new status and new confidence. Her boss has even given her a raise at this evidence of her effect on male customers. The moral seems to be that alcohol's effect on one person can be beneficial to someone else.

TAKING ADVANTAGE

Many people, of course, try to exploit that fact in distasteful ways. The businessman may soften up his potential client with alcohol, if the client allows him to do so. Jonas Chuzzlewit is far too clever to be caught out in that way. 'None of that, thankee,' he says sharply, when Montague offers him a drink in Dickens's *Martin Chuzzlewit*: 'No wine over business.' It is sound thinking, yet soon afterwards he accepts Montague's invitation to dinner and is duly plied with fine wines. The results are disastrous for himself and beneficial to Montague.

Businessmen might argue that drinking with clients is both a necessary and a useful part of the game. Sinclair Lewis makes ironic comments on such matters in *Elmer Gantry*. There is talk of 'securing some telling credit-information by oiling a book-keeper with several drinks'.

Elmer also meets a salesman on a train who says: 'The sales-manager can drink more good liquor than any fellow that's working for him, and believe me, there's some of us that ain't so slow ourselves! Yes-sir, this fool idea that a lot of these fly-by-night firms are hollering about now, that in the long run you don't get no more by drinking with the dealers – all damn foolishness. They say this fellow Ford that makes these automobiles talks that way. Well, you mark my words: by 1910 he'll be out of business.'

At least one other reference to Henry Ford's abstemious views occurs in *Ragtime*, by E.L. Doctorow. There is a scene where Ford has lunch with J.P. Morgan: 'They did not say much as they dined without other company on Chincoteagues, bisque of terrapin, a Montrachet, rack of lamb, a Château Latour, fresh tomatoes and endives, rhubarb pie in heavy cream, and coffee. Ford ate well but did not touch the wine.' The scene is fictional, but I shudder at the thought of leaving wines such as those untouched.

GOOD HEALTH!

G.K. Chesterton was outraged earlier this century when a group of doctors issued a favourable statement about alcohol. The doctors, said Chesterton, in his essay *Wine When It Is Red*, 'are not content with declaring that drink is in moderation harmless; they distinctly declare that it is in moderation beneficial'. Chesterton was worried about drink being prescribed for health reasons, because then 'you are giving it to a desperate person, to whom it is the only form of life. The invalid can hardly be blamed if by some accident of his erratic and overwrought condition he comes to remember the thing as the very water of vitality and to use it as such.'

This is an extreme view. St Timothy does say, after all: 'No longer drink only water, but use a little wine for the sake of your stomach and your frequent ailments' (1 *Timothy* 5.23). In our own culture, mead was clearly felt to be medicinal. The Welsh added spices to it and called it *metheglin*, 'medicinal liquor'. Shakespeare and his contemporaries tended a cold by drinking posset, hot milk curdled with spiced ale or wine.

Others, however, have been worried about equating medicine and alcohol. In 1936, for instance, the Federal Alcohol Administration of America objected to the advertising slogan 'Guinness is good for you'. In response the Guinness company produced hundreds of letters from doctors which said that Guinness was indeed good for anaemia, insomnia, neuralgia, post-influenzal debility and depression. Nevertheless, Codes of Advertising Practice have subsequently made it impossible to claim health-giving qualities for any alcoholic drinks, though modern researchers announce fairly regularly that beer or wine in moderate quantities is beneficial.

FAVOURABLE RESEARCH

Simon de Burgh, of Sydney University's Public Health department, for example, announced in July 1991 that two pints of beer a day could reduce the risk of gall bladder trouble, diabetes, a heart attack or a stroke. This applied to male drinkers: the same Australian National Health Foundation survey concluded that safe levels of drinking for women were 'less clear'. In 1990 a team of cardiological researchers at hospital in Pessac, near Bordeaux, found that red wine 'significantly lowered the amount of potentially harmful cholesterol in patients' blood'.

A French doctor, E.A. Maury, published a book in which, as he described it, he 'took up the challenge to defend the divine beverage which warms the hearts of men'. His book was translated into English by Marie-Luce Monferran-Parker, and was called bluntly: *Wine Is The Best Medicine.*

Dr Maury made specific recommendations for particular categories of people. The obese should drink rosé wines from Provence or Sancerre white wine, both of which are low in sugar and alcohol and have diuretic properties. The old should drink red wines from Aloxe-Corton or light white dry wines, the former being rich in mineral elements, the latter rich in sulphur. Pregnant women, said Dr Maury, should drink light red, 10° Bordeaux wine, rich in calcium and oenotannins, 'and also because it facilitates antitoxic liver function'. Dr Maury also specified how much wine should be drunk: the pregnant women, for example, could have two glasses per meal.

RECOMMENDATIONS IN FICTION

In fiction, references to the medicinal qualities of alcoholic drinks abound. The following selection of quotations shows that a wide range of drinks have long been considered to be beneficial.

'Mr Gray, I find I have some bottles of Malmsey, of the vintage of seventeen hundred and seventy eight, yet left. Malmsey, as perhaps you know, used to be considered a specific for coughs arising from weakness. You must permit me to send you half-a-dozen bottles, and depend upon it, you will take a more cheerful view of life and its duties before you have finished them . . .'

Mrs Gaskell *My Lady Ludlow*

'He has just had a basin of beautiful strong broth, sir,' replied Mrs Bedwin.

'Ugh!' said Mr Brownlow, with a slight shudder; 'a couple of glasses of port wine would have done him a great deal more good.'

Charles Dickens *Oliver Twist*

'I'm going to tell you something about Champagne. Quite seriously. Only yesterday one of the nurses told me it's very good for your bowels.'

Mordecai Richler *Joshua Then and Now*

'I find that it is necessary to have some stimulant in the house in case of sickness. My wife, unfortunately, has been not quite well recently. Brandy is a sure restorative. I sometimes, very seldom, try a little myself, and it has been recommended to me for rheumatism, to which I am a martyr.'

Beverley Nichols *Self*

'Artist's Party, Skagen' by Peter Severin Kroyer (1851–1909).

'I met Dr Corney coming along, and he prescribed hot brandy and water for a wet skin; especially for sitting in it. There's the stuff on the table; I see you have been aware of a singular odour; you must consent to sip some, as medicine; merely to give you warmth.'

George Meredith *The Egoist*

THE NOSTRUM
He would sometimes retire to the sickroom to take his beer; and it was not without much difficulty that he was prevented from forcing Jones to take his beer too; for no quack ever held his nostrum to be a more general panacea than he did this, 'which,' he said, 'had more virtue in it than was in all the physic in an apothecary's shop.'

Henry Fielding *Tom Jones*

[Bounderby to Mrs Sparsit, who has a cold]: 'Take a glass of scalding rum-and-butter after you get into bed.'

Charles Dickens *Hard Times*

'It's not often people get over a stomach wound. Does it affect you at all?'

Vallon grinned. 'Not much. It just makes me like whisky. I find whisky keeps it quiet.'

'Whisky of course is a hypnotic, so is veganin. You'll find veganin is cheaper in the long run . . .'

Peter Cheyney *You Can Call It A Day*

(Nurse speaking): 'We rub brandy on the gums during teething. Matter of fact, we sometimes put a drop in baby's formula when it won't sleep at night.'

Peter de Vries *The Tunnel of Love*

He dipped a rag in whisky and gave it to the baby to suck, and after two or three dippings young Adam went to sleep. Several times he awakened and complained and got the dipped rag again and went to sleep. The baby was drunk for two days and a half. Whatever may have happened in his developing brain, it proved beneficial to his metabolism: from that two and a half days he gained an iron health.

John Steinbeck *East of Eden*

THE DIGESTIVE
While her husband had liked a glass of amontillado well enough before lunch, he had always taken two ounces of Scotch whisky, neat, before his dinner. Mrs Minturn had often heard him say he considered Scotch drunk neat before dinner an excellent digestive, and for years she had followed his custom, despite the fact that she privately thought the taste of Scotch whisky rather nasty.

James Reid Parker
The Merry Wives of Massachusetts

At that moment there walked in one of the chapel deacons for his morning 'medicinal purpose' shot of whisky.

David Brynley *Seth*

Paul Waggett was pouring himself out a carefully measured dram, which he handed to his wife. 'If you'll add sugar and hot water, old lady, I'll drink it when I'm in bed. I rather think I caught a germ at the Manse this afternoon. Mr Morrison really ought to keep that cold of his to himself . . . I think if I drink a double ration of hot grog I may fend it off. That's the beauty of only drinking whisky on rare occasions. One gets the benefit of it when one does drink it.'

Compton Mackenzie *Whisky Galore*

Major Hawkes drank a lot for him, because his pension wouldn't run to more than one bottle of whisky a month at home, and a splendid doctor he knew had said that alcohol was good for his arteries.

Elizabeth Jane Howard *After Julius*

LIFE BEGINS . . . ?

Plato forbiddeth children to drinke any wine before they be eighteene yeares of age, and to be drunk before they come to forty. But to such as have once attained that age, he is content to pardon them, if they chance to delight themselves with it, and alloweth them somewhat largely to blend the influence of Dionysius in their banquets, that good God, who bestoweth cheerfulnesse upon men, and youth unto aged men . . . and in his profitable lawes holds drinking-meetings or quaffing companies as necessary and commendable (alwaies provided there be a chiefe leader amongst them to containe and order them) drunkenness being a good and certaine tryall of every mans nature; and therewithall proper to give aged men the courage to make merry in dancing and musicke; things allowable and profitable, and such as they dare not undertake being sober and settled: that wine is capable to supply the mind with temperance and the body with health.

Michel Montaigne *Of Drunkenness*
(translated from the French by John Florio, 1603)

MOTHER'S MILK

He mixed a great mugful of gin-and-water, and holding it to Smike's mouth, as one might hold a bowl of medicine to the lips of a refractory child, commanded him to drain it to the last drop.

Charles Dickens *Nicholas Nickleby*

Liza: 'They all thought she was dead, but my father he kept ladling gin down her throat till she came to so sudden that she bit the bowl off the spoon.'
Mrs Eynsford Hill: 'But it can't have been right for your father to pour spirits down her throat like that. It might have killed her.'
Liza: 'Not her. Gin was mother's milk to her. Besides, he'd poured so much down his own throat that he knew the good of it.'

G.B. Shaw *Pygmalion*

Doctors of the past were sometimes over-enthusiastic about drink as medicine. The Diary of the Rev. James Woodforde (1740–1803) mentions that his niece who came to live with him had a bad knee. The doctor prescribed 'at least a pint of port wine a day'. To be on the right side the young lady drank 'between a pint and a quart a day.' She was, needless to say, soon obliged to give up the treatment.

DRINKING CONTESTS

The ability to hold one's drink, long associated with masculinity, has often become competitive. A journalist writing in *The Times* on 9 March 1991 recalled his Spanish holidays with an 18–30 club. There were regular competitions amongst the young men to see who could drink most *sangria*. Alan Sillitoe describes another drinking-match in the opening chapter of *Saturday Night and Sunday Morning*. The young hero wins by drinking eleven pints of beer and seven small gins. His opponent, an ex-sailor, remarks in passing that 'we used to have boozing-matches on shore leave'.

T.H. Bird, in his short story *Lord Eglinton and the Flying Dutchman*, makes the point that such contests are not merely a working-class phenomenon. The drinking-match in which his hero takes part is based on champagne, drunk by the bottle. Once again, proof of manhood is felt to be at stake, as well as the money that has been wagered.

There is nothing new about such contests. Washington Irving, in his *Picturesque Views on the Avon*, says that villages in the 17th century used to have teams of topers who challenged one another. He relates a traditional story about Shakespeare, said to have taken part in such a match but obliged to withdraw at an early stage.

Much earlier still one reads of the heroes of Norse mythology and their mighty appetites and thirsts. The man who could withstand the effects of drink the longest was held in great esteem.

Joseph Addison was totally opposed to such thinking. In his *Spectator* essay 'On Drunkenness' he wonders how drunkenness became a vice which 'men are apt to glory in'. As to drinking contests, he implies that if they must occur at all, then we should remember Anacharsis, who 'being invited to a match of drinking at Corinth, demanded the prize very humorously, because he was drunk before any of the rest of the company; 'for,' says he, 'when we run a race, he who arrives at the goal first is entitled to the reward.'

The salesman quoted above is not a little proud of his drinking prowess. His remarks serve as a reminder that the ability to drink a great deal is almost a necessary qualification in certain circles. The journalist Cecil Chesterton (1879–1918) commented on one such group in a lengthy poem called 'A Ballade of Professional Pride'. The first verse runs:

> You ask me how I manage to consume
> So many beers and whiskies multiplied;
> Why I can stand as rigid as a broom
> While others gently sway from side to side;
> Why from the phrase "Ferriferous
>   Vermicide"
> My tongue, all unembarrassed, does not
>   shrink?
> Hear then my city's boast, my calling's pride:
> It was in Fleet Street that I learnt to drink.

LOVING CUPS

At a more personal level, men have long tried for selfish reasons to persuade women to drink. A tipsy woman is more likely to succumb to sexual advances, runs the popular belief, not without reason. J.B. Priestley, in *The Good Companions*, talks of treating girls 'to eighteen-penny glasses of Champagne and other notorious aphrodisiacs'. Modern Australian slang refers more crudely to a strong drink given to a girl as a 'leg-opener'. A really unscrupulous male may attempt to lace or spike a drink that is supposed to be non-alcoholic.

It is obvious that no one, whether potential business client or vulnerable female, should ever drink alcohol so that someone else will benefit. Common-sense dictates that the full circumstances in which one is drinking should always be taken into account, just as the quantity of drink should always be controlled.

The late Margaret Powell expressed a more healthily positive, if slightly risky, point of view in her autobiography, *Below Stairs*. She was speaking of a rather unsatisfactory boy-friend she once had: 'Leaving aside the life you get in a pub, there was another reason I resented George not taking me there and that's the effect drinks have on you. I used to feel amorous after a couple or so and so did any young man. Any fellow I met who had a face like the back of a bus and who I wouldn't have looked at twice if I'd been stone-cold sober, looked like Rudolph Valentino after a beer or so. Mind you, I had to be careful not to have too many, there was a borderline, you wanted enough so that they would kiss you and make a fuss of you and so that you could leave them thinking that next time it might be all right to go a bit further, but you didn't want them dashing at you like madmen the very first time they took you home.'

As Margaret Powell mentions, men are likely to feel amorous after drinking ('whisky makes the heart grow fonder' says a character in *After Julius*, by Elizabeth Jane Howard), but they too must be careful about quantity. Shakespeare does not mention brewer's droop, or its up-market equiva-lent *coq-au-vin*, but the phenomenon would have been in the minds of an Elizabethan audience listening to the drunken porter in *Macbeth*. Drink, he says, provokes and unprovokes lechery: 'It provokes the desire, but it takes away the performance. Therefore much drink may be said to be an equivocator with lechery: it makes him, and it mars him; it sets him on, and it takes him off; it persuades him, and disheartens him; makes him stand to, and not stand to . . .'

L.R.N. Ashley, writing in *Names*, the journal of the American Name Society some years ago, said that the parents of the actress Margaux Hemingway so named her because they thought she was conceived after they had drunk a bottle of Château Margaux together. They gave her the name in the form Margot, but she herself changed the spelling to Margaux to commemorate her conception. Perhaps in parts of Africa there are children called Guinness. The drink there is widely believed to be an aphrodisiac. An unofficial slogan says that there is 'a baby in every bottle'.

WINE IN, TRUTH OUT

There is another way in which a person's drinking may be beneficial to others. 'You can trust a drunken man,' says a character in Graham Greene's *Our Man In Havana*: *'in vino veritas'*. In *Monsignor Quixote* Greene converts this well-known tag, usually translated as 'in wine is truth', into *in vodka veritas*.

Whether this fact is a good thing or not for the individual concerned, will depend on the nature of the truth. A person who is indiscreet under the influence of drink about professional matters is likely to be a menace to himself and his colleagues. But perhaps a psychiatrist would say that it is useful for someone, in his personal life, to lower his defences at times and say what is really on his mind. Many people allow polite social conventions to stifle them. They live in a world of mutually-condoned hypocrisy. If the repressed thoughts emerge from time to time, and if alcohol helps with that spiritual spring-cleaning, that must surely be of value. Naturally, overall circumstances have to be borne in mind. Literature is full of highly comic scenes where inebriated truth emerges at inappropriate moments.

TO CELIA

Drink to me only with thine eyes,
And I will pledge with mine;
Or leave a kiss but in the cup,
And I'll not look for wine.
The thirst that from the soul doth rise,
Doth ask a drink divine:
But might I of Jove's nectar sup,
I would not change for thine.

Ben Jonson

TOASTS AND SALUTATIONS

The custom of drinking someone's health was common in ancient times. It was, in a sense, a human equivalent of the libation offered to the gods. The Romans had *leges compotandi*, or drinking laws, one of which concerned toasting a mistress. According to the poet Martial, it was necessary to drink as many glasses to her as there were letters in her name:

> With six full bumpers Noevia's health
>   be crown'd,
> Let seven at Justina's name go round,
> Let five at Lycas, four at Lyde be;
> But at the name of Ida fill but three.

This clearly provided an excuse for a great deal of drinking. The 17th-century poet Sir John Suckling was even ungallant enough to suggest that the young lady concerned might merely be used as a kind of decoy, or 'stale':

> She's pretty to walk with,
> And witty to talk with,
> And pleasant too to think on:
> But the best use of all
> Is, her health is a stale,
> And helps to make us drink on.

Suckling would not have referred to 'toasting' a lady, though in his day a piece of spiced toast was regularly added to a glass of wine to give it extra flavour. 'Go fetch me a quart of sack,' says Falstaff to Bardolph in *The Merry Wives of Windsor*. 'Put a toast in it,' he adds.

British officers in Sierra Leone, drinking the loyal toast on the Queen's birthday.

It was this toast in the wine which later led to the secondary meaning of the word, the person whose health is pledged. In issue 24 of the *Tatler*, on 2 June 1709, Richard Steele explained: 'It happened that on a public day, a celebrated beauty of those times [i.e., during the reign of Charles II] was in the Cross Bath, and one of the crowd of her admirers took a glass of the water in which the fair one stood, and drank her health to the company. There was in the place a gay fellow, half-fuddled, who offered to jump in, and swore though he liked not the liquor he would have the toast. The whim gave foundation to the present honour which is done to the lady we mention in our liquor, which has ever since been called a toast.'

Steele returned to the subject later and gave a rather simpler explanation: that the name of the lady was like a piece of toast, in that it added flavour to the wine.

OTHER EXCUSES

It was not just the ladies who provided an excuse for male tippling. In a Royal Proclamation Charles II was obliged to state: 'There are likewise another sort of men, of whom we have heard much, and are sufficiently ashamed, who spend their lives in Taverns, Tippling-houses, and Debauches, giving no other evidence of their affection for us but in Drinking our Health.' J.K. Jerome was later to write (*Idle Thoughts of an Idle Fellow*): 'The thirstiness of mankind is something supernatural. We are forever drinking on one excuse or another. We drink one another's healths, and spoil our own. We drink the Queen, and the Army, and the ladies, and everybody else that is drinkable; and, I believe, if the supply ran short, we should drink our mothers-in-law.'

Jerome added the afterthought: 'By the way, we never eat anybody's health,

BUMPERS, HEEL-TAPS, DAYLIGHT AND SKYLIGHT

A formal toast is traditionally drunk with a glass filled to the brim – a 'bumper'. The meaning of this word was later extended into other areas, enabling us to talk about e.g. 'a bumper crop'. Various other words with a basic sense of 'hitting' earlier had the meaning of 'great, huge'. People still talk informally of a whacking great/thumping great/whopping great object.

'I'll give you another one, and I 'umbly ask for bumpers, seeing I intend to make it for the divinest of her sex.'

Charles Dickens *David Copperfield*

Before a toast was proposed, toast-masters in former times would tell guests 'Take off your heel-tap!' – i.e. 'Drain your glasses so that they can be re-filled.' A 'heel-tap' was one of the layers of leather used to build up the heel of a shoe. By the 18th century the word was being commonly used to refer to the liquor left at the bottom of the glass after drinking. 'No heel-taps!' was therefore an exhortation to drain one's glass completely.

'As there was a proper objection to drinking her in heel-taps, we'll give her the first glass in the new magnum.'

Charles Dickens *Nicholas Nickleby*

'Daylight' (sometimes 'skylight') referred to the space between the rim of the glass and the surface of the liquor.

All: 'A toast! a toast!'
Dakry: 'No heel-taps – darken daylights!'

Percy Bysshe Shelley _Oedipus Tyrannus_

'Come, Mick, no skylights – here is Clara's health.'

Sir Walter Scott _St Ronan's Well_

A glee sung by men who are drinking in Thomas Love Peacock's _Headlong Hall_ runs as follows:

A heeltap! a heeltap! I never could
    bear it!
So fill me a bumper, a bumper of
    claret!
Let the bottle pass freely, don't shirk
    it nor spare it,
For a heeltap! a heeltap! I never
    could bear it!

No skylight! no twilight! while
    Bacchus rules o'er us:
No thinking! no shrinking! all
    drinking in chorus:
Let us moisten our clay, since 'tis
    thirsty and porous:
No thinking! no shrinking! all
    drinking in chorus!

always drink it. Why should we not stand up now and then and eat a tart to somebody's success?'

In theory when we tip someone we are providing money for our health to be drunk. This is acknowledged by the French word for 'tip', _pourboire_ – in order to drink. One might see in this a lay equivalent of paying for prayers to be said on one's behalf.

In Scandinavian countries, polite custom dictates that one does not drink in company without saluting someone else who is present. (_Skol_, the word used there to pledge someone's health, derives from an Old Norse word meaning a shallow bowl. From the same source comes the English word 'scale', as in the scales used for weighing.) I remember the lady who sat beside me at a formal banquet in Sweden in the 1960s. She was forced to instruct me on who needed to be toasted next. She herself could not drink until her health was proposed by someone sitting opposite. That person in turn was awaiting my salutation.

WASSAIL

There is less formality in English-speaking countries, but it is nevertheless customary to acknowledge one's drinking companions before starting on a fresh drink. In Old English times _waes hail_, 'may you be healthy', would have been countered with a _drinc hail_, 'drink good health'. The former salutation became fossilised as 'wassail' and was transferred to the drink itself, especially when in the wassail-bowl. The Gaelic equivalent, in its Scottish form, is _Slainte mhath_, 'good health,' which Compton Mackenzie tells us in _Whisky Galore_ is pronounced slahnje vah. The correct reply is _Slainte mhor_, 'great health', pronounced slahnje vor.

'Good health' is still commonly heard as a salutation, though 'Cheers' is even more frequent. The latter expression has become, informally in Britain at least, a multi-purpose tool, serving as a word that means 'goodbye' and 'thank you' as well as 'good health'. It is a modern form of: 'May you be of good cheer.'

Individuals often have their own favourite drinking salutations. Perhaps there are still those who acknowledge a drink bought by a stranger with a performance in miniature, a kind of verbal party-trick. Dickens records an example of the genre in *Great Expectations*:

'Have another glass!'

'With you. Hob and nob,' returned the sergeant. 'The top of mine to the foot of yours – the foot of yours to the top of mine – ring once, ring twice – the best tune on the Musical Glasses! Your health. May you live a thousand years, and never be a worse judge of the right sort than you are at the present moment of your life!'

FICTIONAL FORMULAE

Other novelists comment from time to time on drinking formulae. An old servant toasts newly-weds, in Mrs Gaskell's *Sylvia's Lovers*, with:

Long may ye live,
Happy may ye be,
And blest with a num'rous
Pro-ge-ny.

The equivalent toast in Compton Mackenzie's *Whisky Galore* is: 'Here's long life to you, and may you have a full quiver.'

John Steinbeck, in *Tortilla Flat*, has: 'Health!' said Pablo. '*Salud!*' said Pilon. And in a few moments, '*Salud!*' said Pablo. 'Mud in your eye!' said Pilon. They rested a little while. '*Su servidor,*' said Pilon. 'Down the rat hole,' said Pablo.

Further literary examples:
I proposed an old Russian toast, 'To my wife and my girl friend and to the woman I have yet to meet. I carry gifts for all three.'

Len Deighton *Funeral In Berlin*

'May the skin of your arse never become the head of a banjo!' he exuded and downed his own drink.

'What's that?'

'An old R.A.F. toast. Drink hearty, Timmy!'

Denison Hatch *The Stork*

'Say, jever hear the toast about the sailor?' inquired Elmer.

'Dunno's I ever did. Shoot!'

'Here's to the lass in every port,
And here's to the port-wine in every
lass,
But those tall thoughts don't matter,
sport,
For God's sake, waiter, fill my glass!'

Sinclair Lewis *Elmer Gantry*

I have noted a few other examples while working on this book. They include chin chin! cheerio! (together with cherry-oh!) here's luck! here's to you! skin off your nose! here's how! down the gully! here's lead in your pencil! here's looking up your kilt! here's mud in your eye! bottoms up! down the hatch! bung-ho! up yours! Someone, somewhere, must have a full collection of such terms, but I have yet to see it.

A special toasting custom involves smashing the glass after drinking. It is hardly an English habit, though it is referred to in *A Tale of Two Cities*. Carton and Darnay drink the health of the girl they both love. '"Miss Manette, then!" Looking his companion full in the face while he drank the toast, Carton flung his glass over his shoulder against the wall, where it shivered to pieces; then rang the bell, and ordered another.' The idea, presumably, is to ensure that the same glass is never used to toast a lesser person.

An anonymous punster has commented on this aspect of drinking as follows:

> 'In vino veritas,' they say; but that's a fable,
> A most egregious blunder.
> I've been at many a wine-bibbing ere now,
> And vow,
> For one that told the truth across the table,
> I've seen a dozen *lying* under.
> Besides, as old Sam Johnson said once, I've
>   no patience
> With men who never tell the sober truth
> But when they're drunk, and aren't to be
>   believed, forsooth,
> Except in their *lie-bations.*

COMPOTATIONS

Let us return for a moment to Dean Aldrich's little poem (see p. 24) about the reasons for drinking. His first is 'good wine', which we may interpret a little more liberally as 'any alcoholic drink of good quality'. Throughout this book writers are quoted who praise particular beers, wines and spirits, but in nearly all cases it is made clear that such drinks are being enjoyed in the presence of friends. 'I've heard,' said Jessie in the tones of an oracle, 'that drinking alone is a pernicious habit.' So says a character in O. Henry's short story, *The Rubaiyat of a Scotch Highball*, and the sentiment is echoed by others.

Iris Murdoch, in *The Bell*, has: 'She had drunk a little of her whisky from the tooth mug in her bedroom. But these little celebrations had a surreptitious and dreary quality which had her soon discouraged. She did not like drinking alone.' Somerset Maugham writes, in *The Force of Circumstance*: 'Night after night it was the same. I tried drinking three or four whiskies, but it's poor fun drinking alone, and it didn't cheer me up; it only made me feel rather rotten next day.'

Sir Walter Scott, in *The Monastery*, makes a serious point in a scene not without humour: 'The Abbot opened the conversation by motioning to the monk to take a stool, and inviting him to a cup of wine. The courtesy was declined with respect. "For the stomach's sake, brother," said the Abbot, colouring a little – "you know the text." "It is a dangerous one," answered the monk, "to handle alone, or at late hours. Cut off from human society, the juice of the grape becomes a perilous companion of solitude, and therefore I ever shun it." Abbot Boniface had poured himself out a goblet which might hold about half an English pint; but, either struck with the truth of the observation, or ashamed to act in direct opposition to it, he suffered it to remain untasted before him, and immediately changed the subject.'

Ernest Hemingway presents a rare, opposing view. The Hemingway family preference for Château Margaux has been mentioned above. In *The Sun Also Rises* we have: 'I drank a bottle of wine for company. It was a Château Margaux. It was pleasant to be drinking slowly and to be tasting the wine and be drinking alone. A bottle of wine was good company.' It is quite likely, though, that Hemingway would quickly have agreed that a bottle of wine *and* a friend made for even better company.

THIRSTY WORK

References in literature to Dean Aldrich's third reason for drinking – simple thirst – are rare. D.H. Lawrence is one of the very few to deal with the question. He has a working man remind us, in *Sons and Lovers*, that: 'A man gets that caked up wi' th' dust, you know – that clogged up down a coalmine, he *needs* a drink when he comes home.' A drink at such times must be a restorative and tonic, almost a medicine. In many instances there is no doubt about its medicinal role, as when Ruth saves the life of the heroine in Blackmore's *Lorna Doone* with a few teaspoonfuls of Spanish wine. I discuss separately the important medicinal reasons for drinking alcohol (see pp. 28–31).

With simple thirst we should link the lubrication of the throat when it is used for eating or speaking. In *Our Mutual Friend*, for instance, Wegg is about to begin reading aloud to Mr Boffin. Wegg announces: 'I generally do it on gin and water.' 'Keeps the organ moist, does it, Wegg?'

DRINKING

The thirsty earth soaks up the rain,
And drinks, and gapes for drink again.
The plants suck in the earth, and are
With constant drinking fresh and fair;
The sea itself – which one would think
Should have but little need of drink –
Drinks ten thousand rivers up,
So filled that they o'erflow the cup.
The busy sun – and one would guess
By's drunken fiery face no less –
Drinks up the sea, and when he's done,
The moon and stars drink up the sun:
They drink and dance by their own light
They drink and revel all the night.
Nothing in nature's sober found,
But an eternal health goes round.
Fill up the bowl, then, fill it high,
Fill up glasses there; for why
Should every creature drink but I;
Why, man of morals, tell me why?

Abraham Cowley

asked Mr Boffin, with innocent eagerness. 'N-no, sir,' replied Wegg coolly. 'I should hardly describe it so, sir. I should say, mellers it. Mellers it is the word I should employ, Mr Boffin.'

Other reasons for drinking alcohol mentioned in fiction include:

'You need a drink to steady your nerves.'
John Dos Passos *The Great Days*

Carveth replenished it for me, observing that I was a brandy partisan. 'I drink to make other people interesting,' I said.
Peter de Vries *The Tunnel of Love*

I began drinking because the thought that I was drinking gave me a kind of identity: each time I poured myself a brandy in the deserted afternoon

I could say to myself 'I am a woman who drinks'. It was the positive action rather than the brandy itself that gave me courage.
Penelope Mortimer *The Pumpkin Eater*

On market days, every man drank more than usual; every bargain or agreement was ratified by drink . . .
Mrs Gaskell *Sylvia's Lovers*

Also marked by drink, of course, are occasions worthy of celebration. The fellows of the Cambridge college which forms the background to *The Masters*, by C.P. Snow, are always presenting bottles of claret in the combination room for one reason or another. Jago presents a bottle, for instance, 'to mark a notable discovery completed this day by the junior fellow.'

Weddings, birthdays, arrivals, successes and achievements provide a constant excuse in literature, as in life, for having a drink. Any event which is felt to be of clear significance in a positive way is 'ratified' in this way. In *A World of Difference*, Stanley Price has a character who says: 'Got to float you out to sea' to a friend who is going abroad.

Sometimes the reason for drinking is to be inferred from the context. Insomniacs will see the point of Dickens's comment in *The Pickwick Papers*: 'Long after the ladies had retired, did the hot elder wine, well qualified with brandy and spice, go round, and round, and round again; and sound was the sleep and pleasant were the dreams that followed.'

A CORKING OCCASION

The bottle of Puligny Montrachet 1969 stood practically empty on the table. 'I'm going to keep the cork.' She spoke like a child, gleeful after a treat.

'It hasn't been that memorable, surely?'

Imogen Winn *Coming to Terms*

A favourable comment about drinking may be of a rather general nature:

'Even older men can imagine a lot and forget a lot under the influence of a few drinks. At twenty-one all sorts of things can happen.'
Henry Cecil *Brothers-in-law*

He filled her glass again. Her cheeks were flushed; her eyes were bright. He envied her the generalised sensation of universal wellbeing that he used to get from a glass of wine. Wine was good – it broke down barriers.
Virginia Woolf *The Years*

It is written, indeed, in the Bible, that Noah planted a vine-yard. Was it at divine instigation? Yes, surely, since Noah's mission was to save the human genus and all conducive to its well-being.
Gabriel Chevallier *Clochemerle-Babylon* (translated by Edward Hyams)

INTOXICATION

Man, being reasonable, must get drunk;
The best of life is but intoxication:
Glory, the grape, love, gold, in these
   are sunk
The hopes of all men, and of every
   nation

Lord Byron *Don Juan*

SUMMARY

Dean Aldrich's 'any other reason why' for having a drink, then, can be broken down into many parts. Having a modest drink for any of the above reasons strikes me as being thoroughly justified. There are those, however, who will accept none of them as valid reasons for drinking, and we will look at their views in the next chapter. The difference in viewpoint was amusingly exemplified by Oliver Wendell Holmes. In *The Autocrat of the*

Breakfast Table he tells of a poem he sent to a committee for a celebration. '"It seems," says Holmes, "the president of the day was what is called a 'teetotaller'. He suggested 'some slight changes' to the poem"'.' The last verse, as written by Holmes, was:

Then a smile, and a glass, and a toast, and a
   cheer,
For all the good wine, and we've some of it
   here!
In cellar, and pantry, in attic, in hall,
Long live the gay servant that laughs for us
   all.

The 'slightly-changed' version of this was:

Then a scowl, and a howl, and a scoff, and a
   sneer,
For all strychnine and whisky, and ratsbane
   and beer,
In cellar, in pantry, in attic, in hall,
Down, down, with the tyrant that masters us
   all!

THE OPPOSITION PARTY
Against drinking

THE 17th-century English statesman, Sir William Temple, used to say about drinking: 'The first glass for myself, the second for my friends, the third for good humour, and the fourth for mine enemies.' Everyone has a personal equivalent of Sir William's fourth glass, and the implication is obvious – it should not be drunk. It is likely to convert a feeling of well-being and conviviality into irritation and pugnaciousness. It can change free-flowing wit and intellectual excitement into mental confusion. It may eventually endanger the life of the drinker, or the lives of others. It is the glass which gives drinking a bad name.

Those who drink the fourth glass, and usually many more besides, are of very different kinds. There are drinkers who, enjoying the effect of what they have drunk so far, hardly notice that they have reached a rather critical point. They continue drinking in a rather innocent way, distracted, perhaps, by the conversation and laughter around them. They slip into tipsiness, and may even realise that they have done so. Some will stop drinking at that point; others are relieved to abandon logical reasoning. They are drifting along in a pleasant stream and see little reason to scramble out of the water.

Some, by contrast, are committed to the idea of drinking to oblivion, rather than drinking little and often. Others decide that on this particular occasion, when they sit down for a drink or two, it will be a drink or five, or six, or seven. They are at one of life's high or low points, and a gesture of some kind seems to be called for.

Finally there are those who live in the constant knowledge that after the present drink, however many have gone before, another will soon be desperately needed. These are the drinkers who live in the world of the fourth glass.

DRINKING BY NUMBERS

Three cups of wine a prudent man may
     take:
The first of them for constitution sake;
The second, to the girl he loves the best;
The third and last, to lull him to his rest –
Then home to bed. But if a fourth he
     pours,
That is the cup of folly, and not ours.
Loud noisy talking on the fifth attends;
The sixth breeds feuds, and falling out
     of friends;
Seven beget blows, and faces stained
     with gore;
Eight, and the watch patrol breaks ope'
     the door;
Mad with the ninth, another cup goes
     round,
And the swilled sot drops senseless to
     the floor.

Athenaeus *Deipnosophistai*

IN ALL INNOCENCE

Mr Pickwick, surely, is an example of the innocent drinker. One thinks of him and the cold punch he drinks at a picnic. He certainly has no intention of getting drunk, but as Dickens tells us: 'This constant succession of glasses produced considerable effect upon Mr Pickwick; his countenance beamed with the most sunny smiles, laughter played around his lips, and good-humoured merriment twinkled in his eye. Yielding by degrees to the influence of the exciting liquid, rendered more so by the heat, Mr Pickwick expressed a strong desire to recollect a song which he had heard in his infancy, and the attempt proving abortive, sought to stimulate his memory with more glasses of punch, which appeared to have quite a contrary effect; for, from forgetting the words of the song, he began to forget how to articulate any words at all; and finally, after rising to his legs to address the company in an eloquent speech, he fell into the barrow, and fast asleep, simultaneously.'

Mr Pickwick's friends leave him in the wheelbarrow to sleep it off. He is soon afterwards discovered by others, who wheel him away and put him in the village pound. There he is pelted with vegetables and laughed at by village youths until his friends come to the rescue.

Dickens draws no moral from the incident; readers merely smile as they are meant to do. Nor does Mr Pickwick learn his lesson. He is likely to have convinced himself that it was the sun, not the punch, which caused him to fall asleep. On another occasion, when Pickwick and his friends return the worse for wear from a cricket-club dinner, Jingle explains: 'songs – old port – claret – good – very good – wine, ma'am – wine.'

'It wasn't the wine, ma'am,' murmurs Mr Snodgrass, another innocent. 'It was the salmon.'

'Somehow or other,' says Dickens, 'it never *is* the wine, in these cases.' He is not very severe in his comment. Dickens clearly believed that drunkenness intensified a person's basic character. No amount of alcohol would turn Pickwick into an immoral rogue. The Dickensian view is revealed elsewhere, in *Nicholas Nickleby*, where the author says: 'Beside her was Sir Mulberry Hawk, evidently the worse – if a man be a ruffian at heart, he is never the better – for wine.'

Mr Pickwick as a drinker makes me question the truth of the much quoted 'wine, women and song'. He is not one to become amorous or lustful in his cups; 'wine, women *or* song' would be nearer the truth in his case. When all three do apply I suspect that 'wine, song and women' is more likely to be the order of things, though the phrase in that form has a less happy ring.

DELIBERATE BINGES

It is a different situation when a person whose drinking is usually controlled decides to throw caution to the wind and quite deliberately get drunk. 'Daniel's way of announcing his intention of drinking more than ordinary,' says Mrs Gaskell, in *Sylvia's Lovers*, 'was always the same. He would say at the last moment, "Missus, I've a mind to get fuddled tonight," and be off, disregarding her look of remonstrance.'

The psychological reasons for such bouts of over-indulgence vary greatly. Attempted escape from a permanently depressing situation, or from temporary sorrows, will sometimes provide the motivation. Apprehension or fear of what the immediate future holds may initiate it. Feelings of overwhelming relief, or happiness, may likewise seem to demand that one should drink oneself into oblivion, regardless of the after-effects. There are many occasions, such as at stag parties before a wedding, when for the young, especially, getting drunk is almost a conventional requirement or social ritual. It is also frequently a trial (sometimes a self-imposed one) which forms part of one's initiation into adulthood. Fifty years ago, I might have written manhood in that last sentence, but girls now seem to be subjected to similar pressures as they become women.

FIASCO

We use the word *fiasco* to mean a ludicrous or humiliating failure. In Italian the word simply means 'flask, bottle'. The meaning of the word in English is said to derive from the Italian slang expression *far fiasco* 'to make a bottle', used by Venetian glass-blowers. What that phrase literally meant is unclear, though it must have had something to do with making a mess of things. The phrase was at first metaphorically applied to singing or playing the wrong note during a performance. It has been used in English since the 19th century in a more general sense.

THE MUSIC-LOVER

It was Mr Western's custom every afternoon, as soon as he was drunk, to hear his daughter play upon the harpsichord, for he was a great lover of music . . .

Henry Fielding *Tom Jones*

Those who know that they are going to drink to excess, sometimes try to prepare for it. They eat oily fish, drink pints of milk, and so on. Their stomachs are going to war, and protective armour is needed. No one has yet discovered an armour which infallibly protects all stomachs, though plenty of starchy food, eaten while drinking, is often recommended. Compton Mackenzie, in *Whisky Galore*, says: 'The company had just settled down to the scones, bannocks, girdle-cakes, pancakes, and oatcakes which mixed with tea would provide a solid basis for the whisky . . .'

TYRANNY

The third kind of excessive drinker is a sick person. Alcoholism is of course a serious illness, though that is not always apparent to the sufferer. Thomas Hardy has a scene in *Far From the Madding Crowd* in which some farm labourers, one of whom says that he has been 'drinky once this month already,' discuss alcohol jovially, as if they have it under control: 'Drink is a pleasant delight,' said Jan, as one who repeated a truism so familiar to his brain that he hardly noticed its passage over his tongue. 'Of course, you'll have another drop. A man's twice the man afterwards. You feel so warm and glorious, and you whop and slap at your work without any trouble, and everything goes on like sticks a-breaking. Too much liquor is bad, and leads to the horned man in the smoky house; but after all, many people haven't the gift of enjoying a wet, and since we be highly favoured with a power that way, we should make

the most o't.' '"True," said Mark Clark. '"Tis a talent the Lord has mercifully bestowed upon us, and we ought not to neglect it."'

Hardy makes it quite clear that Mark Clark's belief is a dangerous one. Gabriel Chevallier makes the same point in *Clochemerle-Babylon* (translated by Edward Hyams): 'Arthur believed himself to be armour-plated as a drinker. His vanity misled him. It is folly to defy the god of wine. He can, it is true, when moderately worshipped, cheer and comfort mankind; immoderately, he can equally well kill his man. Torbayon was on the slippery slope of habit, at first pleasant, then insinuating, at last tyrannical. He could no longer exist but with a glass in his hand.'

Chevallier rather implies that it is habitual social drinking which eventually leads to addiction. That may be true in some cases, but there are others in whom a craving appears to be born with the tasting of the first drink. In *Look Homeward, Angel* Thomas Wolfe describes such a case as a 17-year-old boy is allowed to drink whisky at a family Christmas party: 'They lavished fair warnings on him as he lifted his glass. He choked as the fiery stuff caught in his young throat, stopping his breath for a moment and making him tearful . . .

'What he had drunk beat pleasantly through his veins in warm pulses, bathing the tips of ragged nerves, giving to him a feeling of power and tranquillity he had never known. Presently, he went to the pantry where the liquor was stored. He took a water tumbler and filled it experimentally with equal portions of whisky, gin, and rum. Then, seating himself at the kitchen table, he began to drink the mixture slowly.

'The terrible draught smote him with the speed and power of a man's fist. He was made instantly drunken, and he knew instantly why men drank. It was, he knew, one of the great moments in his life – he lay, greedily watching the mastery of the grape over his virgin flesh, like a girl for the first time in the embrace of her lover.

'And suddenly, he knew how completely he was his father's son – how completely, and with what added power and exquisite refinement of sensation, was he Gantian. He exulted in the great length of his limbs and his body, through which the mighty liquor could better work its wizardry. It was greater than all the music he had

DRUNK WITH WORDS

When Sairey Gamp unsteadily makes her way home, in *Martin Chuzzlewit*, the boys who follow her in the street tell her that she is 'only a little screwed'. Dickens adds: 'Whatever she was, or whatever name the vocabulary of medical science would have bestowed upon her malady, Mrs Gamp was perfectly acquainted with the way home . . .'

Dickens was well aware that it was popular slang rather than medical science which bestowed names on Sairey's condition. Elsewhere in the same novel he uses 'swipey' to describe Jonas Chuzzlewit, who is slightly tipsy. The reference there is to 'swipes', weak beer. In *The Old Curiosity Shop*, talking of Dick Swiveller, he says: 'Last night he had had "the sun very strong in his eyes;" by which expression he was understood to convey to his hearers in the most delicate manner possible, the information that he had been extremely drunk.'

Dickens could no doubt have called upon a great many other words to indicate drunkenness. It seems to be a condition which appeals to the popular imagination, challenging everyone's verbal skills. The state provokes a constant source of neologisms or extensions of existing meanings.

Here are some authors displaying their own predilections:

'I think I'll go out and get cockeyed.' Sinclair Lewis *Bethel Merriday*. (The same author elsewhere has: 'I had a beautiful skate on last night.' 'Babbitt was in last night as full as a boiled owl.')

'I wasn't drunk, but I had a top on.'
Arnold Bennett *Clayhanger*

'You've got a load on.'
J.B. Priestley *The Good Companions*

'A giggle when he gets tanked-up.'
Jilly Cooper *Prudence*

'The English feel disgraced if they do something scandalous while under the influence.'
Tallulah Bankhead *Tallulah*

'You look three sheets to the wind again.'
Peter de Vries *The Tunnel of Love*

'We all drank a little rum which Diana brought with her and became what Mark called slightly *beschwippst*.'
Han Suyin *A Many Splendoured Thing*

'Twopence on the can.'
Compton Mackenzie *Whisky Galore*

PERSONAL CHOICE

'Drunk' words appear to be idiolectal in the extreme. Every individual, that is to say, has his personal way of referring to drunkenness, has made a selection from the large number of words that are available. Just how many there are is difficult to say. As a warning against drunkenness, Benjamin Franklin published a list of 228 of them in 1722, words he had heard being used in taverns. Below there follows a selection of such words and phrases, all of which mean 'affected by drink' to a lesser or greater degree.

Afflicted, arseholed, as drunk as David's sow, as drunk as a fiddler, as drunk as a lord, as drunk as a piper, as drunk as a tinker, as happy as a king, as merry as a grig, balmy, been in the sun, beery, blind drunk, blotto, boiled, bombed, boozy, bosky, bottled, breezy, buffy, canned, cast away, caught it, chases geese, chocfull, cocksy-boozy, concerned, corned, cup-sprung, cut, dagged, disguised, drunk as a beggar, drunk as an owl, drunk as a pig, drunk as Chloe, elevated, far-gone, floppy, flushed, flustered, foggy, foxed, fresh, fuddled, full, full-cocked, funny, gilded, ginned up, glassy-eyed, gone, got a dish, got a skinful, got his load, gravy-eyed, groggy, happy, half-cocked, half-seas over, has copped the brewer, has had a drop too much, has had one over the eight, hazy, high, in a quandary, in drink, in his cups, inked, in liquor, inebriated, intoxicated, jagged, legless, lit up, loaded, loppy, lumpy, lushy, maudlin, mellow, miraculous, mops and brooms, muddled, muggy, muzzy, nailed it, nappy, nicely thank you, not able to see a hole through a ladder, obfuscated, oiled, out, overcome, overtaken, pickled, pie-eyed, pious, pissed, plastered, ploughed, raddled, ripe, ripped, screwed, sees double, sewed-up, shot, shows his hobnails, slaughtered, slewed, soaked, soused, sozzled, springy, squiffed, squiffy, stiff, stinking drunk, stinko, stoned, stung, swipy, three sheets to the wind, tiddly, tight, tight as a drum, tipsy, top-heavy, under the influence, under the table, under the weather, weary, well-primed, winey, winged, woozy, worse for wear.

(For some further rhyming slang expressions meaning 'drunk' see p. 20.)

DAVID'S SOW

'As drunk as David's sow' was once a common saying. Its origin was explained in the *British Apollo* (1711) as follows: David Lloyd, a Welshman, kept an ale-house in the town of Hereford, and had a kind of monstrous sow, with six legs, which he showed to customers as a valuable rarity. This David's wife would often make herself quite drunk, and then lie down to sleep an hour or two, that she might qualify herself for the performance of her business.

But one day the house was full, and she could find no other place to sleep in but the hogsty, where her husband kept the sow above-named on clean straw; so she very orderly went in, and fell asleep by her harmonious companion. But the sow no sooner found the door upon the jar, but out she slipt, and rambled to a considerable distance from the yard, in joy for her deliverance.

David had that day some relations come to see him, who had been against his marrying; and, to give them an opinion of his prudent choice, he took occasion to inform them he was sorry his wife was then abroad, because he would have had them see her: 'For,' says David, 'surely man was never better matched, or met with a more quiet, sober wife than I am blest in.'

They congratulated his good fortune, and were after a short time desired by David to go and see the greatest wonder of a sow that had ever been heard of in the world. He led them to his hogsty door, and opening it to its full wideness, the first thing they saw was his good wife in such a posture and condition, as, upon her starting up and calling David husband, gave occasion for a hearty fit of laughter.

ever heard; it was as great as the highest poetry. Why had he never been told? Why had no one ever written adequately about it? Why, when it was possible to buy a god in a bottle, and drink him off, and become a god oneself, were men not forever drunken?'

SHIPS ADRIFT?

Such an extreme response to alcohol does seem to affect some people but not others. Oliver Wendell Holmes, in *The Autocrat of the Breakfast Table*, had an explanation: 'I think you will find it true, that, before any vice can fasten on a man, body, mind, or moral nature must be debilitated. The mosses and fungi gather on sickly trees, not thriving ones; and the odious parasites which fasten on the human frame choose that which is already enfeebled . . . Wherever the wandering Demon of Drunkenness finds a ship adrift – no steady wind in its sails, no thoughtful pilot directing its course – he steps on board, takes the helm, and steers straight for the maelstrom.'

While Holmes allows for the possibility of a physical reaction to alcohol, he clearly favours the theory that lack of moral and mental fibre is the

'The master caused us to have some beer'. Puritans reluctantly celebrating Christmas on arrival in the New World.

LATE STARTERS

'Deacon Worthington was a friend of dear Papa's in Richmond before the war. He was the most straight-laced sober man and highly censorious of others, you understand, until his seventy-first birthday. On that day he was induced to take a sip of liquor. My dear, he never stopped drinking till the day he died.'

John Dos Passos *The Great Days*

Liza hated alcoholic liquors with an iron zeal. Drinking alcohol in any form she regarded as a crime against a properly outraged deity . . . When Liza was about seventy her elimination slowed up and her doctor told her to take a tablespoon of port wine for medicine. She forced down the first spoonful, making a crooked face, but it was not so bad. And from that moment she never drew a completely sober breath. She always took the wine in a tablespoon, it was always medicine, but after a time she was doing over a quart a day and she was a much more relaxed and happy woman.

John Steinbeck *East of Eden*

main cause. This has been a common belief, that addiction to alcohol is merely excessive drinking that is done deliberately. It is assumed that the drinker can stop it at any moment, especially if he is made to feel ashamed. The common punishment for a drunkard in the past was a spell in the stocks, where one remained as a target both for jeering and rotten vegetables. This happened in Newbury, for instance, as late as 1872. Many villages also had a special drunkard's coat – a barrel with holes for the offender's head and arms.

Meanwhile, preachers harangued their congregations. John Bunyan, for example, used simple animal imagery in his *Life and Death of Mr Badman*: 'There was a gentleman that had a drunkard to be his groom, and coming home one night very much abused with beer, his master saw it. "Well" (quoth his master within himself), "I will let thee alone tonight, but tomorrow morning I will convince thee that thou art worse than a beast, by the behaviour of my horse."

'So when morning was come, he bids his man go and water his horse, and so he did; but coming up to his master, he commands him to water him again; so the fellow rid into the water a second time, but his master's horse would now drink no more, so the fellow came up and told his master. Then said his master, "Thou drunken sot, thou art far worse than my horse, he will drink but to satisfy Nature, but thou wilt drink to the abuse of Nature; he will drink but to refresh himself, but thou to thy hurt and damage; he will drink, that he may be more serviceable to his master, but thou, till thou art incapable of serving either God or man. O thou beast, how much art thou worse than the horse that thou ridest on."'

Bunyan later says: 'There are four things which, if they were well considered, would make drunkenness to be abhorred in the thoughts of the children of men.

1. It greatly tendeth to impoverish and beggar

men. The drunkard, says Solomon, shall come to poverty. Yea, many children that have begun the world with plenty, have gone out of it in rags, through drunkenness.

2. This sin of drunkenness, it bringeth upon the body many great and incurable diseases, by which men do in little time come to their end.

3. Drunkenness is a sin that is often times attended with abundance of other evils. Who hath woe? Who hath sorrow? Who hath contention? Who hath babblings? Who hath wounds without cause? Who hath redness of the eyes? They that tarry long at the wine, they that go to seek mixed wine.

4. By drunkenness, men do often times shorten their days; go out of the ale-house drunk, and break their necks before they come home.

GOING THROUGH FIRE

This is all very well, but it shows no understanding at all of the nature of addiction, nor of what causes it. Bunyan has no insight into the difficulties that face the true alcoholic in trying to escape from drink. If such a drinker is made to feel ashamed, then the drinking may be done in secret. Garrison Keillor comments amusingly in *Lake Wobegon Days*: 'His taste for Ever Clear pure grain alcohol was a secret to her for years. . . . She learned about the Ever Clear one morning when the toaster burst into flames and she grabbed his cup and threw the coffee onto the fire. The coffee exploded. Then she had an idea why he always poured his own and what was in the bottle marked DON'T THROW OUT under the sink.'

Charles Lamb was later to show a great deal more sympathy than Bunyan. In his essay *Confessions of a Drunkard* he compares a drunkard's reformation with a 'resuscitation from a state of death almost as real as that from which Lazarus rose but by a miracle'. An alcoholic does not renounce drink, says Lamb, as another person might give up stealing or telling lies, because 'there is no constitutional tendency to do such things'.

Lamb goes on to imagine what happens when an addictive drinker tries to fight the craving: 'What if the beginning be dreadful, the first steps

---

ALCOHOL CONCERN

The modern equivalent of the Temperance Society is still to be found in organisations like Alcohol Concern, which claims that 28 000 people die each year because they drink too much. They also say that five million men exceed the officially recommended 21-units-a-week maximum – a unit of alcohol being a half pint of beer, a glass of wine or a single pub measure of spirit. Over a million men, according to Alcohol Concern, drink more than 50 units a week. The suggested upper limit for women is 14 units a week, but it is thought that some two million women in Britain regularly drink more than that.

A HAIR OF THE DOG

The word 'hangover' has only been in use since the beginning of the 20th century, though we can be sure that many a hangover was experienced before then. In Thackeray's *Vanity Fair*, for instance, Joseph Sedley insists on ordering a bowl of rack [arrack] punch when he visits Vauxhall Gardens. No one else in the party wants to taste it, so Sedley drinks it all. Next morning, needless to say, he suffers. 'What is the rack in the punch, at night, to the rack in the head of a morning?' asks Thackeray. 'To this truth I can vouch as a man; there is no headache in the world like that caused by Vauxhall punch. Through the lapse of twenty years, I can remember the consequence of two glasses! two wine glasses!' Sedley has drunk about a quart of it.

SODA WATER

Thackeray goes on to make a comment about hangover cures. 'Soda water was not invented yet. Small beer – will it be believed? – was the only drink with which unhappy gentlemen soothed the fever of their previous night's potation.'

This is not necessarily a very accurate comment. Thackeray is describing the period around the Battle of Waterloo, which took place in 1815. By 1819 Lord Byron was saying, in his *Don Juan*:
'Let us have wine and women, mirth and laughter,
Sermons and soda-water the day after.'

Later in the same poem Byron says again:
'Get very drunk; and when
You wake with headache, you shall see what then.
Ring for your valet – bid him quickly bring

Some hock and soda-water, then you'll know
A pleasure worthy Xerxes the great king;
For not the blest sherbet, sublimed with snow,
Nor the first sparkle of the desert spring,
Nor burgundy in all its sunset glow,
After long travel, ennui, love, or slaughter,
Vie with that draught of hock and soda-water.'

Soon afterwards Richard Barham was writing, in *The Ingoldsby Legends*:
'We bore him home and put him to bed
And we told his wife and daughter
To give him next morning, a couple of red
Herrings, with soda water.'

Thomas Hughes, in *Tom Brown at Oxford*, writes:
'Some soda water with a dash of bingo [i.e. brandy] clears one's head in the morning.'

The Irish novelist Samuel Lover, however, makes it clear in his novel *Handy Andy* that soda-water was still not generally familiar in the 1840s. When a guest makes a request for some to be brought, the servant is very surprised. He cannot understand why soap and water is needed in the middle of a meal.

Thackeray says that small beer – weak beer, that is – was the only remedy known to gentlemen in the early 19th century, but since at least the 16th century they had been calling for a hair of the dog that bit them. In medieval times it was believed that a wound caused by a dog-bite could be cured by laying a hair of the same dog across it. When that belief was proved erroneous, the saying seems to have been applied metaphorically to alcohol.

FICTIONAL HANGOVER CURES

Writers mention different drinking remedies from time to time. In *East of Eden*, for instance, John Steinbeck says of a woman who has drunk too much: 'She poured dry mustard in a glass, stirred water in it until it was partly fluid, and drank it. She held on to the edge of the sink while the paste went burning down. She retched and strained again and again. At the end of it, her heart was pounding and she was weak – but the wine was overcome and her mind was clear.'

This is presumably before a hangover has had time to set in. If action must be taken next morning, Fernet Branca is sometimes mentioned, as here by Jilly Cooper in *Prudence*:

'Have you got any Alka-Seltzer?'

'You'll never keep it down in that condition,' he said. 'I'll get you a Fernet Branca.' . . .

I gulped it down, then choked.

'You've poisoned me,' I croaked.

For a second I thought I was going to explode. Then suddenly it was a horror film in reverse. The terrified creature being torn apart by Dracula's teeth was transformed into the radiant bride again. Suddenly I was all right. I shook my head three times. It didn't even hurt.

Kingsley Amis specifically tells us that Underberg, which is sold in miniature bottles holding about a pub double, is more effective than Fernet Branca. Alan Sillitoe mentions Indian brandy as being a commonly-used hangover cure. Other people swear by such things as raw eggs in Worcester sauce, or large amounts of vitamins B and C. They obtain the latter by consuming cornflakes and orange juice, followed by potatoes. Another popular suggestion is Black Velvet, a mixture of chilled champagne and Guinness. It is recommended, for instance, by Tallulah Bankhead in her autobiography, *Tallulah*: 'Racked with a hangover I do my muttering over a Black Velvet, a union of champagne and stout.'

TIME ALONE . . .

Miss Bankhead, however, who admits that she is something of an expert on the subject of hangovers, adds: 'Don't be swindled into believing there's any cure for a hangover. I've tried them all: iced tomatoes, hot clam juice, brandy punches. Like the common cold it defies solution. Time alone can stay it. The hair of the dog? That way lies folly. It's as logical as trying to put out a fire with applications of kerosene. . . .'

P.G. Wodehouse introduces us to Jeeves, the perfect butler, in *Jeeves Takes Charge*. Jeeves immediately recommends himself to Bertie Wooster by providing a hangover cure: '"If you would drink this, sir," he said, with a kind of bedside manner rather like a royal doctor shooting the bracer into the sick prince. "It is a little preparation of my own invention. It is the Worcester sauce which gives it its colour. The raw egg makes it nutritious. The red pepper gives it its bite. Gentlemen have told me they have found it extremely invigorating after a late evening."

'I would have clutched at anything that looked like a lifeline that morning. I swallowed the stuff. For a moment I felt as if somebody had touched off a bomb inside the old bean and was strolling down my throat with a lighted torch, then everything seemed suddenly to get all right. The sun shone in through the window; birds twittered in the tree-tops; and generally speaking, hope dawned once more.'

Clement Freud, in *Clement Freud's Book of Hangovers*, offers the following hints for those afflicted:

drink plenty of water, milk or fruit juice before, during and after drinking alcohol;

Paracetamol is better for a hangover headache than aspirin;

nausea may perhaps best be dealt with by taking in an acid substance such as vinegar rather than an alkaline one such as bicarbonate of soda.

NOT THE SAME MAN

'I suppose your old boozing mate's wife was very happy when he reformed,' I said to Mitchell.

'Well, no,' said Mitchell. 'Perhaps it was this way: She loved and married a careless, good-natured, drinking scamp, and when he reformed and became a careful, hard-working man, and an honest and respected townsman, she was disappointed in him. He wasn't the man that won her heart when she was a girl.'

Henry Lawson *The Boozers' Home*

DRYING OUT

I must get out of these wet clothes and into a dry Martini.

Alexander Woollcott

HOME THOUGHTS

A drunkard seldom reforms at home, because he's always surrounded by the signs of the ruin and misery he has brought on the home; and the sight and thought of it sets him off again before he's had time to recover from the last spree. Then, again, the noblest wife in the world mostly goes the wrong way to work with a drunken husband – nearly everything she does is calculated to irritate him. If, for instance, he brings a bottle home from the pub, it shows that he wants to stay at home and not go back to the pub any more; but the first thing the wife does is to get hold of the bottle and plant it, or smash it before his eyes, and that maddens him in the state he is in then. No, a dipsomaniac needs to be taken away from home for a while.

Henry Lawson *The Boozers' Home*

not like climbing a mountain but going through fire? what if the whole system must undergo a change violent as that which we conceive of the mutation of form in some insects? what if a process comparable to flaying alive be to be gone through?'

This, one feels, is rather more to the point than smug comments of writers like Joseph Addison. In his *Spectator* essay 'On Temperance' Addison says: 'Temperance has those particular advantages above all other means of health, that it may be practised by all ranks and conditions, at any season, or in any place. It is a kind of regimen into which every man may put himself, without interruption of business, expense of money, or loss of time. If exercise throws off all superfluities, temperance prevents them; if exercise clears the vessels, temperance neither satiates nor overstrains them; if exercise raises proper ferments in the humours, and promotes the circulation of the

blood, temperance gives nature her full play, and enables her to exert herself in all her force and vigour.'

If John Bunyan's sermons were not necessarily effective, one can understand his extreme concern about drunkenness. He lived at a time when it is estimated that England and Wales had 13 000 licensed premises to serve a population of under five million. Drunkenness had long been identified as a national problem, and official efforts to curb it continued. Between 1604 and 1627 there were seven Acts of Parliament directed against drunkenness and the drink trade. A typical Act of 1606 began: 'Whereas the loathsome and odious sin of drunkenness is of late grown into common use in this realm, being the root and foundation of many other enormous sins, as bloodshed, stabbing, murder, swearing, fornication, adultery, and such like, to the great dishonour of God and our nation, the overthrow of many good acts and manual trades, the dishonour of divers workmen, and the general impoverishing of many good subjects, and wasting the good creatures of God ...' It then went on to limit occasions on which ale could be served in inns.

STAGES OF DRUNKENNESS

I have been talking about 'drunkenness' as if that always means the same thing, but it doesn't. This misapprehension about drinking is summed up by a character in *A World of Difference*, by Stanley Price. His thought is that 'it didn't matter how much he drank now, he was over the brink anyway'. It is not as simple as that. Different stages of drunkenness occur once the brink is passed. Writers label the stages in different ways, but there is agreement that they exist. They may occur in a different order for different people, or the same person may not experience them in the same way each time he drinks, but along with a weakening of mental and physical faculties will come distinct changes of mood.

John Steinbeck, for instance, in *Tortilla Flat*, says: 'Two gallons is a great deal of wine, even for two paisanos. Spiritually the jugs may be graduated thus: Just below the shoulder of the first bottle, serious and concentrated conversation. Two inches further down, sweetly sad memory. Three inches more, thoughts of old and satisfactory loves. An inch, thoughts of old and bitter loves. Bottom of the first jug, general and undirected sadness. Shoulder of the second jug, black unholy despondency. Two fingers down, a song of death or longing. A thumb, every other song one knows. The graduations stop here, for the trail splits and there is no certainty. From this point on anything can happen.'

Dickens puts matters in a different order when he describes Mr Snevellicci in *Nicholas Nickleby*. This gentleman, who 'was a little addicted to drinking; or, if the truth must be told, scarcely ever sober, knew in his cups three distinct stages of intoxication – the dignified – the quarrelsome – the amorous'.

The 'dignified' stage corresponds both to Steinbeck's 'serious and concentrated conversation' and to the 'extreme care' mentioned by James Dillon White, in *Geneviève*: 'She was as

ABSENT FRIENDS

The person you converse with, after the third bottle, is not the same man who at first sat down at table with you. Upon this maxim is founded one of the prettiest sayings I ever me with, which is ascribed to Publius Syrus, *Qui ebrium ludificat, loedit absentum*: He who jests upon a man that is drunk, injures the absent.

Joseph Addison *On Drunkenness*

beautifully poised as ever, but the extreme care with which she moved and spoke was some indication of the scandalous amount she had drunk.' No doubt it is the 'black unholy despondency' mentioned by Steinbeck which leads to the 'quarrelsome' stage of Dickens, though most of us would probably agree with Steinbeck that thoughts of love come first.

Daniel Defoe, writing in the 18th century, would have found a phrase like 'thoughts of love' far too sentimental. He says in *Moll Flanders* that a drunken man 'is in the possession of two devils at once, and can no more govern himself by his reason than a mill can grind without water; vice tramples upon all that was in him that had any good in it. He drinks more when he is drunk already; picking up a common woman, without any regard to what she is or who she is; whether sound or rotten, clean or unclean; whether ugly or handsome, old or young'.

As for the women, their own drunkenness exposes them to sexual abuse. Making the point in his essay *Of Drunkenness*, Montaigne tells the story of a widow in France who was surprised to find that she was expecting a child. She announced through her parish priest that she would marry whoever was responsible.

'A certaine swaine or hyne-boy [household servant] of hers, emboldened by this proclamation, declared how that having one holliday found her well-tippled with wine, and so sound asleepe

'One for the Road' by Henry Gillard Glindoni (1825–1913).

by the chimnie side, lying so fit and readie for him, without awaking her he had the full use of her body. Whom she accepted for her husband, and both live together at this day.'

BEASTLY DRUNK

Thomas Nash (or Nashe), writing at the end of the 16th century, loosely followed Rabbinical tradition in describing the various degrees of drunkenness in terms of animals. In the original Rabbinical story, Satan appeared to Noah while he was planting a vine and killed a lamb, a lion, a pig and an ape to illustrate the four stages of drunkenness, a drunken man being like each animal in turn. Nash says that to be lion-drunk is to be quarrelsome and to be swine-drunk is to be sleepy and puking. For him, though, being ape-drunk means that you 'leap and sing'. Singing apes were not common in his day, but the expression 'to drink wine ape' in the 14th century meant to have reached a state of merriness. The phrase translated the French *avoir vin de singe*.

The nearest Nash gets to 'dignified' drunken behaviour comes in his reference to the 'fox drunk, who is crafty'. He also talks of the 'goat drunk, who is lascivious', and more interestingly of 'the sheep drunk, wise in his own conceit but

TILL THE COWS COME HOME

A minister showed a parishioner a cow who went to a stream, then turned away after satisfying its thirst.

'Let that be a lesson to you,' said the minister.

'But suppose,' said the parishioner, 'another cow had come to the other side of the stream and said: "Here's to you." There's no saying how long they might have gone on.'

Charles Hindley *Tavern Anecdotes and Sayings*

unable to speak'. The latter description seems to fit very well the people I have seen sitting quietly in a corner, apparently listening to the general conversation and thinking wise thoughts. Only when it is time for them to go home does it become apparent that they are almost comatose.

Nash fails to find an animal to illustrate the 'sad' stage of drunkenness, which other writers refer to as the maudlin, lachrymose or tearful state. Nor do any of the writers so far quoted mention the extreme suddenness with which an individual passes from one stage to the next. 'Tipsily mutable,' says Aldous Huxley of Mr Elver, in *Those Barren Leaves*, 'his mood changed all at once from hilarious to profoundly gloomy.' Later: 'Mr Elver had reached the final stage of intoxication. Almost suddenly he began to feel weak, profoundly weary and rather ill. Anger, hilarity, the sense of satanic power – all had left him. He desired only to go to bed as soon as possible; at the same time he doubted his ability to get there.'

DANGEROUS DRINKING

Continued drinking, then, past the equivalent of Sir William Temple's third glass (see p. 41), leads to rapid changes of mood, to a relaxing of the moral code, to a diminution of mental and physical powers.

A.P. Herbert has a humorous comment on the moral question in his musical play *Derby Day*:

Lady Waters: The step is short
From gin and port
To the police-court –
I see it daily.

All: One glass of Hock –
You pick a lock –
And then the dock
At the Old Bailey!

The drunkard in real life, however, is probably as often a victim of crime as a perpetrator. There are gangs in many cities of the world who know how easy it is to 'roll' a drunk, stealing from him while he is physically unable to defend himself. This physical and mental weakness may be dangerous to him in other ways, 'shortening his days'

HOPE ABANDONED?

The Times of London reported in July 1991, that the British Women's Temperance Association had decided to disband itself. The association, based mainly in Scotland, had once claimed more than 500 branches and more than 80 000 members. In 1991 only five branches survived, with less than a 100 teetotal members between them.

The last president of the association, 84-year-old Margaret Duncan, said that it had become impossible to attract young members. Drinking had become a normal part of women's lives and they now thought nothing of going into pubs.

In the same article, reporter Alan Hamilton noted that similar associations, such as the Good Templars and the Edinburgh Total Abstinence Society, had also disappeared, though 'a fragment of the most famous of all, the Band of Hope, survives in Glasgow'. In Edinburgh, said Mr Hamilton, the Independent Order of Rechabites also still existed. He did not mention where the latter group was living, though this would have been of interest. In the *Old Testament*, *Jeremiah* 35, the Rechabites explain: Jonadab, the son of Rechab, our father, commanded us, 'You shall not drink wine, neither you nor your sons for ever; you shall not build a house . . . but you shall live in tents all your days . . .'

TEMPERANCE BY NAME . . .

Temperance societies flourished throughout the 19th century in Britain and America and were strong until the 1920s. Members were mainly women, some of whom would have been Temperance by name. The word was regularly used as a first name until at least the 1850s. A short story by the American writer Sarah Orne Jewett, *Miss Tempy's Watchers*, shows that Tempy was the normal form of the name used in direct address.

The societies appeared to have won substantial victories with the introduction of restricted licensing hours in Britain during the First World War. Federal prohibition followed soon afterwards in the USA. It must have seemed to many people at that time that women might even succeed in getting men to abandon drink. Instead, in an astonishing change of attitude, middle-class women themselves took to it. Membership of temperance societies immediately began to decline.

Even in their heyday, such societies were not without their critics on both sides of the Atlantic. Dickens poked fun at them immediately in *The Pickwick Papers*, describing the Brick Lane Branch of the United Grand Junction Ebenezer Temperance Association. 'The president was the straight-walking Mr Anthony Humm, a converted fireman, now a schoolmaster, and occasionally an itinerant preacher; and the secretary was Mr Jonas Mudge, chandler's shopkeeper, an enthusiastic and disinterested vessel, who sold tea to the members.' The lady members are said to drink vast amounts of such tea, to Mr Mudge's profit.

Dickens later has the hypocritical Stiggins, who loves his pineapple rum and water, come along to address a meeting. He is himself rather drunk, but talks of avoiding 'above all things, the vice of intoxication, which he likened unto the filthy habits of swine, and to those poisonous and baleful drugs which being chewed in the mouth, are said to filch away the memory. At this point of his discourse,' says Dickens, 'the reverend and red-nosed gentleman became singularly incoherent, and staggering to and fro in the excitement of his eloquence, was fain to catch at the back of a chair to preserve his perpendicular.'

HARSHER VIEWS

Twenty years later, in *Hard Times*, Dickens was less inclined to smile at the anti-drink campaigners. 'Then came the Teetotal Society, who complained that these same people *would* get drunk, and showed in tabular statements that they did get drunk, and proved at tea-parties that no inducement, human or Divine (except a medal), would induce them to forego their custom of getting drunk.'

But, said Dickens, 'exactly in the ratio as they worked long and monotonously, the craving grew within them for some physical relief – some relaxation, encouraging good-humour and good spirits, and giving them a vent – which craving must and would be satisfied aright, or must and would inevitably go wrong, until the laws of Creation were repealed.'

Gentle criticism was later to come from Flora Thompson, in her autobiographical *Lark Rise to Candleford*. In this passage she is describing her life in Oxfordshire in the 1880s: 'Uncle James Dowland's chief interest was in the temperance movement, at that time a regular feature of parochial life. His hatred of intoxicating drink amounted to

'Drunks' from a coloured original, 1809.

THE BAR

'Bar' has been used in the sense of a counter over which drinks are served since the end of the 16th century. Its underlying sense is 'barrier'. The word has many other specialised meanings, one of which allows the kind of joke made by Jilly Cooper in *Prudence*:

'Evidently he was called to the Bar younger than anyone else in years.'

'He ought to be called to the bar more often,' I said crossly. 'He hasn't touched his drink. It might make him more jolly.'

Members of the legal profession must be rather used to hearing such comments.

The writer of an anonymous pamphlet against drinking – *The Evils of Drink Traffic* (1915) – made use of the word 'bar' in another sense. His poem 'The Hotel Bar' runs:

A bar to joys that home imparts,
A door to tears, and aching
   hearts;
A bar to manliness and wealth,
A door to want and broken
   health.

A bar to honour, pride, and fame,
A door to grief, and sin, and
   shame;
A bar to hope, a bar to prayer,
A door to darkness and despair.

A bar to honoured, useful life,
A door to brawling, senseless
   strife;
A bar to all that's good and
   brave,
A door to every drunkard's grave.

a phobia, and he used to say that if he saw a workman of his entering a public-house, he would not be a workman of his much longer.

'But he was not content with ruling his own home and business in this respect; the whole town was his mission field, and if he could coax or bribe some unhappy workman into signing away his nightly half-pint he became as exhilarated as if his tender for building a mansion had been accepted. To him the smallest child was worth winning as a temperance convert. He would guide their tiny hands as they signed the temperance pledge and to keep them in the fold he had established a Band of Hope which met once a week to eat buns and drink lemonade at his expense and to sing to his accompaniment on the school harmonium such rousing ditties as "Pray sell no more drink to my father" or:

Father, dear Father, come home with
   me now,
The clock in the steeple strikes one.
You promised, dear Father, that you
   would come home
As soon as your day's work was done,

while, all the time, their own excellent fathers, after a modest half-pint at their favourite inn, were already at home and the singers themselves were likely to get into trouble for being out late.

'Edmund and Laura, that first Sunday, wrote their names on a handsome blue-and-gold illuminated pledge card, thereby promising they would henceforth touch no intoxicating liquor, "so help me God". They were not quite sure what intoxicating liquor was, but they liked the cards and were pleased when their uncle offered to have them framed to hang over their beds at home.'

SIGNING THE PLEDGE

Robert Graves had a similar childhood experience, described in *Goodbye To All That*: 'At seven years old my mother had persuaded me to sign a pledge card, which bound me to abstain by the grace of God from all spirituous liquors so long as I retained it. But my mother took the card away and put it safely in the box-room . . . Since box-room treasures never left the box-room, I regarded myself as permanently parted from my pledge.'

An American view is given by Sinclair Lewis, in *Cass Timberlane*: 'As a member of that earnest sect, the Cross and Crown Covenanters, Benjamin Hearth had read numerous tracts about wives with quarter-loaves and half-candles and starving children who waited shivering at home for drunken husbands, usually coachmen; helpful tracts written in England in 1880, and still circulated in forward-looking America in the 1940s. Benjamin loved to read and to distribute such tracts, and it never occurred to him that in these liberal days, the sexes of the drunks could be switched. His wife, Petal, was a slight, bespectacled, prim-looking woman. She was also a dipsomaniac, a drunk and a dirty drunk. She had always liked hot gin better than Benjamin could have guessed.'

In the novel, Benjamin is eventually forced to recognise his wife's addiction. She sets fire to the house while drunk and ends up in an asylum.

THE PLEDGE

'Pledge' has very different meanings when related to drinking. To pledge someone is to drink that person's health, so that 'pledge' is another word for 'toast'. To 'take the pledge', by contrast, means to give a solemn undertaking to abstain from all forms of alcohol.

TEMPERANCE PUNS

Thomas Hood found in temperance societies, as in everything, an opportunity for puns. He has a 'Drinking Song by a member of a Temperance Society, as sung by Mr Spring at Waterman's Hall.' A typical verse runs:

> Should fortune diminish our cash's
> sum-total,
> Deranging our wits and our private
> affairs,
> Though some in such cases would fly
> to the bottle,
> There's nothing like water for
> drowning our cares.

Hood's last verse refers in passing to 'Mountain', a medium sweet wine from Malaga:

> A fig then for Burgundy, Claret, or
> Mountain,
> A few scanty glasses must limit your
> wish,
> But he's the true toper that goes to
> the fountain,
> The drinker that verily 'drinks like a
> fish!'
> Then hey for a bucket, a bucket, a
> bucket,
> Then hey for a bucket, filled up to the
> brim!
> Or, best of all notions, let's have it by
> oceans,
> With plenty of room for a sink or a
> swim!

as Bunyan puts it. A drunk in John Irving's *The World According to Garp* slips on some ice while walking home and knocks himself unconscious. He freezes to death overnight. George Eliot, in *Adam Bede*, has Adam's father drowning in a brook when returning from a drinking session.

DRIVEN TO DRINK

Modern regulations about drinking and driving recognise rather belatedly a risk that existed long before the invention of motor vehicles. Drivers of horse-drawn vehicles were quite capable of killing themselves and their passengers if they had drunk too much. 'Flitch says the accident occurred through his driving up the bank to save you from the wheels,' says Sir Willoughby, in George Meredith's *The Egoist*. 'Flitch may go and whisper that down the neck of his empty whisky flask,' says Horace De Craye. 'And then let him cork it.'

LIFE-PRESERVER

The horse and mule live 30 years
And nothing know of wines and beers.
The goat and sheep at 20 die
And never taste of Scotch or Rye.
The cow drinks water by the ton
And at 18 is mostly done.
The dog at 15 cashes in
Without the aid of rum and gin.
The cat in milk and water soaks
And then in 12 short years it croaks.
The modest, sober, bone-dry hen
Lays eggs for nogs, then dies at 10.
All animals are strictly dry:
They sinless live and swiftly die;
But sinful, ginful, rum-soaked men
Survive for three score years and ten.
And some of them, a very few,
Stay pickled till they're 92.

Anon (quoted in Arnold Silcock's *Verse and Worse*)

The general acceptance of the idea that a car-driver who has drunk more than a small amount is a hazard to himself and others is now widespread, but is relatively recent. In *The Bell* (1958), for instance, Iris Murdoch was probably reflecting a generally held view when she wrote: 'It was foolish of him to have had that second pint; he was so unused to the stuff now, it had made him feel quite tipsy. But he knew it would be all right once he got into the van; the driving would sober him up.'

Already in 1934, however, F. Scott Fitzgerald was saying in *Tender is the Night* that professional chauffeurs 'could never smell of liquor'. Fitzgerald's hero, Dick Diver, is a doctor who has reached a permanent 'fourth glass' stage. The parents of a young male patient furiously remove their son from his care when the boy smells alcohol on Diver's breath. The doctor reviews his drinking habits. 'He drank claret with each meal, took a night-cap, generally in the form of hot rum, and sometimes he tippled with gin in the afternoons – gin was the most difficult to detect on the breath. He was averaging a half-pint of alcohol a day, too much for his system to burn up.

'Dismissing a tendency to justify himself, he sat down at his desk and wrote out, like a prescription, a regime that would cut his liquor in half. Doctors, chauffeurs, and Protestant clergymen could never smell of liquor, as could painters, brokers, cavalry leaders; Diver blamed himself only for indiscretion.'

DRINK DELUSIONS

That last remark hints at the inability of drinkers to see things as they really are. I have seen people about to take part in radio or television shows make ill-judged use of the hospitality room. Their subsequent meandering speech seems to them either profound or witty. To the sober audience it comes across as repetitious and silly. Dr Johnson's advice should be heeded: 'A man who has been drinking wine at all freely should never go into a new company. With those who have partaken with him he may be pretty well in unison; but he will probably be offensive, or appear ridiculous, to other people.'

Let us take that Johnsonian remark as one of

the charges brought against drink and try to sum up the rest. Most of the comments quoted in this chapter have had to do not with drinking as such, but drinking to excess. Sir William Temple defined that 300 years ago as continuing past the third glass. Modern thinking largely agrees with him, suggesting that three units of alcohol a day are a sensible upper limit for a male drinker. Women are advised to consume only two units a day because their bodies absorb alcohol less easily.

There are individuals, no doubt, who could safely exceed these limits. There are also those for whom half a glass would be too much, because of the craving that would be aroused. A character in *Digby*, by David Walker, says: 'Alcohol, which is the friend and enemy of man, is your enemy. Eschew it, Ross! Let me repeat only the counsel I myself received as a newly-joined subaltern in India – *If you cannot drink like a gentleman, do not drink!*' We might not care to express it in those terms, but we see his point. It is important to know one's own limitations and stay within them.

GOING SOFT

'People have a soft spot in their hearts for alcoholics,' Hawthorne said.

Graham Greene *Our Man In Havana*

Veronica's voice softened. She hated Henry to go drinking, but he knew it was one of his attractions for her; it gave her reforming zeal something solid to bite on. Henry had even, at times, caught himself pretending to be a drunkard, which he wasn't, in order to heighten her interest in him.

Jeremy Brooks *Henry's War*

SONG OF THE DECANTER

There was an old decanter, and its mouth was gaping wide; the rosy wine had ebbed away and left its crystal side; and the wind went humming – humming up and down: the wind it blew, and through the reed-like hollow neck the wildest notes it blew. I placed it in the window, where the blast was blowing free, and fancied that its pale mouth sang the queerest strains to me. 'They tell me – puny conquerors! the Plague has slain his ten, and war his hundred thousand of the very best of men; but I '– 'twas thus the Bottle spake – 'but I have conquered more than all your famous conquerors, so feared and famed of yore. Then come, ye youths and maidens all, come drink from out my cup, the beverage that dulls the brain and burns the spirits up; that puts to shame your conquerors that slay their scores below; for this has deluged millions with the lava tide of woe. Tho' in the path of battle darkest streams of blood may roll; yet while I killed the body, I have damn'd the very soul. The cholera, the plague, the sword, such ruin never wrought, as I in mirth or malice on the innocent have brought. And still I breathe upon them, and they shrink before my breath, and year by year my thousands tread the dusty way of death.'

Anonymous poem included by Carolyn Wells in her *Whimsey Anthology*

THE THIRTEEN YEARS

American temperance societies such as the Women's Christian Temperance Union (founded 1874) and the Anti-Saloon League (founded 1893) became increasingly militant towards the end of the 19th century. Together with the Prohibition Party, a minor political group, they helped bring about national Prohibition in the USA. The Volstead Act of 1919 provided for strict enforcement of the Eighteenth Amendment, though in practice this proved to be impossible. During the Roaring Twenties Americans drank as never before, easily obtaining liquor from illegal sources. As H.L. Mencken says, in *The American Language*: 'Prohibition multiplied the number of American boozers and made the whole nation booze-conscious.'

The effects of Prohibition were soon to be seen in everyday language. Everybody was aware of the 'rum runners', 'hijackers', 'bathtub gin', 'law enforcement', and so on. The vast upsurge of crime made familiar a great many terms: 'big shot', 'trigger man', 'the mob', 'gorilla', 'hot' (of a stolen object), 'racketeer', etc. 'Rum' to the Prohibitionists meant any alcoholic drink. 'Hijack' is said to derive from the customary command to raise the hands in the air – 'Up high, Jack!' – used by those who intercepted and robbed the rum-runners.

At least one well-established word virtually disappeared as a result of Prohibition, which was repealed in 1933 by the Twenty-first Amendment. Those who campaigned for repeal had to promise that the old-time 'saloons' would not be revived. In a purely linguistic sense they were not, but taverns, cocktail lounges, taprooms, grills and bars appeared on all sides.

WRY COMMENTS

One of the writers who commented wryly on the effects of Prohibition was Sinclair Lewis. In *Gideon Planish*, for instance, occurs: 'There was no Prohibition-era drinking at Kinnikinick, which was moral through Episcopal. There were no saloons in town; Holy Communion was drunk in grape-juice; and at large public dinners, the bishop and the football team were toasted in Coca-Cola. The students carried abstinence so far that they never drank in the dormitories, except in the evening, and perhaps afternoons. The president had to be known as a teetotaller, and it was only in the houses of the professors who had married money that there were any very large private cellars.

'Not having had a drink since he had left his rooms at Mrs Hilp's, the Professor chummily helped Teckla crack the ice, open the White Rock bottle, and look over her Prohibition stock; four bottles of Bourbon whisky, two of Scotch, twenty-seven gin, and a bottle of rock-and-rye like an anatomical specimen in a museum.'

In *Babbitt*, which is set during the same period, Lewis has: 'Besides the new bottle of gin, his cellar consisted of one half-bottle of Bourbon whisky, a quarter of a bottle of Italian vermouth, and approximately one hundred drops of orange bitters. He did not possess a cocktail shaker. A shaker was proof of dissipation, the symbol of a Drinker, and Babbitt disliked being known as a Drinker . . .'

THE PROBLEMS

Beyond those limits lie the problems, all of which concern excessive drinking, not the moderate drinking of the normal, sensible adult. We have a truer knowledge now of what constitutes moderation. An 18th-century squire might well have consumed three bottles of claret at a sitting. Ordinary 19th-century drinkers ordered brandy by the half-pint.

Times have changed. Already in 1889 Jerome K. Jerome was saying, in his *Idle Thoughts of an Idle Fellow*: 'Drinking is one of those subjects with which it is inadvisable to appear too well acquainted. The days are gone by when it was considered manly to go to bed intoxicated every night, and a clear head and a firm hand no longer draw upon their owner the reproach of effeminacy. On the contrary, in these sadly degenerate days, an evil-smelling breath, a blotchy face, a reeling gait and a husky voice are regarded as the hall-marks of the cad rather than of the gentleman.'

If not the cad, then still the butt of other people's jokes. When James Boswell got drunk while touring in the Hebrides, Dr Johnson paid him a morning visit. He had not come to sympathise with Boswell's hangover, but to advise him to become drunk again straight away. '"Then", said Johnson, "we can laugh at you all day. It is a poor thing for a fellow to get drunk at night, and skulk to bed, and let his friends have no sport."'

'Gin Lane', engraving after an original by Hogarth. Published 1751.

LITERARY DRINKING
Drinking in literature

PASSING references to drinks and drinking occur in a great many literary works. Sometimes drinking itself provides the major theme of a novel, play or short story. A social commentator such as Charles Dickens touches on innumerable aspects of the subject, telling us what was drunk by what type of person, when and where throughout the 19th century. He offers his readers many philosophical reflections about drinking and reports on both the use and abuse of alcohol.

Other writers describe in loving detail their favourite drinks, or are lyrical about the charms of fine wines. It is usually vintage wines that stir their imaginations and turn the most prosaic of writers into poets.

OPENING WORDS

A reader turning to *Elmer Gantry*, by Sinclair Lewis, might imagine that he was about to read the story of an alcoholic. The opening sentences of the book are: 'Elmer Gantry was drunk. He was eloquently drunk, lovingly and pugnaciously drunk.' Lewis himself was an alcoholic but this, as it happens, is merely a description of a lively young man who is sowing his wild oats while he can. His drunkenness is a lusty, thoughtless celebration of his young manhood. It is a temporary escape from thoughts of difficulties and trying times that lie ahead.

There is a very similar scene at the beginning of *Saturday Night and Sunday Morning*, by Alan Sillitoe. The young hero is there shown to be rather revoltingly drunk, but getting drunk from time to time is almost normal for any young working-class man who spends most of his days in a factory. Sillitoe's Arthur Seaton and Lewis's Elmer Gantry will pursue very different paths through life, but they are alike as they try to come to terms with adult life. Neither of them, according to their creators, has or will have in the future a drinking problem. Both are responding to appetites which, for the moment, they can barely control.

In Stan Barstow's *A Kind of Loving*, another young working-class hero responds not so much to appetites as specific pressures when he eventually goes out on a spree. He is faced with problems which appear to be insurmountable. Beer and brandy offer temporary relief, and in this case usefully bring a family crisis to its head. Barstow offers no philosophical thoughts about whether such behaviour constitutes a use or abuse of drinking. The average reader will probably agree with the novelist's assumption that in such circumstances, a young man of this background would act in the way described. Comment would only have been required had the young man's wife reacted in a similar way, drowning her sorrows in drink.

WOMEN DRINKERS

The idea that young women might also occasionally use alcohol for temporary relaxation and relief, without there being any sinister overtones, has surfaced only very recently in literature. The normal assumption has been that a woman who drinks is a woman with a serious problem. A typical scene involving a woman and drink occurs in John Steinbeck's *The Wayward Bus*. Alice is left alone, feeling depressed and neglected. A glass of whisky seems a good idea. Steinbeck describes in fine detail what happens next: 'She waved the glass and drank slowly. She did not toss it. She let the hot, straight whisky ease and burn and flow over her tongue and in back of her tongue, and she swallowed slowly and

MRS FREELAND'S EPITAPH (IN EDWALTON CHURCHYARD)

She drank good ale, strong punch and wine,
And lived to the age of ninety-nine.

Quoted by E.V. Lucas *Her Infinite Variety*

felt the bite on her palate, and the warmth of the whisky went into her chest and into her stomach. Even after she had emptied the glass she still held it to her lips. She put down the glass and she said, "Ah!" and breathed outward harshly.

'She could taste the sweet whisky again on her returning breath. Now she reached for the tumbler of beer. She crossed her legs and drank very slowly until the glass was empty. . . . She poured two fingers of whisky in one glass and four fingers of beer in the other glass.

"There's more than one way to skin a drink," she said, and she tossed the whisky in and tossed the beer right in after it. Now there's an idea. It doesn't taste the same. The way you drink changes the taste. Why had no one else ever found that out, only Alice . . . She poured half a glass of beer and filled the glass with whisky. "I wonder if anybody ever tried this before?" "Your health, kid." And she drank the beer and the whisky the way a thirsty man drinks milk.'

This is clearly serious drinking, in no way similar to the careless swilling of the young men. It is not just that Alice is drinking alone. She is far too interested in the drink itself. The deliberation of the drinking ritual, beautifully described by Steinbeck, is another sign of real danger.

DRINKING COUPLES

Some wives operate on the principle that what is good for the gander is good for the goose. Examples in literature of women who hold their own with their partners include Martha, in Edward Albee's *Who's Afraid of Virginia Woolf?*

The whole play is a massive drinking scene, with an occasional specific comment:

George 'Martha's tastes in liquor have come down . . . simplified over the years . . . crystallized. Back when I was courting Martha she'd order the damnedest things! We'd go into a bar . . . a whisky, beer, and bourbon bar . . . and what she'd do would be, she'd screw up her face, think real hard, and come up with . . . brandy Alexanders, crème de cacao frappés, gimlets, flaming punch bowls . . . seven-layer liqueur things.'
Martha 'They were good . . . I liked them.'
George 'Real lady-like little drinkies.'
Martha 'Hey, where's my rubbing alcohol?'
George 'But the years have brought to Martha a sense of essentials . . . the knowledge that cream is for coffee, lime juice for pies . . . and alcohol pure and simple . . . here you are, angel . . . for the pure and simple. For the mind's blind eye, the heart's ease, and the liver's craw. Down the hatch, all.'
Martha 'Cheers, dears!'

Few readers, perhaps, would think of Dickens's Sairey Gamp as one of a marital drinking partnership, but she was certainly so at one time. Mr Gamp is already dead when Sairey comes on the scene in *Martin Chuzzlewit*, bulging out of the rusty black gown which is very much the worse for snuff. We are told that the couple had previously long been separated, 'on the ground of incompatibility of temper in their drink', but Mr Gamp was obviously as formidable a drinker as

MAN'S WORK

She made the appropriate oos and ahhs, and pretended with him that opening the champagne bottle was a difficult and dangerous masculine task.

Len Deighton *Close-up*

Sairey herself. She says of her late husband: 'the blessing of a daughter was denied me; which, if we had had one, Gamp would certainly have drunk its little shoes right off its feet, as with our precious boy he did, and afterwards send the child a errand to sell his wooden leg for any money it would fetch as matches in the rough, and bring it home in liquor. . . .'

Sairey herself has no wooden leg to sell, but fortunately does not need one. Her employment brings in enough money to cater for some of her considerable needs; her employers usually make up the difference by supplying liquid refreshment. Dickens remarks that: 'Mrs Gamp in her drinking was very punctual and particular, requiring a pint of mild porter at lunch, a pint at dinner, half a pint as a species of stay or holdfast between dinner and tea, and a pint of the celebrated staggering ale, or real Old Brighton Tipper, at supper; besides the bottle on the chimney-piece, and such casual invitations to refresh herself with wine as the good breeding of her employers might prompt them to offer.'

It is hardly surprising then, that 'the face of Mrs Gamp - the nose in particular - was somewhat red and swollen, and it was difficult to enjoy her society without becoming conscious of a smell of spirits'.

In her own mind, of course, the drinking has some justification. As a professional nurse, she spends much time with the dying and the dead. She explains to Mr Pecksniff: 'If it wasn't for the nerve a little sip of liquor gives me (I never was able to do more that taste it), I could never go through with what I sometimes has to do. "Mrs Harris," I says, "leave the bottle on the chimney-piece, and don't ask me to take none, but let me put my lips to it when I am so dispoged . . ."' She also claims a practical reason for drinking the powerful Brighton Tipper when she has to work all night: 'it being considered wakeful by the doctors'.

When she is at home, Sairey resorts to her teapot, but not because she feels the need for something non-alcoholic. It is in that innocent-looking container - 'from motives of delicacy' - that she keeps her personal supply of spirits.

WOMEN WRITERS

In recent times far more women have appeared in fiction who drink when they feel like it. They are not ignorant sluts, nor do they expect to be labelled as dipsomaniacs. The heroine of Jilly Cooper's *Prudence*, for instance, has a cheerfully open attitude to drink, using it liberally to oil the social wheels. The novels of the past had the women retiring discreetly to leave the men with the port. A more modern attitude is displayed by Pamela Hansford Johnson in *An Error of Judgement*: 'She said, at last, "We won't separate the sexes tonight. I adore port, and I shall have it here."'

One can hardly imagine a woman writer of the past commenting on drink in such a way. Jane Austen, in *Pride and Prejudice*, rarely mentions the subject. There is a passing reference to 'when the gentlemen had joined them', to indicate that the usual separation after dinner had occurred, but no real discussion of drinks or drinking. The one exception is when Mrs Bennett is allowed to make her views known:

'If I were as rich as Mr Darcy,' cried a young Lucas, who came with his sisters, 'I should not care how proud I was. I would keep a pack of foxhounds, and drink a bottle of wine every day.' 'Then you would drink a great deal more than you ought,' said Mrs Bennett; 'and if I were to see you at it, I should take away your bottle directly.'

Anne Brontë's *The Tenant of Wildfell Hall* is unusual in that drinking is the major theme of the book. It examines in detail the problems caused to a wife by her husband's excesses and is perhaps the first novel in English to do so. Miss Brontë did not have a drunken husband herself, but she had had the experience of seeing her brother Branwell rapidly going downhill with drink and dissipation.

In the story the tenant of Wildfell Hall is known as the widow, Mrs Graham, though she is really the estranged wife of Arthur Huntingdon. In the latter's social group, drinking is equated with manliness - by some of the women as well as the men themselves. When Lord Lowborough, for instance, renounces the after-dinner drinking and joins the ladies, his wife sneers: 'It looks so silly to be always dangling after the women.'

THE FELLOWSHIP

Sweet fellowship in shame!
One drunkard loves another of the
name.

William Shakespeare *Love's Labour's Lost*

Lowborough himself knows that once he starts drinking, he will not be able to stop. The next man to appear says that he has managed to escape in spite of his friends' jeers and comments. We can fairly assume that Branwell Brontë had been subjected to similar pressure by his peer group.

An innocent discussion about drinking is introduced near the beginning of the story. The Reverend Millward is visiting the Markhams, and tells his hostess: 'I'll take a little of your home-brewed ale. I always prefer your home-brewed to anything else.' Flattered at this compliment (says Gilbert Markham, narrator at this point), 'my mother rang the bell, and a china jug of our best ale was presently brought and set before the worthy gentleman who so well knew how to appreciate its excellences.

'"Now THIS is the thing!" cried he, pouring out a glass of the same in a long stream, skilfully directed from the jug to the tumbler, so as to produce much foam without spilling a drop; and, having surveyed it for a moment opposite the candle, he took a deep draught, and then smacked his lips, drew a long breath, and refilled his glass. "I'm sure I'm glad you like it, sir. I always look after the brewing myself, as well as the cheese and the butter."'

AVERSION THERAPY

Mrs Graham, however, soon afterwards reveals that her six-year old son, Arthur, detests the very sight of wine and the smell of it almost makes him sick. 'I have been accustomed to make him swallow a little wine or weak spirits and water, by way of medicine when he was sick, and, in fact, I have

done what I could to make him hate them.' The company find this amusing, though Mrs Graham and her son do not join in the laughter. 'By that means,' says the young woman, 'I hope to save him from one degrading vice at least.'

There follows a long passage in which she justifies her philosophy, defending herself against the accusation of over-protecting her child, turning him into a milksop, etc. Frederick Lawrence supports her: 'Some parents have entirely prohibited their children from tasting intoxicating liquors; but a parent's authority cannot last for ever: children are naturally prone to hanker after forbidden things; and a child, in such a case, would be likely to have a strong curiosity to taste, and try the effect of what has been so lauded and enjoyed by others, so strictly forbidden to himself. Which curiosity would generally be gratified on the first convenient opportunity; and the restraint once broken, serious consequences might ensue.'

There is something in that for any modern parent to think about. A mutually-agreed parental policy is needed, and outright prohibition may be an over-simplification.

Some might argue that *The Tenant of Wildfell Hall* is almost a temperance tract in disguise. It is certainly not very subtle, but Anne, youngest and gentlest of the sisters, must have been deeply distressed by what was happening to her brother. She had no real insight into what caused a man to drink excessively, but was right to identify group pressure as a major factor. She also had first-hand knowledge of the difficulties faced by a woman who wants to prevent a man's self-destruction. In the book Huntingdon blames his

DRINKING HOURS

'I don't drink at this hour.'
'It was the English who made hours for drinking, not the Scotch. They'll be making hours for dying next.'

Graham Greene *Our Man In Havana*

wife for her constant recriminations, and drinks again to escape them. No doubt Branwell reacted to his sister in a similar way.

MACHO DRINKING

It would have been interesting to hear Ernest Hemingway's comments on the Anne Brontë novel. His own works consistently celebrate drinking, and were a great influence on several generations. *A Farewell To Arms*, published in 1929, reacted against the over-literary styles that had gone before, replacing them with a simplified journalese that was, at the outset, very refreshing. To the modern reader the lack of variety can become an irritation, and the constant macho-imagery does not necessarily accord with current thinking.

The novel is in one sense a kind of drinking diary. References to drinks and drinking occur on almost every page. A brief distillation of the book from that point of view would reveal references to Asti, grappa, white capri, fresa, Barbera, Margaux, Cognac, vermouth, Marsala, capri, Chianti, Kümmel, St Estèphe, Champagne, *Glühwein*, whisky, beer. There are additional references to Strega (an Italian liqueur made from herbs), Cinzano, sherry in an egg nog, whisky and soda, clear red Barbera, Martini and Champagne cocktails.

The pregnant heroine of the book says that a doctor has advised her to drink beer. It will be good for her and keep the baby small. In passing she remarks that 'brandy is for heroes', an allusion to a well-known comment by Dr Johnson: 'Claret is the liquor for boys; port for men; but he who aspires to be a hero must drink brandy.'

'The Wine Tasters' by J. P. Hasencleven (1843).

COLOURFUL DRINKING

David Niven, in *The Moon's A Balloon*, tells of his meeting with 'an enchanting middle-aged American much exercised by the thought of going home to face the rigours of Prohibition.

"Dave," he said, "I've gotta great idea . . . tonight you and me are gonna drink by colours."

'We settled ourselves at the bar and he decided to drink the colours of the national flags of all the countries he had visited on his trip – Stars and Stripes first of course. Red was easy – port. White was simple – gin, but blue was a real hazard till the barman unveiled a vicious Swiss liqueur called gentiane. The French and British flags fell easily into place but a horrible snag was placed in our path by the Belgians. Black, yellow and red. Black beer was used to lay a foundation for yellow chartreuse and Burgundy, but it was the green crème de menthe of the Italian flag that caused me to retire leaving my new-found friend the undisputed champion'.

In R.D. Blackmore's *Lorna Doone* the colour of the wine proves a girl's love. Reuben Huckaback sends his granddaughter Ruth to the cellar to get a bottle of wine for him and John Ridd. She brings it, and the following conversation occurs: 'Marry some sweet little thing if you can. We have the maid to suit you, my lad, in this old town of Dulverton.'

'Have you so, sir? But perhaps the maid might have no desire to suit me.'

'That you may take my word she has. The colour of this wine will prove it. The sly little hussy has been to the cobwebbed arch of the cellar, where she has no right to go, for anyone under a magistrate. However, I am glad to see it and we will not spare it, John.'

This long hymn in praise of alcohol of any kind (for a *real* man) was published while Prohibition was still in force in America. That was perhaps one of the reasons for it – the 'artist' was rebelling against conventional control. But it established for countless young men an image of heroism firmly connected with being able to drink anything that was put on the table. A personal knowledge of a wide range of drinks became an essential aspect of a young man's education. Getting drunk was not part of this philosophy; being able to hold one's drink was very much part of the creed. Girls, if they followed Hemingway, learned that it was all right for them to sip a little of what their menfolk consumed in quantity. That was certainly Hemingway's view of their role. Though his constant macho-imagery is not necessarily fashionable today, his basic views are probably still widely held.

Hemingway himself, like Sinclair Lewis, was an alcoholic, and seems to assume in most of his novels that his astonishing capacity for alcohol was normal. In *Across the River and Into the Trees* Colonel Cantwell begins his evening with three very dry double Martinis, a gin and Campari and three Montgomerys (gin with the faintest splash of vermouth). At dinner he shares with his girlfriend a bottle of Capri Bianco, two bottles of Valpolicella, a bottle of dry Roederer Champagne and another of Perrier-Jouet. The two then retire to the bedroom and make love, refreshing themselves with more Valpolicella.

Before a young writer tries to emulate Hemingway, he should perhaps read a book such as *The Thirsty Muse*, by Tom Dardis, which examines the terrible effects of alcoholism not only on Hemingway, but on William Faulkner, Scott Fitzgerald and Eugene O'Neill. Of these it was only O'Neill who managed to conquer the addiction. The plays he then wrote, *The Iceman Cometh* and *Long Day's Journey Into Night*, deal with the problem of alcoholism.

Before the Dardis study, Frederick R. Karl had pointed out, in his biography *William Faulkner*, that heavy drinking had been a special problem for American writers. Others who were at least near-alcoholics included John Steinbeck, Theodore Dreiser, Thomas Wolfe, Edgar Allen Poe, Jack London, Robert Lowell and Dashiell Hammett. Karl's explanation was that writing in the United States was not thought of as a masculine pursuit, so that manhood had to be proved in other ways. It is an interesting theory that could be extended to journalism, then into fields such as acting.

VOLCANIC DRINKING

Geoffrey Firmin, in Malcolm Lowry's *Under the Volcano*, is far from being a macho drinker. The novel is a totally convincing study, based on personal knowledge, of what it means to be an alcoholic. Firmin is a highly intelligent and sensitive man who has to continue drinking, though aware that he is rapidly descending into personal degradation. We believe him when he says that nothing in the world is more terrible than an empty bottle, unless it is an empty glass.

The novel is set in Mexico, where Firmin drinks mainly mescal, according to the spelling used in the book. This is the American version of Mexican mezcal. The spelling is of some significance: the drink is a spirit made from the Blue Maguey cactus, not the cactus mescal, from which the drug mescaline derives. Almost no mezcal is exported, though in some areas of Mexico it is consumed in great quantities. Mexicans themselves claim that 'for everything bad, it is good, and also for everything good'.

Firmin catalogues at one point some of the other drinks he has taken in his lifetime, the bottles and glasses, as he expresses it, in which he has hidden himself. He talks of 'aguardiente (brandy), anis, Jerez, Highland Queen, Oporto, tinto, blanco, Pernod, Oxygenée (an American aniseed-flavoured absinthe substitute), absinthe, Calvados, Dubonnet, Falstaff (an American beer, though there is also a British beer called Falstaff Mild), rye, Johnny Walker, *Vieux* Whisky, *blanc Canadien, aperitifs, digestifs, demis, dobles,* tequila – the millions of gourds of beautiful mescal'.

There is no boasting, overt or implied, in Firmin's thoughts about a life-time's drinking. He is obsessed by drink, possessed by it. He remembers the names, tastes and smells. Of a return trip to England he writes: 'How strange the landing at Liverpool, the Liver Building seen once more through the misty rain, that murk smelling already of nosebags and Caegwyrle Ale . . .'

METHYLATED SPIRITS

One of the more bizarre characters in literature is Mr Krook, a rag and bone merchant who appears in a minor role in *Bleak House*, by Charles Dickens. He is unmarried, old, eccentric, cadaverous and withered. The breath issues from his mouth in visible smoke 'as if he were on fire within', says Dickens. He is constantly drinking gin, and the unwholesome air of his shop 'is so stained with this liquor, that even the green eyes of the cat upon her shelf as they open and shut, and glimmer on the visitors, look drunk'. Mr Jobling has an appointment with Krook at midnight, but he finds the room full of smoke and the window-panes covered with a dark, greasy deposit. There is a small heap of ashes on the floor in front of the fire. These, Dickens would have us believe, represent all that is left of Mr Krook. He had become so saturated in spirits that he eventually burst into flames spontaneously and was burned to death.

The incident aroused much controversy in 1852, when *Bleak House* was first published. Dickens was apparently convinced that spontaneous combustion of a human being could occur in real life, though there were many who pointed out the absurdity of such a notion. No harm could have been done by the story of Krook, and perhaps a few hardened gin-drinkers were worried enough temporarily to ease up on their intake.

Hemingway's narrator, in *A Farewell to Arms*, drinks a great deal, but appears to be in control of his drinking. Perhaps that is because we are always aware of Hemingway's conscious control of his writing. Malcolm Lowry, a far more poetical wordsmith than Hemingway, writes from within his subject. When we read his description of a Mexican bar, for instance, we see not only what

Firmin sees, but instantly picture Firmin himself, sitting there and absorbing the scene:

'Behind the bar hung, by a clamped swivel, a beautiful Oaxaquenan gourd of mescal de olla, from which his drink had been measured. Ranged on either side stood bottles of Tenampa, Berreteaga, Tequila Anejo, Anis doble de Mallorca, a violet decanter of Henry Mallet's *"delicicoso licor"*, a flask of peppermint cordial, a tall voluted bottle of Anis del Mono, on the label of which a devil brandished a pitchfork.'

DEVILISH DRINKING

The label of that particular bottle seems to have fascinated Lowry. He was well aware of its symbolism. On another occasion he writes: 'M. Laruelle poured himself another anis. He was drinking anis because it reminded him of absinthe. His hand trembled slightly over the bottle, from whose label a florid demon brandished a pitchfork at him.'

Firmin's wife drinks only to quench her occasional thirst, and has no serious need of alcohol. At one point, however, when she is with her brother-in-law, she makes an attempt to understand what it is that enslaves her husband:

'*Mescal, por favor*. I've always wanted to find out what Geoffrey sees in it.'

Sickly, sullen, and ether-tasting, the mescal produced at first no warmth in her stomach, only, like the beer, a coldness, a chill. But it worked. It had in the end the quality of a good hard drink. She selected a lemon from the table and squeezed a few drops into her glass.

'How's the mescal?' Hugh said.

'Like ten yards of barbed-wire fence. It nearly took the top of my head off.'

Firmin himself describes the effect of drink rather differently. 'The Consul, sucking a lemon, felt the fire of the tequila run down his spine like lightning striking a tree which thereupon, miraculously, blossoms.' Tequila is another Mexican drink, rather better known abroad than mescal. It takes its name from a town and is made from the distilled fermented sap of a succulent plant, the *agave tequiliana*, normally referred to as a cactus. It is a white spirit when first made, but becomes golden if aged for several years in wood.

Lowry himself, of course, does not pause in his narrative to give facts such as those I have just supplied. *Under the Volcano* is a totally subjective response to drinks and drinking, not an objective survey of the subject. There is just an occasional hint of awareness that scholarly discussion would be possible, as with the reference to Hindu religious practices, but it is not pursued: 'He was talking of *soma*, Amrita, the nectar of immortality, praised in one whole book of the Rig Veda – *bhang*, which was, perhaps, much the same thing as mescal itself.'

Under the Volcano is a literary masterpiece which describes a deeply moving tragedy. Malcolm Lowry was presumably aware, as he wrote, of the fate that awaited him. 'I'm on the wagon now,' he has Firmin say at one point to his peevish neighbour. 'The funeral wagon I'd say, Firmin,' is the accurate reply.

JOYCEAN DRINKING

A portrait in miniature of an alcoholic is to be found in *Counterparts*, a short story by James Joyce. Joyce is not demonstrating in this piece his idiosyncratic verbal tricks (in *Finnegan's Wake*, for example, Sir Arthur Guinness is transformed into Guinnghis Khan, Allfor Guineas, Ser Artur Ghinis, Mooseyeare Goorness). Instead we get an accurate report of Irish drinking language earlier this century.

Counterparts is about a lower middle-class drunkard and the seediness of his life. Joyce's

POLITICAL PROGRESSION

'Given the benefit of a couple of drinks,' Antonio said, 'we're all republicans here. A few more stiff ones, and we're Communists. But come four o'clock in the morning, man, every self-respecting Spaniard is an anarchist.'

Mordecai Richler *Joshua Then and Now*

ALE AND SHERRIS-SACK

Shakespeare refers to a relatively small range of alcoholic drinks in his plays. The gentlemen drink wines from France, Spain, Portugal, Germany and Greece; the working-men sup their 'ale' – the term used far more frequently than 'beer'. When a trick is played on Christopher Sly in The Induction to *The Taming of the Shrew*, a servant offers him a cup of sack. He demands instead a pot of small ale, and specifically says: 'I ne'er drank sack in my life.'

A 'cup of sack' in modern times would be a 'glass of dry sherry', ('sack' being from French *sec* 'dry'.) 'Cup' seems a slightly unusual word in this context, but 'glass', to Shakespeare and his contemporaries, would have more immediately suggested a mirror than a container for drink. The Elizabethan 'cup' was like a chalice, or the kind of cup we now award as a sporting prize. It certainly had no associations with tea or coffee, neither of which was as yet being drunk in Shakespeare's England.

Another Elizabethan drinking vessel which is mentioned in the plays is the 'stoop', or 'stoup' as we would now usually spell it. The word survives in its sense of a container for holy-water, but at one time it had the more general sense of 'flagon'.

In *Measure for Measure* there are references to brown and white bastard wine, so-called because it was adulterated with honey. Elsewhere Shakespeare mentions Charneco, a sweet wine named after a Portuguese village. Other Shakespearean wines are mostly still familiar – Canary, Madeira, Muscadel, etc. – though his 'claret wine' was not necessarily the red Bordeaux it would be today. 'Claret' was originally applied to wine which was neither red nor white but 'clear' and 'light'.

The Merry Wives of Windsor has some especially interesting references to drinks. At one point Ford says: 'Page is an ass, a secure ass; he will trust his wife; he will not be jealous; I will rather trust a Fleming with my butter, Parson Hugh the Welshman with my cheese, an Irishman with my aqua-vitae bottle . . .' *Aqua-vitae* is the Latin equivalent of Irish *uisge beatha*, 'water of life', and this appears to be a clear reference to Irish whiskey. Later in the play the Welsh parson Sir Hugh Evans says of Falstaff that he is a man 'given to taverns, and sack, and wine, and metheglins . . .' Metheglin was a kind of mead drunk in Wales, but Shakespeare seems to have assumed that it would be familiar to London theatre-goers. He mentions it again in *Love's Labour's Lost*, when Berowne asks the Princess of France for 'one sweet word'. 'Honey, and milk, and sugar; there is three,' she replies. He adds 'Metheglin, wort and malmsey' as three more.

SOME PEOPLE CONNECTED WITH DRINKING

A bellarmine is a large beer mug or jug which has a bearded man's face and a large belly. Such a mug was produced by Dutch Protestants in order to mock Cardinal Bellarmine (Roberto Francesco Romolo Bellarmino (1542–1621)) an Italian theologian who defended Roman Catholic dogma. The mug is also known as a greybeard.

Saint Benedict of Nursia (*c.*480–*c.*543) founded the Benedictine order of monks and therefore gave his name to the liqueur Bénédictine. The latter was originally produced by Benedictine monks at the abbey of Fécamp, Normandy.

At one time the terms Gladstone claret and Gladstone sherry were used. William Ewart Gladstone (1809–98) reduced the duty on such drinks when he was Chancellor of the Exchequer (1860). He was later four times prime minister.

Jeroboam I was King of Israel (*c.*912 BC). For this 'mighty man of valour' is named the large champagne bottle, roughly four standard bottles. Two jeroboams = one rehoboam.

Methuselah is the oldest man named in the bible; he supposedly lived 969 years. A champagne bottle of six quarts is named after him.

Rehoboam was the son of King Solomon. The champagne bottle named for him is six standard bottles in size.

St Martin of Tours (*c.*315–399) is the patron saint of inn-keepers and publicans. St Martin's evil means drunkenness and Martin drunk means extremely drunk. (Notes adapted from Cyril Leslie Beeching, *A Dictionary of Eponyms*.)

THE TASTE TEST

Can you name the following drinks from the description of their taste given by various writers? Some additional clues are provided.

1. It was ice-cold and seemed to have a faint taste of strawberries. It was delicious. (Drunk by James Bond and Tiffany Case in Ian Fleming's *Diamonds Are Forever*.)

2. 'That enough water?'
   'Touch more.' She took a gulp and it was like bitter burned honey. She made a face.
   'Don't like?'
   'Not quite sure yet.'
   'Take slowly.'

3. The drink smelt and tasted like the flower of geranium. Warbeck explained that it was a favourite drink of stokers and Cornish miners. (It's also described as 'horrible brown stuff'.)

4. It had a peaty tang to it that was incomparable without a doubt.

5. Boldly she drained her glass, too, in one gulp. For a second or so, nothing happened but a curious aniseedy taste as the liquor slipped over her palate, but then, suddenly, it was if an incendiary bomb had burst in her throat and sent white fire racing down every channel of her body. She gasped, laughed, coughed, all at once.

6. When you add water it turns milky. It tastes like liquorice and it has a good uplift, but it drops you just as far.

7. Tim took a sip. The potion had an interesting, nutty flavour. 'What's this?'
   'Nectar of the gods!'

8. Samuel sipped from the bottle. 'Tastes

a little like rotten apples,' he said.

'Yes, but nice rotten apples. Take it back along your tongue toward the roots.'

(The drink is described as 'almost black'.)

9. It tasted like honey: rich and sweet.

10. 'Don't think I ever tasted it. Any good?'

'Sweet. And warm without being sordid.'

ANSWERS

1. They're drinking Clicquot Rosé, a vintage Champagne.

2. From Sumner Locke Elliott's *Edens Lost*. The girl has just been told: 'I want you to know you're drinking real Kentucky bourbon.'

3. 'It's Dog's Nose.'
'Dog's nose? Are you studying botany?'
'No, sir.'
'Oh, I see; it's a drink, and not a wild flower.'
'It's for my friend Warbeck. Beer and gin.'
Henry Williamson *The Dream of Fair Women*

Mrs Gaskell refers to the same drink in *Sylvia's Lovers*: 'The sergeant brought up his own mug of beer, into which a noggin of gin had been put (called in Yorkshire 'dog's nose').'

4. The only malt whisky fit to offer his old friend, 'that stuff from Islay'.
Michael Innes *Honeybath's Haven*

5. J.B. Priestley says in *Angel Pavement* that Miss Matfield 'had never tasted vodka before, never remembered ever having seen it before, but of course it was richly associated with her memories of romantic fiction of various kinds, and was tremendously thrilling, the final completing thrill of the afternoon's adventure.

'Come along, Miss Matfield,' said Mr Golspie, looking at her over his raised glass. 'Down it goes. Happy days!' And he emptied his glass with one turn of the wrist.

'All right,' she cried, raising hers. 'What do I say? Cheerio?'

6. Ernest Hemingway introduces this in *The Sun Also Rises* with:
'Well, what will you drink?' I asked.
'Pernod.'
'That's not good for little girls.'
'Little girl yourself.'
Hemingway adds the information that: Pernod is greenish imitation absinthe.

In *Men Without Women* Hemingway talks of another liquorice-flavoured drink:
'Anis del Toro.'
'Could we try it?'
'Do you want it with water?'
'Is it good with water?'
'It's all right.'
'It tastes like liquorice,' the girl said.

7. Denison Hatch, in his novel *The Stork*, has the last speaker continue: 'Irish whiskey. Old Bushmill eight-year-old.'

8. The drink under discussion is ng-ka-py, a Chinese brandy much favoured by Lee in *East of Eden*, by John Steinbeck. Lee also says: 'As a matter of fact it's a brandy with a dosage of wormwood. Very powerful. It softens the world.' Later he refers to it as 'Chinese absinthe'.

9. The remark about the taste is preceded by: The beer made me full, so I laid the can in the sand and poured Scotch instead.
Joe McGinnis *The Dream Team*

10. This is Angela Snow's reply to Pop Larkin's question about Madeira in H.E. Bates's story, *When the Green Woods Laugh*.

'hero' is Farrington, an incompetent clerk who, as the story begins, is humiliatingly told off by his boss. He sneaks out of the office soon afterwards to get a 'g.p.' as he calls it – a glass of plain. The barman who serves him is described as the 'curate'. We learn that this is the fifth time during the day that Farrington has been out for a drink.

The clerk gets very angry with the office and everyone in it. He thinks about the coming evening, 'a night for hot punches'. When he returns to the office he is insolent to his boss, but is humiliated again by being forced to apologise. The working day over at last, and in need of money for a drink, he goes off to pawn his watch.

In the pub he joins his cronies and boastfully narrates the story of his insolence. He is stood a 'half-one', then: 'O'Halloran stood tailors of malt, hot, all round.' They 'name their poisons' and have another. An office colleague arrives and confirms the story of how Farrington braved the lion in his den. Joyce has time to supply some visual as well as linguistic detail. Farrington, for example, is drawing forth any stray drops of liquor from his moustache.

He and two others go off to another pub. They meet a man who drinks a small Irish and Apollinaris while they have their whiskey hot. The man they have met gets them to 'have just one little tincture at his expense'. They go off to have 'small hot specials' in another pub. Farrington indulges in arm wrestling and loses. He begins to get very angry at the world in general. He has had a very bad day at work, pawned his watch, spent all his money and is still fairly sober. When he gets home his wife is out at the chapel. In his rage he starts to beat his young son.

The literary quality of *Counterparts* can be shown by comparing it with short stories by O. Henry, say, which also have alcohol as a theme. Joyce has managed to capture with brilliant economy the thoughts and feelings of a man who cannot control his drinking. He is dealing with truth. We are almost unaware of the literary skills he employs to bring us into the presence, and into the mind, of an alcoholic. In O. Henry the artificial conventions of plotting are obvious, and are meant to be enjoyed at a superficial level.

In *The Lost Blend*, for instance, McQuirk and Riley decide to establish an American bar in Nicaragua. When they arrive they learn that a 48 per cent tax has been imposed on imported bottles, but there is no duty on liquor in barrels. They pour all their bottles, wines and spirits, into two barrels. The resulting mixture in one barrel is awful. In the other the men have, by chance, created a superb cocktail. 'The stuff in that second barrel was distilled elixir of battle, money and high life. It was the colour of gold, and it shone after dark like the sunshine was still in it.'

The story concerns their search for the magic blend. Eventually they realise that Apollinaris is the missing ingredient, and the cocktail is recreated. O. Henry does not give its ingredients, but its effect is shown when a waiter drinks two or three drops of it. He immediately finds the courage to propose to the girl he loves.

DRINKING GALORE

Compton Mackenzie's *Whisky Galore* is a humorous account of whisky's role in the imaginary Scottish island of Todaidh Mor. At the beginning of the book, whisky and other alcoholic drinks have almost disappeared from the island because of the Second World War. The effects of the shortage are seen to be terrible. The local doctor, for instance, is forced to make a tragic announcement about Captain MacPhee, who 'for the last fifteen years, to my knowledge, drank his three drams of whisky and three pints of beer every night of his life and on such a tonic he might have lived to a hundred. He's not had a drop of whisky for twelve days, and before that only one dram a night for nearly a month. And tonight he wasn't able to get his third pint of beer. Well, it's killed him.'

Not everyone reacts quite so extremely, but another speaker says: 'They're all feeling the effect of the shortage. They haven't been without whisky for thousands of years. It's like depriving them of the very air they breathe.'

'They drink far too much whisky when they can get it,' said Captain Waggett austerely.

'And I wouldn't say that, sir, either. Put it this way. A fish doesn't drink water all the time, but you take a fish out of water, and where is the poor animal? It's the same with the people here. They don't want to drink whisky all the time, but they want to feel it's there.'

'The Artist's Breakfast' by Peter Severin Kroyer (1851–1909).

Fortunately for the islanders, the *Cabinet Minister*, bound for America with a cargo of whisky, is shortly afterwards wrecked on the shore. Its crew abandon the 'liquid gold' in its holds, and the local men quietly salvage it. There follows a lyrical account of the treasure:

'In one wooden case of twelve bottles you might have found half a dozen different brands in half a dozen different shapes. Besides the famous names known all over the world by ruthless and persistent advertising for many years, there were many blends of the finest quality, less famous perhaps but not less delicious. There were Highland Gold and Highland Heart, Tartan Milk and Tartan Perfection, Bluebell, Northern Light, Prestonpans, Queen of the Glens, Chief's Choice, and Prince's Choice, Islay Dew, Silver Whistle, Salmon's Leap, Stag's Breath, Stalker's Joy, Bonnie Doon, Auld Stuarts, King's Own, Trusty Friend, Old Cateran, Scottish Envoy, Norval, Bard's Bounty, Fingal's Cave, Deirdre's Farewell, Lion Rampant, Road to the Isles, Pipe Major, Moorland Gold and Moorland Cream, Thistle Cream, Shinty, Blended Heather, Glen Gloming, Mountain Tarn, Cromag, All the Year Round, Clan McTavish and Clan MacNab, Annie Laurie, Over the Border, and Cabarfeidh.'

The choice is bewilderingly complicated, but expert advice is available. A visiting English lady, after much thought, is offered All The Year Round – 'Just the smallest sensation, Mistress Odd. Oh, really beautiful stuff. You'll just think you're sipping cream. Really a baby in arms would hardly know it was whisky. *Uisge beatha.* Water of Life!' The pronunciation of the Gaelic words is described in passing as 'something between a sneeze and a yawn'. More usefully, perhaps, English readers are told to say 'ooshki beh-ha'.

Light-hearted comments on whisky occur throughout the book. 'Love makes the world go round? Not at all. Whisky makes it go round twice as fast,' says one character, ambiguously. A typical exchange elsewhere is: 'I drink whisky any time of the year. I don't drink so much of it that I must give it up in Lent.'

'Then what difference will Lent make?' the Sergeant-major asked in perplexity.

'Man, we always allow ourselves a few extra drams before Lent begins. You don't understand what a solemn sort of time Lent is.'

Whisky Galore was suggested by a real-life incident. The S.S. *Politician* went aground in 1941 in the shallow Sound of Eriskay, in the Hebrides. It was carrying six casks and 243 600 bottles of whisky, bound for the US. When the crew had gone, the islanders moved in. It is said that an orgy of drunkenness followed such as had never before been seen.

VINTAGE DRINKING

Gabriel Chevallier, in his novels *Clochemerle* and *Clochemerle-Babylon*, celebrates his native wines even more than Compton Mackenzie celebrates his native whisky. Mackenzie writes of appreciative drinkers: Chevallier speaks of those whose lives are devoted to the production as well as the consumption of wine. Edward Hyams provides the fine translation: 'The quality of the years was measured by the bouquet, the texture and colour of the vintages. The life of the town centred upon its wine, which nourished that life with a faith, the ideal of a noble duty common to all. The honour of Clochemerle was involved in the quality of its vintages. These wines, that honour, were tended in the town's cellars, in darkness, where the temperature remained always even; in neatly ranged barrels, regularly visited, the contents tested to see how the stronger wines, those of 12 and 13 degrees, were evolving as they aged. Clochemerle allocated to itself the mission of preparing for mankind such nectars as sustain the body, and enchant the mind.

'The old priest died in the apotheosis of a great year, famous for its wine, one of those years whose fragrant soul is destined to be poured, later, from bottles, to rejoice the heart of man, to celebrate earth's abundance, the memories of happy days and perfect summers.

'It was undoubtedly by favour of a benevolent Providential decree that the old priest died in that year. For thereafter, when speaking of the most exquisite wine their vines had yielded in thirty years, the Clochemerlins could say, "It's the wine of Ponosse's year." Indeed, when that wine had become scarce and venerable, people spoke simply of "the Ponosse wine". Surely a fine posthumous reward for an old Beaujolais parson who, when he yet lived, had believed that the

LIQUID ENCHANTMENT

It is traditional among the Beaujolais wine-growers to open their cellars to visitors, for they are proud of their wine and anxious to see it appreciated. It is a point of honour among them to make their visitors drunk.

The novice has no suspicion. Drawn directly from the wood and drunk at the temperature of the cellar, Beaujolais seems very smooth and safely light. Uncountable are those presumptious ones who have been obliged to revise this judgement, and that when in postures hardly compatible with the dignity of an investigator. For the wine of Clochemerle is at once exquisite and treacherous: it charms first the nose, then the palate, finally the entire man. Mark well that if it makes a man drunk it does not do so malignantly. It produces an enchanting light-heartedness, an intellectual sparkle which liberates the drinker from the constraints and conventions which bind him in his daily life. Thus, for example, it may happen that he, the drinker, is brought to declare that he does not give a damn for his wife and the account which he will have to render her of his behaviour; that he does not give a damn for the boss, either, nor for the police, the tax collector, bills, appointments, nor, in general, for anyone or anything which might prevent a free citizen from conducting himself in such a manner as shall seem to him good and pleasant and contributing to his touchy, drunkard's dignity. And such declarations of independence are much enjoyed by the Clochemerlins.

Gabriel Chevallier *Clochemerle-Babylon* (translated by Edward Hyams)

tending of vines and the pains taken with wine of quality are two of the principal tasks of mankind here below.'

SUB-THEMATIC DRINKING

Drinks and drinking occur as sub-themes in literature in various other ways, both serious and light-hearted. A slightly tongue-in-cheek serious approach is shown in Graham Greene's *Monsignor Quixote*. The quality of local wines is first discussed, it being pointed out that 'no wine can be regarded as unimportant since the marriage at Cana'. Later there are reflections on the writings of a German moral theologian: 'I've never drunk out of vice in my life. I drink when I have a fancy and to toast a friend. Here's to you, monsignor. What does Father Jone say about drinking?'

'Intoxication that ends in complete loss of reason is a mortal sin, unless there is sufficient reason, and making others drink is the same unless there is a sufficient excuse.'

'How he qualifies things, doesn't he?'

'Curiously enough, according to Father Jone, it is more readily permissible to be the occasion of another's drunkenness – what you are guilty of now – at a banquet.'

Monsignor Quixote says later: 'Father Heribert Jone found drunkenness a more serious sin than gluttony. I don't understand that. A little drunkenness has brought us together, Sancho. It helps friendship. Gluttony surely is a solitary vice. A form of onanism. And yet I remember Father Jone writing that it is only a venial sin. "Even if vomiting is produced." Those are his very words.'

No such serious discussions take place in *Poet's Pub*, by Eric Linklater, in spite of the setting. The latter comes about rather negatively: 'I'm useless as a shipper, exporter or broker,' he said, 'and not much good as a poet. What shall I do?'

'Have a drink,' Quentin suggested.

'I can't make a profession of that.'

'Why not? You boast about your palate. You can tell the difference between a tenpenny Medoc and a Lafite. Be a wine-shipper.'

'I haven't a ship.'

'Then keep a pub.'

There is some discussion later about drinks of former times, and the invention of blue cocktails is celebrated. The pub mainly serves, however, as a convenient excuse for bringing people of very different backgrounds under one roof. They then become involved in adventures of a mildly exciting nature.

Yet another way of using drinks in fiction is shown by Peter de Vries in *The Tunnel of Love*. The author has a lot of fun with his hero, a man who has become a keen student of wine and is keen to impart his new-found knowledge. When he sees some Piesporter being sold at a bargain price he struggles home with 12 bottles, supposedly as an anniversary present for his wife.

'"It's a Spätlese," I pointed out, tapping the label of a bottle which I had picked up. "That means it's from selected grapes which have been allowed to become dead ripe, which is when those grapes are at their best. It's a condition the Germans call *edelfaul*, when the grapes are *edelreif*. The French have a term for it too – *pourriture noble*. It means a noble ripeness. When the grapes get so they're ready to fall off the vine. Age is a guarantee of body and perfume."

'I poured and served the Moselle with style. I toasted the occasion, and we drank.

"God," I said, working my lips. "Beautiful?"

"Mm," she agreed, nodding. "Quite nice."

"Get that delightful fruitiness characteristic of all your fine Moselles." I was relieved to find the wine good, because I'd suddenly remembered something about Moselles having to be drunk young, which meant that mine was pushing senility, and also shed a little light on it as a shopping coup.'

As de Vries gets into his full comic stride, the wife points out that the husband tends to buy presents for her which he wants himself: '"You're really getting to like wine, aren't you? Especially white wines."

"What do you mean by that?"

"I mean you like white wine," she answered, a flintiness in her voice which recalled the great Chablis. "You'd love to lay in cases of it, have a cellar, but it's too expensive."

"I remember distinctly you were crazy about the wine we drank at Hans's. You exclaimed about the Piesporter we had first, and you exclaimed about the bottle he opened later. It was a 1937 Rüdesheimer Hinterhaus Riesling Auslese – '

'You *have* to exclaim at Hans's. Or he sulks.'

'I remember that bottle because I memorized the label, as a sort of gag. It was a Rüdesheimer Hinterhaus Riesling Auslese Wachstum und Original Abfüllung Grafen von Franken-Sierstorpff."'

This is verbal slapstick, but de Vries is quite able to write prose of high quality. It is pleasant to find sentences like: 'She set her glass down after looking in surprise at its contents, as though sobered by the realization of the effect alcohol had on you.'

COMIC DRINKING

The more usual comic drinking scene in literature involves drunken behaviour, such as that of Kingsley Amis's Lucky Jim. Practical jokes played on drunks are less common, but have their own tradition. Shakespeare's victim for the latter treatment is Christopher Sly, the drunken tinker in *The Taming of the Shrew*. He is discovered asleep before 'an ale-house on a heath' by a passing lord who is returning from hunting. Sly is gently conveyed to a bed in a rich chamber. When he wakes, he is told that he has 'been in a dream' for 15 years and that he is really a rich nobleman. His supposed wife appears – a page called Bartholomew dressed as a lady. Sly dismisses the servants and wants his 'wife' to come to bed: instead the couple watch the players perform the play.

A similar trick is played in *The Arabian Nights*, 'The Sleeper Awakened'. Shakespeare could also have found the idea in Goulart's *Admirable . . . Histories* (1607).

Dickens has Mr Pickwick trundled away in a wheelbarrow while drunk, but I am rather fond myself of the joke played on M'Garry in Samuel Lover's *Handy Andy*. M'Garry has been holding forth about galvanism, the latest sensation. There is a discussion about whether it is possible to bring a dead person back to life by applying an electric shock. M'Garry gets very drunk and falls into a deep sleep. When he wakes up his friends pretend that he has died and is in a state of temporary animation.

DICKENSIAN DRINKING

Having mentioned Charles Dickens at the beginning of this chapter, it is now fitting to return to him. He mentions many different drinks and drinkers, sometimes in telling little asides. When Jingle is in full conversational flow we are told that he takes 'an occasional glass of ale, by way of parenthesis'. A group of young gentlemen who have been drinking heavily continue to pour down the wine, 'like oil on blazing fire'. Pecksniff, drinking brandy from a stone bottle as he rides in a coach, makes a philosophical remark. Then: 'he corked the bottle tight, with the air of a man who had effectually corked the subject also'.

This is the same Pecksniff who falls into the fireplace when drunk and has to be rescued by the lodgers. As they carry him off to bed he asks frequently for something to drink. The youngest gentleman of the company proposes water and is called 'opprobrious names' for his trouble. We picture the scene as easily as we see Mr Tuckle, who has been drinking large quantities of sweetened gin and water with his fellow men-servants. 'Mr Tuckle no sooner got into the open air, than he was seized with a sudden desire to lie on the curbstone.'

Dickens is thoroughly acquainted with the behaviour of committed drinkers, and little seems to have changed since his time. There are still plenty of ladies like Mrs Weller, who 'began by protesting that she couldn't touch a drop – then took a small drop – then a large drop – then a great many drops'. In any pub there are still men like Krook, responding to a drink that has been put before them with: 'You're a nobleman, sir. You're a baron of the land.'

In essays Dickens wrote of gin palaces and discussed the temperance question. In his fiction he mentions drinking in many different ways, and is always aware of what he is doing. Two scenes in *A Tale of Two Cities* demonstrate the point. Early in the book, a large cask of wine has been dropped and broken in a Parisian street. Dickens describes how the people scoop up the wine in any way they can. 'There was no drainage to carry off the wine, and not only did it all get taken up, but so much mud got taken up along with it, that there might have been a scavenger in the street.'

SPLIT PERSONALITY

Robert Louis Stevenson's *Dr Jekyll and Mr Hyde* could be seen as a deliberately over-exaggerated portrait of a man whose personality is changed by drink. It is perhaps surprising that no one has invented a Jekyll and Hyde cocktail, though if it behaved like the mixture described by Stevenson, which began 'to effervesce audibly and to throw off small fumes of vapour', there are probably few drinkers who would care to sample it.

We are told that Dr Jekyll's drink 'was at first of a reddish hue'. It then 'changed to a dark purple, which faded again more slowly to a watery green'. Its immediate effect is similar to that induced more slowly by strong alcohol. Dr Jekyll reels and staggers, while his features seem to melt and alter.

But on this occasion, Dickens is not so much concerned with people's behaviour, horrifying though it is. The cask had contained red wine, and its symbolism is more important. Dickens reminds us that the time would soon come when blood would run in those same streets as freely as the wine.

The climax of the story is Sydney Carton's supreme sacrifice, replacing Darnay in the condemned cell, but Carton has been established as a heavy drinker. His early companion is Stryver, and 'what the two drank together, between Hilary Term and Michaelmas, might have floated a king's ship. Carton was rumoured to be seen at broad day, going home stealthily and unsteadily to his lodgings like a dissipated cat'.

Such a man is hardly heroic material, but Dickens is careful to make it clear that Carton has not decided to take Darnay's place while under the influence of drink. 'For the first time in many years, he had no strong drink. Since last night he had taken nothing but a little light thin wine, and last night he had dropped the brandy slowly down on Mr Lorry's hearth like a man who had done with it.' The gesture paves the way for the final, better rest that awaits him.

SOMETHING BREWING

Beers, ales, stouts

LET US turn now from thoughts about drinking to the drinks themselves. It seems fitting to begin with one which is so much a part of the Anglo-Saxon heritage that the word used to describe it simply means 'drink'. 'Beer' was adapted by our ancestors from a Latin word *biber* 'a drink', itself a late development of *bibere* 'to drink'. As an English word 'beer' dates from the sixth or seventh century; German 'Bier' is from the same period. An earlier English word was 'ale', derived from Old Norse.

In many countries, beer has long had something of an image-problem. It is the drink of the working-man, rather than the traditional gentleman or the modern middle-class professional man. It is the drink of quantity, rather than quality. It is the bread-and-cheese drink, rather than the drink that accompanies a gourmet meal.

Christopher Finch, in his *Beer: Connoisseur's Guide to the World's Best*, has attempted, in a lavishly and beautifully illustrated book, to correct such ideas, but he is fighting against great odds. Current television commercials for Australian lager, for instance, reinforce both the association with working-class male drinkers and with quantity. It is all done in an amusing way, but the advertisers have no doubts about the market at which they are aiming.

Christopher Finch imagines a very different world, where male and female guests at society dinner-parties sip Mackeson's sweet stout as an aperitif, drink Guinness with their oysters or a Pilsner Urquell with their caviare, then proceed to a beer carefully chosen to match the food: Grolsch with Dover sole, Worthington White Shield with game, Beck's with roast pork, and so on.

It's an interesting idea, but its very strangeness makes the point that most of us do not think of beer in that way. Nor is this down-market

ROYAL DISH

'For a quart of ale is a dish for a king.'

William Shakespeare *The Winter's Tale*

image of beer a recent phenomenon. For centuries, those who could afford to do so have drunk imported wines and spirits, leaving the

A punning French advertisement for Guinness.

home-produced beer to the labourers. Beer was usually quite literally 'home-produced', its making supervised by the same housewives and farmers' wives who saw to the baking of the bread.

In ancient history, the connection between bread and beer is a very strong one. It is generally assumed that beer was first produced accidentally from dough or bread that became wet, then came into contact with yeast spores in the air. The yeast would have caused a natural fermentation to occur. Spontaneous fermentation is still used today in the production of lambic beers, brewed in the region of Brussels in Belgium. As for bread, stale rye bread forms the basis, as it has done for centuries, of the Russian beer-like drink called kvass.

AN EARLY HICCUP

This is rushing along somewhat, and we should go back to the beginning. In the case of most mod-ern beers, that means going back to barley. Grain from other cereals, such as wheat, maize, millet, oats and rice, could be used instead, and in modern brewing may be used as well as barley, but barley has for centuries been beer's basic raw material. The connection between beer and barley is so strong that some have been tempted to link the two words, as if both came from the same original, but their vague similarity is a coincidence.

What is needed to make beer, in more general terms, is a source of carbohydrate. Barley happens to be relatively easy to grow in many countries, including Britain. It is also especially good for brewing beer – a fact that was known to the ancient Egyptians at least 5000 years ago. The name of their beer, incidentally, is variously transliterated as *hek*, *hequ* or *hequp*. Ivor Brown preferred the latter form because it reminded him, very appropriately, of *hiccup*.

Barley is turned into malt before it is used in brewing. To the etymologist there is a connection

Harvesting the barley.

between the words *malt* and *melt*. If you melt something, you turn it into a liquid. In the malting process the barley grains are not exactly liquefied, but steeped in water. Excess water is then drained away and the grains begin to germinate, or sprout.

MODERN METHODS

In the old-time brewery, germination usually continued for 10 or 11 days and the whole process had a human touch. The maltster regulated the temperature in the maltings by opening or closing windows, while men with wooden shovels came in to turn the grain. This prevented too much heat building up in the grain bed and stopped the shoots binding together. Mechanical screws now do the latter job, while forced ventilation circulates air at a computer-controlled temperature.

Just as the modern brewer wants to speed up the malting process, so the farmer tries to ensure a good crop. He will have used fertilisers to achieve that aim, and will probably have chosen a short-strawed variety of barley which has been tested in malting and brewing trials for its commercial potential. The different strains of barley, incidentally, have their own names. Approved

varieties for a recent growing season included Natasha, Halcyon, Maris Otter and Golden Promise.

Let's get back to our typical modern brewery and continue our tour. We had reached the point where the barley grain had been steeped in water and allowed to germinate. That germination has to be stopped after 'modification', as brewers express it, has taken place. It is a feature of the brewing industry that a number of such common words are given a specific meaning, while other words are used which are not met with elsewhere. An example of the former is 'liquor', which inside a brewery means 'water'. 'Sparge' and 'wort' are examples of specialised brewing terms which we will come to shortly.

An attempt was made to deal with this language of brewing in *Word for Word*, an anonymous little book published by Whitbread in 1953. It bore the sub-title 'An Encyclopaedia of Beer', but rather more than the book's 38 pages would have been needed to do justice to the subject. A more

---

BREWSTER

There was a William Brewster on *The Mayflower*. He was the son of the bailiff of the manor of Scrooby, Nottinghamshire, where there was an important Puritan congregation. His family name indicated an ancestor who was a brewer. Until the 13th century, the –ster ending would have pointed to a woman who did the brewing, but a brewster could later be a man or a woman. Other variants of the surname in English, German and Dutch include Brewer, Breuer, Brauer, Breier, Breyer, Breger, Breu, Brei, Preuer, Preyer, Bruyer, Braumann, Breymann, Brauermann, De Brouwer, Brower, Brouwers.

ENORMOUS PROFITS

In *David Copperfield* Mrs Micawber says of her husband: 'I have long felt the brewing business to be particularly adapted to Mr Micawber. Look at Barclay and Perkins! Look at Truman, Hanbury and Buxton! It is on that extensive footing that Mr Micawber, I know from my own knowledge of him, is calculated to shine; and the profits, I am told, are e-NOR-mous!'

Mr Micawber applies to the breweries mentioned, offering his services 'in an inferior capacity', but they decline to answer his letters.

Breweries do not feature strongly elsewhere in the works of Charles Dickens. In *Great Expectations* Miss Havisham owns one, having been tricked into buying her brother's share of it, but it is disused.

---

recent publication is the *CAMRA Dictionary of Beer*, by Brian Glover. *Word for Word* has no entry for 'modification'. The CAMRA dictionary defines it as: 'the germination stage of the malting process (after steeping), when the barley starts to sprout shoots and the chemical actions begin.'

GRIST FROM THE MILL?

The modified barley, then, is fed into a kiln, where it is dried or cured. That completes the initial process, and the barley is now malt. The colour of the malt, which will affect the colour of the beer, will have been controlled by varying the temperature during kilning. The malt is next milled, or 'cracked', and becomes 'grist'. This use of the term is confusing, since 'it's all grist to the mill' is a fairly common expression. Grist normally refers to corn that is ready for grinding, but has not yet been ground. The saying 'grist to the

---

THE UNKNOWN X

Breweries have long used X, XX, XXX, XXXX, etc., as an indication of beer-strength. Various explanations for the use of X have been suggested. One says that it was originally the sign of the cross, used by monastic brewers as a guarantee that the brew was of good quality. No evidence has been produced, however, to support this claim. Written references to X in relation to beer occur from only the 17th century, after taxes had been imposed. X may therefore have been the Roman numeral, indicating the multiples of ten pence that were to be paid as tax. More tax would have been paid on stronger beers, so the number of Xs would have given some indication of strength.

By the 17th century, XX was being used for mild ale, while XXX was used for stronger beer. In modern times some brewers use a string of Xs to imply that their beer is especially strong, but no official scale is recognised.

---

mill' means something like 'it all helps; it's all useful; it can all be turned to profit'. In a brewery one would presumably have to say 'it's all grist *from* the mill' to mean the same thing. A brewer with a keen interest in words might argue, however, that 'grist' is related to 'grind' and does not indicate whether the grinding is about to occur or has already happened.

Grist from the brewery mill is stored in a large hopper known as a grist case. There it is likely to be mixed with other raw materials, known as brewing adjuncts, some of which have also been through the mill. These adjuncts have been in use since the beginning of the 20th century and are nearly always of cereal origin.

A major reason for their use, according to the Brewers' Society, is the brewers' need to limit the nitrogen content of malt. This must be done, it seems, to help improve the stability of the beer and prolong its shelf life. The adjuncts are also said to 'aid head retention in the glass'. I assume that it is the head of the drink itself which is meant by that phrase (from *How Beer is Brewed*) but a pleasant alternative is suggested. The writer could equally well have said that adjuncts were meant to aid 'nose retention in the glass'.

ADDING THE ADJUNCTS

By varying the quantities of the adjuncts, a brewer can produce a wide variety of beers. A pale, American-type lager, for instance, may contain up to 30 per cent of maize or rice. It is obvious that yet more reasons for the use of adjuncts have cynically been suggested at one time or another. The Brewers' Society says defensively: 'Some adjuncts used to be considered as cheap substitutes for malted barley, but it is a fact nowadays that some are more expensive than malt.'

How We Brew Our Beer, the booklet produced by Scottish and Newcastle Beer Production Ltd, explains clearly how adjuncts are introduced at different stages of the brewing process. Solids such as torrefied wheat and wheat pellets go through the malt mill and then join the crushed malt in the grist case. The word 'torrefied' derives from Latin *torrere* 'scorch' and means 'roasted'. The final colour of the beer is also thought about again at this stage. If necessary, a

PAIL ALE

Now David Pryce had one darling vice;
Remarkably partial to anything nice,
Nought that was good to him came
 amiss,
Whether to eat, or to drink, or to kiss!
Especially ale! – if it was not too stale
I really believe he'd have emptied a
 pail.

Richard Harris Barham *The Ingoldsby
Legends*

controlled amount of a special coloured malt, such as caramalt, crystal malt, chocolate malt, black malt, or barley that has been roasted without being malted, can be milled and fed into the grist case. Directly into the same hopper go adjuncts such as flaked maize and wheat flour which do not need to be milled.

WATERY LIQUOR

Everything in the grist case is now ready to be transferred to the mash mixer or mash tun (called a 'kieve' in Dublin), where it will be mixed with hot liquor. There is some justification, incidentally, for calling water in a brewery 'liquor'. The brewer will almost certainly have made adjustments to the mains water supply. It is no longer necessary for breweries to be built in certain areas because of the water that happens to be there, though that is one of the reasons why Edinburgh, Newcastle, Burton and Dublin, for example, became famous for their beers. The modern brewer treats water by adding, if necessary, salts such as gypsum to create the brewing liquor he needs. There is even a treatment known as Burtonisation which aims to recreate the type of water that is found naturally in the wells around Burton.

Breweries use a great deal of water, about six pints for every pint of beer produced. Most of it is used for heating, cooling and cleansing, but 90 per cent of every pint of beer is water.

ENTER THE ENZYMES

The word 'mash' is related to 'mix'. In the mash mixer, hot liquor is added to the grist and adjuncts to form a porridge-like mass. Other adjuncts may now be added in a liquid form. If maize grits, for instance, are to be used, they will themselves have been mixed with liquor and cooked in a cereal cooker. In the form of a hot slurry they can then be fed into the mash mixer. Using the standard British infusion system of mashing, the combined mixture that is now there is left for several hours. During that time the starches in the grist and adjuncts dissolve in the hot liquor and are converted by enzymes into fermentable sugars.

Enzymes were only identified and named at the end of the last century, but they now seem to be popping up all over the place. They are a feature of modern washing powders which can break down biological stains (i.e. made by grass, blood, wine, eggs and the like), but they need time to do their work. The mashing process in the brewery

PLUS JE BOIS
MIEUX JE CHANTE!

is therefore somewhat similar to clothes being left to soak overnight. Enzymes are hard at work during this period, breaking down large biochemical structures into molecules.

The European system of mashing, used in the production of lager-type beers, is slightly more complicated and is known as decoction. The Latin word *decoquere* means to 'boil down', and decoction refers to the process of extracting an essence by that method. It can also mean the liquor that is obtained by such a process. Decoction mashing differs from the infusion method in varying the temperature of the liquor and grist at different stages. The brewers who use it argue that some enzymes favour lower temperatures, some higher, and that the system therefore leads to better results.

It is interesting that brewers have only in relatively recent times been able to explain in biochemical terms what happens during such processes as mashing and fermentation. For thousands of years they had known how to make beer (and wine) without knowing how or why their methods worked. Towards the end of the 19th century, when Pasteur and his contemporaries first introduced microscopes into the breweries and demonstrated what was happening, there must have been many who felt like Monsieur Jourdain in Molière's *Le Bourgeois Gentilhomme*. He was the gentleman who discovered that for more than 40 years he had been speaking prose without knowing it.

THE WORZEL GUMMIDGE CONNECTION

Back in the brewery, the next task for the brewer is to extract the sugary solution from the mash. The traditional method, according to *How We Brew Our Beer*, was to spray the mash with hot liquor in the mashing vessel and run off the strained liquid. In brewery language, the mash was sparged to extract the sweet wort. 'Sparge' is from Latin *spargere*, which means 'to sprinkle'. The term is known to any plumber as well as brewers. A sparge pipe is one which has holes to allow water to spray out.

'Wort' (pronounced *wert*) is simply the infusion of sugary liquid derived from malt. It has been

called wort for at least a thousand years and could set us off on an interesting etymological trail. The word links ultimately with plant names such as liverwort, St John's wort. In such names wort means 'plant' and is a first-cousin of the word 'root'. Perhaps the connection in meaning is shown by German *Würze*, 'spice, flavouring'. The modern German word for wort is *Bierwürze*, literally 'beer-flavouring'. 'Root' in German is *Wurzel*, which was adapted slightly by Barbara Euphan Todd for a whole series of stories about a certain scarecrow called Worzel Gummidge.

In modern breweries mashing takes place in a mash mixer. Extraction of the sweet wort then takes place in a separate vessel which naturally has a word to itself: it is the lauter tun. This must surely have been a German invention, *lauter* meaning 'pure' in that language, and a purifying process being involved. Other types of extraction systems in use are known as the Strainmaster and the Mash Filter. Whichever type is used, removal of the sweet wort leaves behind spent grains, or 'draff'. 'Draff' means 'dregs', and the word has been used by brewers since the Middle Ages. In spite of its sound and meaning, draff is by no means something that goes to waste. It is sold by the breweries as cattle feed and is a valuable by-product of the beer-making process.

We have reached the stage, then, in our verbal tour of a modern brewery, where sweet wort has been extracted from a mash of malted barley and adjuncts. Other adjuncts may be added at this stage, in the form of sugar or cereal syrups. These do not contain starch and are readily fermentable. After these additions, the sweet wort is ready to be introduced to the hops.

HOP IT!

Hops were first used by British brewers in the 15th century, and a mighty fuss was made about them at the time. Until then the English had drunk unhopped ale, very sweet and thick, and there were many who wanted to keep it that way. Hops were described as a 'pernicious weed', with several local authorities imposing a ban on their use. Even the Brewers' Company demanded in 1484 that ale should be brewed from water, malt and yeast and nothing else.

In his *Compendyous Regyment or Dyetary of Health* (1542) a certain Andrew Boorde wrote: 'Beer is made of malte, hoppes and water; it is the natural drink for a Dutcheman, and now of lete dayes it is much used in England to the detryment of many Englysshe people; specyally it kylleth them the which be troubled with the colyke; for the drynke is a cold drynke, yet it doth make a man fat, and doth inflate the bely, as it doth appere by the Dutche men's faces and belyes.'

The idea of using hops had been introduced by Flemish traders, some of whom may indeed have had beer-bellies. But they had been drinking hopped beer for a very long time and knew that its

flavour and aroma made it superior to unhopped ale. English brewers also noticed that beer could be stored for longer periods than the traditional ale. Hopped beer gradually won general favour and became the norm. When it was no longer necessary to distinguish between unhopped ale and hopped beer, 'beer' and 'ale' reverted to being loose synonyms. 'Beer' is now slightly the more general term, covering ales, lagers and stouts. 'Ale' would not be applied to a stout: other than that it is simply a word for 'beer' used with greater or lesser intensity in different dialects, or in the vocabularies of individual drinkers.

Hop fields are a familiar sight in south-eastern English counties such as Kent, and in Hereford and Worcester. Also to be seen are the distinctively-shaped oast-houses, where the hops are dried after being harvested. Mechanisation long ago put an end to the harvesting that was once done by whole families on a working holiday, and there have been other changes. Hops used in English beers, for instance, may actually have been imported from Germany or Yugoslavia.

THE DREADED WILT

Even the English hops that have been used are unlikely to be the same as those used in the 15th century. Just as new varieties of barley are continually being introduced, so plant breeders seek to develop new varieties of hops. The Hop Research Department of Wye College is pioneering the development of dwarf varieties which will be easier to grow and harvest. It is also hoped that they will be more resistant to diseases such as Verticillium wilt (*not* a hop-growing equivalent of brewer's droop) and will have a high alpha acid content. It is the alpha acid which imparts the bitterness to beer.

New varieties of hops will have new names, and familiar names may disappear. It will be a sad day when a Fuggle is no longer to be seen in the hopfields. This was introduced by a Mr Fuggle of Kent in 1875, and was the dominant variety of hop in England for 70 years. Alas, Fuggles are susceptible to wilt and have a low alpha acid content. Their excellent aroma may not be enough to save them. Goldings is another famous English hop, while Borthdown, Wye Challenger and Target are newcomers. The Yeoman hop was introduced in 1980 and is said to mature early and have a high alpha acid content, but to need careful handling.

Dried hops used to arrive at the brewery in large sacks, called pockets. More recently it has been usual, after kiln-drying, to press them into small pellets which are then hermetically sealed. This reduces the bulk that has to be transported and makes the hops less perishable. It seems highly likely that in future the acids and oils in the hops which give beer its bitterness and aroma will simply be extracted in the hop-growing areas.

They will then be supplied to the breweries in extract form.

BOILING THE KETTLE

If hop pellets are still used by the brewery, they are boiled in a wort kettle, or copper (usually made of stainless steel in modern times), with the sweet wort. Boiling usually lasts for about an hour, causing evaporation and an increase in strength of the liquid that remains. Any living organisms that might have been present are killed off, and the activity of the enzymes ceases. What is left is a sterile hopped wort, but it contains solid material that has clumped together during boiling. 'These solids,' says *How We Brew Our Beer*, 'are called trub.'

'Trub' in that sense defeats my copy of the *Oxford English Dictionary*. The learned editors say that trub is an obsolete or dialectal word for a truffle, connected with Latin *tuber* 'hump, swelling'. They also mention that in the 17th and 18th centuries, a trub or trubtail was 'a little squat woman, a slut'. Trub, to the brewers, is something that has to be removed from the hoppped wort. The wort is therefore drained ('cast') from the copper into a whirlpool machine. As this spins round the trub remains at the centre and the clarified liquid is drawn off from the edges. The hopped wort, free of trub, is then cooled and is ready for its transformation into beer.

Hops may make an appearance again later in the beer-making process. In what is called 'dry hopping' a small quantity of hops or hop oils is added loose to the beer to improve flavour and aroma. In quite a different way, spent hops are

---

MOCK BEERS

The villagers in Flora Thompson's *Lark Rise to Candleford* make what is called a 'yarb beer'. Yarb is a dialectal form of 'herb', and the herb in this case was the yarrow. Beer-like drinks can also be made from ginger, nettles, elderflowers, bran, spruce, parsnips and other ingredients.

squeezed and sold as compost to gardeners. Hops that have been strained from the wort may add aroma to roses and rose-growers are therefore especially keen customers.

If the processes described above appear to be complicated, it is only a case of technical terms obscuring a simple story. What has happened is remarkably simple. Essentially, barley grains were steeped in water and were left to germinate. Germination was stopped at the right moment by heating and the barley was now malt. The malt was milled and the crushed grains were mixed with hot water, left to stand, then strained, boiled with hops and strained again. Small proportions of other grains were added along the way. This simple series of operations has produced a sugar-rich liquid known as hopped wort.

FRATERNAL DRINKING

Most monasteries in the Middle Ages brewed their own beer. Occasionally the monks made notes about their brews. The friars of the Abbey of St Thomas the Martyr, in Dublin, said: 'Ale shoulde not be drunk under V days olde. Newe Ale is unwholesome for all men. And sowre ale, and dead ale; and ale the while doth stand a tylte is good for no man.'

Having made the beer, the monks got on with drinking it. Richard Erdoes, in his _1000 Remarkable Facts About Booze_, quotes a saying:
'To drink like a Capuchin is to drink poorly,
To drink like a Benedictine is to drink deeply,
To drink like a Dominican is pot after pot,
But to drink like a Franciscan is to drink the cellar dry.'

Certain abbots found it necessary to issue warnings: 'If any monk through drinking too freely gets thick of speech so that he cannot join in the psalms, he is to be deprived of his supper.' The abbots themselves also drank, however. A local legend in Burton says:
'The Abbot of Burton brewed good ale,
On Fridays when they fasted,
But the Abbot of Burton never tasted his own
As long as his neighbour's lasted.'

THE MAGIC COMPONENT

All this has been a mere prelude to the really dramatic action which is now to take place. Everything has been prepared for the entrance of the star performer – yeast. Even the Information Brief of The Brewers' Society waxes lyrical at this point. 'Yeast,' it says, 'could almost be described as the magic component of brewing. It is responsible for spectacular changes in the composition of the wort that enters the fermenting vessel during the later stages of the brewing process, yet its properties were very much a mystery until relatively recently.'

Magic and mystery – a distinct improvement on lauter tuns, draff and trub. Yeast has also been known as leaven and barm, while a dialectal term for it seems to have been God-is-good. The latter reflects the sense of wonder that early brewers must have felt as they watched the effect of yeast. 'Barm' refers specifically to yeast in the form of froth, seen on liquor while it is fermenting. The British slang term 'barmy', meaning crazy or stupid, is derived from it, implying that the person so-described has nothing in his head but froth.

How Beer is Brewed says: 'There are hundreds of species of yeast, all of them composed of individual cells of microscopic fungi. They are all around us, on cereals, fruit, plants and even in the air. Wort, left open to the atmosphere, would soon be seeded by yeasts and other micro-organisms, and begin to ferment, which must have been the way the ancient brewers of Babylon achieved their results.'

Yeast grows and multiplies by feeding on various types of sugar. It turns the sugar into energy, some of which it uses for its own growth. Quite a lot of the energy it transforms into heat. In passing it produces carbon dioxide gas and alcohol,

NINKASI

Norman Hammond, archaeology correspondent of *The Times*, reported on 5 August 1991 that Solomon Katz of the University of Pennsylvania, working with Fritz Maytag of the Anchor Brewery, had recreated one of the world's earliest beers. The two men used a recipe contained in a hymn to Ninkasi, the Sumerian goddess of brewing. The beer they produced was said to have 'the smoothness of champagne and a slight aroma of dates'.

Honey and barley flour were mixed to make *bappir*, a sweet bread. Dates were used for what the original recipe referred to as 'sweet aromatics', but because of modern US food regulations were added to the brew later rather than being mixed with the bread. Since it had not been possible to identify the preservative used in ancient times, the beer was flash-pasteurised.

To taste the beer, the researchers used long straws and jugs in the Sumerian fashion. Seven months later a further tasting led to the assessment: 'a dry flavour lacking in bitterness, similar to a hard apple cider but retaining the fragrance of dates'.

and is followed by a succession of mini-fermentations until the right quantity is produced. A fresh culture is prepared when the yeast has been used ten times or so. There is a National Collection of Yeast Cultures at the Food Research Institute in Norwich.

A brewer refers to 'pitching' the yeast, in a slurried form, into the cooled stream of wort as it is on its way to the fermenting vessel. Old-style fermenting vessels were open at the top, and the thick frothy head that appeared on the surface as fermentation took place could clearly be seen. Typical examples of such vessels can be seen at Tetley's brewery in Leeds, where they are called Yorkshire Squares and have been in use since Georgian times. Modern fermenters are closed and use a foam control agent to reduce the frothy heads. To the brewer the latter are a nuisance since they reduce the amount of space available for the beer. The foam control agent is, of course, a modern innovation, and its name reflects what is happening in the brewing industry as the scientists take control. It goes by the catchy name of dimethylpolysiloxane.

THE GREAT ESCAPE

Tetley's Brewery issued a challenge in 1911 to the famous escape artist, Harry Houdini. In his act he used to escape from a padlocked trunk submerged in a tank full of water. Tetley's offered instead to replace the water with beer for one special performance. Houdini accepted the challenge and the tank was duly filled with beer for his second evening performance on 9 February.

In the event, Houdini was unable to cope with the alcohol. He was hauled out of the tank half conscious and suffered what was, perhaps, his only defeat.

In 1983, at the Tetley Gala Day, the escapologist David De Val took up the same challenge. He emerged from the tank safe and sound after 1 minute 41 seconds.

both of which, from the yeast's point of view, are waste products. Some of the carbon dioxide dissolves in the beer, giving it its fizz. The rest has to be treated with great caution by the brewer and dispersed safely.

A major part of the brewer's skill is employed in keeping his yeast happy while this fermentation process is taking place. Yeast is a sensitive, living organism. Too much or too little heat, for instance, will cause it to stop working. I refer deliberately to the brewer and 'his' yeast. I mentioned earlier that some Flemish brewers of lambic beers still rely on air-borne yeasts, but most other brewers propagate and maintain their own cultures. Propagation starts in the laboratory

A MATTER OF GRAVITY

When the wort reaches the fermentation vessel its specific gravity (SG) is measured by comparing its weight with that of the same volume of water. Since the wort is a sugary solution, it is about four per cent heavier than water, though a reading would not be expressed in that way. The specific gravity of water is 1.0; that of the wort might be between 1.035 and 1.045. Brewers do not like working with decimals, so they multiply such figures by 1000. They then refer to specific gravities as 'ten thirty five', 'ten forty five', etc., or, since such figures always begin with 10, the 'ten' can be omitted. A brewery worker would understand a comment that the 'SG is forty' to mean that the specific gravity was 1040 (1.040).

The gravity of the wort at the start of fermentation is called the original gravity (OG), and it is this figure on which duty is assessed by the Customs and Excise. It is also the figure which will tell the brewer how strong his beer will be after fermentation. If the original gravity is not right for his purposes, he will correct it before fermentation begins. This adjustment, made by adding sterile liquor to the wort, is known in the trade as 'cutting' the brew.

When a brew has first been pitched with yeast, there is a short pause while the yeast takes stock of its new surroundings. It then realises that it is surrounded by a wonderful supply of sugars and starts to feed. Fermentation has begun, and the sugars are steadily replaced with alcohol. During this attenuation process the density of the liquid decreases, as a series of so-called 'present gravity' readings informs the brewer. He is thus able to bring the fermentation process to an end when the correct gravity is reached. He does this by cooling the fermentation vessel to a point where

Pub scene, 1870, by Fred Barnard. Published in Fun.

the yeast refuses to go on working. The final gravity now reveals the strength of the beer – probably between 1008 and 1015. The higher the final gravity, the more sugar that has remained in the beer.

BEER IN STORE

The yeast strain used in lager production is not the same as that used for making traditional British beers. If a brewery is making both kinds of beer, it must be careful to keep the different yeasts apart. The lager yeast cells sink in the fermenting vessel, and bottom fermentation occurs. This leaves a clearer brew and forms less of a head, but is a much slower process than top fermentation and has to occur at a lower temperature. Since we are talking of lager, the other main differences between it and traditional British beer can be mentioned. As already noted, the decoction rather than infusion system is used for mashing the brew. The brewer's liquor is also different, being low in mineral salts. Continental hops are used which have less alpha acid. Finally there is the process which gives lager its name. The word in German means 'a store', and lager beers are kept in a store where they undergo secondary fermentation for several weeks. The very best lager, Pilsner Urquell, is stored in wooden casks for three months.

This secondary fermentation needs a really cool environment, and until the 19th century it was only possible to make a lager beer in areas where natural cold storage was available. Since the foothills of the Alps had caves that could, if necessary, be packed with ice from the higher slopes, Bavaria and Bohemia became the main lager-producing centres. Industrial refrigeration subsequently made it possible for lager-type beer to be brewed anywhere, though purists would argue that a lager bought in Britain, Australia or the USA differs markedly from true European lager.

But we had not quite finished our tour of the brewery. We had reached the point where the brewer decided that fermentation should cease. At that point he needs to remove the yeast from the beer, perhaps by means of a centrifuge, a machine like a spin dryer. Fermentation has pro-

---

THE MOTHER AND FATHER OF DRINKS

Mum seems to be a strange name for a beer, but it was popular enough in former times for there to be special mum-houses in London. Samuel Pepys tells us that he went to such a tavern in June, 1664 with his uncle Wight. 'There drinking, he do complain of his wife most cruel as the most troublesome woman in the world . . .'

Mum had nothing to do with the familiar word for 'mother'. It was the English version of German Mumme, which in turn was probably the family name of a 15th-century brewer. The beer was first sold in Braunschweig (Brunswick), in northern Germany.

Pop was once a colloquialism for champagne. Evelyn Waugh, in *Vile Bodies*, has:

. . . drinking what Lady Throbbing, with late Victorian *chic*, called 'a bottle of pop', and Mrs Blackwater, more exotically, called '*champagne*', pronouncing it as though it were French.

Pop is still a childish slang name for a fizzy, non-alcoholic drink. In both cases the name originally referred to the popping sound heard when a bottle is opened.

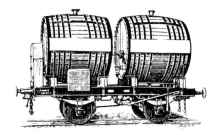

duced more yeast than the brewer began with, so the surplus can be sold off. It goes to distillers, or to food manufacturers who make yeast extracts such as Marmite. Some goes to farmers who feed it to pigs.

'A River Side Street' by Gustav Doré.

THE BEER-DRINKER'S TRAGEDY

'A Lay of St Dunstan' is one of the *Ingoldsby Legends*, by Richard Harris Barham. It concerns Peter, a lay-brother, who overhears St Dunstan issuing commands to a magic broomstick. Peter decides to make use of the broomstick himself, but the results are disastrous:

> Peter, full of his fun,
> Cries, 'Broomstick! you lubberly son of a gun!
> Bring ale! – bring a flagon! – a hogshead – a tun!'

> No doubt you've remarked how uncommonly quick
> A Newfoundland puppy runs after a stick,
> Well, so potent the spell,
> The Broomstick perceived it was vain to rebel,
> So ran off like that puppy; – some cellar was near,
> For in less than ten seconds 'twas back with the beer!
> Peter seizes the flagon; but ere he can suck
> Its contents, or enjoy what he thinks his good luck,
> The Broomstick comes in with a tub in a truck;
> Continues to run at the rate it begun,
> And, *au pied de lettre*, next brings in a tun!
> A fresh one succeeds, then a third, then another,
> Discomfiting much the astounded lay-brother;
> Who, had he possessed fifty pitchers or stoups,
> They all had been too few; for, arranging in groups
> The barrels, the Broomstick next *started the hoops*;

> The ale deluged the floor, but, still through the door,
> Said Broomstick kept bolting, and bringing in more.
> And Peter, who did not expect such a rough visit,
> Cried, lustily, 'Stop! – That will do, Broomstick!
> *Sufficit!*'

> But ah, well-a-day! The Devil, they say,
> 'Tis easier at all times to raise than to lay.
> The longer he roared, and the louder and quicker,
> The faster the Broomstick was bringing in liquor.
> The poor lay-brother knew not on earth what to do –
> He caught hold of the Broomstick and snapped it in two.
> Worse and worse! Like a dart each part made a start,

And he found he'd been adding more
    fuel to the fire,
For *both* now came loaded with
    Meux's entire;
Coombe's, Delafield's, Hanbury's,
    Truman's – no stopping –
Goding's, Charenton's, Whitbread's
    continued to drop in,
With Hodson's pale ale, from the Sun
    Brewhouse, Wapping;
The firms differed then, but I can't put
    a tax on
My memory to say what their names
    were in Saxon.
Now extremely alarmed, Peter
    screamed without ceasing,

For a flood of brown stout he was up
    to his knees in,
Which, thanks to the Broomstick,
    continued increasing;
He feared he'd been drowned, and he
    yelled till the sound
Of his voice, winged by terror, at last
    reached the ear
Of St Dunstan himself, who had
    finished *his* beer,
And had put off his mitre, dalmatic,
    and shoes,
And was just stepping into his bed for
    a snooze.

His Holiness paused when he heard
    such a clatter;

RICE-BEER

The Japanese national drink is sake (or saki). It causes some confusion among westerners, who are aware of it as an alcoholic drink and perhaps know that it is served warm at the table from small ceramic flasks. These are known as *tokkuri*; the tiny drinking bowls from which the sake is actually drunk are called *sakazuki*. Sake itself takes its name from the city of Osaka, where it was first produced, according to tradition, in the eighth century.

When they mention sake (pronounced as two syllables *sah-kee*), English writers tend to be very unclear about its nature. Dictionaries hedge their bets by calling it an 'alcoholic beverage', not specifying whether it is a beer, wine or spirit. The fact that it derives from a grain makes it beer-like; its alcoholic strength puts it into the fortified-wine category; it is served as if it were a spirit.

Sake is in fact a slightly sweet rice-beer. It is non-carbonated and of a light colour. When it is made, steamed rice is first allowed to ferment for four weeks; a secondary fermentation with added rice then brings its alcohol content up to about 18 per cent. This makes it as strong as sherry and other fortified wines and accounts for its common description as rice-wine. It has more in common with barley-wine, though, than with wine derived from the grape or other fruits.

It would be possible to distil sake, but I can find no references to such a spirit. I am not sure, therefore, why *The Penguin Book of Spirits and Liqueurs*, by Pamela Vandyke Price, says firmly that 'Sake is a rice-based spirit'. She has perhaps been misled by the fact that sake is occasionally used as a cocktail ingredient. Miss Price herself mentions the Sakini, which is one part sake to three parts gin. There is also a Sake Manhattan, which mixes one part sake with two parts rye whiskey.

The Times reported early in 1991 that special bottles of Mozart K.001 sake were on sale in Japan, commemorating Mozart's death in 1791. The connection with the composer was a little tenuous – the sake had been fermented to the strains of his music.

He could not conceive what on earth was the matter.
Slipping on a few things, for the sake of decorum,
He issued forthwith from his *Sanctum sanctorum*,
And calling a few of the lay-brothers near him,
Who were not yet in bed, and who happened to hear him,
At once led the way, without further delay,
To the tower where he'd been in the course of the day.
Poor Peter! – alas! – though St Dunstan was quick,
There were two there before him –

Grim Death, and Old Nick! –
When they opened the door out the malt-liquor flowed,
Just as when the great vat burst in Tottenham Court Road;
The lay-brothers nearest were up to their necks
In an instant, and swimming in strong double-X;
While Peter, who, spite of himself now had drunk hard,
After floating awhile, like a toast in a tankard,
To the bottom had sunk, and was spied by a monk,
Stone-dead, like poor Clarence, half drowned and half drunk.

A FISHY STORY

Not all the yeast is removed in the centrifuge. The rough ('green') beer is therefore allowed to stand for a time in a process known as maturation. The maturation vessels are large – those at Tetley's brewery, for instance, hold 1200 barrels each. Isinglass is added to help any remaining yeast and solid particles settle out. 'Isinglass' is a curious word for a curious substance. The word is an English attempt to cope with the obsolete Dutch word *huisenblas*, 'sturgeon's bladder'. The substance is a kind of gelatine obtained from the air-bladders of fish such as the sturgeon. It serves as a 'fining', a refining or clarifying agent. As isinglass finings pass through the beer they attract to themselves particles of other matter. Isinglass does not affect the flavour of the beer, but settles out with the yeast and is itself removed.

Isinglass is not the only odd substance to come into contact with beer during brewing. Additives

---

ANIMAL SPIRITS

The Reverend James Woodforde recorded in his *Diary of a Country Parson* (1758–1802) that his two pigs had drunk some beer grounds from one of his barrels. They 'got so amazingly drunk by it, that they were not able to stand . . . I never saw pigs so drunk in my life.' The two pigs were still unable to walk next day. 'They tumble about the yard and can by no means stand at all steady yet.'

There is a well-known pub in Hawkshead, Lancashire, called *The Drunken Duck*. The traditional story behind the name is that a former landlady found several of her ducks lying as if dead in the backyard. They were in a drunken stupor, having eaten grain soaked in ale from a leaking barrel.

Some dog-owners allow their animals to drink beer, for which they sometimes develop a liking. Horses have also been known to enjoy an occasional pint.

NAMING NAMES

O Beer! O Hodgson, Guinness, Allsop,
  Bass!
Names that should be on every infant's
  tongue!
Shall days and months and years and
  centuries pass,
And still your merits be unrecked,
  unsung?
Oh! I have gazed into my foaming
  glass,
And wished that lyre could yet again
  be strung
Which once rang prophet-like through
  Greece, and taught her
Misguided sons that 'the best drink was
  water'.

C.S. Calverley *Beer* (one of 15 verses)

and processing aids are used 'to increase the performance of the raw materials', as the Brewers' Society expresses it. They are lost or filtered out later and are no longer present in the beer that reaches the customer. As a typical customer, I am glad to know that, since additives include alginates and carrageenan (seaweed extracts) and sulphur dioxide. Carbon dioxide is added to brewery-conditioned beer and does remain, but this is said to be replacing what has been lost in the brewing process.

Some beer is brewery-conditioned, with the maturation process occurring in large vessels. Other rough beer, however, is transferred, or 'racked', directly from the fermentation vessel into casks so that the fining and maturing happens there. The yeast that remains in the rough beer also allows a slow, secondary fermentation to occur. This leads to the cask-conditioned beer known to many enthusiasts as 'real ale'.

In the brewery, rough beer is filtered after maturation and is then stored in 'bright' beer tanks. The beer is drinkable at this stage, but will probably be subjected to pasteurisation – sterilisation by heat treatment. It gets to the customer, finally, by means of cans, bottles, kegs or cellar tanks.

STOUT-HEARTED MEN

So far, I have described the production of traditional British bitter beer and mentioned how it differed from beer that is lagered. It remains to say something of stout, and to do that we must step back in time. The first reference to 'stout' as a drink occurs in a manuscript letter of 1677: 'We will drink your healths both in stout and best wine.' In 1719 Thomas D'Urfey has: 'We will frolick in stout, and banish all care in a mug.' The meaning of the word at this time was recorded by Dr Johnson in 1755: 'a cant name for strong beer'. An earlier term for this had been huff-cap, implying that drinking such beer would huff or raise one's cap.

Stout, then, was at first any strong beer. Later the word was also applied to 'porter', or 'entire'. The latter term was invented by a brewer named Ralph Harwood, according to J. Feltham, *Picture of London* (1802). He says that in the London alehouses and taverns of the early 18th century it had been 'the practice to call for a pint of *three threads*, meaning a third of ale, beer and twopenny (the strongest beer, costing twopence a quart). A brewer of the name of Harwood conceived the idea of making a liquor which should partake of the united flavours of all three . . . calling it *entire* or *entire butt*.'

Harwood's entire was highly hopped, strong and dark. It was brewed with soft rather than hard water. The term 'entire' is first recorded in the 1720s. Within a few years entire was also being referred to as porter – short for porter's ale or beer – because the porters of the London street markets were especially fond of it. Porter that was extra strong was known as stout porter, and eventually as 'stout'. In Ireland it also came to be known as 'plain'.

GUINNESS

Whereas beer in general is associated with many long-established and famous breweries in different countries, many people now associate stout with Guinness. They do so because of a decision made by Arthur Guinness in 1799 to concentrate on that style of beer. Forty years earlier, at the age of thirty-four, Arthur Guinness had taken over a small, disused and ill-equipped Dublin brewery. In Dublin at that time, brewing was not a thriving industry. This was partly due to the quality of the beer being produced. A ballad of 1725, 'The Old Cheese,' said of it:

'This beer is sour – thin, musty, thick and stale And worse than anything except the ale.'

Another factor was the habit of the rural Irish to distil whiskey, gin and poteen (illegally) and drink that instead of beer.

My Goodness –

My GUINNESS

A 1942 press advertisement by John Gilroy.

A PINT OF PLAIN

When things go wrong and will not
   come right,
Though you do the best you can,
When life looks black as the hour of
   night –
A PINT OF PLAIN IS YOUR ONLY
   MAN.

When money's tight and is hard to get
And your horse has also ran,
When all you have is a heap of debt –
A PINT OF PLAIN IS YOUR ONLY
   MAN.

When health is bad and your heart
   feels strange,
And your face is pale and wan,
When the doctors say that you need a
   change –
A PINT OF PLAIN IS YOUR ONLY
   MAN.

When food is scarce and your larder
   bare
And no rashers grease your pan,
When hunger grows as your meals are
   rare –
A PINT OF PLAIN IS YOUR ONLY
   MAN.

In time of trouble and lousy strife,
You have still got a darling plan,
You still can turn to a brighter life –
A PINT OF PLAIN IS YOUR ONLY
   MAN.

Brian (Flann) O'Brien *At Swim-Two-Birds*

Nevertheless, some two hundred or so Irish brewers were competing with one another. Arthur Guinness at first brewed traditional Dublin ale, but impressed with the dark porter exported to Dublin from London in the 1770s, he added that to his repertoire.

Arthur Guinness the Second took over the brewery in 1803. A period of expansion was followed by a slump after the Napoleonic Wars. In 1824 sales were below the level they had reached at the beginning of the century. A decision was taken to brew a stronger 'lasting' beer, using more hops and only the best materials. Fellow brewers who tried to cut costs failed to survive, and by 1833 Guinness had the largest brewery in Ireland. By this time the drink had apparently changed its image and was being drunk at all social levels. In a letter to his sister on 21 November 1837, Benjamin Disraeli writes: 'The division took an hour. I then left the house at ten o'clock, none of us scarcely having dined. The tumult and excitement unprecedented. I dined or rather supped at the Carlton with a large party of the flower of our side off oysters, Guinness, and broiled bones, and got to bed at half past 12. Thus ended the most remarkable day hitherto of my life.'

It has to be said that it was probably what had happened in the House of Commons, where there had been a division on the Address in Queen Victoria's first Parliament, that made this such a remarkable day for Disraeli – not his Guinness and oyster supper.

In that same year Dickens had published his *Pickwick Papers*. One of the original illustrations by Phiz shows the Wellers, father and son, with Sam in the throes of composing his Valentine to Mary. In the background is a card advertising 'GUINES'S DUBLIN STOUT'. People clearly found it as difficult to spell Guinness then as they do today.

OUTSIDE A PINT

Benjamin Lee Guinness later took over the brewery and greatly increased its size. He was followed in turn by his third son, Edward Cecil Guinness. The drink was by this time being recommended to nursing mothers, and others believed in its medicinal qualities. Robert Louis Stevenson wrote a letter aboard the S.S. *Mariposa*, 19 February 1893 in which he said: 'Fanny ate a whole fowl for breakfast, to say nothing of a tower of hot cakes. Belle and I floored another hen betwixt the pair of us, and I shall be no sooner done with the present amanuensing racket than I shall put myself outside a pint of Guinness.'

Dylan Thomas later recounted humorously that he had put himself outside rather more than a single pint of Guinness: 'Don't you call me morbid, George Ring. I remember once I drank forty-nine Guinnesses straight off and I came home on top of a bus. There's nothing morbid about a man who can do that. Right on top of the bus, too, not just the upper deck.'

Rather more subtle humour was shown in a *Comic English Grammar* published in 1840: The Possessive Case is distinguished by an apostrophe, with the letter *s* subjoined to it: as 'My soul's idol!' – 'A pudding's end' . . . When the singular terminates in *ss*, the letter *s* is sometimes dispensed with: as 'For goodness' sake!' Nevertheless, we have no objection to 'Guinness's Stout'.

The story of Guinness is obviously on-going and need not be pursued here. The drink is known throughout the world and the company continues to expand. It now has at least 60 principal subsidiaries. A major factor in its success since 1929 has been its advertising campaigns, made necessary at that time by a slump in sales. Many of the poster advertisements, such as those featuring John Gilroy's distraught zookeeper or the man carrying the girder, became famous in their own right. Those with a special interest in such matters should see *The Book of Guinness Advertising*, by Brian Sibley. The drinks industry in general seems to have been particularly successful with its advertising. Various companies have inspired the creation of striking images and effective slogans, many of which continue to amuse readers and television viewers.

ROLL OUT THE BARREL

If a brewery must advertise its products to generate a demand, it has an even more fundamental need to get its products to the customer. In this area, as in the beer-making process itself, there have been great changes in modern times. Most of the traditional oak casks have disappeared, as have the coopers who made them. It seems that another era has almost come to an end. In Britain the Samuel Smith brewery is one of the very few to continue using the old-style casks.

Brewers' casks were made of oak – since the time of Elizabeth I mostly imported from Baltic ports such as Memel (now renamed Klaipeda). The oak staves were bound with iron hoops, splayed to fit the curvature of the wood. Metal bushes (lining) for the bung staves and the tap holes were of brass or gun metal. Rushes, known to the coopers as flags, were inserted between the joints of the cask-head and sometimes in the stave joints. If a cask had dried out, causing shrinkage, the flags would expand rapidly when it was next filled, acting as a temporary seal until the staves themselves absorbed the moisture and expanded.

Popular casks for centuries were the butt (108

CELTIC DRINKING

The beer of the ancient Celts is variously referred to as korma, courmi or coirm.
The second-century Greek physician and writer on medicine, Dioscorides, said that 'Coirm, being drunk by the Irish instead of wine, produces headaches, is a compound of bad juices, and does harm to the muscles'.

From time to time, in the Irish epic tale *Tain Bo Cuailnge*, King Conchubar is said to spend a third of each day feasting, a third watching young warriors wrestle, a third drinking coirm until he falls asleep.

---

gal), puncheon (72 gal), hogshead (54 gal), barrel (36 gal), kilderkin (18 gal), firkin (9 gal) and the pin (4½ gal). Some casks had names which differed in different parts of the country. Once they reached the pubs, they were supported on wooden cradles, variously known as stillions, stillages, thralls or thrawls. If a cask was stacked on top of two others it was known as 'horsing'.

The names for the casks were fairly generally known, but were only a tiny part of the special vocabulary used by coopers. Each stave was 'listed', 'backed', 'hollowed out' and 'dressed' as it was shaped. The hoops were 'dingees' or 'booges', and the cask itself, part way towards completion, was called a 'gun'. The tools used by the cooper also had special names like 'box chiv', 'croze', 'inside shave', 'swift' and 'buzz'. On completion the cask had to be 'pickled' by filling it with a solution of salt and sodium carbonate. This was left for three days to neutralise the tannin in the wood.

An early Guinness drinker, 1794.

DIFFERENT DRINKING

It was his habit to enjoy a half-pint about this time every evening, before he began his night's work at the theatre. Sometimes he liked a quiet, peaceful, meditative half-pint, and at other times he preferred a noisy, gregarious half-pint. It depended upon his mood. When a glass of beer is one of a man's few pleasures and luxuries, he will not casually swill it down, not caring when or where he drinks it. He will exercise to the full his power of choice. That is why places like Bruddersfield are full of public houses. To the outsider, anybody who does not understand such matters, these public houses look all alike, but to Mr Oakroyd and his friends they are as different from one another as the books in a bedside shelf are to an old reader, and a pint at one of them is entirely different from a pint at the next one.

J.B. Priestley *The Good Companions*

It is pleasant to think that there was a man whose special job was to smell the interior of the casks after they had been washed and before they were filled with beer. He was ensuring that the casks were 'sweet', and was actually known as a smeller.

The widespread introduction of aluminium kegs in the 1950s drastically reduced the practitioners of this ancient and highly skilled craft. Many dedicated beer-drinkers were saddened by the change-over to metal kegs. They felt that time spent in the oak casks added something special to the flavour of the beer.

Associated with the casks of former times were the draymen's carts and Shire horses. They are still to be seen at summer shows in Britain, attracting admiring crowds. A Shire horse is likely to weigh nearly a ton, and when it stands erect the tips of its ears are some eight feet from

SAMUEL DOUBLE TOP

A game of darts is one of the most popular activities associated with downing a pint of beer in a British pub. A story is told of a vicar who was especially fond of the game. One Sunday he announced that the text of his sermon would be 'The First Book of Samuel, Double Top'. He meant Samuel I, chapter 20, verse 20. This reads: 'And I will shoot three arrows to the side of it, as though I shot at a mark.'

the ground. In spite of its bulk and strength, it has to be treated delicately. Its small stomach means that four small meals a day are required, with plenty of time allowed for digestion.

During the First World War, many of the brewery Shires were called up for war service. They served with ambulance brigades, but were also asked to haul heavy guns through the Flanders mud. Few of the horses were later returned to the breweries.

For the average drinker the most common reminders of the Shires are the horse brasses which decorate his local pub. They were originally amulets or charms, meant to ensure safe journeys. Similar ornaments have been found in early Mediterranean tombs, but brass objects were only made in England from the 16th century. Brasses hand-made before 1800 are now extremely valuable, but most of those on display are modern replicas.

The pub may also have a Shire horseshoe as a symbol of good luck. Popular tradition says that the open end should be pointing upwards so that the good luck does not drain away. Blacksmiths usually prefer to nail a horseshoe over the door with the open end downward. The theory is that if a devil tries to cross the threshold, the shoe will fall and catch him round the neck. Perhaps two shoes, one pointing each way, should be used.

THE INN-SECT

In Britain, pubs continue to be the main points of sale for beers. For every pint of light or brown ale, stout or lager consumed at home, three pints are drunk in pub or hotel bars. Care in delivering the beer from the cellar to the customer at the bar is of great importance. Even more important is the pub's general atmosphere and appearance. Older customers would probably prefer to drink in Dickensian coaching inns, but in cities older drinkers are not a pub's best customers. In

THE ALE-CONNER

The ale-conner was an official appointed by a manorial authority in former times. He was a professional drinker, whose job was to taste ale that was on sale to the public to ensure that it was of good quality. He also inspected the measures that were used. Frederick W. Hackwood, in *Inns, Ales and Drinking Customs of Old England*, quotes a 17th-century description of a very red-nosed man who had been an ale-conner for seven beery years.

Perhaps because of the effects on the officials of so much drinking, ale-tasters later became ale-testers. Hackwood reports that: 'The official ale-tester wore leather breeches. He would enter an inn unexpectedly, draw a glass of ale, pour it onto a wooden bench, and then sit down in the little puddle he had made. There he would sit for thirty minutes. He would converse, he would smoke, he would drink with all who asked him to, but he would be very careful not to change his position in any way. At the end of the half-hour he would rise, and this was the test of the ale; for, if the ale was impure, if it had sugar in it, the tester's leather breeches would stick to the bench, but if there was no sugar in the liquor the tester would not stick to the seat.'

attempts to please the young, much redesigning of pub interiors has occurred. Traditionalists like myself do not much like the results, but pubs have been evolving steadily since the Middle Ages. They have probably survived because of their constant adaptation. Fortunately, there is still a wide variety of pubs to be found in most districts; a search for the right one can be a pleasant enough task.

There are a surprising number of people in Britain (mostly men, it must be said) who take their pubs very seriously indeed. The first member of the inn-sect, as the enthusiasts sometimes call themselves, that I can remember meeting was the late John Leaver. John's special interest was in the names of pubs, and he collected them for 60 years. When John died, he left copies of the large volumes that contained his collection to Gordon Wright and myself. Gordon has made a life-time study of pubs, especially those of his native Nottinghamshire. Some years ago he and

I co-wrote *A Dictionary of Pub Names*. There is also a chapter which introduces this topic in the *Guinness Book of Names*.

Many men have decided to have a drink in as many pubs as possible, touring the country in order to add to the score. Others make the tour with a camera, photographing inn signs. At least one enthusiast known to me specialises in photographing only those pubs and pub signs which have a railway connection. Then there are those who collect beer bottle labels, beer mats and other point-of-sale advertising items.

In many countries a certain amount of caution has to be exercised where beer mats are concerned. If drinks are not paid for at the time of ordering, as in Britain, the beer mat may well be used by a waiter or waitress to record what a customer has drunk. Trying to remove the mat before paying one's dues would not be looked on with favour. There is a reference to the custom in Len Deighton's *Funeral In Berlin*. At a bar in

London pub scene, 1872, by Arthur Boyd Houghton. From the Graphic.

Prague 'groups of men shouted for slivovice, borovicka [a kind of gin] or Pilsner Urquell, and the waiters kept a tally of their progress by marking each man's beer mat with strange pencil marks.'

A Dictionary of Collectors' Terms, by Alfred Lubran, assures us that a collector of beer bottles is known as a 'labeorphilist', a collector of beer bottle tops as a 'capglazerite', a collector of beer mats as a 'tegestologist'. Those who collect the horse brasses discussed earlier should be called 'hippornurgists', says Mr Lubran, suggesting also that collectors of inn signs should answer to the name of 'hostelaphilists'.

These are not very happy inventions on the whole. 'Labeorphilist' appears to be a mixture of Latin and Greek, with a meaning something like 'a lover of big lips'. 'Capglazerite' is an attempt to suggest 'covering glass with a cap'. 'Tegestologist' is based on the Latin word for a 'mat', which is *teges*. A Greek ending has been added. In 'hippornurgist' I recognise Greek *hippos* 'horse', but from there on I am lost. 'Hostelaphilist' is again an ugly mixture of languages.

Mr Lubran does not include the word 'canologist'. This is said to be an American term for someone who collects beer cans. Canologists are likely to belong to Beer Can Collectors of America, an organisation which claims 80 000 members. Collectors' gatherings are said to be known as 'canventions'. This is more like it – I am all in favour of ghastly puns.

The only canologist I have actually met preferred to call himself a collector of beer cans. Julien Zickwolff, of Rio de Janeiro, told me enthusiastically of the 4000 empty cans which he has at home. His collection is a mixed one, since he began with cola cans and then switched to beer. I learned from Mr Zickwolff about the variations in can capacity, ranging from 135 millilitres to five litres, about magazines such as *Balcao*, *Recycle* and *Loot* in which beer cans are advertised for

sale or exchange, about the weekly collectors' fair in the Passeo Publico in Rio, where beer cans feature strongly. Passionate discussions take place amongst collectors on the subject of technical details – whether a rip-top can should be opened as intended, or pierced with two holes at the bottom – and etiquette. It is not pleasant, said Mr Zickwolff, to receive a beer can through the mail which the previous owner has not bothered to wash.

Beer-related collections, then, occur outside as well as inside the pub. I will leave the subject of pubs for the moment; those who are interested can turn to many excellent books on the subject. As we gathered information about pub names, Gordon Wright and I consulted some 300 of them, and there are many more. A good pub is worth its weight in gold; it remains the best place to drink a well-brewed pint of beer.

Bar scene, 1909, by L. Burret. From Fantasia.

HOME-BREWING

Some who might disagree with that statement are those who brew their own beer at home. Kits are now available to make life relatively easy, though friends who have tried this hobby tend to speak of the 'hassle' involved. Those home-made beers I have sampled have usually had a distinctive taste and been decidedly potent.

References to home-brewing are common in the literature of the past, especially when it is set in country areas. In George Eliot's *Adam Bede*, for example, we are told that the farmer Martin Poyser 'was not a frequenter of public-houses, but he liked a friendly chat over his own home-brewed'. One of the subjects discussed would be the beer itself. When Adam Bede visits Poyser, he 'had to give his opinion of the new tap . . . and then followed a discussion on the secrets of good brewing, the folly of stinginess in "hopping", and the doubtful economy of a farmer's making his own malt . . .'

BREAKFAST ALE

Be mine each morn with eager appetite,
And hunger undissembled, to repair
To friendly buttery, there on smoking
   crust
And foaming Ale to banquet
   unrestrain'd.
Material breakfast! Thus, in ancient
   times,
Our ancestors, robust with liberal cups,
Usher'd the morn, unlike the languid
   sons
Of modern days; nor ever had the
   might
Of Britons brave decay'd, had thus they
   fed,
With English Ale improving English
   worth.

Thomas Warton (1728–90)

Farm labourers and servants in rural districts depended on their employers for their allowance of beer, and for its strength and quality. Weak beer was usually the reflection of a mean employer. William Thackeray reports in *Vanity Fair*: 'There was always a good glass of ale in the kitchen of the Rectory for the Hall people, whose ordinary drink was very small – and, indeed, the Rector's lady knew exactly how much malt went to every barrel of Hall beer . . .'

An extra strong beer was brewed for special occasions. In *Adam Bede*, for instance, the 21st birthday is celebrated of Arthur Donnithorne, grandson and heir of the local squire. The whole community gathers, with the men sitting at separate tables. George Eliot says, of the women and children, 'There was none of the strong ale here, of course, but wine and dessert – sparkling gooseberry for the young ones, and some good sherry for the mothers.'

As the 19th century wore on, home-brewing became less common. Flora Thompson comments, in *Lark Rise to Candleford*: 'The custom of home brewing was fading out in farmers' and tradesmen's households; it saved trouble and expense to buy the beer from the brewery in barrels; but a few belonging to the older generation still brewed at home for themselves and their workmen. At the Candleford Post Office Laura issued about half-a-dozen four-shilling home-brewing licences a year.'

Such licences, of course, are no longer required.

WORKSHOP ALES

I mentioned a moment ago the drinking of beer at a special occasion. Workmen in the past seem to have been ingenious in finding excuses to drink. William Ryland, describing life in 1865 in some Birmingham workshops, says: 'The masters were not very strict in the discipline of their works. "Foot ales" and "marriage ales", "child ales", "walking-stick ales", "change-of-place ales", "ales charged for making a new article", "journey ales" with numerous others, supplied a constant excuse for extending the five o'clock rest; for "tea" was scarcely known as a beverage in any works. The man who "paid his ale" paid a shilling,

the shopmates putting down threepence each.'

An 'ale' in the sense used by Ryland meant 'an occasion when ale was drunk', or as the modern slang expression has it, a 'beer-up'. Foot (or footing) ales were of at least two kinds, the most common being that signalling a new man starting work. The newcomer 'paid his ale', which in mining communities could mean the equivalent of his first day's wages. Any stranger in a rural community might also be asked to stand his footing ale. Some parents had a footing ale when their child took its first steps.

The marriage ale was far more commonly known as the bride ale, or bridal. 'Bridal' had become a noun meaning 'a marriage feast' by the 11th century. Its use as an adjective in phrases like 'the bridal gown' came much later. Child ales celebrated the birth of children. Because a woman was said to be brought or put to bed when she had a child, they were also known as bed ales. In Cornwall they were known still more graphically as 'groaning ales'. These were not to be confused with 'dirge ales', otherwise known as 'soul ales', which marked funerals.

The journey ales mentioned by Ryland no doubt marked the end of an apprenticeship, when the young man concerned became a journeyman. From now on he would be paid for each day's work. The modern meaning of 'journey' rather obscures the fact that the word derives from French *journée*, referring to a period of a day. Early meanings of the word in English had to do with the distance one could travel or the amount of work one could do in a day.

NO HARM DONE

He drank rather heavily, though not more than many miners, and always beer, so that whilst his health was affected, it was never injured. He practically never had to miss work owing to his drinking.

D.H. Lawrence *Sons and Lovers*

One can only guess at what was meant by Ryland's 'walking stick ale'. It may have occurred when a man returned to work after an accident or illness, using a walking stick as an aid. If so, it was stretching things rather far, at a time when

COCK ALE

Samuel Pepys mentions in his *Diary* (e.g. 2 February 1663; 4 June 1666) that he has drunk Cock ale. This was ale mixed with the jelly or minced meat of a boiled cock, plus other ingredients. A 17th-century recipe for making it runs as follows:

'First catch your cock of half a year old, kill him and truss him well, and put into a cask 12 gallons of ale, to which add four pounds of raisins of the sun, well picked, stoned, washed and dried; sliced dates, half a pound; nutmegs and mace two ounces. Infuse the dates and spices in a quart of canary 24 hours, then boil the cock in a manner to a jelly, till a gallon of water is reduced to two quarts: then press the body of him extremely well, and put the liquor into the cask where the ale is, with the spices and fruit, adding a few blades of mace: then put to it a pint of new ale yeast, and let it work well for a day, and in two days, you may broach it for use, or in hot weather, the second day, and if it proves too strong, you may add more plain ale to palliate this restorative drink, which contributes much to the invigorating of nature.'

In *The Language of Drink*, by Graham and Sue Edwards, a completely different explanation is given. The authors claim that cock-ale was 'a mixture of spirits fed to fighting cocks in the eighteenth century'. They go on to say that 'this would also be consumed by the winning punters with a number of tail feathers in the drink showing the number of ingredients in the drink'. No evidence of any kind is supplied for either of these dubious statements.

excuses for extra drinking hardly seemed to be necessary. A hundred years earlier Benjamin Franklin had recorded daily beer consumption in a London printing house. Everyone had a pint before breakfast, a pint with breakfast, a pint between breakfast and dinner, a pint at dinner, a pint at six o'clock and a pint at the end of the working day. Elsewhere it is recorded that the ordinary working man's allowance of beer in the 18th century was a gallon a day. This fairly heavy drinking had no doubt continued into the Birmingham workshops a century later.

HOLY ALES

Those Birmingham workmen were in fact continuing a tradition that had existed for many centuries in rural communities. Ales of one kind or another were a normal part of life, sanctioned by the church. Shakespeare refers to them as 'holy ales'. Philip Stubbes, in his *Anatomie of Abuses* (1583), said that 'against a Christmas, an Easter, Whitsunday, or some other time, the Churche-wardens provide half a score or twenty quarters of maulte . . . which maulte being made into very strong ale or beere, is set to sale, either in the Churche or some other place assigned to that purpose. They repair their Churches and Chappels with it . . . they buy books for service.'

The Puritan Stubbes would have liked to abolish the church ales, but they continued. Churches also seem to have sanctioned special clerk ales, where proceeds from the sale of beer went to the parish clerk. In more general terms, a 'bid ale' might be arranged for any honest man who was down on his luck. It was a kind of benefit night, to which a general bidding or invitation was given. If parishioners were lucky they might be invited to a 'give ale', where everything was provided free and they were not expected to help others. The money for such annual parochial celebrations usually came from bequests.

The *Oxford English Dictionary* records that there was once a 'cuckoo ale', defined as 'ale drunk out of doors as a celebration of the cuckoo's return'. A 'lamb ale', in Oxfordshire, was an annual celebration at lamb-shearing.

Historical references to these various ales reassure us that human nature has not changed a

18TH-CENTURY DRINKING SONG

Ye true honest Britons who love your
    own land
Whose sires were so brave, so
    victorious, so free,
Who always beat France when they
    took her in hand –
Come join honest Britons in chorus with
    me.

Let us sing our own treasures, Old
    England's good cheer,
The profits and pleasures of stout British
    beer;
Your wine-tippling, dram-sipping
    fellows retreat,
But your beer-drinking Britons can
    never be beat.

The French with the vineyards are
    meagre and pale,
They drink of their squeezings of half-
    ripened fruit;
But we, who have hop yards to mellow
    our ale,
Are rosy and plump, and have freedom
    to boot.

great deal. If friends and neighbours were to help us with a task, we might no longer talk about having a 'help ale' to mark its completion. It is only the name that has gone: we almost certainly do have a drink to say thank you and to celebrate a job well done. We still instinctively want to celebrate significant moments in our domestic and professional lives, as did our ancestors. For centuries such celebrations were so closely associated with the drinking of beer that the word 'ale' in itself meant a 'party'. There can be no better indication of the part beer has played in our national life.

BEER BIOGRAPHIES

At a far more personal level, Ernest Hemingway reflected in his *Green Hills of Africa* on beers that had played their part in his life: 'I was thinking about beer and in my mind was back to that year in the spring when we walked on the mountain road to the Bains d' Alliez and the beer-drinking contest where we failed to win the calf . . . and the brown beer sitting at the wood tables under the wistaria vine at Aigle when we came in across the Rhône Valley from fishing . . . and later there was the good beer at Lipp's at midnight . . .'

Hemingway goes on to sum up his memories of beer-drinking in various countries: 'We outgrew some countries and we went to others but beer was still a bloody marvel.' His comments provide what a 17th-century writer, using a word that was fashionable at the time, might have called a nippitate testimony, a hymn of praise to good beers based on personal knowledge. When he was holding forth in a bar about his drinking experiences, Hemingway was a man who would have commanded the respect of other drinkers.

'Down to the Dregs' by John Seymour Lucas (1849–1923).

WASHING IT DOWN

Elizabeth I thought that beer was 'an excellent wash'. She drank a quart of it for breakfast. When she visited Hatfield House, the Earl of Leicester hastily wrote to Lord Burleigh: 'There is not one drop of good drink for her there. We were fain to send to London and Kenilworth and divers other places where ale was; her own beer was so strong as there was no man able to drink it.'

Stephen Potter comments on that important aspect of pubmanship, incidentally, in one of the essays in *Pub*, a volume edited by Angus McGill. Mr Potter deals humorously with such important subjects as how to get someone else to pay for your drink.

Another essay in the volume is 'The Glory That Is Beer', by Vincent Mulchrone. This is a mixed bag of interesting fact and comment. Examples: beer should not be sipped because the taste-buds which respond to bitterness are at the back of the tongue; Babylon had the first barmaids. 'They gave good measure, too. The penalty for a short pull was death by drowning.'

Mr Mulchrone also quotes a lament which came from the Society for the Preservation of Beers from the Wood:

'Keg, or not to keg; that is the question.
Whether 'tis nobler for the gut to suffer
The effect of CO_2 in dustbin beer
Or take arms against the sea of bubbles
And, by boycott, to end them . . .'

CAMRA (details on p. 110) later took up the cause of maintaining traditional beer standards, but a new generation of beer drinkers seems to have different criteria. Michael Jackson lists 1500 or more beers in his *Pocket Beer Book*, many of which could be described as exotic. There is a Beer Shop in north London which offers 500 of them, including some with names such as Old Fart, Willie Warmer, Baz's Bonce Blower and Son of a Bitch. This hints at a world of commercialised, trendy, novelty drinking rather than knowledgeable appreciation, but beer is flexible enough to cope with those who come to it for whatever reason. Not for nothing has it survived triumphantly for more than 5000 years.

GOOD ENOUGH

'And no ports,' I said. 'I don't believe in ports for young girls. Beer was good enough for Queen Elizabeth, and it's good enough for little pieces that ought to be in bed with a feeding bottle.'

Joyce Cary *The Horse's Mouth*

Glossary of beer words and names

Adam's ale – water, and therefore sometimes applied to weak beer. The Scottish version is Adam's wine.

Air pressure – a beer-dispensing system used mainly in Scotland. Compressed air in the cask forces the beer up to the dispenser at the counter.

Alcohol content – normal beers are within the range 3%-6%. The Frog and Parrot pub brewery in Sheffield serves a beer called Over and Out, 16.9%, claiming that it is the strongest draught beer in the world. Brewers tend to say that a beer of more than 8% is undrinkable.

Ale – a synonym for beer. (See p. 79.) Also a festival or social occasion at which ale was drunk, normally prefixed by another word – bride-ale, groaning-ale, etc. (See pp. 104–6.) A slightly unusual use of the word occurs in *David Copperfield*, by Charles Dickens. Betsey Trotwood has been forced by loss of her money to switch from her usual wine to a half-pint of ale. She says – 'If nothing worse than Ale happens to us, we are well off.' Swift's Stella was apparently unable to spell 'ale' – 'Sept. 29, 1710 – I drink no *aile* (I suppose you mean *ale*), but yet good wine every day, of five and six shillings a bottle.' Jonathan Swift *Journal to Stella*.

Aleberry – ale boiled with spice and sugar and pieces of bread. References to it are found between the 15th and 17th centuries. The word originally was alebrew, which changed to alebrey, alebery.

Ale-conner – an ale-inspector. (See p. 100.)

Alecost – costmary (plant used to flavour ale).

Alecy – a word invented by Lilly in 1598 to describe ale-lunacy, caused by drinking too much ale.

Alegar – malt vinegar. Made by home-brewers before vinegar became readily available.

Ale-hoof – the herb ground ivy, supposedly used to add bitterness to ale before hops were introduced. 'Hoof' = 'hove', a plant name.

Ale-house – for centuries this was the normal word for 'pub'.

Ale-knight – a derisive name for someone who visited an ale-house too frequently. Common in the 16th and 17th centuries.

Ale passion – used by a 16th-century writer to describe the headache ('pain in the pate') caused by drinking too much ale. 'Passion' is presumably used in its religious sense of 'suffering'.

Ale-stake – a post set up outside an ale-house, normally bearing a bush or garland to indicate that ale was sold.

Ale-taster – another word for ale-conner.

Ale-wife – a woman who kept an ale-house.

All-nations – a mixture of dregs from bottles, tap-droppings, etc. Also known as 'alls'.

Altbier – copper-coloured German ale style; especially popular around Düsseldorf.

Amber fluid – also amber liquid. Australian slang for beer. This and other Australian expressions listed here are from G.A. Wilkes *A Dictionary of Australian Colloquialisms*.

Anker – a cask holding an anker (10 old wine gal, 8.5 imp gal) of beer. The word may be present in some pub names as 'Anchor'.

Arval – a funeral ale or feast. The word is of Scandinavian origin and was used in the north of England. Now obsolete or dialectal.

Attemperation – temperature control of wort as it ferments.

Audit ale – ale specially brewed at certain colleges for use on audit days.

Barbed wire – Australian slang for beer, derived from the XXXX symbol.

Barley-bree – also barley-broth. Words formerly used for strong ale.

Barley-cap – to wear a barley-cap formerly meant to be tipsy. A man who was a barley-cap was therefore a tippler.

Barley-hood – a fit of drunkenness.

Barley wine – dark, sweet beer, usually sold in nips (third of a pint) because of its extra strength.

Barm – the frothy yeast head that forms on top of fermenting malt liquor. By the 17th century the adjective barmy was being used to describe a frothy-headed, silly person.

Beer – for the etymology see p. 79. An alcoholic drink normally made from yeast-fermented malt, flavoured by hops. Early religious writers sometimes referred confusingly to God as 'the beer'. They meant the be-er, the one who has being, who exists.

Beeregar – malt vinegar, a synonym for alegar.

Beer engine – the old name for the hand-pump used to draw beer from the cellar to the bar.

Beer garden – garden attached to a pub.

Beer mat – a small table-mat for a beer-glass, used by the breweries for advertising purposes. Collected by tegestologists.

Beer-up – a heavy drinking session.

Best – used for 'best bitter', a commercial rather than realistic description.

Bevvy – slang for 'drink', usually beer. From 'beverage'. The older term was 'bever'. At Eton College 'Bever days' were those when extra beer was served to the boys.

Bitter – the driest, most highly-hopped beer. Also called light, pale, IPA.

Black and Tan – stout and mild, mixed half-and-half. Name is now out of favour.

Bock – applied to German beer, a strong lager of at least 6% alcohol content. Asking for *un bock* in France and Belgium will usually result in a small glass of light lager.

Bottle-conditioned – a beer which has been subject to secondary fermentation in the bottle. Such beer must be poured carefully to avoid transferring the sediment to the glass.

Bottoms – sediment left in the bottom of a cask.

Bragget – a drink made of honey and ale fermented together. From Welsh *bragawd*. The word was later used of a spiced ale. In Lancashire they once celebrated Bragget Sunday, Mid-Lent Sunday, from the custom of drinking such ale on that day. Thomas Love Peacock, in *The Misfortunes of Elphin*:

'The ale-froth is white, and the
     mead sparkles bright;
They both smile apart, and with
     smiles they unite –
The mead from the flower, and the
     ale from the corn,
Smile, sparkle, and sing in the
     buffalo horn.'

Brew – (to make) beer. 'Brew' is mainly northern English slang for a glass, bottle or can of beer. American college students use 'brew' or 'brewski'.

Brewer's inch – the last inch of a bottle of bottle-conditioned beer, containing the bottoms or lees. Peter McCall in his *Brewer's Dictionary* says it is rich in vitamin B and health-giving.

Brewery-conditioned – tank or keg beer, filtered and pasteurised at the brewery.

Brewery Tap – the pub attached to a city brewery.

Brewex – British brewery trade fair.

Brewster – originally a female brewer, but a synonym of brewer by the 14th century.

Brown ale – usually a bottled mild ale, dark and sweetish.

Bung – Australian slang for a publican.

Burdock – one of the herbs that was used to flavour ale before hops became normal.

Burton – Burton-upon-Trent became a major English brewing centre because of the quality of water available in local wells. Breweries elsewhere can now 'Burtonise' their own local water supply – adjust its chemical composition to that of Burton water.

Butcher – a measure of beer in Australia. Usually 170 ml.

Buttered ale – beer with cinnamon, sugar and butter, drunk in the 17th century.

CAMRA – the Campaign for Real Ale. An association of British beer-drinkers formed in 1971 to fight against bland keg beer, pub closures, high beer prices, brewery takeovers, etc. Currently has 30 000 members. For details write to: 34 Alma Road, St Albans, Herts AL1 3BW, or telephone 0727 867201.

Cauliflower – a term used to describe the layer of yeast that forms on top of a fermenting vessel.

Chaser – a glass of beer drunk immediately after a glass of spirits, usually whisky or rum.

Cocktail hour – beer and rum session of Australian sheep-shearers after work.

Codswallop – a British expression of unknown origin meaning 'nonsense'. The 'wallop' has caused some to explain this as Codd's wallop, after an American Mr Codd who invented a particular kind of ginger-beer bottle. The explanation provides a good example of codswallop.

Cold gold – Australian slang for a can of beer (from advertising).

Coldie – can or bottle of cold beer in Australia, where coldness is the main requirement. Howard Jacobson, in *Redback*, his novel about his experiences in Australia, has – 'the beer was so cold that it anaesthetised my teeth and gums. I could have bitten off half the glass and not noticed.'

Collar – the froth between the top of beer and the rim of a glass, though used by some to mean the space between the beer surface and the measure line.

Condition – the carbon dioxide in beer, which gives it freshness and sharpens the flavour, provided the right amount of the gas is present.

Copper – wort and hops are boiled in a brewery copper – now usually made of stainless steel.

Costmary – an aromatic plant formerly used to flavour ale. Also known as alecost.

Dagger ale – a slang term for inferior ale in the 17th century. Sold by a tavern in London, called The Dagger.

Dark – mild beer is often described in this way.

Decoction – a system of mashing used for lager-type beers. (See p. 84.)

Depth charge – Budweiser beer with a shot of bourbon in it.

Diät beer – this is beer which is suitable for diabetics, not for those on a diet. It normally contains less carbohydrates but more calories than normal beer. Alcohol content is also higher, at around 6%.

Dog's nose – beer with a measure of gin added to it.

Doppelbock – an extra-strong German beer, with an alcohol content of 7.5% or more.

Draught beer – beer which is *drawn* to the counter of the pub from the cellar.

Dray – the traditional horse-drawn vehicle used to deliver beer from the brewery. The word refers to a vehicle that is *drawn* along.

Drip mat – earlier term for beer mat.

Dry beer – Japanese beer style, popularised by Asahi Super Dry. Has the characteristics of dry white wine. Ostensibly similar to Diät Pils.

Dry hopping – fresh hops added to a cask of beer. (See p. 86.)

Dunkel – Describes German 'dark' beer.

Eisbock – the strongest kind of German bock beer. Alcohol content is over 12%. The German word *Eis* 'ice' refers to the freezing process used to make the beer.

Export – a term used for premium beers. In the past beers were made of extra strength to help preserve them in store or while travelling.

Faro – a sweet version of Lambic.

Flat – describes beer which has no head or bead.

Flip – beer with a tot of brandy, sometimes with sugar and spices added and often mulled.

Fob – excessive froth on beer, an indication of over-carbonation or high temperature.

Free house – British term for a pub that is not tied to a particular brewery. Offers a wide range of beers.

Froth – the head of a glass of beer. There was at one time an Ancient Order of Frothblowers who mixed their beer-drinking with charitable activities.

Glass – this can mean half a pint of beer in Ireland. In British criminal slang, to glass someone means to slash him with a bottle or glass.

Grandma – also Granny. A mixed pint, old or mild, or sweet stout and mild.

Gravity – a measure of beer-density. Specific, Original and Final Gravity. (See pp. 89–90.)

Green beer – beer which has finished fermentation but has not matured.

Grist – malt and brewer's adjuncts after milling. (See p. 82.)

Grog up – Australian slang = beer up.

Grout – a former name for the infusion of malt before it started to ferment. In the 18th century it also meant weak beer.

Gueuze – blended Belgian lambic beers.

Gush – another term for fob.

Gyle – a quantity of beer brewed at one time. The word has also been used of fermenting wort, contained in a gyle-fat (= vat). A gyle-number is stencilled on to a cask.

Half-and-half – usually a half-pint of mild mixed with half of bitter, but the term can apply to various other combinations.

Head – the froth on top of a glass of beer.

Heavy – in northern England used of a strong beer with a high specific gravity.

Hequ – also Hequp. Ancient Egyptian beer. (See p. 80.)

Hell – describes German 'light' beer.

High gravity brewing – a system whereby beer of very high gravity is brewed and then watered down to the required strength.

Huff cap – strong ale.

Humming ale – strong ale with a good head. The 'humming' is variously explained as referring to the hum in the head after drinking, the noise that

frothing beer makes, or a corruption of 'spuming' = effervescent.

Infusion – the British system of mashing. (See p. 83.)

I.P.A. – India Pale Ale, so-called because it was originally made for export to British troops in India. The letters I.P.A. became synonymous with high-quality beer.

Jar – British slang = a glass of beer.

John Barleycorn – personification of barley, then by extension, of ale or beer. Often made a knight and called Sir John Barleycorn.

Jug – a dimpled beer glass with a handle, used as an alternative to a straight-sided glass. (See below under Sleeve.)

Keg – a small barrel used for 'brewery-conditioned' beer, usually made of stainless steel. The word is also used of the beer itself. Keg beer was first developed by Watney's for use by the Sheen Tennis Club, which needed a beer that would keep and not require the skills of an experienced cellarman when served. The processing of keg beer (e.g. filtering and pasteurisation) adversely affects its taste and makes it sterile, unable to undergo a secondary fermentation. Carbon dioxide is not generated naturally and is therefore injected artificially. The gas is also used to force the beer from the cellar to the bar. CAMRA (see entry above) has successfully waged war against keg beer, forcing breweries to revert to more traditional brewing methods. (See also below: Real ale.)

Kettle – another name for the brewery copper.

Kilning – the roasting of barley in a kiln to end germination. The barley is then malt.

Kölsch – a top-fermented golden ale; popular in the Cologne area of Germany.

Kriek – a cherry-flavoured lambic. Another Belgian fruit-flavoured beer is Framboise (raspberry).

Kvass – a Russian beer-like drink made from fermented rye bread. Most reference sources say that it is at least lightly alcoholic, though a Russian to whom I spoke in 1991, who had been drinking it all her life, labelled it non-alcoholic.

Labologist – collector of beer-bottle labels.

Lager – beer made by the bottom-fermentation method. (See p. 90.)

Lager lout – the *Oxford English Dictionary of New Words* says that this term was inspired by a speech made by John Patten MP in September 1988, when he was Home Office Minister of State responsible for crime prevention. Mr Patten talked of trouble-makers who had nothing better to do with their leisure time than drink too much beer, and used the phrase 'lager culture'. Within weeks journalists were using 'lager lout' to mean a young man who consistently drank too much lager and indulged in aggressive, rowdy behaviour.

Lambic beer – Belgian wheat beer fermented by wild, airborne yeasts.

Lamb's wool – ale mixed with spices, sugar and the pulp of roasted apples. Often used in the wassail bowl. Popular from the 17th to the 19th century. Robert Herrick says in 'Twelfth Night':

> 'Next crowne the bowle full
> With gentle Lamb's Wool;
> Add sugar, nutmeg, and ginger,
> With store of ale too;
> And thus ye must doe
> To make the Wassail a swinger.'

Light ale – light-bodied bottled beer of less alcoholic strength than bitter.

Liquor – in a brewery this means the (treated) water used to make the beer.

Local – pub with a local trade; neighbourhood pub.

Malt liquor – American beer-style, high in alcohol content. Breaker and Colt 45 are well-known brands.

Medium – in Ireland = half-pint of draught Guinness. It is more often called simply a 'glass'.

Merry-go-down – formerly a common name for strong ale.

Middy – a measure of beer in Australia.

Mild – beer of fairly low alcoholic content and not densely hopped.

Milk stout – so-called because it was sweetened with lactose, the main sugar found in milk. The name is now considered to be misleading and cannot be used commercially, though it remains in the normal speech of older drinkers.

Modification – as a brewing term. (See p. 81.)

Mother-in-law – a slang name for stout and bitter.

Mug-house – an 18th-century term for an ale-house.

Nappy ale – formerly used of strong, foaming ale. Sometimes nappy was used by itself to refer to such ale.

Naturally-conditioned beer – refers to beer that continues to undergo a secondary fermentation in the cask or bottle. Often called 'real ale'.

Near beer – American term for non-alcoholic beers, originally produced during the Prohibition.

Nigerian lager – British criminal slang = Guinness.

Niner – Australian slang for a 9-gal keg of beer.

Nippitate – a term of unknown origin used in the 16th and 17th centuries for 'good ale'.

Nog(g) – a kind of strong beer brewed in East Anglia. It was this word which led to the original egg-nog.

October – a strong ale brewed in October. The term was commonly used in the 18th century. '"Ale – strong ale – old October; brewed, perhaps, when I was born." "It must be curious; is it good?" "Excessively good." "I should like a little," said Paulina. "I never had any old October; is it sweet?" "Perilously sweet," said Graham . . . "It smells of spice and sugar. I find it anything but sweet; it is bitter and hot, and takes away my breath. Your old October was only desirable while forbidden."' Charlotte Brontë *Villette*.
'We are plagued here with an October Club; that is, a set of above a hundred Parliamentmen of the country, who drink October beer at home, and meet every evening at a tavern near the Parliament, to consult affairs.' Jonathan Swift *Journal to Stella*.

Pale ale – a bottled beer, heavily hopped and carbonated, similar to bitter.

Pancake – another word for the cauliflower head which forms on fermenting yeast.

Pewter pots – used by some pub regulars, illegally in most cases when the pots do not have a government stamp. Otherwise now mainly for decoration and awarding as prizes.

Pig's ear – rhyming slang for beer. 'What about some more pig's ear? 'Ere, I'm paying for this lot. Same again, boys?' J.B. Priestley *The Good Companions*.

Pipkin – name of a barley malt; also of a party-size can of beer.

Plain – used in Ireland for porter.

Porter – a beer formerly favoured by market porters. Its popularity is indicated by a tragedy which occurred in 1814, when a vat of porter burst at Meux's Horseshoe Brewery in Tottenham Court Road. Hurford Janes relates in *The Red Barrel* that the vat contained 20 000 barrels. The flood caused two or three houses nearby to collapse, and eight people were killed. (See also p. 96.)

Pot – a beer tankard, or measure of beer that varies in different parts of Australia.

Pundy – the free allowance of beer given to brewery workers.

Purl – originally ale infused with wormwood or other bitter herbs. Later it became a drink similar to Dog's Nose, made with hot beer and gin, sometimes with added ginger and sugar. It was supposed to be a good morning drink. Charles Dickens, in *Our Mutual Friend*, has – 'they mulled your ale, or heated for you those delectable drinks, Purl, Flip, and Dog's Nose. The first of these humming compounds was a speciality of the Porters, which, through an inscription on its door-posts, gently appealed to your feelings as, "The Early Purl House". For, it would seem that Purl must always be taken early; though whether for any more distinctly stomachic reason than that, as the early bird catches the worm, so the early purl catches the customer, cannot here be resolved.'

Rauchbier – see Smoked beer.

Real ale – The definition given in Brian Glover's *Camra Dictionary of Beer* is 'Draught or bottled beer brewed from traditional ingredients, matured by secondary fermentation in the container from which it is dispensed, and served without the use of extraneous carbon dioxide, also called "cask-conditioned" and "naturally-conditioned" beer.'

Rhyming slang – terms which have been used for 'beer' at various times include pig's ear (usually abbreviated to pig's), Charlie Freer, far and near, never fear, oh my dear, red steer, Crimea, fusilier. Lace curtain rhymed on Burton (ale), Daily Mail on ale. Julian Franklyn, in his *Dictionary of Rhyming Slang*, also mentions – apple fritter, giggle and titter (bitter); photo-finish (Guinness); day and night (light ale); hod of mortar, Liffey water (porter); in and out, salmon and trout (stout).

Russian stout – an especially strong stout originally exported to the Baltic countries.

Scotch ale – used in northern England of strong dark bottled beer.

Shandy – beer and lemonade mixed half-and-half. The original 19th-century form of the word was shandygaff, of unknown origin, though a pint of beer in the London slang of the time was a 'shant of gatter'. A shanty was a public-house; gatter may have been a corruption of water.

Sherbet – Australian slang for beer.

Skinful – to have had a skinful is to have drunk a large amount of beer.

Sleeve – a name used for a thin, straight-sided pint glass, as opposed to the thicker dimpled jug. Bartenders often ask a customer to specify the kind of glass required, since some people have strong feelings on the subject. The sleeve is sometimes said to be northern English and working-class, the jug southern middle-class, but many would argue that the beer can be better assessed in the straight glass. It is also unkindly said that the chunky jug is preferred by those who feel a need to demonstrate their masculinity.

Small beer – an archaic term for weak or inferior beer. Extended to anything else of a trivial nature. At one time to think small beer of oneself meant to have low self-esteem.

Smoked beer – German *Rauchbier*. Produced in parts of Bavaria. The malt has been dried over beech-wood logs.

Steam beer – a method of brewing used by one or two Californian breweries. It uses bottom-fermenting lager yeasts at top-fermenting temperatures to produce a sparkly beer of 5% alcohol content. The 'steam' may refer to effervescence released when a cask is tapped, but is more likely to refer to the steam-powered breweries which were in use when the beer was first produced. Newquay Steam Beer is a marketing invention based on an association with steam engines used in Cornish tin mines.

Stingo – ale strong enough to sting the drinker as it is consumed. The -o ending is fanciful. In use as a general description since the 17th century. Later adopted as a trade name by several breweries for their barley wines.

Stout – originally used as a general description for strong beer. Now specifically a very dark, heavy, highly hopped bitter with a thick, creamy head.

Stubby – Australian slang for a small beer bottle.

Submarino – San Miguel lager with a shot of tequila in it.

Suds – Australian and American slang for beer. In Britain over-lively beer is likely to be referred to by this term.

Suk – the Korean equivalent of sake. (See p. 93.)

Swankey – a 19th-century dialectal term for weak beer.

Swipes – originally used of poor, weak beer. Now refers to waste beer that spills over the top of the glass when pouring. To swipe in some English dialects once meant to drink hastily.

Tankard – a tall one-handled mug, mainly used for beer-drinking. Some tankards have a lid.

Tank beer – beer delivered in bulk to outlets and pumped into cellar tanks.

Tap – to insert a tap into a cask in order to draw off the contents. The tap itself.

Three threads – beer of three kinds mixed together. (See p. 96.)

Tinnie – Australian slang for a can of beer.

Wallop – beer. There may be some connection with pot-walloper, itself a corruption of pot-waller = pot-boiler. In former times this meant a man entitled to vote because he was a householder, owning his own hearth where he could boil his pot.

Pot-walloper was in use, in that sense, in the 18th century. It associated 'wallop' with 'pot', the usual vessel from which beer was drunk. The more common explanation refers to the wallop that strong beer gives the drinker once it has been drunk.

Wang-tsai – a Chinese beverage made from fermented rice.

Weiss – 'cloudy' white beer made from wheat instead of barley. Also called Weizen. Popular in Germany and Belgium.

Winter ale – another term for October ale, made especially strong so that it would last through the winter.

Wort – liquefied malt before the fermentation process which converts it into beer. (See p. 84.)

Yard of ale – long glass with a bulbous end, holding between 2 and 4 pints, used in drinking contests.

Zymurgy – the art and science of brewing. Words beginning with zym- or zymo- all have to do with fermentation, since they are based on the Greek word for 'yeast'. Zymotic (infectious) diseases were so-called because it was thought that a process similar to fermentation caused them.

BEER CONSUMPTION PER HEAD

Litres per head

Country	1970	1975	1980	1984	1985	1986	1987	1988	1989
European Community									
Belgium	131.8	130.0	131.0	126.0	121.0	120.0	121.0	119.0	115.0
Denmark	108.5	129.0	130.7	134.0	129.8	130.0	125.2	126.0	126.5
France	41.3	44.9	44.3	41.2	40.1	40.4	38.9	39.2	40.8
Greece	9.4	14.8	26.3	31.2	33.9	34.4	38.3	40.0	39.0
Ireland, Rep. of	101.0	131.2	121.7	108.4	109.0	104.5	94.0	94.4	90.3
Italy	11.3	12.8	16.7	19.5	21.6	23.0	23.0	23.1	21.8
Netherlands	57.4	79.0	86.4	83.2	84.4	86.0	84.5	83.3	87.6
Portugal	13.3	32.7	37.9	35.5	36.9	39.5	47.0	53.1	63.8
Spain	38.5	47.0	53.4	59.0	61.0	62.6	66.8	68.7	72.4
West Germany	141.1	147.8	145.9	144.7	145.4	146.5	144.3	143.0	142.9
UK	103.0	118.5	118.3	110.9	110.1	109.7	110.4	110.9	110.4
Rest of Europe									
Austria	98.7	103.8	101.9	107.7	111.6	115.9	116.2	118.0	119.3
Bulgaria	36.5	48.4	57.3	63.6	63.6	64.3	66.4	66.5	70.3
Czechoslovakia	139.9	143.4	137.8	140.1	130.8	133.5	130.0	131.7	131.8
East Germany	95.7	119.7	139.1	142.2	141.6	142.1	141.3	143.0	146.5
Finland	48.8	54.7	57.4	59.5	61.7	65.4	68.1	73.7	80.4
Hungary	59.4	72.3	87.0	87.0	92.4	99.1	100.2	101.0	103.0
Iceland	13.2	11.9	14.4	17.1	17.0	15.8	16.0	17.8	30.7
Norway	37.8	45.4	48.3	46.8	47.5	50.9	51.4	52.5	51.8
Poland	31.4	36.8	30.4	29.3	29.5	29.7	30.4	30.8	31.3
Romania	21.6	34.1	43.8	45.0	45.0	47.2	44.0	51.0	50.9
Sweden	57.5	60.1	48.0	44.5	46.8	50.0	51.6	56.0	58.0
Switzerland	78.5	71.8	69.0	68.6	69.2	69.4	69.3	69.4	69.9
USSR	17.5	22.4	23.1	24.1	23.8	21.5	18.2	19.8	21.0
Yugoslavia	28.0	37.7	44.2	50.2	48.8	50.9	50.0	48.5	46.0
Africa									
Nigeria	..	..	..	..	..	..	..	7.7	6.4
South Africa	12.1	19.5	28.6	39.3	39.4	42.2	45.0	50.0	54.4
Asia									
China	..	..	..	..	..	..	..	..	..
Japan	28.7	35.2	39.0	38.5	40.6	42.0	43.8	47.2	49.7
Korea, Rep. of	..	..	..	..	..	..	21.0	24.7	28.1
Philippines	7.6	9.8	14.5	18.3	12.2	13.8	..	..	23.3
Australasia									
Australia	119.4	136.5	132.3	117.8	114.5	115.5	111.7	110.8	113.1
New Zealand	116.0	132.4	118.0	116.2	114.8	118.9	120.8	114.8	117.0
North America									
Canada	74.0	87.0	86.1	83.0	82.2	81.8	82.8	81.5	80.2
USA	70.4	81.8	91.1	90.5	89.7	90.9	90.1	89.7	88.6
Central and South America									
Argentina	15.4	16.8	7.7	13.2	13.0	17.6	18.5	16.3	18.6
Brazil	10.6	14.9	18.9	21.4	22.3	31.6	33.6	32.4	43.8
Chile	17.9	12.7	17.2	15.0	16.0	16.4	20.7	20.7	22.1
Colombia	34.0	32.8	43.9	50.0	55.2	54.2	56.0	52.0	57.1
Cuba	16.5	22.2	24.4	26.0	25.6	28.7	29.0	31.9	33.1
Mexico	29.1	33.0	39.0	33.0	35.0	34.0	34.0	38.0	37.5
Peru	18.2	28.0	30.4	27.5	30.0	35.8	43.0	43.0	27.4
Venezuela	49.5	47.8	74.0	70.2	59.5	60.7	72.4	75.0	61.8

POMONA'S JUICES
Cider

CIDER, as we shall see later, acts as a bridge between beer and wine. Perhaps the most surprising thing about it is that it is not now as important a drink in western countries as one might expect. Apples grow wild in all temperate zones, and seem to have been cultivated since early times. The discovery that fermented apple-juice was a pleasant and powerful drink was made at a very early stage.

Henry David Thoreau, in his essay on *Wild Apples*, hints at the way the discovery could have occurred. Talking of apples that have fallen to the ground naturally and become frozen while sound, he says: 'Let a warmer sun come to thaw them – for they are extremely sensitive to its rays – and they are found to be filled with a rich, sweet cider, better than any bottled cider that I know of, and with which I am better acquainted than wine. All apples are good in this state, and your jaws are the cider-press.'

THE CIDER CONQUEST

Nevertheless, specific references to cider occur in English only after the Norman Conquest. Normandy is still an important area of cider production, and the Normans may have brought with them a taste for the drink. They certainly seem to have brought to England the word 'cider' itself. *Cider-Making*, by Alfred Pollard and Frederick Walter Beech, claims that 'the first documentary evidence of English cider-making comes in the reign of King John, for cider was being made in Norfolk in 1205. In 1282 there are references to cider-making near Richmond in Yorkshire . . .' The earliest reference to the word 'cider' in the *Oxford English Dictionary*, however, is dated 1315. (For the etymology of the word see p. 13.)

The belief that fermented apple-juice must have been drunk in England before the Norman Conquest has led some scholars to suggest that it was referred to loosely as 'wine'. Some have even argued that early English references to vineyards really mean orchards, but this is supposition. The verbal evidence leads to the very surprising conclusion that cider was unknown in England before the Middle Ages.

It was not until the second half of the 17th century that cider became really fashionable. By that time a reasonably efficient apple-mill had been invented, and a number of books and pamphlets

Apple orchard, 18th century. From The King *1904.*

GOLDEN FIRE

Rosie scratched about, turned over a sack, and revealed a stone jar of cider. Huge and squat, the jar lay on the grass like an unexploded bomb. We lifted it up, unscrewed the stopper, and smelt the whiff of fermented apples. I held the jar to my mouth and rolled my eyes sideways, like a beast at a waterhole. 'Go on,' said Rosie. I took a deep breath . . .

Never to be forgotten, that first long secret drink of golden fire, juice of those valleys and of that time, wine of wild orchards, of russet summer, of plump red apples, and Rosie's burning cheeks. Never to be forgotten, or ever tasted again.

Laurie Lee *Cider With Rosie*

appeared, giving opinions about the best cider apples. The orchards of Hereford, especially, were singled out for praise. A book published in 1656 described them as 'a pattern for all England'.

RED-STREAKS

In 1708 those orchards, with their Red-streak apples, were further praised in a long poem by John Philips. Philips talks, incidentally, of 'cyder' rather than 'cider'. I was told as a boy that the area in which the drink was made affected the spelling, but that was merely a convention of the trade, not a fact of linguistic history.

The poem *Cyder* is in blank verse and imitates Virgil's Georgics. There can be few drinks which have received treatment of this kind:

'Let every tree in every garden own
The Red-streak as supreme, whose pulpous fruit
With gold irradiate, and vermilion shines

Tempting, not fatal, as the birth of that
Primeval interdicted plant that won
Fond Eve in hapless hour to taste, and die.

This, of more bounteous influences, inspires
Poetic raptures, and the lowly Muse
Kindles to loftier strains: even I perceive
Her sacred virtue. See! the numbers flow
Easy, whilst, cheer'd with her nectareous
     juice,
Hers and my country's praises I exalt.

Hail Herefordian plant, that dost disdain
All other fields! Heaven's sweetest blessing,
     hail!
Be thou the copious matter of my song,
And thy choice nectar; on which always
     waits
Laughter, and sport, and care-beguiling wit,
And friendship, chief delight of human life,
What should we wish for more? or why, in
     quest
Of foreign vintage, insincere and mixt,
Traverse th'extremest world? why tempt the
     rage
Of the rough ocean? when our native glebe
Imparts, from bounteous womb, annual
     recruits
Of wine delectable, that far surmounts
Gallic, or Latin grapes, or those that see
The setting sun near Calpes' towering
     height,
Nor let the Rhodian, nor the Lesbian vines
Vaunt their rich Must, nor let Tokay contend
For sovereignty . . .'

In spite of such eulogies, the drinking of cider in urban areas decreased in England throughout the 18th century. Cheap gin became available in the towns; cider was only drunk in the areas where it was made.

This situation seems to have continued into the 19th century. Thomas Hardy, for instance, refers to the farm labourers in *Far From the Madding Crowd* who quickly became drunk when forced to drink brandy by Sergeant Troy. 'Having from their youth up been unaccustomed to any liquor stronger than cider or mild ale, it was no wonder that they had succumbed after the lapse of about an hour.'

SCRUMPY

Many labourers would only have been used to drinking ciderkin, or water-cider, made by re-pressing the pulp (pomace or pommey) of the apples. Troy's men appear to have drunk the rough unsweetened cider known as scrumpy. Bathsheba asks for a few gallons to be taken into the farm-house and says that she will 'make some cider-wine'. She would presumably have added sugar and then stored the cider for a considerable time. 'Scrumpy', now sometimes used commer-cially for a particularly strong cider, is based on a word which means 'shrivelled'. To 'scrump' origi-nally mean to collect wind-fall apples which had shrivelled while lying on the ground. By the time I was a boy, 'to go scrumping' had acquired the more exciting meaning of raiding a garden or orchard to steal a few apples.

NOBLE WINE

Herefordshire cider is so exquisite, that when the earl of Manchester was ambassador in France, he is said frequently to have passed this beverage on their nobility for a delicious wine.

William Hone *The Every-day Book*

Writing a few years before Hardy's novel was published, William Chambers had this to say about cider in his *Book of Days*: 'As a summer drink, cider is a most palatable and refreshing one, though its extended use seems to be con-

Worlidge's cider-mill, 1678. From The King *1904.*

fined to the western counties of England, where it occupies the place in popular favour held, in other parts of the country, by beer. We retain a most affectionate remembrance of the liquor in connection with the fairy nooks of Devon, and the rich pastures of Somerset, through which, some years ago, it was our good fortune to ramble.'

Chambers goes on to invoke the blessings of Pomona, the Italian goddess of fruit, and adds: 'Long may her refreshing juices cheer the heart of the thirsty and way-worn traveller!'

At the end of the 19th century a conscious effort was made by some of those living in the cider-producing regions to re-introduce Pomona's 'refreshing juices' on a national scale. Farmers became suppliers of apples for bulk cider-production instead of making the drink themselves, and a successful industry was established. Various kinds of cider are now available in pubs and bars throughout the country. They probably surprise American visitors who, when they ask for cider, usually expect to get the unfermented drink that the British call 'apple-juice'. Americans wanting the alcoholic drink tend to ask for 'hard cider'.

FOXWHELP

The *Oxford English Dictionary* appears to be rather baffled by Robert Southey's reference, in *The Doctor*, to 'Foxwhelp, a beverage as much better than Champagne, as it is honester, wholesomer and cheaper.' The Dictionary editors can only tell us that Foxwhelp is 'some kind of drink' – a pity in view of Southey's recommendation. I think there is little doubt that he was extolling the virtues of cider, especially that made from the Foxwhelp apple.

Pollard and Beech, in their *Cider-Making*, remark: 'The revived interest in science during the Restoration produced eulogies of the best cider apples of the day. Most of these have long since gone but we still have the Foxwhelp as evidence of their standard of vintage quality.' In *Just Around the Corner* Humphrey Phelps writes: 'He kept reciting the names of cider apples: "Coccagee and Bloody Butcher, Slack-ma-girdle, Red Soldier and Lady's Finger, Kingston Black, Bloody Turk, Foxwhelp, Pawson, Tom Putt,

Bitter Sweet and Fatty Mutt."' Phelps rather carelessly adds a remark about the 'deep, rich *fruity* voice of the speaker'.

It was certainly the practice to refer to cider on occasion by the name of the apple used to produce it. I have quoted John Philips above on the qualities of the famous Red-streak apple. Later in the same poem he refers to drinking Red-streak. The *Oxford English Dictionary* also has a quote from 1671: 'I have had as good Red-streak as ever I drank in any place.'

These apple-names are no longer familiar to most of us, but they were widely known in former times. Phelps mentions the Bitter Sweet, for instance, which already bore that name at the end of the 14th century. Shakespeare was certainly aware of it, and expected his audiences to pick up on an allusion. 'Thy wit,' says Mercutio to Romeo, in *Romeo and Juliet*, 'is a very bitter sweeting; it is a most sharp sauce.'

Apples used in modern cider-making have no doubt been specially developed by scientists for the purpose. Experiments were already being conducted two centuries ago to see which apples were most suitable. Thoreau reported: 'Apples of a small size are always, if equal in quality, to be preferred to those of a larger size, in order that the rind and kernel may bear the greatest proportion to the pulp, which affords the weakest and

French cider press, 1875. From Merveilles de l'Industrie.

most watery juice. To prove this, Dr Symonds, of Hereford, about the year 1800, made one hogshead of cider entirely from the rinds and cores of apples, and another from the pulp only, when the first was found of extraordinary strength and flavor, while the latter was sweet and insipid.'

Since 1800, an astonishing number of apple cultivars have been created. The *National Apple Register of the United Kingdom*, by M.W.G. Smith, lists some 6000 of them which have been grown since 1853. No doubt many more have appeared since the Register appeared in 1971. Cider seems to be a simple drink based on the apple, but 'apple' is far from being a simple term.

PERRY

In a similar way the word 'pear' acts as an umbrella term for a large number of pear varieties, only some of which, such as the Longland, are suitable for producing the cider-like drink known as perry. Good perry is said to be very difficult to make. It has a more delicate flavour than cider, resembling a light white wine. In modern times it has been successfully marketed in a sparkling form as Babycham.

An interesting point about Babycham is that it is drunk as a wine. Cider is traditionally classed with beer, presumably because it is beer-like in strength and is associated socially with farm labourers rather than city gentlemen. The basis of all beers, however, is a malt derived from grain. Clearly that does not apply to cider.

Since cider and perry are fermented juices, they are more accurately described as wines – wines that happen to derive from fruit other than the grape. Plums, cherries, blackberries, elderberries and loganberries are amongst other fruits used to make similar wines. Ordinary grape-wine, as we shall see in the next chapter, can be fortified with brandy. Fruit wine can be strengthened in the same way, using a distillation derived from whichever fruit was used to make it in the first place. Like ordinary wines, fruit wines can be produced in still or sparkling form.

Cider is far more wine-like, then, than beer-like. What is interesting is the way its social associations, more than simple technical details, influence the way we think about it. Where cider is concerned, even the most intensive advertising campaign might not manage to change its image. The commercial success of Babycham was partly due to the fact that perry was less clearly placed in the liquor hierarchy of the average drinker. Clever use of a brand-name, coupled with a reminder of the drink's claim to be a wine, brilliantly did the rest.

LIQUID MAGNANIMITY
The wines of the world

THE unromantic compilers of our dictionaries are content to define *wine* as 'fermented grape juice' and leave it at that. Such verbal brutality comes as something of a shock if you have been immersed in the literature on the subject. Books on wine published in English-speaking countries now tend to be written in a language of their own. Apart from the use of a large number of words in specialised senses, there is a general atmosphere of reverence and adoration. It would have seemed appropriate to the ancient devotees of Dionysus, the wine god.

THE LANGUAGE OF WINE

Of all alcoholic drinks, wine seems to be the one most likely to arouse passion and unleash a torrent of emotive words. A passage in Mrs Gaskell's *Wives and Daughters* might serve in general terms to describe the appeal of wine. 'It cannot be defined,' says Mrs Gaskell, 'or rather it is so delicate a mixture of many gifts and qualities that it is impossible to decide on the proportions of each. Perhaps it is incompatible with very high principle; as its essence seems to consist in the most exquisite power of adaptation to varying people and still more various moods; "being all things to all men".'

As it happens, Mrs Gaskell was there trying to describe the mysterious charm which some young ladies possess, a natural sex-appeal. I see no reason not to apply her remarks on human beings to wine, since particular wines are often described in human terms. Raymond Postgate, in the *Pan Book of Wine*, once commented on the silliness of descriptions he had read in a handbook about Swiss wines. Those of Neuchâtel, for instance, were: 'Flippant at times, indeed irrever-

ent; they surprise first, then arouse interest, finally inspire lasting friendship.' Other Swiss wines were said to be 'crisp, playful, a bit naughty, sometimes even daring' or were 'boisterous and waggish.'

Roald Dahl has a short story, *Taste*, in which Richard Pratt is apt to talk of wine as 'rather diffident and evasive, but quite prudent', or 'benevolent and cheerful – slightly obscene, perhaps, but nonetheless good-humoured'. Such comments are still to be heard or read, though Dahl was not alone in making fun of them. More traditional wine-language makes use of words like full, robust, vigorous, rich, clean, warm, elegant, velvety, or soft to comment favourably in a general

Treading the grapes, 15th century.

way. An unsatisfactory wine is light, poor, thin, weak, insipid, thick, harsh, sharp, unbalanced, heavy. Specific comments on colour, sugar content and aroma are made with words like sumptuous or dull, mellow or sugary, fruity or flat.

Meanwhile, for her part, Mrs Gaskell adds that the effects of a young lady's charms 'are only manifested in the susceptible'. That, too, might be said of wine. There are some of us who, stumbling across the latest purple prose of the journalistic wine-writer, wonder what all the fuss is about. Amongst the latter are probably to be counted the majority of those who live in the main wine-producing countries. An average French family, for instance, spends little time discussing wine, though its members have probably drunk it twice a day throughout their adult lives. Wine is bought economically at the local grocer's or supermarket, and is merely red or white. It is appreciated as a natural adjunct to food, but is drunk without

THE LAST BIN

In his last bin Sir Peter lies,
Who knew not what it was to frown:
Death took him mellow, by surprise,
And.in his cellar stopped him down.
Through all our land we could not boast
A knight more gay, more prompt than
    he,
To rise and fill a bumper toast,
And pass it round with three times
    three.

He kept at true good humour's mark
The social flow of pleasure's tide:
He never made a brow look dark,
Nor caused a tear, but when he died.
No sorrow round his tomb should dwell:
More pleased his gay old ghost. would
    be,
For funeral song, and passing bell,
To hear no sound but three times three.

Thomas Love Peacock

much comment. There is nothing surprising in that. Members of a typical English family do not spend much time discussing tea, though they may drink it in great quantities.

UPPER CLASS TRADITIONS

In the Anglo-Saxon world an interest in wine is felt to make a statement about social and intellectual status. That this is so has to do with some obvious facts about the history of wine-drinking in England. The Domesday Book (1086) recorded some 40 vineyards in England, but they were rendered uneconomical when huge quantities – up to three million gallons a season – of what was probably poor quality wine flooded into England after 1152. In that year Prince Henry (later Henry II) married Eleanor of Aquitaine and acquired for England many of the French wine regions,

WASHING IT DOWN

We washed it down with a dark Spanish wine George Elbert bought by the gallon from an Asturian who got it off the Havana car ferry.

John Dos Passos *The Great Days*

including Bordeaux. The amount of wine shipped from there declined drastically when England lost control of Bordeaux in 1453.

Hugh Johnson says in *Wine* that during the Middle Ages 'claret was part of the staple diet, even of the ordinary man'. He is led to that conclusion by the sheer amount of wine imported compared with the relatively small population. It is clear, however, that a great quantity of beer was also being brewed at the time. My own belief is that the descendants of the Norman noblemen, still the rulers of the country, were drinking the wine while the ordinary Englishman drank his beer. We have clear evidence by the 17th century that this was the case. Christopher Sly, in Shakespeare's *Taming of the Shrew*, calls for a 'pot of small ale', indignantly protesting that he 'ne'er drank sack'. The groundlings in the theatre would no doubt have echoed his protest.

Benjamin Disraeli, in *Sybil*, later describes a 19th-century scene where he specifically says that the rioting workmen had never before tasted wines: 'In the meantime the castle was in the possession of the mob. The first great rush was to the cellars ... This was not a crisis of corkscrews: the heads of the bottles were knocked off with the same promptitude and dexterity as if they were shelling nuts or decapitating shrimps: the choicest wines of Christendom were poured down the thirsty throats that ale and spirits alone had hitherto stimulated: Tummas was swallowing Burgundy; Master Nixon had got hold of a batch of Tokay; while the Bishop himself alternatively quaffed very old Port and some Madeira of many voyages ...'

A BUSY BUTLER

The little butler was indefatigable with his corkscrew, which is reported on one occasion to have grown so hot under the influence of perpetual friction that it actually set fire to the cork.

Thomas Love Peacock *Headlong Hall*

After the 15th century, wine continued to be imported, especially from Spain, Portugal and Italy. It was relatively expensive, and only the upper classes could afford it. Even they sometimes complained about the cost. 'We only had a scurvy dinner at an ale-house,' Jonathan Swift tells Stella, on 9 January 1711. 'He made me go to a tavern, and drink Florence, four and sixpence a flask; damned wine!' It is curious how Swift, in such passages, manages to give the impression that he is rather proud of spending such sums on wine.

Wine-drinking spread downwards from aristocrats to gentlemen, later to those who wished to

ape gentlemanly ways. The gentlemen themselves, once corks had been invented to make it possible for wine to mature in bottles, became more concerned with quality, though they continued to drink very large amounts. Each man who dined with a typical 18th-century squire would expect to get through three bottles of wine. If the male guests left the table completely sober, the host thought himself insulted.

By the 19th century, amongst the upper social classes, an interest in wine was a natural family inheritance, passed on from father to son. P. Morton Shand, for instance, in his *Book of French Wines*, remarks that 'my earliest recollection of

MAKING A SHOW

Mrs Garstin hated to spend money. She flattered herself that she could make as much show as any one else at half the price. Her dinners were long and elaborate, but thrifty, and she could never persuade herself that people when they were eating and talking knew what they drank. She wrapped sparkling Moselle in a napkin and thought her guests took it for champagne.

Somerset Maugham *The Painted Veil*

what I suppose would now be called "the cultural importance of wine" was the excitement caused by confidential club reports of the 1893 vintage of Bordeaux and the wonderful future predicted for it. For some months little else was discussed over the dinner table by my father's friends.' The author goes on to remember unpacking the cases of wine in which his father invested heavily, much to the latter's subsequent regret.

There are those who were not born into such a tradition but would like to imply that they were. They seem to believe that they can do this, now that wine of reasonable quality is within reach of all, by putting the emphasis not on wine-drinking as such, but on the drinking of fine wines. It is when that is done for reasons other than a well-developed palate and a genuine appreciation of quality that we have our wine snob. He is the man, as has been said, who drinks the label and the price in order to boast about it afterwards. As it happens, thanks largely to the combined efforts of the wine snobs themselves and the commercial instincts of the wine producers, the price of wine now reflects the laws of supply and demand but is not always related to intrinsic quality.

Wine-making. From a 15th-century French manuscript.

QUALITY WINES

The word 'quality', in relation to wine, needs to be thought about. In his essay *On Wine*, Evelyn Waugh once commented on the categories established in 1855 for the wines of Bordeaux. Only the châteaux of Lafite, Margaux, Haut Brion and Latour were placed in the first class. 'It is rather,' says Waugh, 'as though a committee had decided that Virgil, Dante and Shakespeare stood in a class apart. They would not thus make Milton and Tolstoy "second-rate" writers.'

This analogy could be considerably extended. Even the highly literate are not always in the mood to read Virgil, Dante or Shakespeare. Dickens or Thackeray, Jane Austen or George Eliot may be preferred, or for those not in a literary

mood, Agatha Christie or Ian Fleming may suit. For daily consumption, newspapers and magazines serve a very real purpose. Different qualities of wine may be thought of as corresponding to these various literary levels. All of them are able to provide enjoyment of one kind or another. To enjoy Shakespeare properly, however, the reader needs a considerable amount of background knowledge, acquired by many years of study. That study, in turn, will only have been undertaken by those who have discovered in themselves an instinctive love of language and literature. The wine connoisseur must have discovered an analagous instinct.

WINE IS . . .

Wine is bottled poetry.

Robert Louis Stevenson

WINE SNOBBERY

What, then, of the wine snob we hear about so often? It would be ridiculous to imply that everyone who shows more than a passing interest in wine is a snob. Wine snobs exist, but so do beer and whisky snobs: the wine snobs have simply been more vocal and attracted more ridicule to themselves in modern times than have the others. They have also made it necessary for those who have become genuinely fascinated by wine to think twice before enthusing about their interest. It is better if they are in the company of like-minded people before they say too much.

Even then, a little honesty does no harm. The appreciation of fine wine is not just a language, which can be learned by a mental process, but a tuning of the palate allied with a training of the sensual memory. A long and complex learning process is involved, to be taken in stages. No harm is done by admitting that one has recently begun that process and is feeling one's way along.

Books about wine can obviously help as guides, but the right kind of author needs to be found. P. Morton Shand, for instance, instinctively writes for those like himself, people who have drunk good wine all their lives and are interested in fine details. There are other, more helpful books, written for those willing to admit that they are beginners. They may be written by authors

Monks in the cloisters, 16th century.

who themselves came fresh to wine, with no family traditions behind them. They must at least be written by those who can begin at the beginning and explain more obvious points. Too often writers about wine do little more than describe the cosy and privileged world in which they live.

For those who think it might actually be useful to be known as a wine snob, there is the *Official Guide to Wine Snobbery*, by Leonard S. Bernstein. Mr Bernstein's thesis is that those people who appear to know a lot about wine may well arouse the hatred of their friends, but those friends will secretly envy them. The 'secretly' is a nice touch; it gives a licence to the wine snob to go on boring his victims while ignoring their signs of suffering.

THE WINE LIST

The earlier stages of the dinner had worn off. The wine list had been consulted, by some with the blank embarrassment of a schoolboy suddenly called on to locate a Minor Prophet in the tangled hinterland of the Old Testament, by others with the severe scrutiny which suggested that they have visited most of the higher-priced wines in their own homes and probed their family weaknesses. The diners who chose their wine in the latter fashion always gave their orders in a penetrating voice, with a plentiful garnishing of stage directions. By insisting on having your bottle pointing to the north when the cork is being drawn, or calling the waiter Max, you may induce an impression on your guests which hours of laboured boasting might be powerless to achieve. For this purpose, however, the guests must be chosen as carefully as the wine.

Saki (Hector Hugh Munro) *The Chaplet*

WINE SNOBBERY

A wine-snob dialogue competition was set in *Wine Mine*, Winter 1970, by Arthur Marshall. The conversation submitted by A.G. Cairns Smith included the following exchange:

A: What's the grape do you think? *Kabinet Semolina?*

B: Possibly, although are we not too far south for that? More likely a *Pompidou Noir.*

A: But surely we're north of the river?

B: . . . but south of the petrol station . . .

A: . . . but facing *east* on that slope between Henri's bistro and the cross-roads.

B: Even so, until Jean-Jacques went down with his *foie troublé* most of this wine was made from the vines beside the *abattoir* – which were, of course, pre-haemophilia *pompidous.*

A: (suddenly) Have another look now: I think the wine is trying to tell us something (swill swill, sniff sniff, gurgle gurgle, gargle, cough, splutter, choke . . .)
(A falls to the floor. His face assumes the colour of a *cru supérieur Châteauneuf-du-Pape* in an off year. He expires.)

B: (Sniffing with great concentration) Yes, *Pompidou Noir*, definitely.

ELEMENTARY PRINCIPLES

Many of the points made by Mr Bernstein will not necessarily turn his reader into a wine snob. He mentions such things as opening a bottle of Champagne carefully, so as to avoid the pop, and explains what to do if a wine-waiter presents you with the cork when he opens your bottle (put it in the ash-tray). He tells you to hold a glass of white wine by the stem, since cupping it not only looks ugly but warms the wine.

Complying with such common-sense directions could only make someone a wine snob if such things were done with great ostentation and were meant to convey an impression of esoteric knowledge. There are certain elementary principles about wine-drinking which have become established over a long period. There is fairly general agreement, for instance, that red wine is not the best accompaniment for fish and that it is best drunk at room temperature. Equally, sweet white wines do not go well with main courses and taste better when cool.

If they are going to drink more expensive wines, most serious drinkers prefer an untinted glass which allows them to appreciate the wine's colour: they may smell the wine before drinking to confirm that it is in good condition and add to their sensual experience. Since the better wines have different tastes and qualities which make one rather than another more suitable for a particular meal or occasion, it is logical rather than snobbish to choose them carefully.

Nor can any person be a wine snob who has genuinely enjoyed drinking a particular wine and talks about it to someone who in turn will describe his own wine-drinking experiences. The snob distinguishes himself by insisting on discussing wine, in extravagant language, with an audience which clearly has no interest in the subject. The listeners are usually well aware that the object of the exercise is not to pass on information but to transmit a status-message.

THE WINE CELLAR

Wine snobbery is not merely to do with a display of wealth. In England, especially, it is still linked with the notion of high birth and social superiority. The wine snob would probably like to see himself as a gentleman of former times. As our literature makes clear, wine was a very real part of the life led by such a man among his social equals. The cellars of his house, where his stocks of wine were kept, were a masculine domain, visited only by himself and his butler. That servant's title was derived from Old French *bouteillier* 'bottler', a clear indication that his principal duty originally was to take charge of the wine cellar. The importance attached to that function led to his becoming the chief servant in the household.

THE WINE CELLAR

A house having a great wine stored below, lives in our imagination as a joyful house fast and splendidly rooted in the soil.

George Meredith *The Egoist*

In Chancery, by John Galsworthy, has a fine passage which gives us an insight into the way a man might think about the wine in his cellar:

'Look here, Warmson, you go to the inner cellar, and on the middle shelf of the end bin on the left you'll see seven bottles; take the one in the centre, and don't shake it. It's the last of the Madeira I had from Mr Jolyon when we came in here – never been moved; it ought to be in prime condition still. I was keeping it for our golden wedding,' said James suddenly, 'but I shan't live three years at my age.' 'Nonsense, James,' said Emily, 'don't talk like that.' 'I ought to have got it myself,' murmured James, 'he'll shake is as likely as not.' And he sank into silent recollection of long moments among the open gas jets, the cobwebs and the good smell of wine-soaked corks, which had been appetizer to so many feasts. In the wine from that cellar was written the history of the forty-odd years since he had come to the Park Lane house with his young bride; its depleted bins preserved the record of family festivity – all

PEACE OFFERING

The Manor was said to be haunted by a ghost. The Squire called in the parson to lay the ghost, and the ceremony of exorcism was completed by bricking in a barrel of wine in the cellar to pacify the evil spirit. As Fred Wheatcroft said to me: 'Thur be things as appears as we beunt meant to understand.'

Fred Archer *Under the Parish Lantern*

the marriages, births, deaths of his kith and kin.

Here is no wine snob, but a man for whom wine is a very real complement to life. Many other writers speak of such men. Thackeray makes a passing remark of Joseph Sedley, for instance, in *Vanity Fair*: He began praising his father's wine. That was generally a successful means of cajoling the old gentleman. 'We never get such Madeira in the West Indies, sir, as yours.'

With this advice on how to please a man we can compare Thackeray's view, expressed elsewhere in the novel, that to please a woman you should praise her children.

THE EGOIST

The wine and wine cellars of a country house are given special significance in George Meredith's comedy *The Egoist*. Meredith creates a character called Dr Middleton who is a fanatical lover of vintage wine. His daughter Clara is engaged to Sir Willoughby, but announces that she wishes to break the engagement. Sir Willoughby decides to enlist her father's help on his behalf.

'My cellars are worth a visit,' he tells his prospective father-in-law. 'Cellars are not catacombs,' replies that gentleman solemnly. 'They are, if rightly constructed, rightly considered, cloisters, where the bottle meditates on joys to bestow, not on dust misused!' Soon afterwards he bestows his benediction on the cellars themselves: 'North

SAFE RETURN

Oh! God of Wine deliver me
Now half across life's stormy sea
From snares and gins of every sort
And bring me safely back to port.

Neil Hogg

side and South. No musty damp. A pure air! Everything requisite. One might lie down oneself and keep sweet here.'

It can be imagined what a man who can be so enthusiastic about wine cellars can say about a vintage wine. Dr Middleton is a classical scholar, with a reverence for the past. Sir Willoughby offers him a 90-year-old port, which inspires the reverend doctor to discuss, in rapturous terms, port, Hock and Hermitage:

A tonel of port wine, holding 620 gallons.

A 1907 advertisement for Chromo, a French beer.

(Above) One of John Gilroy's famous Guinness
advertisements – 'The man with the girder'.

(Below) The grape-harvest in Burgundy; a
painting by an unknown artist, Musée de Dijon.

An early advertisement for Victor Clicquot Champagne. The company later became Veuve Clicquot.

'Approved', by Tito Conti (1842–1924).

(Above) 'Monks in a cellar', by J. Haier (1816–91).

(Below) 'The public bar', by John Henry Henshall (1856–1928).

An early advertisement for Dubonnet.

An early French advertisement for Hurard rum.

An advertisement for Cointreau liqueur.

'Observe, I do not compare the wines; I distinguish the qualities. Let them live together for our enrichment; they are not rivals like the Idaean Three. Were they rivals, a fourth would challenge them. Burgundy has great genius. It does wonders within its period; it does all except to keep up the race; it is short-lived. An aged Burgundy runs with a beardless Port. I cherish the fancy that Port speaks the sentences of wisdom, Burgundy sings the inspired Ode. Or put it, that Port is the Homeric hexameter, Burgundy the Pindaric dithyramb.'

CLASSICAL ALLUSIONS

Speeches like this brought charges of obscurity and affection on to Meredith's head. The passage is certainly obscure to the modern reader, but usefully reminds us that a classical education was once normal for the upper classes. One of its side-effects was to give its members a range of allusions which constituted a social dialect, a private language for the initiated. In former times it could have been claimed on behalf of that language that it was fitting for the discussion of wine, being internationally understood by educated people.

BACCHUS

The names Denis, Dennis and Denise derive ultimately from Dionysus, the Greek God of wine. He was otherwise known to both Greeks and Romans as Bacchus (a name meaning 'the god who is worshipped with loud cries'). The Roman festival dedicated to Bacchus was called the Bacchanalia, and that word is sometimes used in English to describe a drunken revelry. Bacchanal, with the adjective bacchanalian, is used in the same sense.

References to Bacchus and bacchanalian revels are regularly found in literature. Shakespeare refers to 'tipsy bacchanals' in *A Midsummer Night's Dream*. In *Antony and Cleopatra*, Enobarbus asks: 'Shall we dance now the Egyptian bacchanals and celebrate our drink?' The song that follows is:

'Come, thou monarch of the vine,
Plumpy Bacchus with pink eyne!
In thy vats our cares be drowned,
With thy grapes our hairs be crowned.
Cup us till the world go round,
Cup us till the world go round!'

John Wilmot, Earl of Rochester, was responsible for:

'Cupid and Bacchus my saints are;
May drink and love still reign!
With wine I wash away my cares
And then to love again.'

Thomas Love Peacock, in *Headlong Hall*, has:

'Comus and Momus were the deities of the night; and Bacchus of course was not forgotten by the male part of the assembly (with them, indeed, a ball was invariably a scene of *tipsy dance and jollity*), the servants flew about with wine and negus . . .'

Thomas Hood, in his light-hearted poem *The Green Man*, says:

'. . . Bacchanalian revels
Bring very sad catastrophes about;
Palsy, Dyspepsy, Dropsy, and Blue
    Devils,
Not to forget the Gout.'

There is a poem called *Bacchus* by Ralph Waldo Emerson, but it is rather obscure. It contains the thought:

'Wine which Music is – Music and
    wine are one.'

Used by a present-day writer it would lead to bewilderment. Readers would be irritated by references to the 'Idaean three', though Sir Willoughby must have had no trouble identifying Hera, Aphrodite and Athene, judged by Paris on the slopes of Mount Ida. He would have known, too, that the 'dithyramb' was a wild choral hymn in praise of Dionysus, god of wine.

Meredith himself argued not just for classical allusions in the discussion of wine. His thesis, rather tortuously expressed in the passage below, is that a classical background best prepares a man for the appreciation of vintage wine.

'Of all our venerable British of the two Isles professing a suckling attachment to an ancient port-wine, lawyer, doctor, squire, rosy admiral, city merchant, the classical scholar is he whose blood is most nuptial to the webbed bottle.

'The reason must be, that he is full of the old poets. He has their spirit to sing with, and the best that Time has done on earth to feed it. He may also perceive a resemblance in the wine to the studious mind, which is the obverse of our mortality, and throws off acids and crusty particles in the piling of the years, until it is fulgent by clarity. Port hymns to his conservativism. It is magical: at one sip he is off swimming in the purple flood of the ever-youthful antique.

'By comparison, then, the enjoyment of others is brutish; they have not the soul for it; but he is worthy of the wine, as are poets of Beauty.'

We can be sure that Meredith's Sir Willoughby and Dr Middleton derived no little pleasure from their learned conversation. Both would have felt that their appreciation of classical literature, and of good wine, set them apart, elevated them above their fellow men. The 'sound mind in a sound body', prescribed by the educationists for a normal well-rounded person, would have fallen short of their own ideal. At very least they would have wished to add 'a fine palate' to the formula.

Meredith makes the point himself, as his two self-satisfied characters congratulate themselves on their own refinement. I suspect that, translated into more modern idiom, their conversation is one which could take place today between two wine enthusiasts.

'But here is the misfortune of a thing super-excellent - not more than one in twenty will do it justice.'

LIQUID GOUT

... the old-established Bull's Head fruity port: whose reputation was gained solely by the old-established price the Bull's Head put upon it, and by the old-established air with which the Bull's Head set the glasses and D'Oyleys on, and held that Liquid Gout to the three-and-sixpenny wax-candle, as if its old-established colour hadn't come from the dyer's.

Charles Dickens *Refreshments for Travellers*

Sir Willoughby replied: 'Very true, sir, and I think we may pass over the nineteen.'

'Women, for example: and most men.'

'This wine would be a sealed book to them.'

'I believe it would. It would be a grievous waste.'

'Vernon is a claret man: and so is Horace De Craye. They are both below the mark of this wine. They will join the ladies. Perhaps you and I, sir, might remain together.'

WOMEN AND WINE

The remark about women is condescending in the extreme, but there was probably some truth in it. In the polite society of the 18th and 19th centuries, women left the room after dinner so that the men could continue with their serious drinking. A lady did not admit to appreciating wine, even if she happened to enjoy it. Needless to say, there are now women journalists who are acknowledged wine experts. The average woman in a restaurant, however, still seems to pass the wine list to the man, even though she may be paying for the meal.

Meredith, I am sure, had his tongue firmly in cheek when he made the learned but pompous Dr Middleton put women even more firmly in their place. 'Ladies are creation's glory, but they are

RARA AVIS

'She has the reputation, rather rare in your sex, of being a wonderfully sound judge of wine.'

Saki (Hector Hugh Munro)
The Unbearable Bassington

anti-climax, following a wine of a century old . . . Can they, dear though they be to us, light up candelabras in the brain, to illuminate all history and solve the secret of the destiny of man? They cannot; they cannot sympathize with them that can.'

These are by no means Meredith's own views, but in Dr Middleton he has created a character who can exclaim at one point: 'I have but a girl to give!' He means that he can only offer his daughter in exchange for the vintage port in his host's cellar. Clara herself reluctantly begins to suspect that her father is being hoodwinked by Sir Willoughby. 'How: through wine? the thought

Women drinking, Paris.

was repulsive . . . What was there is this wine of great age which expelled reasonableness, fatherliness? . . . The strangeness of men, young and old, the little things (she regarded a grand wine as a little thing) twisting and changing them, amazed her . . . Would women do an injury to one they loved for oceans of that – ah! pah!'

Sir Willoughby fails in his attempt to buy Clara with his vintage port, though not because her father comes to his senses. Dr Middleton, minor comic character though he is, deserves more recognition. He must surely rank as the supreme example in literature of a wine lover. He is not an alcoholic, in the grip of forces which he cannot control, but is ready to sacrifice his daughter's happiness for the exquisite taste of a fine wine. We are meant to laugh at him, yet his plausibility makes us wonder whether he could exist in real life.

THE MAGNANIMITY OF WINE

It is a pity about Meredith's obscure style, for he offers interesting thoughts on wine (and life in general) which are sometimes difficult to decipher. As a literary craftsman, he pares his sentences to the minimum, where sometimes expansion would be justified. He makes the point, for example, that a man who loves wine differs from the man who loves a woman in an important respect. A man jealously wants to keep the woman he loves to himself; the wine-lover's pleasure is increased when he shares with another. Meredith has Dr Middleton express this as: 'Note the superiority of wine over Venus! – I may say, the magnanimity of wine; our jealousy turns on him that will not share!' 'The magnanimity of wine,' in the sense that Meredith uses it, is a beautiful phrase, deserving attention.

In *Jaffery*, by William J. Locke, there is a more normal reference to the 'generosity' of vintage port. In this case the remark applies to the fullness and richness of the port itself, but the whole passage strikes a false note. Here is an author who feels obliged to be poetic on this subject. He is going through the motions:

'I sipped my port. I recognized Cockburn 1870. "When one has 1870 port to drink," said I, "why fritter away its flavour in vain words?"

DRAWING A VEIL

One of the most famous names associated with port is Cockburn. The name is usually pronounced Co-burn. The editors of *A Dictionary of Surnames*, published by Oxford University Press, say that this pronunciation is apparently meant 'to veil the imagined delicacy of the first syllable'.

'"It is a damned good port," Adrian admitted.

'"Earth holds nothing better," said I.

'I confess that I rather surrendered myself to the wine. A little taper for cigarettes happened to be in front of me; I held my glass in its light and lost myself in the wine's pure depths of mystery and colour; and my mind wandered to the lusty sunshine of "Lusitanian summers" that was there imprisoned. I inhaled its fragrance, I accepted its exquisite and spacious generosity. Wine, like bread and oil – "God's three chief words" – is a thing of itself – a thing of earth and air and sun – one of the great natural things, such as the stars and flowers and the eyes of a dog. Even the most mouth-twisting new wine of Northern Italy has its fascination for me, in that it is essentially something apart from the dust and empty racket of the world; how much more then this radiant vintage suddenly awakened from its slumber in the darkness of forty years. So I mused, as I think an honest man is justified in musing, soberly, over a great wine . . .'

With this we may compare a passage by Charles Dickens. For him the thought of all those years that a vintage wine spends in the cellar arouses other ideas. In *Bleak House* he shows us Mr Tulkinghorn in his chambers at Lincoln's Inn Fields, chambers as dusty as the cellar from which he fetches his wine:

'Mr Tulkinghorn sits at one of the open windows, enjoying a bottle of old port. Though a hard-grained man, close, dry, and silent, he can enjoy old wine with the best. He has a priceless binn of port in some artful cellar under the Fields, which is one of his many secrets. When he dines alone in chambers, as he has dined today, and has his bit of fish and his steak or chicken brought in from the coffee-house, he descends with a candle to the echoing regions below the deserted mansion, and, heralded by a remote reverberation of thundering doors, comes gravely back, encircled by an earthy atmosphere, and carrying a bottle from which he pours a radiant nectar, two score and ten years old, that blushes in the glass to find itself so famous, and fills the whole room with the fragrance of southern grapes.

'Mr Tulkinghorn, sitting in the twilight by the open window, enjoys his wine. As if it whispered to him of its fifty years of silence and seclusion, it shuts him up the closer. More impenetrable than ever, he sits, and drinks, and mellows as it were, in secrecy . . .'

Here, it would seem, is the justification for applying to wine Mrs Gaskell's words: 'its essence seems to consist in the most exquisite power of adaptation to varying people and still more various moods; "being all things to all men".'

FERMENTED GRAPE JUICE

For a less abstract description of wine we must leave literature and return to the dictionary definition: 'fermented grape juice'. We immediately have to ask: which grape? 'Grape' is another of those umbrella words, like 'hop' and 'apple', which covers a very large number of individual varieties.

Wine-grapes are mostly derived from a single species, *Vitis vinifera*, which is known to have been growing in Europe since before the advent of Man. Amongst the best known used to produce red wines are the Barbera, Cabernet-Franc, Cabernet-Sauvignon, Carignan, Cinsault, Gamay, Grenache, Kadarka, Malbec, Merlot, Pinot Noir, Syrah and Zinfandel. For white wines the best-known grapes are the Alvarinho, Chardonnay, Chasselas, Chenin-Blanc, Colombard, Folle Blanche, Gewürztraminer, Kerner, Malvasia, Müller-Thurgau, Muscat, Palomino, Pinot Blanc, Riesling, Sauvignon Blanc, Semillon and Sylvaner.

In some parts of the world, such as the USA, a varietal description of wine is favoured. This contrasts with the traditional French preference for pin-pointing the vineyard where the grapes were

CATAWBA WINE

This song of mine
Is a Song of the Vine
To be sung by the glowing embers
Of wayside inns,
When the rain begins
To darken the drear Novembers.

It is not a song
Of the Scuppernong,
From warm Carolinian valleys,
Nor the Isabel
And the Muscadel
That bask in our garden alleys.

Nor the red Mustang
Whose clusters hang
O'er the waves of the Colorado,
And the fiery flood
Of whose purple blood
Has a dash of Spanish bravado.

For richest and best
Is the wine of the West
That grows by the Beautiful River;
Whose sweet perfume
Fills all the room
With a benison on the giver.

And as hollow trees
Are the haunts of bees,
For ever going and coming;
So this crystal hive
Is all alive
With a swarming and buzzing and
   humming.

Very good in its way
Is the Verzenay,
Or the Sillery soft and creamy;
But Catawba wine
Has a taste more divine,
More dulcet, delicious and dreamy.

There grows no vine
By the haunted Rhine,
By Danube or Guadalquivir,
Nor on island or cape,
That bears such a grape
As grows by the Beautiful River.

Drugged is their juice
For foreign use,
When shipped o'er the reeling Atlantic,
To rack our brains
With the fever pains,
That have driven the Old World frantic.

To the sewers and sinks
With all such drinks,
And after them tumble the mixer;
For a poison malign
Is such Borgia wine,
Or at best but a Devil's Elixir.

While pure as a spring
Is the wine I sing,
And to praise it, one needs but to name
    it:
For Catawba wine
Has need of no sign,
No tavern bush to proclaim it.

And this Song of the Vine,
This greeting of mine,
The winds and the birds shall deliver
To the Queen of the West,
In her garlands dressed,
On the banks of the Beautiful River.

Henry Wadsworth Longfellow

Robert Joseph has pointed out that many fine red wines from Bordeaux make no use of that grape. The examples he mentions in *The Wine Lists* include: Château Belair, 60% Merlot, 40% Cabernet-Franc; Château Cheval Blanc, 66% Cabernet-Franc, 32% Merlot, 2% Malbec; Château Grand-Barrail-Lamarzelle-Figeac, 90% Merlot, 10% Cabernet-Franc; Château Pavillon-

grown. In favour of the French way of doing things is the fact that a vineyard usually grows and makes use of more than one variety of grape. Penning-Rowsell, in *The Wines of Bordeaux*, tells us that a typical fine Médoc vineyard may be planted with 55% Cabernet-Sauvignon, 20% Cabernet-Franc, 20% Merlot and 5% Malbec; whereas a common 'blend' in St Emilion might be 60% Merlot, 30% Bouchet and 10% Pressac (Malbec).

A particular type of wine is associated with the grape principally used to make it: the Gamay with Beaujolais, the Pinot Noir with Burgundy. The reputation of claret, or red Bordeaux, is rightly founded on the Cabernet-Sauvignon, though

Cadet, 50% Merlot, 50% Cabernet-Franc. Those interested to know which grapes make up their favourite Bordeaux should certainly consult Mr Joseph, though he points out that a château may vary the proportions year by year.

Many pests and diseases attack vines, the most famous being the yellow plant-louse, or aphid, known as Phylloxera. This was native to North America, but managed to stowaway, probably on a bunch of table grapes, and reach Europe. By the late 1870s, reproducing itself at a terrifying rate, laying large numbers of eggs eight times a season, it was destroying millions of vines.

Wine-making, an Italian engraving.

CHÂTEAU

This well-known French wine-word literally means a castle, or country house. It comes from Latin *castellum*, a fortified dwelling, a diminutive of *castrum*, fort. In the language of wine it has come to mean 'Bordeaux wine-growing estate'. There are nearly 4000 such estates in the Bordeaux region, many of which have no building at all attached to them. We could compare the use of 'arms' in English pub-names, where the word has ceased to have heraldic significance and has become almost a synonym of 'inn'.

Château has almost become an English word meaning a winery. It is already used, for example, by the Château Wente in California, Yaldara in Australia, Yelas in New Zealand, Windsor in Israel and Alphen in South Africa. In France, when applied to wine, it normally continues to indicate a red or white wine from the Bordeaux region. Exceptions usually come about because *château* is a fairly frequent element in French place-names, rather like -cester, -chester, etc., in English place-names, which come from a closely-related Latin word. Examples of non-Bordeaux château wine-names include Châteauneuf-du-pape, used for red and white wines from the southern Rhône valley, and Château-Chalon in the Jura, known for a famous 'yellow-wine' rather like a light sherry. Château Grillet, in the northern Rhône valley, was formerly the smallest vineyard in France to have its own *appellation*, but

Château de Corton-Grancey, built 1749.

the area under vines has been enlarged. It produces a rare and expensive white wine.

It would be tempting to think that a Chateaubriand steak, cut from a beef fillet, was named because of the wine that was meant to accompany it, but there is no wine called Chateaubriand. John Ayto points out in his *Glutton's Glossary* that the steak is named after the French writer and statesman François René, Vicomte de Chateaubriand, ambassador in London in the 1820s.

AD-HOC CHÂTEAU

The word château is sometimes used to create ad-hoc wine-names. In *The Wrecker*, by Robert Louis Stevenson and Lloyd Osbourne, occurs: 'My first sip of Château Siron, a vintage from which I had long been estranged, startled me into speech.' The reference here is to house-wine served at an inn run by the Siron family. I could equally well offer house-guests a Château Dunkling, on the well-known principle that an Englishman's home is his château. A

CHÂTEAU CHOICE

'We'll have a marvellous talk. And our compotations shall be in Château Léoville-Poyferré. Business is a little slack, you know, but I can still, praise God, run to a decent claret.'

. . . The Léoville Poyferré (which turned out to be 1966, an outstanding year) did Lightfoot no good.

Michael Innes *Honeybath's Haven*

similar creation of an individual wine occurred in an article by the sports-writer Simon Barnes. Discussing the possibility of the English footballer Paul Gascoigne playing in Italy, he asked: 'Is Château Gascoigne a wine that travels?'

The French themselves have long been using *château* to create new names. Château la Pompe, for instance, is an ironic reference to water or to wine that has been much watered down.

A Dictionary of Contemporary Slang, by Tony Thorne, reports that 'château'd' has become a British adjective meaning drunk. It is said to be 'a colourful upper-class and yuppie expression of the late 1980s playing on "shattered" and implying that it is an expensive claret (Bordeaux) or other château-bottled wine which has caused the inebriety.'

I have not heard the word being used in such a way, but the joke is to be found in *The Wine Graffiti Book*, by 'The 4 Muscateers', published in 1982: 'After a tour of the Loire Valley, I was absolutely châteaued.' The same book has some individual château puns: 'Yquem, Ysaw, Yconquered;' 'Margaux is better than butter.' It also admits that some of the puns 'are bordeauxing on the viniculous'.

Phylloxera (composed of two Greek words meaning 'dry leaf') almost put an end to wine-production in countries as far apart as Italy, Australia, South Africa and the USA, as well as France. It was not until the 1890s that a defence to it was discovered. Certain vines from the eastern United States were found to be resistant to the aphid. The vines themselves produced very poor wine, but scions (shoots) from the European varieties could be grafted on to their root-stocks. Some four million acres of land were eventually replanted with the grafted vines. There was subsequently much argument as to whether post-phylloxera plants produced wine of pre-phylloxera taste and quality.

Before phylloxera there was the oidium, a small mushroom growth which caused whitish spots to cover the vine-leaves and branches. The grapes split and dried up. The application of sulphur solved that problem. After phylloxera, Bordeaux suffered from a plague of mildew, but this could be cured by spraying the grapes with copper sulphate. Proprietors of some vineyards were already doing this on the vines nearest roads and paths. The idea was to discourage a different kind of pest – passers-by who felt like helping themselves to a few grapes.

Grapes, then, require much care and attention as they grow. When ripe, their juice is extracted and allowed to ferment. Since the juice of nearly all wine-producing grapes, whether dark or light-skinned, is pale yellow, red wines are obtained by allowing the skins and grape-juice to remain in contact throughout the whole fermentation process. For lightly-coloured rosé wines, the skins are removed after a short time. White wines are produced from must (grapes in pulp form) which has had the skins removed before fermentation begins. Fermentation itself takes several days and is much as described in an earlier chapter (see pp. 87–8). The necessary wine-yeasts, together with other wild-yeasts, are present in the vineyards, having collected on the grape-skins as they grow.

Old-style books on wine speak with reverence of the cellar-masters who control the wine-making process. By the early 1970s L.W. Marrison was admitting, in his *Wines and Spirits*, that 'expert chemists and biologists are supplementing and even supplanting *monsieur le maître*'. As

CALIFORNIA PROPHECY

Wine in California is still in the experimental stage; and when you taste a vintage, grave economical questions are involved. The beginning of vine-planting is like the beginning of mining for precious metals: the wine-grower also 'prospects'. One corner of land after another is tried with one kind of grape after another. This is a failure; that is better; a third best. So, bit by bit, they grope about for their Clos Vougeot and Lafite . . . The smack of Californian earth shall linger on the palate of your grandson.

R.L. Stevenson *The Silverado Squatters* (1883)

with brewing, the scientists and technologists continue to take over. The effect has been to increase the efficiency of wine-producers everywhere, making great quantities of acceptable wine available at reasonable prices. Inevitably, much of the romance of wine is disappearing, though the magnificent château surrounded by its vines may still exist. Behind the scenes, peasant traditions have given way to scientific exactitude and objectivity.

TYPES OF WINE

We can sub-divide the word 'wine' in many ways. A primary distinction is by colour, distinguishing broadly between red, rosé and white wines. (*Verde* 'green' is used to describe some northern Portuguese wines, which are usually white. The colour reference means that the wines are like Cleopatra in her salad days, when she was green in judgement. There are also the famous *vins jaunes* 'yellow wines' of the Jura (see p. 166). The rosé wine of the same region is known as *vin gris* 'grey wine'.) Wines are still or sparkling, dry or sweet, natural or fortified. We can also distinguish between flavoured and unflavoured wines, the former (mostly of the vermouth family) having been mixed with herbs and spices before being put on sale.

The vast majority of those who buy wine would probably be content with a label that gave factual information about a particular wine in terms of the categories just mentioned, plus two or three others. Together with the all-important indication of quality which is normally inherent in the price, customers might want to know exactly what quantity of wine they were buying, of what alcoholic strength. As with other products, they would be interested in the country of origin. A best-consumed-by date would be more useful to many buyers than a vintage year.

The wines referred to here are of ordinary quality, drunk by most people most of the time. They are wines which are used to wash down a meal cheerfully in an unpretentious way. For such wines, the labels which exist at present, in their confusing variety of languages, are a hindrance rather than a help. They would be considered absurd if applied to other products. Imagine for a moment pots of strawberry jam on a supermarket shelf, with labels saying in which village, and on which farm owned by whom, the strawberries were grown. Imagine labels which told you which particular variety of strawberry had been used to make the jam, and whether it was made at the farm itself or in a nearby factory. All this in French, German, Spanish, Italian and other languages.

For a connoisseur of strawberry jam, such details would be relevant, but we accept the fact that most people who eat it are not connoisseurs – they are content if it is of reasonable price, quality and taste. That description applies to nine wine drinkers of every ten. For them, the labelling complexities that delight the specialists are totally irrelevant. A restaurant wine list is especially meaningless if it simply mentions a string of names. The average customer orders by price and feels intimidated, as if his own ignorance had been exposed.

SECONDARY LABELS

The better supermarkets and wine-shippers have taken to substituting descriptive labels of their own, giving some indication of a wine's basic qualities. Back labels or neck tags may instead be used for this purpose. For instance, the Lambrusco sold by Marks and Spencer has a label saying that it is a 'medium sweet white wine, produce of Italy, alcohol 9% by volume, contents 70 cl'. A suggestion is added that it should be served chilled. For some reason, instead of 'semi-sparkling', the Italian phrase *vino frizzante gassificato* is also there, perhaps to add a little touch of exoticism. Ned Halley remarks in his *Cheap Wine Guide* that the popularity of this wine is spiralling upwards in spite of its being an 'alcoholic version of lemonade'. That may well have something to do with the fact that customers know what they are buying.

Some secondary labels also make suggestions as to whether a wine might be drunk before, during or after a meal, and recommend the food it might accompany. Restaurant wine lists should do the same, unless the wine waiter is properly qualified to advise his customers.

In some supermarkets, such information and suggestions are attached to the shelf where the wine is standing. This is better than nothing, but the substitute, or preferably the secondary-label idea should be extended for ordinary wines. An international set of symbols could probably be introduced to indicate degrees of sweetness, fruitiness and the like. A star system indicating overall quality, such as that applied to hotels, could be applied.

There is no reason why the original labels should not remain. They have evolved over a long

---

ELEVENSES

I must have a drink at eleven,
It's a duty that must be done;
If I don't have a drink at eleven,
Then I must have eleven at one.

Anon

---

period and are steeped in their own traditions and there are clearly plenty of enthusiasts who are content with them as they are. Secondary

SOMETHING EXTRA

'What about champagne?'
Both Ma and Mariette said they adored champagne. That was a brilliant idea. Something extra nice always happened, Mariette said, when you had champagne.

H.E. Bates *The Darling Buds of May*

MELODIOUS WINE

We no longer talk about canary, meaning wine from the Canary Isles, but it was familiar to Shakespeare and remained popular until at least the 18th century. There is a famous mention of it in Keats's poem *The Mermaid Tavern*, which begins:

> Souls of Poets dead and gone,
> What Elysium have ye known,
> Happy field or mossy cavern,
> Choicer than the Mermaid Tavern?
> Have ye tippled drink more fine
> Than mine host's Canary wine?

A less famous reference occurs in Samuel Lover's novel *Handy Andy*: 'When I want to sing particularly well,' said Tom, 'I drink *canary*.'

---

labelling, in the form of back labels or neck tags, would be like translations of texts, making them accessible to vast numbers of people who do not happen to have a passing acquaintanceship with several languages. Other help is provided by an increasing number of journalists who tell us, in newspaper columns and on television programmes, about the merits of a particular wine which is now on special offer around the corner.

QUIZ

No firm rules say that wines and spirits come in bottles, or are drunk from glasses of specific shapes and sizes, but certain conventions are recognised fairly widely. Can you name the drink or region associated with the glasses and bottles seen here?

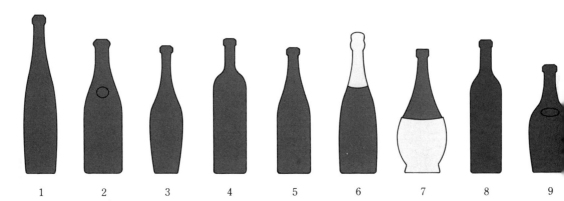

WINE NAMES AND WORDS

Certain names and words are common to all discussions of wine. I say names and words, but the dividing line between the two is not always clear. Bordeaux remains the name of a French region, but many writers would use a phrase like 'red bordeaux'. Similarly, Champagne is the name of a region, but champagne with a small 'c' is often used to describe the drink; claret has always been a word, derived ultimately from Latin and meaning 'clear'. It was applied originally to pale red wine, but is now generally used of any red wine, especially if it comes from Bordeaux. (In this book we have tended to capitalise names of wines and grapes.)

We would have no hesitation is saying that sherry and port are words, but both began as names. Shakespeare refers to sherry more correctly as sherris, an English form of Jerez (formerly Xeres, and Scheris in its Moorish form). The wine came from Jerez de la Frontera, a town in the Cadiz province of Andalusia, Spain. Scholars such as Walter Skeat and Eric Partridge

BACHELOR BLISS

Algernon: 'Why is it that at a bachelor's establishment the servants invariably drink the champagne? I ask merely for information.'
Lane: 'I attribute it to the superior quality of the wine, sir. I have often observed that in married households the champagne is rarely of a first-rate brand.'
Algernon: 'Good heavens! Is marriage so demoralising as that?'

Oscar Wilde *The Importance of Being Earnest*

believe that Jerez was named in honour of Caesar, as was Jersey in the Channel Islands. The Roman name for the town, however, given by Sturmfels

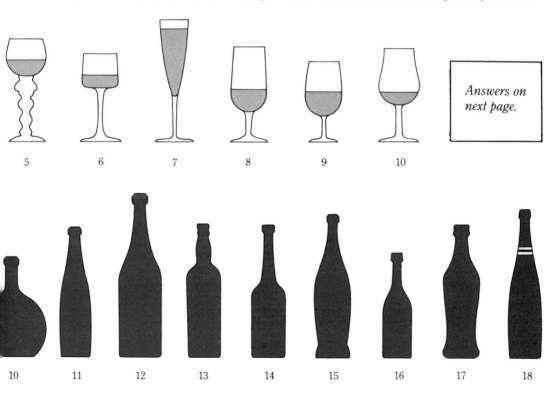

5   6   7   8   9   10

Answers on next page.

10   11   12   13   14   15   16   17   18

and Bischof in *Unsere Ortsnamen*, seems to have been *Asta Regia*. It's a pity: it would be pleasant to connect the drink indirectly with the Roman emperors.

For students of language, sherry is interesting in another way. 'Sherris', as used by Shakespeare and his contemporaries, was an unfamiliar foreign word at the time. Because of the -s ending it was mistakenly thought to be a plural: sherry was invented as the singular form. A similar fate befell French *cerise* 'cherry', which originally came into English as 'cherris'.

Port is short for port-wine, which came from Oporto, in Portugal. There is a connection with 'port' meaning a harbour, since Oporto in turn means 'the (chief) port'. The country is named for the town, since an early Count of Oporto conquered the lands around him.

FORTIFIED WINES

I have linked sherry and port as words of similar origin, both derived from place names. They are also linked in that both fall into the category of fortified wines. These are wines which have been strengthened by the addition of spirits, during or after fermentation, to raise their alcohol level. The fortification was originally intended to preserve wines which were otherwise, as L.W. Marrison expresses it in his *Wines and Spirits*, 'subject to many ills'.

The image of sherry in Britain appears to be changing, with a gradual turning-away from the social ritual in which it had become an ingredient. In my own youth it would certainly have been possible to apply these words from *Edens Lost*, by Sumner Locke Elliott, to any English city:

'What is this Sydney thing about sherry?'

'It's mostly offered. It has a kind of decorum about it. Very proper old ladies can get quietly potted. And clergymen. Won't you have a drink, Reverend? Oh, just a spot of sherry for me if you're all . . . I mean, my mother, for instance. When we were quite young we all had a glass of sherry before dinner because it's supposed to spark the appetite and be quite harmless.'

The Englishness of the drink is remarked upon in passing by Han Suyin, in *A Many Splendoured Thing*: 'Mark asked me why I liked Martinis. "I could not remember any cocktail's name except Martini, so I said that. Sherry sounds so English, and you are so English already. I did not want to ask for a respectable English drink for a lady."'

Social distinctions within the general description of Englishness could still be maintained. A.J. Cronin, in *The Citadel*, writes: 'She must have everything of the best. When on his sixth visit she unbent to offer him a glass of sherry he observed that it was Amontillado of the year 1819.'

Comments like that would probably seem bizarre to Americans, for whom sherry has a very low social image indeed. In the US what is described as sherry by the Californian producers is a cheap drink, much favoured by down-and-out alcoholics. It would not be thought of as a suitable aperitif.

Californian sherry has something in common

CALIFORNIAN BURGUNDY

15 January 1932 . . . It was past midnight before I realised that dinner was over. It was a beautiful dinner, with Californian burgundy served, and it was really lovely wine. So often at American dinner parties the idea of entertainment is to serve you raw whiskey, than which there is nothing more sickening.

Edgar Wallace *My Hollywood Diary*

with British sherry. Both serve as a reminder that imitations of Spanish sherry are produced in several other countries, including South Africa and Australia. Of Cyprus sherry Kingsley Amis had

Advertisement for Sandeman wines, from The Tatler, *1935.*

this to say in his novel *Girl, 20*: 'Cyprus sherry, they call it. A more exact description would be Cyprus raisin tea with some spirits in it. They soak the raisins in a water tank in the sun and either it ferments on its own or they make it ferment – I'm not quite clear which – and then they strain it and put the spirits in it. But perfectly wholesome.'

BURNT SHERRY

Sherry was drunk in very different ways in the past. Shakespeare's Falstaff drank it in great quantities as sack, adding sugar to it. It was often heated: 'Come, come, I'll go burn some sack,' says Sir Toby Belch, in *Twelfth Night*. In *Our Mutual Friend*, Charles Dickens gives us a full description of how this was done in the early 19th century. 'They burn sherry very well here,' says one of the customers in the Six Jolly Fellowship-Porters. A bottle is ordered and the pot-boy comes in with a steaming jug. Dickens continues: 'He carried in his left hand one of those iron models of sugar-loaf hats, into which he emptied the jug, and the pointed end of which he thrust deep down into the fire, so leaving it for a few moments while he disappeared and reappeared with three bright drinking-glasses.

'He watched the wreaths of steam, until at the special instant of projection he caught up the iron vessel and gave it one delicate twirl, causing it to send forth one gentle hiss. Then he restored the contents to the jug; held over the steam of the jug each of the three bright glasses in succession; finally filled them all, and with a clear conscience awaited the applause of his fellow-creatures.'

This heating of the drink seems to have made a big difference to the taste. Eugene Wrayburn tries drinking it a little later when it has cooled: 'Pooh,' said Eugene, spitting it out among the ashes. 'Tastes like the wash of the river.'

In *Great Expectations* there is another reference to the drink: 'I have brought you, as the compliments of the season – I have brought you, Mum, a bottle of sherry wine – and I have brought you, Mum, a bottle of port wine.' Every Christmas Day he presented himself, as a profound novelty, with exactly the same words, and carrying the two bottles like dumb-bells.

LIQUID GOUT

This is Uncle Pumblechook visiting the Gargery family. His annual present again links the two great fortified wines. It thoughtfully provided the Gargerys with sherry to be drunk before the meal, port after it, if they were aware of such a convention.

Port is brandified wine, and is basically of three types. Vintage port, which is capable of arousing the kind of raptures in English breasts quoted earlier in this chapter, is the product of a single year. It matures in the bottle for at least 10 years and must be carefully decanted before being drunk. Crusted port is not quite up to vintage standard, and is a blend of different years. Ruby and tawny ports are the more ordinary blended varieties.

The export of Portuguese wine to England increased substantially from the beginning of the 18th century. For political reasons there was a treaty between the two countries which favoured the Portuguese at the expense of the French and others. As Raymond Postgate puts it, in his *Plain Man's Guide to Wine*, it was to have the effect of turning 'the upper reaches of the Douro Valley almost into a British colony'.

Portuguese wine at the time was apparently not very good. The English wine merchants established in Oporto worked hard at improving it, bearing in mind the English taste for sweetness. They discovered that adding brandy to the fermenting wine would bring fermentation to an end, leaving a considerable amount of unconverted sugar. There was still a problem – the resulting wine was undrinkable until it had matured for many years. This maturing process is now well understood, but its effects must have been far from obvious at first.

The success of port in England was astonishing. Connoisseurs took to vintage port, but the less expensive kinds were drunk in great quantities at all social levels. It sometimes had a severe effect upon the health, but Dickens remarks in passing that Mr Pickwick had 'finished his second pint of particular port' and that benign old gentleman seems not to have suffered as a result. Elsewhere Dickens refers to port as 'liquid gout' (see p. 130).

LAUREATE'S LIBATION

Lord Tennyson has a well-known, long, light-hearted poem *Will Waterproof's Lyrical Monologue*, supposedly written at the Cock Inn. I quote a few of its verses below:

O plump head-waiter at the Cock,
To which I most resort,
How goes the time? 'Tis five o'clock.
Go fetch a pint of port:
But let it not be such as that
You set before chance comers,
But such whose father-grape grew fat
On Lusitanian summers.

For since I came to live and learn,
No pint of white or red
Had ever half the power to turn
This wheel within my head,
Which bears a season'd brain about,
Unsubject to confusion,
Tho' soak'd and saturate, out and out,
Thro' every convolution.

For I am of a numerous house,
With many kinsmen gay,
Where long and largely we carouse
As who shall say me nay:
Each month, a birth-day coming on,
We drink, defying trouble,
Or sometimes two would meet in one,
And then we drank it double;

Whether the vintage, yet unkept,
Had relish fiery-new,
Or, elbow-deep in sawdust, slept,
As old as Waterloo;
Or stowed (when classic Channing died)
In musty bins and chambers,
Had cast upon its crusty side
The gloom of ten Decembers.

The Muse, the jolly Muse, it is!
She answered to my call,
She changes with that mood or this,
Is all-in-all to all:
She lit the spark within my throat,

To make my blood run quicker,
Used all her fiery will, and smote
Her life into the liquor.

And hence this halo lives about
The waiter's hands that reach
To each his perfect pint of stout,
His proper chop to each.
He looks not like the common breed
That with the napkin dally;
I think he came like Ganymede,
From some delightful valley.

Head-waiter of the chop-house here,
To which I most resort,
I too must part: I hold thee dear
For this good pint of port.
For this, thou shalt from all things suck
Marrow of mirth and laughter;
And, wheresoe'er thou move, good luck
Shall fling her old shoe after.

As with sherry, port-type wines are made in other countries. Constantia, a sweet red dessert wine, lighter than port, appeared in South Africa at the end of the 18th century. It took its name from the farm near Cape Town where it was grown. Its flavour of muscat causes it to be described as such by some modern writers, who add that it became very popular with ladies in the early 19th century. America has a range of ruby, tawny and white port-style drinks, the California white variety being artificially decolorised. In Portugal white port has been made with white grapes. Also found in California, and similar to the white port, is Angelica. It is a sweet, white dessert wine which has been fortified with brandy.

MADEIRA

Madeira is another kind of fortified dessert wine, especially popular in countries like France, Sweden and Denmark. It comes from the island of the same name, owned by Portugal, which is in the Atlantic Ocean. Madeira means 'wooded', as the island once was. The varieties of Madeira are mainly named for the grapes which produce them; Malmsey (from the Malvasia grape, the sweetest type of Madeira), Bual (Boal), Verdelho and Sercial.

BOTTLED HAPPINESS

The delicacies of the season, flavoured by a brand of old Madeira which has been the pride of many seasons. It is the Juno brand; a glorious wine, fragrant, and full of gentle might; a bottled-up happiness, put by for use; a golden liquid, worth more than liquid gold; so rare and admirable, that veteran wine-bibbers count it among their epochs to have tasted it! It drives away the heart-ache, and substitutes no head-ache! It would all but revive a dead man!

Nathaniel Hawthorne *The House of the Seven Gables*

The Bastardo grape is also used, but in modern times is blended with others. It formerly named its own kind of Madeira, and it is tempting to think that this was the Bastard wine drunk in Shakespeare's time. Eric Linklater certainly thought so, judging by comments in his *Poet's Pub*: 'In the cellar Keith anxiously examined the Malmsey he had apparelled, the white Bastard and the Sack. For some time he had been experimenting with the elegant mixtures of our ancestors. Sweetness and heaviness might be urged against them, but if they had not been too heavy to clog the nimble wits nor sweet enough to make sickly the subtle flame at "The Mermaid", why should "The Pelican" be frightened of them?'

A particular blend of Sercial, the driest type of Madeira, is known as Rainwater. Rupert Croft-Cooke, in his *Madeira*, suggests that the name indicates wine made on high slopes where the soil is irrigated only by rain, not rivers. Hugh Johnson says instead that an American distributor bestowed the name, 'perhaps because he had the curious habit of leaving his casks outside, like rainwater butts'. In *The Wine Lists* Robert Joseph says that it was named 'after a consignment of well-liked Madeira diluted by a sudden storm whilst standing on the quay'.

MALMSEY

Apart from Madeira itself, Malmsey is the word with which most of us are familiar. There is a famous scene in Shakespeare's *King Richard the Third* where the Duke of Clarence awakes in his cell and calls for a cup of wine. 'You shall have wine enough, my lord, anon,' says the man standing beside his bed. Clarence realises that he is in the presence of men who have come to kill him. He pleads eloquently for his life, but is stabbed, then drowned in the butt of Malmsey which is in the next room. Modern historians now think that Clarence was drowned in a bath, but the butt of Malmsey appealed strongly to Shakespeare's contemporaries and still lives in popular imagination.

Madeira has aroused the enthusiasm of other writers. Nathaniel Hawthorne writes, in *Lady Eleanore's Mantle*: 'Our host, in due season, uncorked a bottle of Madeira, of such exquisite perfume and admirable flavour, that he must surely have discovered it in an ancient bin, down deep beneath the deepest cellar, where some jolly butler stored away the Governor's choicest wine, and forgot to reveal the secret on his death-bed. Peace to his red-nosed ghost, and a libation to his memory! This precious liquor was imbibed by Mr Tiffany with peculiar zest . . .'

In *Dombey and Son* Dickens makes much of some Madeira owned by Uncle Solomon. The last but one bottle is drunk near the beginning of the book, when it is said: 'You shall drink the other

THE WINE GLASS

Who has woe? Who has sorrow? Who has strife? Who has complaining? Who has wounds without cause? Who has redness of eyes? Those who tarry long over wine, those who go to try mixed wine. Do not look at wine when it is red, when it sparkles in the cup and goes down smoothly. At the last it bites like a serpent and stings like an adder.

Old Testament (Revised Standard Version): *Proverbs* xxiii, 29–32

bottle, Wally, when you come to good fortune; when you are a thriving, respected and happy man.' That last bottle is mentioned again nearly 800 pages later. Solomon decides not to drink the last bottle of old Madeira yet, even though Walter and Florence have just married. They are not yet reconciled to Florence's father.

The last chapter of the book begins: 'A bottle that has been long excluded from the light of day, and is hoary with dust and cobwebs, has been brought into the sunshine; and the golden wine within it sheds a lustre on the table. It is the last bottle of the old Madeira. "You are quite right, Mr Gills," says Mr Dombey. "This is a very rare and most delicious wine."'

The reconciliation has been achieved. Dickens then builds his final chapter around the idea of people maturing and mellowing like buried wine. Not everyone, unfortunately, ages as well as Madeira wine; it is said to maintain its quality for ever.

Evelyn Waugh, in *Vile Bodies*, refers to eating 'black Bradenham ham with Madeira sauce', indicating one use to which Madeira is put. It is not used, however, for the more familiar (in Britain)

Madeira cake, made with plenty of eggs and lightly flavoured with lemon. Its name simply commemorates the fact that it was once eaten in mid-morning to accompany a glass of the wine.

MARSALA AND MALAGA

Marsala is a dark, dessert wine that comes from Sicily. It can be treacle-sweet, though a drier variety exists. An Englishman called John Woodhouse had the idea of exploiting it towards the end of the 18th century. He was well acquainted with sherry and no doubt with port; he therefore fortified Marsala to make it suitable for the English market. It resembles sherry, though Thackeray has a character say, in *The Book of Snobs*: 'I prefer sherry to marsala when I can get it.'

Not everyone would agree with that judgement, and anyone who likes sherry should try Marsala. A good quality Marsala, more difficult than sherry to obtain because it is less fashionable, is usually cheaper than sherry of equal quality. Perhaps for that reason it is often used in the kitchen.

The drink is not mentioned often in literature, though Hemingway includes it amongst the vast array of drinks consumed by the hero of *A Farewell to Arms*. Horace Annesley Vachell, in his novel *The Actor*, has: 'I got a little parcel of marsala the other day, wonderful value at eighteen

NERVOUS DISORDER

At the other end of the bar was the real business; a case of Bourbon, half a case of Scotch, and a cocktail-shaker of the size and menace of a trench-mortar, all guarded by the club bar-tender. As to wine, most prominent citizens of Grand Republic, including Cass, were unaware of it except as something you nervously ordered on a liner.

Sinclair Lewis *Cass Timberlane*

shillings the dozen. Give you a glass at luncheon tomorrow. I hate bad wine. To get good sound wine cheap is no easy job.' 'Parcel' in this quotation means a case: the word was once in general commercial use to refer to a quantity of goods offered for bulk sale.

Marsala was popular at one time with Lord Nelson, who once said in a letter to Lord Keith that 'Marsala wine is so good that any gentleman's table might receive it; and it will be of real use to our seamen.' Acting on the latter belief, Nelson later placed an order for some 5000 gallons of the wine to be delivered to the ships at Malta. For this he paid 1s 5d (7.5 pence) per gallon.

Málaga, yet another wine known by a place name – in this case that of a port on the south-east coast of Spain – also has associations with the Royal Navy. In 1694 Admiral Edward Russell, commanding the Mediterranean Fleet, gave an entertainment at Alicante. Contemporary reports say that a fountain was converted into a punch bowl, into which were poured four hogsheads of brandy, one pipe of Málaga wine and 20 gallons of lime juice. Lemons, fine white sugar, nutmegs, toasted biscuits and eight hogsheads of water were also added. Six hundred guests were invited to the party.

Málaga is once again a fortified dessert wine. It is found in a wide variety of types, but is best known as a dark and very sweet wine. In the 17th century it was closely bracketed with sherry, so that it was also known as sack. A medium sweet variety was found in England under the name of Mountain. Málaga is still exported, but mainly to Switzerland, Germany, Belgium and Poland.

ENRICHED WINES

The process of 'fortifying' wine has been mentioned in passing: the French talk about *enrichissement*, the 'enrichment' of wine. The justification for adding alcohol to wine, it should be remembered, is that it increases not only the alcohol level of a wine but conserves the sweetness of the grape-sugar. The extra alcohol, which may be anything from brandy to rectified neutral alcohol, has the effect of 'muting' the must during vinification. In other words, it stops yeast continuing to convert the sugar in the grape-juice to alcohol, since the yeast can no longer function above certain alcohol-levels.

'Enrichment' is perhaps justified as a term. The yeast could, after all, be stopped in its tracks by other methods. In the production of cheap sweet wines, in any of the wine-producing countries, fermentation is muted by adding chemicals that kill the yeast, or pasteurising the wine, which has the same effect.

The French cleverly exploit the fact that 'natural' sugar has been retained in fortified or enriched wines by calling them *vins doux naturels* (V.D.N.), 'natural sweet wines'. That name, of course, manages to convey the idea that no interference has taken place. If a great deal of alcohol has been added, a more honest term is used. The wines become *vins de liqueur*. For foreigners, the most familiar French wines of this type bear names like Roussillon, Muscat de Frontignan, Muscat de Minervois. They are not often exported, but are found in the south of the country. The Roussillon Plain is near the eastern Pyrenees; the other wines are from Languedoc, a little further to the north-east.

Foreign visitors have been sampling these wines over a long period. A literary recommendation is found in *The Wrecker*, by Robert Louis Stevenson and Lloyd Osbourne: 'The restaurant was no great place, but boasted a considerable cellar, and a long printed list of vintages. This I was perusing with the double zest of a man who is fond of wine and a lover of beautiful names, when my eye fell (near the end of the card) on that not very famous or familiar brand, Roussillon. I

COMING OUT IN THE WASH

'I can't place the tangy flavour,' I said. 'Vim probably. Marcia mixed it in the wash basin.'

Jilly Cooper *Prudence*

remembered it was a wine I had never tasted, ordered a bottle, found it excellent, and when I had discussed the contents, called (according to my habit) for a final pint. It appears they did not keep Roussillon in half-bottles. "All right," said I, "another bottle".'

In this instance the second bottle does not prove to be a good idea, but the so-called natural sweet wines of France are certainly worth sampling.

The French also produce a drink, *Pineau des Charentes*, which tastes like a fortified wine but is really brandy diluted with grape juice. In the 19th century, brandy producers in the Charentes region found themselves with surplus stocks. One of them mixed brandy with grape juice in such a way that the alcohol level immediately reached a level – between 18 and 22 per cent – where fermentation could not begin. *Pineau* could be called the ultimate muted wine.

OKAY TOKAY

14 September 1710: I dined with Stratford at a merchant's in the city, where I drank the first Tokay wine I ever saw; and it is admirable, yet not to the degree I expected.

Jonathan Swift *Journal to Stella*

VERMOUTHS

Vermouths are technically fortified wines, though some make use of wine that has completed its fermentation in the normal way. (They can also be described as flavoured wines, since most have been mixed with herbs and spices.) The word vermouth is one that can lure any would-be philologist into a tangled maze. It was taken into English from French at the beginning of the 18th century, at first with something like its French pronunciation, *ver-moot*. The French had in turn taken the word from German *Wermut*, in which our Anglo-Saxon ancestors would have recognised their *wermod*. That was their name for the shrub we now call wormwood, which quite wrongly suggests that it is a habitat for woodworm. The original form of the name shows that it meant something like 'manliness', perhaps because it was in early use as an aphrodisiac. At various other times it has been used as a tonic and as a protection against moths and fleas in bedding.

Wormwood has a decidedly bitter flavour, making it useful in the brewing of beer. Its better known application to drinks, however, has been in vermouth and absinthe. The full Latin name of the plant is *Artemisia Absinthium*, the first word linking it with the goddess Artemis, the second meaning 'devoid of delight', a reference to its bitterness and bad smell.

What we now call vermouth is wine which has been fortified with some kind of spirit, to which has been added sugar, colouring and extracts of wormwood and other plants. The precise ingredients of a particular vermouth, as with patent aperitifs such as Byrrh and Dubonnet, is known only within the company that produces it, but elder flowers, forget-me-nots, gentian, ginger, lime, hyssop, mint, sage, thyme, cloves, nutmeg, angelica, mace, coriander and cinnamon are likely to be included with the wormwood.

CLEOPATRA'S DRINK

Cleopatra disdaining to be vanquished in any excess by a Roman, laid a wager with Antony that she herself would receive into her body at one supper the value of fifty thousand pounds, which to Antony was thought in a manner to be impossible. The next day Cleopatra prepared for Antony a right sumptuous supper, but whereat Antony nothing marvelled, knowing the value thereof by his accustomed fare. Then the Queen smiling called for a goblet, whereinto she did pour a quantity of very tart vinegar, and taking a pearl which hung at one of her ears, she quickly did let it fall into the vinegar, wherein being shortly dissolved (as it is the nature of the pearl) she immediately drank it.

Sir Thomas Elyot *The Book Named the Governor*

GERMAN INTERESTS

The German peasant and poorer classes have, like the English proletariat, always preferred beer; when they drink wine, it has been for some solemn or festive occasion, for which they are prepared to pay relatively high prices. The result of this is that down the ages the great vine-growing capacity of the Rhine and its tributaries, the Mosel, the Main and the Nahe, have been adapted to a different clientele, to producing exclusively high quality wine for the rich and mighty of this world.

Anthony Rhodes *Princes of the Grape*

Vermouths come in three basic forms – dry white, sweet white and sweet red. There is a tradition in England of referring to French vermouth as dry, Italian as sweet. That geographical description is not justified, as the very name of the dry Martini cocktail indicates. Perhaps the tradition is fading: when I asked in a pub recently for a 'gin and it', the blank gaze of the young barmaid made me correct it to 'gin and Italian', then to 'gin and sweet vermouth'.

If the most famous French vermouth is Noilly Prat, the best is said to be Chambéry, made in a town near the Italian border. It has a version called Chamberyzette which includes the flavour of wild Alpine strawberries. Italian vermouths include Carpano, Martini & Rossi, Cinzano, Riccadonna, Cora, Bosca and Fratelli. Carpano, the first company to sell vermouth, is especially well-known for its Punt e Mes ('point and a half'). The name is said to have originated with a Turin stockbroker.

A number of drinks which are known by a commercial name derive from a type of vermouth. Dubonnet, for example, is based on red wine, quinine and *mistelle* (grape juice fortified with brandy). There is a slight suggestion of raspberry flavour. Because of the quinine, a favourite ingredient in such drinks, it was once marketed as Quinquina Dubonnet. Lillet is vermouth with added Armagnac; St Raphael is again quinine-based. The inventor of the latter drink is said to have lost his sight, then regained it when he prayed to St Raphael, patron of the blind. Byrrh is vermouth plus quinine and Pyrenean herbs; Pikina is a wine, bitter orange and quinine mixture. Cap Corse, from Corsica, presumably contains some of the many aromatic herbs that grow on that island.

A familiar name that may be mentioned here is Gauloise. This was an early kind of aperitif wine which had dry, medium and sweet versions. The well-known cigarette was named after it. Another drink that has disappeared is Raspail, invented by the chemist François Raspail in 1947. Such drinks, which are now only of interest to the social historian, remind us that our drinking habits are always changing and evolving. Perhaps it is true that every drink has its day.

BEADED BUBBLES

Champagne, of course, has managed to become the drink of the special day. It is the drink we associate with wedding days, birthdays, anniversaries, high days and holidays. We use it to launch ships and celebrate victories. There is a reference to its being drunk from a lady's slipper in *The Connoisseur* of 6 June 1754. It is certainly the best known of the sparkling wines, our next general category. For many people Champagne is the most expensive drink they are likely to buy. The very word is even used metaphorically to describe a special excitement: 'Mrs Soames! She mightn't take much, but she would appreciate what she drank,' says John Galsworthy, in *The Man of Property*. 'It was a pleasure to give her good wine ... The thought of her was like Champagne itself.'

There is a similar comment in *All That Glitters*, by Thomas Tryon: 'I recalled how someone had

dubbed Maude Antrim the "Champagne Lady"; the name had stuck.'

What is this magical elixir that occupies such a special place in our imagination? An objective description does not make it sound very exciting. In his *Book of French Wines*, P. Morton Shand describes Champagne as a 'manufactured, blended, and (in non-vintage years) standardised sparkling wine'. That makes it sound decidedly ordinary, and it has had its opponents. They are answered by John P. Marquand, in *Women and Thomas Harrow*: 'Alfred was refilling his glass, and after all, there was nothing like good Champagne. It was occasionally called the beverage of the parvenu, an artificially charged wine that had

'Fizz', an illustration in The Sketch, *1898.*

none of the subtle strength of a fine Burgundy –
but neither had Burgundy the gaiety, the power
of partially restoring youth or of resurrecting
memory.'

Expanding his description of Champagne, P.
Morton Shand points out that the sparkle comes
from cane-sugar that is added after the natural
sugar in the grape juice has been converted to
alcohol. The wine itself is a mixture of several still
wines which come from different vineyards. It is
made from both black (Pinot Noir, Pinot
Meunier) and white (Chardonnay) grapes. In a
poor year it is reblended with wine of finer vintages to bring it up to a standard quality. What
gives individual Champagnes their special taste
depends on how much sugar is added and which
wines are blended.

CHAMPAGNE NAMES

It is not surprising, then, that true French Champagnes are identified by the names of their
blenders and shippers. They include names as
famous as Ayala, Bollinger, Heidsieck, Krug,
Lanson, Louis Roederer, Mercier, Moët &
Chandon, Mumm, Perrier–Jouët, Pol–Roger,
Pommery & Gréno, Ruinart, Veuve Clicquot.
There are scores of others, less well-known but
still producing a Champagne of the highest quality. In *The Wine Lists*, for instance, Robert Joseph
mentions 'four good, inexpensive Champagne
houses: Lambert, Boizel, Duval Leroy, Massé'.

The word 'Champagne' itself, incidentally, in
Britain as in France, can only be used of a wine

The Moët family home at Epernay, France, 1862.

SPARKLING NAMES

A gracious table light fell upon Mrs
Abrams' face, cooked to a turn in
Veuve Clicquot . . .

F. Scott Fitzgerald *Tender is the Night*

Some epicures like Burgundy,
Hock, claret and Moselle,
But Moët's vintage only
Satisfies this Champagne swell.

George Leybourne *Champagne Charlie*

'We've got some Oeil-de-Perdrix –' His
lips pursed as though he were tasting it.
  'What's that?' Cal asked.
  'Champagne– but very pretty, same
colour as a partridge eye – pink but a
little darker than pink, and dry too.
Four-fifty a bottle.'
  'Isn't that high?' Aron asked.

John Steinbeck *East of Eden*

'A bottle to my table, please. The
Heidsieck 'fifty-two.'

William Haggard *The High Wire*

And then the Champagne that we
drank, not the quantity but the quality!
Well, it was Pol-Roger, '84, and quite
good enough for me.

E. W. Hornung *Raffles*

'I find Champagne at midday has such
a calamitous effect on my working day
that I am tempted to coin the word
"bollingering", meaning much the same
as malingering, only nicer.'

Humphrey Lyttelton

that comes from the Champagne region. In North
America and other parts of the world it is loosely
used of a champagne-style drink.

The discovery of true Champagne is traditionally attributed to a Benedictine monk, Dom
Pérignon, born near Rheims in 1639. He became
the cellarer of the Abbey of Hautvillers in 1668
and was a skilled taster and blender. He is said to
have been able to taste any wine from the Champagne region and immediately identify the vineyard from which it came.

Dom Pérignon noticed that the white wine in
his cellars was usually in a semi-sparkling state
each spring. We would now say that a secondary
fermentation was occurring. The yeast would
have lain dormant during the cold weather, then
begun its work again as temperatures rose. The
monk wanted to retain the sparkle in the wine
and discovered that he could do so if he corked

*Dom Pérignon discovers the secret of making
good champagne.*

OPENING CEREMONY

Cyril Ray rightly points out in *Bollinger* that there is more ceremony attached to uncorking Champagne than any other drink. The silver foil is first removed. It is there to cover the wire which holds in the cork and which has probably become rusty in the cellar. Perfectly dry glasses have to be at the ready, since Champagne poured into a wet glass kills the bubbles. The cork shouldn't pop on opening. Youngman Carter once said that the gas should escape from a bottle of Champagne with a sigh, 'as from a well-contented woman'.

the bottles. Until that time bottles had been ineffectually sealed with rags. Corks made it possible for the wine to continue its secondary fermentation inside the bottle. The carbon dioxide that was produced was also trapped and was absorbed by the wine.

There were still many technical problems to overcome. The cork, and the bottle itself, had to be able to withstand the pressure that built up as fermentation proceeded. Even when all went well, and the process was completed, the wine contained a cloudy deposit of dead yeast. If the bottle was opened and the wine filtered, the gas escaped.

VEUVE CLICQUOT

The credit for solving that problem is normally ascribed to a woman. As Anthony Rhodes points out, in his *Princes of the Grape*, 'no business in the world can have been as much influenced by the female sex as that of Champagne'. The women concerned were all widows of men who ran Champagne houses. They inherited the companies, then proved that they had all the commercial abilities needed to remain as their heads. Amongst this special group of ladies were the widows Heidsieck, Pommery, Roederer, Bollinger and Pol-Roger. The first of them, and

the one who had most influence on Champagne production, was *Veuve* Clicquot.

The widow Clicquot acquired that title in 1805 when she was only twenty-three. Her husband, only five years older, had been making a great success of his wine business, but died suddenly of a fever. The young woman, born in Rheims as Nicole-Barbe Ponsardin, immediately changed the name of the company to *Veuve Clicquot-Ponsardin et Cie* and carried on. It was quite a remarkable thing to do, given the views that prevailed at the time about women being engaged in commerce at management level. The young widow also had a baby daughter to raise. There were many problems to overcome, not least the technical one of the sediment in the Champagne bottles.

Veuve Clicquot introduced the system of storing bottles with their necks downwards. Men turned the bottles every day and tapped the

THE HUMAN CHAMPAGNE BOTTLE

In Edgar Allan Poe's short story, *The System of Dr Tarr and Prof. Fether*, the narrator visits an asylum. He is told of a patient 'who very pertinaciously maintained himself to be a Cordova cheese, and went about, with a knife in his hand, soliciting his friends to try a small slice from the middle of his leg.'

This is capped by mention of the man who thought he was a bottle of Champagne. 'Here the speaker, very rudely, as I thought, put his right thumb in his left cheek, withdrew it with a sound resembling the popping of a cork, and then, by a dextrous movement of the tongue upon the teeth, created a sharp hissing and fizzing, which lasted for several minutes, in imitation of the frothing of Champagne.'

The narrator subsequently learns that he is talking to the patients themselves, who have locked up the staff and taken over the asylum.

bottoms to dislodge the sediment and make it gather in the neck. The men who did this job were *remueurs*; the process *remuage*. When all the sediment was in the bottle-neck, after some three months of *remuage*, the corks were removed and the deposit poured away (*degorgement*). The bottles were then immediately topped up and re-corked.

The task of the *degorgeurs* was subsequently made slightly easier when a man called Walfard had the idea of freezing the bottle-necks. The sediment becomes enclosed in a plug, or pellet, of ice and emerges as a single entity.

CHAMPAGNE SUGAR

The wine used for the topping up, known as the *dosage*, had another function to perform. With the secondary fermentation now complete, all the natural sugar in the wine had been converted to alcohol. The widow Clicquot knew that many of her customers preferred a fairly sweet wine. The *dosage* therefore contained sugar – and usually a little brandy – so that it adjusted the final sweetness of the Champagne. Champagne producers still control the sweetness of their product by adding more or less sugar at the topping-up stage. Wines intended for different national markets vary considerably.

Labels on Champagne bottles give information on this point, but can be confusing. The description Extra Dry, for instance, by no means refers to the driest type of Champagne. Those wanting such a drink should look for labels saying *Brut Zéro*, *Brut Intégral* or *Brut Sauvage*. The word *Brut* on its own indicates a Champagne which is marginally sweeter: then come Extra Dry (*Extra-Sec*), Dry (*Sec*), Semi-Dry (*Demi-Sec*) and Sweet (*Doux*). *Brut*, incidentally, is pronounced something like our word 'brute' and is derived from the same source. Applied to Champagne its meaning is raw, unsweetened.

As can be seen from the above description, the production of Champagne by the true Champagne method was a long process, requiring the attention of a great many skilled workmen. It was expensive to make and therefore expensive to buy. In the past the workmen must often have been in a dangerous situation. Until the bottle

THE WARNING

Only a glass of Champagne
But it led a poor girl into sin,
Only a glass of Champagne,
Was the door where the devil crept
    in . . .
Now all you young maidens
Take warning by her,
If you go out with a lord or a sir,
See that you don't let the same thing
    occur,
All through a glass of Champagne.

Music-hall song by Noel Gay

manufacturers had solved their own technical problems, bottles regularly exploded as pressure built up inside them.

Inevitably modern technology has introduced many changes. *Remuage* can now be carried out in long racks that are controlled by a computer. Traditional skills have been passed from workmen with a lifetime's experience to the computer programmers. Production costs have been cut, but the prestige of the wine will probably see to it that its cost remains high. André Simon makes the point, in *The Pan Book of Wine*, that 'there are people who drink Champagne because they like it; but there are also people who drink Champagne because it is an expensive wine and they wish the world to know that they can afford it'.

CHAMPAGNE SUBSTITUTES

Advice for those who cannot afford it is offered by L.W. Marrison in *Wines and Spirits*: 'Order an Asti Spumante if your companion has a sweet tooth, or a sparkling Saumur or hock or Moselle if not, and laugh the matter off by saying, "Champagne's too serious for an occasion like this", or "Hope you don't mind, but Champagne always tastes like soapy water to me" (this requires fortitude).'

Robert Joseph has also suggested possible alternatives to Champagne. His list includes Blanquette de Limoux, Saumur Mousseux, Crémant d'Alsace, Crémant de Bougogne, Schramsberg (California), Domaine Chandon (California). To these we could add Fontanafredda, Ca del Bosco, Equipe 5, Ferrari Brut, Pinot de Pinot (Italy); Château Remy (Australia); Clairette de Die Tradition, Dopff au Moulin, Poniatowski Clos Baudouin Vouvray (France); Deinhard Leila (Germany); Piper Sonoma (USA). Such substitutes seem especially appropriate if the intention is to mix the wine with something else and make, for instance, a Buck's Fizz.

The sparkle in these less-expensive wines is usually obtained by cheaper production methods. Secondary fermentation can take place in a tank instead of in the individual bottles. Filtering then takes place under pressure. This process is known by various names, such as *cuvé close, Charmat, Chaussepied* or simply as the Tank Method.

CHANGING TIMES

The Club bar was empty except for Kwaku, the old steward, who stood behind the counter, his shrunken shoulders hunched inside the white drill jacket as he polished doggedly a battered Champagne bucket. Johnnie wondered how many people drank Champagne these days.

'Use this one much, Kwaku?'

The old man shook his head. 'No, sah. On'y small-small, dis time. Dis one, he too cost. Long time pas', Eur'pean use dis one – oh, plenty, plenty.' He chuckled softly, perhaps recalling those munificent years, and the 'dash' given by the drinkers of Champagne to a young stewardboy, quick on his feet, strong, princely in white robe and turban and vivid cummerbund.

Margaret Laurence *This Side Jordan*

A compromise between the Champagne Method and Tank Method is popular in the USA. In what is called the Transfer Method, secondary fermentation takes place in bottles, but the wine goes into a tank to be filtered. The wine is then re-bottled. American labels therefore distinguish between 'fermented in this bottle' and 'fermented in the bottle'.

It is also possible to put wine into a pressurised tank and inject carbon dioxide into it. This is known as the Impregnation Method. When bottles of such wine are opened, they give off large bubbles which quickly disperse, leaving the wine to go flat. Fizzy lemonade is made in this way, and is probably to be preferred to impregnated sparkling wine.

But this section should end, as it began, with Champagne itself, and the last word should go to Thomas Moore. In a few witty lines from *Illustrations of a Bore* he personifies the drink and turns it into an exuberant old friend:

'If you've ever been to a party
Relieved of the presence of Ned,
How instantly joyous and hearty
They've grown when the damper was fled.
You may guess what a gay piece of work,
What delight to Champagne it must be,
To get rid of its bore of a cork,
And come sparkling to you, love, and me.

OTHER WINES

Beyond the convenient islands of fortified and sparkling wines lies the vinous mainland. It is natural to use a geographic image when thinking of the thousands of other red, white and rosé wines of the world, drunk while at table or whenever a conversational lubricant is needed. In modern times they come from a wide range of European countries, from the USA, South America, Australia, South Africa.

For historical reasons, the literature of the subject devotes a great deal of space to the wines and wine language of France, then to those of a few other European countries. Wine language consists of words, but also of many names that are used allusively.

Words can usually be translated; names

require explanation. If I said, for example, that I spent most of my working life at Bush House, only the initiated would recognise that name as the headquarters of the BBC World Service. John Dos Passos writes, in _The Great Days_: 'The Tuba was plentiful and strong. We were highly exhilarated by the time we got up to start back to camp.' He is being equally allusive, referring to a wine made in the East Indies from coconuts and rice.

Certain names can be used with more justification than others in this allusive way. Someone who tells me that he once met Marilyn Monroe, say, or Frank Sinatra, has a right to expect that I will recognise the famous name. So it is with G.B. Stern when she writes: 'The 1906 Château Haut-Brion was a mellow charmer.' Haut-Brion names one of the super-stars of the wine world. Amongst its many claims to fame, it seems to have been the first wine château to be mentioned by name in English. Samuel Pepys writes on 10 April 1663: 'Ho Bryan; that hath a good and most particular taste that I ever met with.'

Other Bordeaux super-stars include the Châteaux Lafite-Rothschild, Margaux, Latour, Mouton-Rothschild, Cheval Blanc, d'Yquem, Coutet, Climens, and Pétrus. One or two of these names must be treated with caution. There are about 80 châteaux which mention La Tour, for instance, spelt as two words, and their wines vary in quality. Some of the super-stars themselves are like their human counterparts. Their performance in a particular year may not equal that of the past, though it is also true that they can suddenly reach yet new heights. To continue the analogy for a moment, with wines as with actors there are those who remain in relative obscurity though they deserve – and may one day achieve – far greater fame. What now tends to happen is that buyers for wine merchants, supermarkets and other outlets discover them, the wine journalists make them known.

BEEFING ABOUT CHAMPAGNE

'I don't know what's been planned in the way of wine, but if it isn't Champagne, we'll have Champagne.'

'Darling,' Emily said, 'we're having roast beef.'

'Let us not forget that Champagne goes with everything.'

John P. Marquand _Women and Thomas Harrow_

The glossary on pp. 157–166 includes some historical and specialist words and names which confront the average customer who is buying wine and does not find back labels or neck tags to help him. While words and names are interesting in themselves, there is probably no other ordinary product which requires customers to be familiar with such an international linguistic mish-mash. I stress the words 'ordinary product', since that is what wine of a reasonable quality has now become in the English-speaking countries. The high-quality wines, which are drunk by a small minority, constitute a special product. It is true that every area of specialisation develops a special language but again it has to be said that it should not be found in the retail market-place without a translation. It confuses the customer and presumably hinders sales. While it remains it will act as a barrier to countless people who might otherwise experience the magnanimity of wine.

Glossary of wine words and names

Abboccato – Italian; slightly sweet.

Abocado – Spanish; sweet.

AC – see *Appellation Contrôlée*.

Affenthaler – a German red wine produced in the Baden region. Sold in bottle embossed with a monkey.

Ahr – one of eleven German wine regions of designated quality (*Qualitäts-Anbaugebiete*). Names of particular significance within the region (according to wine-experts) – Ahrweiler, Altenahr, Bachem, Bad Neuenahr, May Schoss, Walporzheim.

Ahrtaler Landwein – see *Landwein*.

Ahrweiler – see Ahr.

Alella – a demarcated Portuguese wine region.

Algarve – a demarcated Portuguese wine region.

Alicante – a demarcated Spanish wine region.

Almansa – a demarcated Spanish wine region.

Aloxe Corton – see Côte de Beaune.

Alsace – A French wine-growing area. Most of the wines from this region have the name of the grape variety on the label, e.g. Chasselas, Sylvaner, Muscat, Traminer, Pinot Blanc, Pinot Gris, Riesling, Gewürztraminer, Auxerrois. Blended wines are described as *Zwicker* and *Edelzwicker*, the latter being of better quality.

Altenahr – see Ahr.

Altrheingauer Landwein – see *Landwein*.

Alzey – see Rheinhessen.

Amabile – Italian; fairly sweet.

Amaro – Italian; bitter-flavoured.

Ampurdan-Costa Brava – a demarcated Spanish wine region.

Amtlich-geprüfter Qualitätswein – German. Describes wine from Austria officially recognised as being of superior quality.

Anjou – see Loire Valley.

Appellation Contrôlée – French; a government certification that guarantees the geographical area of origin mentioned on the label. It also guarantees that the area's standards of production have been maintained. It is normally assumed that an AC wine is of the highest possible quality, and this will be reflected in the price.

Arbois – French; principal appellation of the Jura region, south-east France.

Asciutto – Italian; dry.

Assemblage – French; blending. Used to describe the grape varieties blended to produce a wine.

Assmannshausen – see Rheingau.

Asti Spumante – an Italian sparkling wine made at Asti.

Ausbruch – German; used in Austria to describe a quality of wine between *Beerenauslese* and *Trockenbeerenauslese*. See QmP.

Auslese – German; special selection. Describes a German or Austrian wine made from selected late-harvested grapes. See *Prädikatswein*.

Australia – described by an enthusiastic British commentator as 'the most exciting new wine-producing country in the world'. Varietal descriptions are usual, though some generic terms – claret, Burgundy, Chablis, etc. – also occur. The largest wine-producing area is the Riverina District of New South Wales, but it does not dominate as California dominates the USA.

Austria – has four wine-growing regions, each of which has many named districts. Produces mainly white wines. Gumpoldskirchen is well-known, especially for its *Königswein*. Voslauer wines are of good repute.

Auxey-Duresses – see Côte de Beaune.

Ayl – see Mosel-Saar-Ruwer.

Bacharach – see Mittelrhein.

Bachem – see Ahr.

Bad Dürkheim – see Rheinpfalz.

Baden – one of the 11 German wine regions of designated quality (*Qualitäts-Anbaugebiete*). Names of particular significance within the region (according to wine experts) – Durbach, Freiburg, Heidelberg, Ihringen, Markgraflerland, Meersburg.

Bad Kreuznach – see Nahe.

Bad Neuenahr – see Ahr.

Bairrada – a demarcated Portuguese wine region.

Balgarske Slanske – see Bulgaria.

Bandol – much-praised wines from Provence, in southern France.

Barbaresco – one of the better-known red wines of the Italian province of Piedmont.

Barbera – Italian red wine from the Piedmont region. Barbera d'Asti said to be best type.

Bardolino – well-known, light red Italian wine from the province of Verona.

Barolo – well-known Italian red wine from the Piedmont region.

Barsac – a Bordeaux AC, known for its sweet white wines.

Bayerischer Bodensee Landwein – see *Landwein*.

Beaujolais – an area in southern Burgundy, France, known for its red table wine. Important place names that fall within the Beaujolais region include Brouilly, Chénas, Chiroubles, Côtes de Brouilly, Fleurie, Juliénas, Morgon, Moulin-à-Vent, St Amour.

Beaujolais Cru – wine from nine villages which produce the best Beaujolais.

Beaujolais Nouveau – wine from the most recent harvest, usually made available around the third Wednesday in November.

Beaujolais Supérieur – Beaujolais of slightly increased alcoholic strength.

Beaujolais Villages – wine from a specified group of villages in the Beaujolais area, usually of higher quality than Beaujolais itself.

Beaumes de Venise – sweet wine made from the Muscat grape. See Loire Valley.

Beaune – see Côte de Beaune.

Beerenauslese – German; special berry selection. A German or Austrian wine made from even riper grapes than those described as *Auslese*. See *Prädikatswein*.

Beeswing – light floating crust found in some ports.

Bensheim – see Hessische Bergstrasse.

Bergerac – a vineyard covering most of the Bergerac area of the Dordogne. See South-West France.

Bernkastel – see Mosel-Saar-Ruwer.

Bianco – Italian; white.

Bingen – see Rheinhessen.

Blanc de blancs – French; white of white, i.e. white wine made exclusively from white grapes.

Blanc de noirs – French; white of black, i.e. white wine made exclusively from black grapes.

Blanco – Spanish; sweet.

Blanquette de Limoux – sparkling and still white wines from the Languedoc-Roussillon region in France.

BOB – Buyer's Own Brand (of Champagne).

Bocksbeutel – German; name of the flagon bottle used for Frankenwein and some wines from Baden. The same shape is used for Mateus Rosé wine.

Bodega – Spanish; wine cellar.

Bodensee – German name for Lake Constance, used to identify *Tafelwein*.

Body – term used to describe the density of wine.

Boppard – see Mittelrhein.

Bordeaux – the largest wine-growing region in France, producing wine of mostly high quality. It contains many communes which have their own AC and are famous in their own right. Amongst them are Barsac, Côtes de Bourg, Côtes de Fronsac, Entre-deux-Mers, Graves, Haut-Médoc, Margaux, Médoc, Pauillac, Pomerol, Saint-Emilion, Saint-Estèphe, Saint-Julien, Sauternes. The red wines from this area are known as claret. Bordeaux white wine has a reputation for being sweet but dry white wine is now increasingly produced.

Bordeaux Supérieur – Bordeaux wine of slightly increased alcoholic strength.

Bouquet – term used to describe the perfume of a wine.

Bourgogne – Burgundy.

Bourgueil – see Loire Valley.

Bouzy – the name of a wine-producing village in the Champagne region, derived from a Gaullish personal name. There is no reason to think that it is connected with the word booze.

Boy – in *Bollinger*, Cyril Ray recounts how 'boy' came to be a slang word for Champagne amongst a select group. When Edward VII was Prince of Wales, a boy was responsible for a wheelbarrow of champagne packed in ice. The repeated cry of 'Boy!' led to the drink being referred to as a 'bottle of the boy'.

Branco – Portuguese; white.

Brauneberg – see Mosel-Saar-Ruwer.

Bristol Milk – sherry.

British champagne – an ironic name for gooseberry wine, often passed off as champagne in former times.

British wine – see England.

Brouilly – see Beaujolais

Brut – French; rather dry Champagne. See p. 154.

Bubble water – a 19th-century American term for champagne.

Bucelas – a Portuguese demarcated wine region.

Buckfast – a proprietary tonic wine.

Bulgaria – wines from this country have been amongst the best bargains in recent years. Quality is usually good, and prices relatively low. Fancy names, normally a danger signal, do not seem to be too ominous in this instance. Wines include Donau Perle (pearl of the Danube) a sparkling wine, Sonnenküste (sun coast), Klosterkeller (monastery cellar), Balgarske Slanske (Bulgarian sun), Slantchev Birag (sunshine coast).

Bull's Blood – (*Egri Bikaver*) A deep red wine from Hungary.

Burgundy – a famous wine region in East Central France. Divided into the areas Beaujolais, Chablis, Côte d'Or

(= Côte de Nuits and Côte de Beaune), Mâconnais, Region de Mercurey. The general term Burgundy normally describes a red wine from this region, though white Burgundy is also produced. 'Though he had contented himself with simple claret before, nothing now but the most precious Burgundy would serve his purpose.' Henry Fielding *Tom Jones*. 'Burgundy in all its sunset glow.' Lord Byron *Don Juan*. 'Burgundy' is used as a generic term by wine-makers in the USA.

Cahors – see South-West France.

California – main wine-producing region in the USA.

Calvi – see Vin de Corse.

Carcavelos – a demarcated Portuguese wine region.

Cardinal – archaic slang for mulled red wine.

Carinena – a demarcated Spanish wine region.

Carmignano – a recommended Italian 'claret'.

Cassis – an area in Provence, southern France, producing white wines of good quality. The blackcurrant cordial of this name is made in the Burgundy region.

Castell – see Franken.

Castel San Michele – a recommended Italian 'claret'.

Castello di Roncade – a recommended Italian 'claret'.

Cava – Spanish; cellar, but used to describe a good-quality wine made by the Champagne Method.

Cave – French; cellar.

Chablis – see Burgundy. '. . . a gloomy retainer always seeming to say, after "Chablis, sir?" – "You wouldn't if you knew what it was made of."' Charles Dickens *Our Mutual Friend*. 'Chablis' is used as a generic term by wine-makers in the USA.

Chai – French; a wine store at ground level where the vinification operation takes place (i.e. not a cellar).

Chambolle-Musigny – see Côte de Nuits.

Chambré – French; (of red wines) at room temperature.

Champagne – the northernmost wine-growing area of France. For a discussion of Champagne, the drink, see pp. 150–155. 'Champagne' is used as a generic term by wine-makers in the USA.

Champers – colloquial name for Champagne. 'There's some champers in the ice-box.' Len Deighton *Close-up.*

Chaptalisation – the addition of sugar to fermenting wine so as to raise its alcoholic strength. The word commemorates Jean André Chaptal (1756–1832), a chemist who became Minister of the Interior under Napoleon. He wrote a book on wine-production.

Chassagne-Montrachet – see Côte de Beaune.

Château Grillet – see Rhône Valley.

Chateauneuf-du-Pape – see Rhône Valley.

Chénas – see Beaujolais.

Cheste – a demarcated Spanish wine region.

Chianti – well-known Italian wine. Best types are Chianti Classico and Chianti Putto. Chianti is used as a generic term by wine-makers in the USA.

Chiantishire – a nickname for Tuscany, because of the number of English people who live there and drink chianti.

Chiaretto – Italian; rosé produced south of Lake Garda.

Chicha – a Bolivian wine made from molasses and corn. 'She filled his earthenware mug with more *chicha*.' Imogen Winn *Coming to Terms.*

Chinon – see Loire Valley.

Chiroubles – see Beaujolais.

Clairet – a very light red wine.

Claret – English term for red wine from Bordeaux; also used of other wines based on the Cabernet Sauvignon grape. 'It's not one of the great Bordeaux . . .' 'I prefer the word "claret",' someone else put in, 'it's so full of English history.' 'You mean,' retorted Pflaumen, 'English history is so full of it.' Mary McCarthy *The Genial Host.* 'Gustav entered a public house where they drew wines and spirits from the wood. In the

mahogany interior he put back mugs of claret reading a little sign against the decanter stand –' 'Claret is a close friend to take wherever you go.' J.P. Donleavy *Gustav G.* 'As he sat before the coffee-room fire, his (Mr Lorry's) mind was busily digging, digging, digging, in the live red coals. A bottle of good claret after dinner does a digger in the coals no harm, otherwise than as it has a tendency to throw him out of work.' Charles Dickens *A Tale of Two Cities.*

Clarete – Spanish, Portuguese; light red wine.

Classico – Italian; from a delimited area. Best wine in region.

Clos – French; walled vineyard (Burgundy).

Cochem – see Mosel-Saar-Ruwer.

Colares – a Portuguese demarcated wine region, of special interest because vines were not affected by phylloxera.

Col Sandago – a recommended Italian 'claret'.

Commandaria – a rich sweet dessert wine produced in Cyprus.

Condado de Huelva – a demarcated Spanish wine region.

Condrieu – see Rhône Valley.

Copita – Spanish; a rosebud-shaped sherry glass. 'He was holding in his hand a copita of sherry, now almost empty.' Iris Murdoch *A Word Child.*

Corbières – see Languedoc-Roussillon.

Corked – said of wine which has had its taste affected by an inferior cork. A weeevil may also have penetrated the cork, allowing air to get to the wine. Corky is perhaps a more accurate term.

Cornas – see Rhone Valley.

Corsica – see Vin de Corse.

Corvo – a well-known red or white Italian wine.

Cortese di Gavi – yellow Italian wine highly recommended by Cyril Ray.

Costières du Gard – see Languedoc-Roussillon.

Costozza Cabernet – a recommended Italian 'claret'.

Coteaux d'Ajaccio – see Vin de Corse.

Coteaux de Layon – see Loire Valley.

Coteaux du Cap Corse – see Vin de Corse.

Côte de Beaune – a Burgundy region. Important names within it include Aloxe-Corton, Auxey-Duresses, Beaune, Chassagne-Montrachet, Meursault, Monthélie, Pernand Vergelesses, Pommard, Puligny Montrachet, St-Aubin, St-Romain, Santenay, Volnay.

Côte de Brouilly – see Beaujolais.

Côte de Nuit – a Burgundy region. Important names within it include Chambolle-Musigny, Fixin, Gevrey Chambertin, Marsannay-la-Côte, Morey St Denis, Nuits-St-Georges, Vosne-Romanée, Vougeot.

Côte Rôtie – see Rhône Valley.

Côtes de Bourg – a Bordeaux AC.

Côtes de Buzet – see South-West France.

Côtes de Duras – see South West France.

Côtes de Fronsac – a Bordeaux AC.

Côtes de Provence – white, red and rosé wines fom southern France.

Côtes du Frontonnais – see South-West France.

Côtes-du-Rhône – see Rhône Valley.

Côtes du Roussillon – see Languedoc-Roussillon.

Côtes du Roussillon-Villages – see Languedoc-Roussillon.

Crémant – French; lightly fizzy.

Crémant de Loire – see Loire Valley

Crépy – see Savoie.

Crozes-Hermitage – see Rhône Valley.

Cru – French; growth. Indicates wine of repute. *Cru classé* wines have been officially classified and are considered to be of outstanding quality. In Bordeaux *cru bourgeois* means good but not great wine. *Cru exceptionnel* also means not of *grand cru* standard.

Cuvée – French; the contents of a *cuve*, or vat. Used of Champagne, cuvée refers to wine from the first (and best) pressing of the grape. Otherwise it refers to blended wine.

Cyprus – Known mainly for sherry-style wines and Commandaria, a rich sweet dessert wine.

Dago red – early American slang for red wine.

Dão – a Portuguese demarcated wine region producing good table wines. Better quality wine indicated by *reserva* or *garrafeira* on the label.

Decant – Remove wine from its bottle to another container, usually a decanter, in order to separate it from sediment and allow it to breathe

Deidesheim – see Rheinpfalz.

Demi-sec – French; semi-dry.

Denominacion de Origen – Spanish. Equivalent of the French *Appellation Controlée*.

Denominazione di Origine Controllata – Italian. Equivalent of the French *Appellation Controlée*.

Denominazione di Origine Controllata e Garantita – Italian; a guarantee of the quality of certain DOC wines.

Derry-downderry – a rhyming slang expression for sherry, formerly used by actors.

Dhron – see Mosel-Saar-Ruwer.

Didn't ought – an old rhyming slang expression for port, based on a traditional reaction by Cockney ladies to the offer of a glass. Also known as pimple and wart.

DOC – Italian; see *Denominazione di Origine Controllata.*

DOCG – Italian; see *Denominazione di Origine Controllata e Garantita.*

Doce – Portuguese; sweet.

Doctor – Brown sherry used to be called this in England, because it was a doctored drink.

Dolce – Italian; sweet.

Dôle – a Swiss red wine from the Valais area, made from the Pinot Noir or Gamay.

Domaine – French; estate. The Burgundy equivalent of chateau.

Donau Perle – see Bulgaria.

Dorsheim – see Nahe.

Douro – Portuguese demarcated wine region known mainly for port.

Doux – French; sweet.

Dulce – Spanish; sweet.

Durbach – see Baden.

Edelfäule – German; noble rot.

Edelzwicker – German; noble mixture. Alsatian wine made from a blend of grapes.

Eiswein – German; ice-wine. Made from grapes that are fully ripe, but which have been left on the vine to freeze. Harvested while still frozen. Conditions for its production occur rarely.

Eitelsbach – see Mosel-Saar-Ruwer.

Eltville – see Rheingau.

Embotellado de origen – Spanish; estate bottled.

Emu – a proprietary tonic wine.

Enervin – a proprietary tonic wine.

Enkirch – see Mosel-Saar-Ruwer.

Engarrafado – Portuguese; bottled by . . .

England – There are at least 50 vineyards in England, mostly fairly small. English wine has a curiosity value, apart from inherent quality. British wine is quite different, made from imported grape concentrate and added sugar.

Eno Friulia – a recommended Italian 'claret'.

Entre-deux-Mers – a Bordeaux AC. The name means 'between two seas' but the area is between the rivers Dordogne and Garonne. Known for its relatively cheap white wine.

Erbach – see Rheingau.

Erden – see Mosel-Saar-Ruwer.

Erzeugerabfüllung – German; estate bottled.

Escherndorf – see Franken.

Espumante – Portuguese; sparkling.

Espumoso – Spanish; sparkling.

Est! Est!! Est!!! – Latin; Est = here it is! A white from Trebbiano and Malvasia grown by Lake Bolsena in Italy. Supposedly named when Bishop Fugger sent his servant ahead to try local wines while journeying to meet the Pope in the 12th century. He was asked to write Est on the door of each inn whose wine was particularly good.

After trying the wine at Montefiascone, the servant left the enthusiastic message Est! Est!! Est!!! The bishop apparently died of intoxication.

Faro – one of the better-known Italian wines, grown around Messina.

Fendant – white Swiss wine from Valois; Switzerland's most famous.

Fermentazione naturale – Italian; natural fermentation, i.e. a sparkling wine made by either the Champagne or Tank Method. (See p. 154.)

Ferreira – well-known shippers of vintage port. 'An advancing decanter came under Fitch's hand. "Ah!" Fitch said. "As you will have observed, Ferreira '45. And Oporto bottled. You may be prompted to hint a criticism. You may judge us precipitate, since it will undoubtedly further develop and improve. But there is plenty downstairs, so we have indulged ourselves." He filled his glass . . .' J.I.M. Stewart *The Last Tresilians.*

Fiasco – Italian; flask, specifically the wicker-covered Chianti bottle, holding two litres. The plural is *fiaschi*. Our word 'fiasco' is from this origin – see p. 42.

Figari – see Vin de Corse.

Fiorano Rosso – a recommended Italian 'claret'.

Fitou – see Languedoc-Roussillon.

Fixin – see Côte de Nuits.

Fizz – champagne. 'I had champagne, too. Used to sleep all morning, then breakfast with my pint of fizz.' Robert Louis Stevenson and Lloyd Osbourne *The Wrecker.*

Fleurie – see Beaujolais.

Flor – a wild yeast found mainly in Jerez. It gives fino sherry its special taste. Also accounts for individual taste of *vin jaune* in the French Jura region.

Foianeghe Rosso – a recommended Italian 'claret'.

Foolish water – a 19th-century American term for champagne.

Forst – see Rheinpfalz.

France – see regional notes under Alsace, Bordeaux, Burgundy, Champagne, Corsica, Jura, Languedoc-Roussillon, Loire Valley, Rhône Valley,

South-West France, Savoie. Qualities – see *Appellation Controlee, VDQS (Vin Délimité de Qualité Supérieure), Vin de pays, Vin de table.*

Franken – one of the 11 German wine regions of designated quality (*Qualitäts-Anbaugebiete*). Names of particular significance within the region (according to wine experts) – Castell, Escherndorf, Hammelburg, Iphofen, Randersacker, Rodelsee, Volkath, Würzburg.

Fränkischer Landwein – see *Landwein.*

Frascati – one of the best Italian dry white wines.

Freiburg – see Baden.

Freundstück – see Rheinpfalz.

Frizzante – Italian; semi-sparkling.

Gaillac – see South-West France.

Geisbohl – see Rheinpfalz.

Geisenheim – see Rheingau.

Germany – see regional notes under Ahr, Baden, Franken, Hessische Bergstrasse, Mittelrhein, Mosel-Saar-Ruwer, Nahe, Rheingau, Rheinhessen, Rheinpfalz, Württemberg. Classifications – see *Tafelwein, Landwein,* QbA (*Qualitätswein bestimmter Anbaugebiete*), QmP (*Qualitätswein mit Prädikat*). See also Affenthaler, Liebfraumilch, Moselblümchen. The country is best-known for its white wines

Gevrey Chambertin – see Côte de Nuits.

Gigondas – see Rhône Valley.

Givry – see Région de Mercurey.

Glühwein – German; mulled red wine, with sugar, lemon and spices.

Goon – a flagon of wine in Australian slang.

Graach – see Mosel-Saar-Ruwer.

Grand Cru – French; great growth. Usually the classification of the highest quality wine.

Graves – a Bordeaux AC, known for its relatively cheap white wine, dry to medium sweet. The reds are said to be better.

Greece – known mostly for Retsina, but other wines include Amynteon, Cambas rosé, Castel Danielis, Cava Tsintalis, Château Carras, Demestica,

Imperial, Kleoni, Malvasia, Mantinea, Mavrodaphne, Muscat (of Patras, Rhodes, Rion, Samos), Naoussa, Nemea, Othello, Patras, Santa Helena, Tegea, Verdea.

Gumpoldskirchen – a fruity white Austrian wine from a village south of Vienna. 'This is a Gumpoldskirchner,' Garp would say, explaining the wine. 'It goes very well with the Schweinebraten.' 'What funny words,' Jenny remarked. John Irving *The World According to Garp.* Gumpoldskirchner Steinwein is a white variety.

Guntersblum – see Rheinhessen.

Halbtrocken – German; medium-dry.

Hallgarten – see Rheingau.

Hammelburg – see Franken.

Hattenheim – see Rheingau.

Haut-Médoc – a Bordeau AC.

Heidelberg – see Baden.

Herb – German; normally the word means harsh or bitter, applied to wine it means dry.

Hermitage – see Rhône Valley.

Hessische Bergstrasse – one of the 11 German wine regions of designated quality (*Qualitäts-Anbaugebiete*). A name within the region of particular significance (according to wine-experts) – Bensheim.

Heuriger – German; of this year's vintage.

Hipping – see Rheinhessen.

Hochheim – see Rheingau.

Hock – originally applied in English to wine from Hochheim, on the River Main. Now mainly applied to white wine from the Rhineland, sweet or dry.

Hohesburg – see Rheinpfalz.

Hospices – French; old people's home. Hospices de Beaune and Hospices de Nuit are named for institutions funded by the sale of wine from vineyards donated to them.

Hungary – famous historically for its Tokay and Bull's Blood, but Pecs Olaszriesling is well-known abroad. Hungary's other wines, mostly white, are mainly sold under varietal names. The wines from Somlo are said to help produce male children and impart long life.

Ihringen – see Baden.

Imbottigliato all' origine – Italian; estate-bottled.

Inferno – one of the better-known Italian wines, from Lombardy.

Iphofen – see Franken.

Italy – produces more wine than any other country, but to quote T.E. Carling, *The Complete Book of Drink,* 'The Italians are not vintage-minded.' Wines have varietal, geographical and fanciful names (Lacryma Christi 'Christ's tears'; Sangue di Guida 'Judas's blood'). Quality wines are now classified by the DOC (DOCG) system. Italy's best-known wines include – Asti Spumante, Barbaresco, Barbera, Bardolino, Barolo, Chianti, Corvo, Cortese di Gavi, Est! Est!! Est!!!, Faro, Frascati, Inferno, Lambrusco, Moscato d'Asti, Orvieto, Picolit, Soave, Spanna, Torgiano, Trentino, Valpantena, Valpolicella, Verdiccio. Wines described in the word-list as Italian 'clarets' are based on the Cabernet Sauvignon grape. All are recommended by Robert Joseph in *The Wine Lists.*

Jerez – a demarcated Spanish wine region.

Jesuitengarten – see Rheinpfalz.

Johannisberg – see Rheingau.

Juliénas – see Beaujolais.

Jumilla – a demarcated Spanish wine region.

Jura – a French wine region. Its specialities are *vin jaune* (Château-Chalon), *vin de paille* and *macvin.*

Jurançon – see South-West France.

Kabinett – German; lowest and driest of the five German grades of quality wines. See QmP.

Kallstadt – see Rheinpfalz.

Kanzem – see Mosel-Saar-Ruwer.

Kasel – see Mosel-Saar-Ruwer.

Kiedrich – see Rheingau.

Kirchenstück – see Rheinpfalz.

Klosterkeller – see Bulgaria.

Königswein – see Austria.

Lacryma Christi – also found as Lacrima Christi, 'tears of Christ'. Italian wine found in many versions: white, red and rosé; the best as

Lacryma Christi del Vesuvio. The legend is that Christ cried at the thought that so much wickedness could occur in a place as beautiful as the Bay of Naples. 'So now, Signor Giovanni, drink off your glass of lachryma.' Nathaniel Hawthorne *Rappaccini's Daughter.*

La Mancha - a demarcated Spanish wine region.

Lambrusco - Italian, popular sweet pink wine, though variously referred to as 'dental mouthwash' and 'alcoholic lemonade' by wine writers.

Lancers - a carbonated Portuguese rosé well known in the USA.

Landwein - German; country wine, the equivalent of French *vin de pays.* One step up from *Tafelwein*. The designated names are Ahrtaler Landwein, Bayerischer Bodensee Landwein, Frankischer Landwein, Landwein der Mosel, Landwein der Saar, Nahegauer Landwein, Pfalzer Landwein, Regensburger Landwein, Rheinburger Landwein, Rheinischer Landwein, Schwäbischer Landwein, Starkenburger Landwein, Südbadischer Landwein, Unterbadischer Landwein.

Languedoc-Roussillon - a wine-producing area in southern France. Important names within the region include Blanquette de Limoux, Corbières, Costières du Gard, Côtes du Roussillon, Côtes du Roussillon-Villages, Fitou, Minervois, St Chinian.

Liebfraumilch - trade name of a German wine, originally Liebfrauenstiftwein, after a church dedicated to the Virgin Mary. Produced in the Rheinhessen, Rheinpfalz, Nahe and Rheingau regions.

Lieser - see Mosel-Saar-Ruwer.

Lirac - see Rhône Valley.

Lisbon - formerly used of white wine produced in the province of Estremadura and exported from Lisbon. 'When the cloth was removed, and we had each made a tumbler of negus, of that liquor which hosts call Sherry, and guests call Lisbon, I perceived that the stranger seemed pensive . . .' Sir Walter Scott *The Monastery.*

Loire Valley - a French wine-producing area. Mainly white wines, including Muscadet (grape variety that produces white wine of the same name). Other important names in this region are Anjou, Beaumes de Venise, Bourgueil, Chinon, Coteaux de Layon, Crémant de Loire, Montlouis, Pouilly Fumé, Quincy, Reuilly, Saint Nicolas de Bourgueil, Sancerre, Saumur, Saumur Champigny, Savennières, Touraine, Vouvray.

Longuich - see Mosel-Saar-Ruwer.

Macvin - an aperitif wine produced in the Jura region of France. Red wine is mixed with marc and herbs.

Mâconnais - a Burgundy region. It includes Pouilly-Fuissé.

Madeira - a demarcated Portuguese wine region. See pp. 145-6. 'Madeira' is used as a generic term by wine-makers in the USA.

Madiran - see South-West France.

Main - German river name used to identify *Tafelwein.*

Malaga - a demarcated Spanish wine region. 'Malaga' is used as a generic term by wine-makers in the USA.

Manchuela - a demarcated Spanish wine region.

Margaux - a Bordeaux region which includes the famous Château Margaux and many other wines of top quality. 'Craig has ordered the oldest and most expensive wine on the menu, a 1953 Château Margaux.' Robert Daley *Only A Game.*

Markgraflerland - see Baden.

Marques de Murrieta - a wine-producer in the Rioja region of Spain. 'Sancho gave the order for two portions of sucking-pig and a bottle of the Marques de Murrieta's red wine. "I'm surprised that you favour the aristocracy," Father Quixote remarked. "They can be temporarily accepted for the good of the Party, like a priest."' Graham Greene *Monsignor Quixote.*

Marsannay-la-Côte - see Côte de Nuits.

Mateus Rosé - a well-known Portuguese carbonated rosé, sold in a flagon-shaped bottle.

Maximin-Grünhaus - see Mosel-Saar-Ruwer.

May Schoss - see Ahr.

Médoc - a Bordeaux AC.

Meersburg - see Baden.

Mentrida - a demarcated Spanish wine region.

Meursault - see Côte de Beaune.

Minervois - see Languedoc-Roussillon.

Mittelheim - see Rheingau.

Mittelrhein - one of the 11 German wine regions of designated quality (*Qualitäts-Anbaugebiete*). Names within the region of particular significance (according to wine experts) - Bacharach, Boppard, Oberwesel, Rheinburgengau, Siebengebirge Königswinter, Steeg.

Monbazillac - see South-West France.

Montagny - see Région de Mercurey.

Monthélie - see Côte de Beaune.

Montilla-Moriles - a demarcated Spanish wine region.

Montlouis - see Loire Valley.

Montravel - see South-West France.

Morey St Denis - see Côte de Nuits.

Morgon - an important Beaujolais area.

Mori-Vecio - a recommended Italian 'claret'.

Moscatel de Setubal - a Portuguese demarcated wine region, where an old classic grapey dessert wine is produced.

Moscato d'Asti - one of the better-known Italian wines.

Mosel - German river name used to identify *Tafelwein.*

Moselblümchen - German trade name ('little flower of the River Mosel') for a wine similar to Liebfraumilch.

Moselle - English name for white (light green) wine from the Mosel wine region in Germany. Also used as a generic term by wine-makers in the USA.

Mosel-Saar-Ruwer - one of the 11 German wine regions of designated quality (*Qualitäts-Anbaugebiete*). Names within the region of particular significance (according to wine-experts) - Ayl, Bernkastel, Braunenberg, Cochem, Dhron,

Eitelsbach, Enkirch, Erden, Graach, Kanzem, Kasel, Lieser, Longuich, Maximin-Grünhaus, Mülheim, Oberemmel, Ockfen, Piesport, Saarburg, Serrig, Traben-Trarbach, Trier, Trittenheim, Urzig, Waldrach, Wawern, Wehlen, Wiltingen, Zell.

Moulin-à-Vent - see Beaujolais.

Mountain - a term used in the 18th and 19th centuries for a variety of wine from Malaga, Spain. Made from grapes grown on the mountain sides.

Mousseux - French; sparkling.

Mülheim - see Mosel-Saar-Ruwer.

Mulled wine - wine heated by means of a red-hot poker being plunged into it. Sugar and spices often added. 'The mulled claret made me begin to feel a little mulled myself.' Peter de Vries *The Tunnel of Love.*

Münster-Sarmsheim - see Nahe.

Muscadet - see Loire Valley.

Nackenheim - see Rheinhessen.

Nahe - one of the 11 German wine regions of designated quality (*Qualitäts-Anbaugebiete*). Names within the region of particular significance (according to wine-experts) - Bad Kreuznach, Dorsheim, Münster-Sarmsheim, Niederhausen, Norheim, Schlossbockelheim, Traisen.

Nahegauer Landwein - see *Landwein.*

Napa Valley - see USA.

Nature - French; still (not sparkling).

Navarra - a demarcated Spanish wine region.

Neckar - German river name used to identify *Tafelwein.*

Nero - Italian; deep red.

Niederhausen - see Nahe.

Nierstein - see Rheinhessen.

Noble rot - *Botrytis cinerea*, a mould that affects white grapes in certain conditions, increasing the natural sugar content.

Norheim - see Nahe.

Nuits-St-Georges - see Côte de Nuits.

Oberemmel - see Mosel-Saar-Ruwer.

Oberrhein - German river name used to identify *Tafelwein.*

Oberwesel - see Mittelrhein.

Ockfen - see Mosel-Saar-Ruwer.

Oenology - The science of wine-making.

Oeschle - German; scale measuring sweetness of wine.

Oestrich - see Rheingau.

Oppenheim - see Rheinhessen.

Orvieto - one of the better-known Italian white wines. Comes in sweet and dry versions.

Pacherenc - see South-West France.

Palm wine - wine made from the fermented sap of tropical palm trees. 'We boys stopped to stare at the lorries that passed, or we loitered beside the palm shelters where palm-wine was sold in old beer bottles.' Margaret Laurence *This Side Jordan.*

Pastoso - Italian; medium-dry.

Patrimonio - see Vin de Corse.

Pauillac - a Bordeaux region which includes the famous Châteaux Lafite, Latour and Mouton.

Penedes - a demarcated Spanish wine region.

Perlant - French; very slightly sparkling.

Perlwein - German; light sparkling wine.

Pernand Vergelesses - see Côte de Beaune.

Pétillant - French; semi-sparkling.

Pettenthal - see Rheinhessen.

Pfalzer Landwein - see *Landwein.*

Picolit - one of the better-known Italian wines.

Piesport - see Mosel-Saar-Ruwer.

Pinkie - Australian slang for cheap wine.

Pipe - a cask for wine, 105 gallons (2 hogsheads). 'They look as though they'd been quarrelling.' 'Probably over whether to buy another pipe, or something like that. The sort of pipe that is an enormous barrel of port, and' - casting round in his mind for something else they might buy, he was assisted by memories of Edgar Allan Poe - 'and casks of Amontillado.' J.I.M. Stewart *The Last Tresilians.*

Pomerol - a Bordeaux region which includes the famous Château Petrus.

Pomino - a recommended Italian 'claret'.

Pommard - a Burgundy. See Côte de Beaune. 'I had scarce decency to let the man set the wine upon the table or put the butter alongside the bread, before my glass and my mouth were filled. Exquisite bread of the Café Cluny, exquisite first glass of Old Pommard tingling to my wet feet . . .' Robert Louis Stevenson and Lloyd Osbourne *The Wrecker.*

Pop - a light-hearted colloquialism for Champagne.

Porto-Vecchio - see Vin de Corse.

Portugal - mainly known for port, Madeira and the carbonated rosé wines, of which Mateus Rosé and Lancers are the largest producers. The Portuguese demarcated regions are Algarve, Bairrada, Bucelas, Carcavelos, Colares, Dão, Douro, Madeira, Moscatel de Setubal, Vinhos Verdes. Much undemarcated table wine of good quality is also produced. '12 Mar 1713 - I can't drink now at all with any pleasure. I love white Portugal wine better than claret, Champagne or Burgundy.' Jonathan Swift *Journal to Stella.*

Pouilly Fumé - see Loire Valley.

Pouilly-Fuissé - see Mâconnais. 'He had celebrated in verse the golden wines of the Pouilly-Fuissé, or the ruby ones of Clochemerle, Juliénas, Morgon, Moulin à Vent, etc.' Gabriel Chevallier *Clochemerle-Babylon* (trans. Edward Hyams).

Pourriture noble - French; noble rot.

Premier cru - French; first growth, but the second rank of Burgundy.

Priorato - a demarcated Spanish wine region.

Puligny-Montrachet - see Côte de Beaune.

QbA - German; the letters stand for *Qualitätswein bestimmter Anbaugebiete*, an official classification for wine of middle-quality. Grape varieties and sugar content are specified. Subject to analytical and taste tests.

QmP - German; the letters stand for *Qualitätswein mit Prädikat*, an official classification for distinguished wine of the highest quality. Sub-divisions of QmP wine, made from grapes that are rich enough in sugar to need no artifical enrichment, in ascending order are *Kabinett, Spätlese, Auslese, Beerenauslese – Ausbruch* (Austria only), *Trockenbeerenauslese, Eiswein.*

Quincy – see Loire Valley.

Quinta – Portuguese; estate.

Randersacker – see Franken.

Rasteau – a sweet fortified wine from the Rhône Valley, in France.

Rauenthal – see Rheingau.

Récolte – French; crop, vintage.

Redders – Oxford University slang for red wine.

Red ink – early American slang for red wine.

Red Ned – Australian slang for red wine.

Regensburger Landwein – see *Landwein.*

Région de Mercurey – a Burgundy region. Important names within it include Givry, Montagny, Rully.

Reserva – Spanish, Portuguese; aged in the cask.

Retsina – Greek; adaptation of Italian *resina* 'resin'. White wine with added pine-resin, popular in Greece for 3000 years. In central Greece 80% of the wine produced is retsina. 'The whole village turned out to give us the promised farewell dinner of lamb on the spit and gold rezina wine.' Lawrence Durrell *Clea.*

Reuilly – see Loire Valley.

Rhein – German river name used to identify *Tafelwein.*

Rheinburgengau – see Mittelrhein.

Rheinburger Landwein – see *Landwein.*

Rheingau – one of the 11 German wine regions of designated quality (*Qualitäts-Anbaugebiete*). Names of particular significance within the region (according to wine experts) – Assmannshausen, Eltville, Erbach, Geisenheim, Hallgarten, Hatenheim, Hochheim, Johannisberg (the best), Kiedrich, Mittelheim, Oestrich, Rauenthal, Rüdesheim, Winkel.

Rheinhessen – one of the 11 German wine regions of designated quality

(*Qualitäts-Anbaugebiete*). Names of particular significance within the region (according to wine experts) – Alzey, Bingen, Guntersblum, Hipping, Nackenheim, Nierstein, Oppenheim, Pettenthal, Rothenberg, Worms.

Rheinischer Landwein – see *Landwein.*

Rheinpfalz – one of the 11 German wine regions of designated quality (*Qualitäts-Anbaugebiete*). Pfalz is 'the Palatinate' (territory in south-west Germany once ruled by feudal lords with supreme judicial authority over a province). Names of particular significance within the region (according to wine experts) – Bad Durkheim, Deidesheim, Forst, Freundstück, Geisbohl, Hohesburg, Jesuitengarten, Kallstadt, Kirchenstück, Ruppertsberg, Ungstein, Wachenheim.

Rhenish – wine from the German Rhineland; hock.

Rhine – used as a generic term by wine-makers in the USA.

Rhône Valley – a French wine-growing area. Most of the wine is sold as Côtes-du-Rhône or Côtes-du-Rhône Villages. Other important names from this region are Château Grillet, Châteauneuf-du-Pape, Condrieu, Cornas, Côte Rôtie, Crozes-Hermitage, Gigondas, Hermitage, Lirac, St-Joseph, St-Peray, Tavel, Tricastin.

Ribeiro – a demarcated Spanish wine region.

Rioja – the best-known Spanish wines apart from sherry come from this region, which has the sub-divisions Rioja Alta, Rioja Alavesa and Rioja Baja. Wines of Rioja Alta are considered to be the best. Red Riojas are matured in oak casks and can have an oakey flavour.

Rise and shine – also silk and twine, string and twine. American rhyming slang terms for wine mentioned by Julian Franklyn in his *Dictionary of Rhyming Slang.*

Riserva – Italian; aged in the cask.

Rodelsee – see Franken.

Romania – the country has a wine-making history which stretches back to the 14th century. Its Tirnave Riesling, from Transylvania, is well-known, but other wines are of a generally high standard.

Rosado – Spanish, Portuguese; rosé.

Rosato – Italian; rosé.

Rosé – French; pink wine.

Rosé d'Arbois – a high quality rosé wine from the Jura region.

Roséwein – German; rosé wine.

Rosso – Italian; red.

Rosso Armentano – a recommended Italian 'claret'.

Rothenberg – see Rheinhessen.

Rotwein – German; red wine.

Rüdesheim – see Rheingau.

Rully – see Région de Mercurey.

Ruppertsberg – see Rheinpfalz.

Saarburg – see Mosel-Saar-Ruwer.

Sack – also sherris-sack. (See p. 70).

St-Amour – see Beaujolais. (Since *amour* means 'love' there is a pleasant local legend that the name arose when a Roman soldier married a girl from the village. The name is more likely to derive from a 5th-century bishop whose name was Amator.)

St-Aubin – see Côte de Beaune.

St Chinian – see Languedoc-Roussillon.

St Emilion – a Bordeaux AC, named after a picturesque medieval town. Its best-known wine is Château Cheval-Blanc.

St-Estephe – a Bordeaux AC.

St-Joseph – see Rhône Valley.

St-Julien – a Bordeaux AC, described by wine-writer Robert Joseph as 'amongst the top levels of the aristocracy'.

St Nicolas de Bourgueil – see Loire Valley.

St-Peray – see Rhône Valley.

St-Romain – see Côte de Beaune.

Salvagnin – red Swiss wine from the Vaud region.

Sancerre – see Loire Valley

San Leonardo – a recommended Italian 'claret'.

Santenay – see Côte de Beaune.

Sartene – see Vin de Corse.

Sassicaia – a recommended Italian 'claret'.

Saumur - see Loire Valley.

Saumur Champigny - see Loire Valley.

Sauternes - a Bordeaux AC, known especially for its sweet, golden wines. 'Sauterne' is used as a generic term by wine-makers in the USA.

Savennières - see Loire Valley.

Savoie - a French wine-producing region. The most important names from this region are Crépy and Seyssel.

Schaumwein - German; sparkling wine of higher quality than *Perlwein*, lower quality than *Sekt*.

Schlossböckelheim - see Nahe.

Schwäbischer Landwein - see *Landwein*.

Sec - French; dry.

Secco - Italian; dry.

Seco - Spanish; dry.

Sekt - German; originally from French *sec* 'dry', but it now means good quality sparkling wine.

Serrig - see Mosel-Saar-Ruwer.

Seyssel - see Savoie.

Sherry - see pp. 141-43.

Siebengebirge Königswinter - see Mittelrhein.

Sillery - a high quality still white wine produced in the Champagne region of France. Frequently referred to in 19th-century English literature. The name of a French marquis who was the first to ship wines from the Champagne region to England in the 17th century.

Slantchev Birag - see Bulgaria.

Soave - white Italian wine, best drunk young.

Solera - a system whereby new wine is gradually blended with mature wine. Used especially in the production of sherry and Madeira.

Sonnenküste - see Bulgaria.

South Africa - the Cape Province is the main wine-producing area, especially of brandy, sherries and ports. The country has Wine of Origin Superior (WOS) laws. These designated 14 wine-growing areas and established rules about the use of varietal names and vintage years. The best vineyards are allowed to use the word 'estate' on the label.

South-West France - wines from this region include Bergerac, Cahors, Côtes de Buzet, Côtes de Duras, Côtes du Frontonnais, Gaillac, Jurançon, Madiran, Monbazillac, Montravel, Pacherenc.

Spain - mainly known in the past for sherry, Malaga and Montilla (see pp. 141-47). Quality of its wines has improved dramatically since the 1960s. The demarcated wine regions are - Alella, Alicante, Almansa, Ampurdan-Costa Brava, Carinena, Cheste, Condado de Huelva, Jerez, Jumilla, La Mancha, Malaga, Manchuela, Mentrida, Montilla-Moriles, Navarra, Penedes, Priorato, Ribeiro, Rioja, Tarragona, Utiel-Requena, Valdeorras, Valencia, Valdepeñas, Yecla. The best-known of these are Rioja, Penedes, Ribeiro, Tarragona, Valdepeñas.

Spanna - one of the better-known Italian wines.

Spätlese - German; late gathering. Wine made from grapes harvested late.

Spitzenwein - German; top (quality) wine.

Spritzig - German; semi-sparkling, slightly fizzy.

Spumante - Italian; sparkling.

Starkenburger Landwein - see *Landwein*.

Steam - Australian slang for cheap wine or methylated spirits.

Steeg - see Mittelrhein.

Steinwein - German; traditional name for wine from Franconia.

Südbadischer Landwein - see *Landwein*.

Tafelwein - German; table wine. The name of the nearest river or lake is used to identify it - Bodensee, Main, Mosel, Neckar, Oberrhein, Rhein.

Tarragona - a demarcated Spanish wine region.

Tavel - a dry rosé wine from the Rhône Valley, the best of its kind. 'It was hardly done to drink Tavel so early in the morning but I could never resist the colour or the taste; Toby, true to taste, gulped at an *anisette*'. Lawrence Durrell *Monsieur*.

Tent - deep red Spanish wine. The word is found in the 17th century and is a corruption of Spanish *tinto*.

Tiganello - a recommended Italian 'claret'.

Tinto - Spanish, Portuguese; red.

Tokay - famous ultra-sweet wine from north-east Hungary. Said to have medicinal properties. The highest quality is known as Tokay escencia. 'Tokay' is used as a generic term by wine-makers in the USA.

Tonic wines - mainly port or Burgundy-type wines with added medicinal ingredients. Leading brands include Buckfast, Emu, Enervin, Vibrona, Wincarnis.

Torgiano - one of the better-known Italian wines.

Torre Ercolano - a recommended Italian 'claret'.

Touraine - see Loire Valley.

Traben-Trarbach - see Mosel-Saar-Ruwer.

Traisen - see Nahe.

Trentino - one of the better-known Italian wines.

Tricastin - see Rhône Valley.

Trier - see Mosel-Saar-Ruwer.

Trittenheim - see Mosel-Saar-Ruwer.

Trocken - German; dry.

Trockenbeerenauslese - German; the highest quality of German and Austrian wine, made from grapes which have become exceptionally concentrated in flavour and sugar content after being attacked by noble rot. See *Prädikatswein*.

Ungstein - see Rheinpfalz.

Unterbadischer Landwein - see *Landwein*.

Urzig - see Mosel-Saar-Ruwer.

USA - the Napa Valley of California is the most famous wine-growing region in the USA, and California generally is to America what the Bordeaux region is to France. Oregon is perhaps as important as the Burgundy region, and wineries of high repute are to be found in Idaho, Maryland, Missouri, New Jersey, New York, Virginia and Washington. Many other states produce wine of good quality. Wines are described by grape variety, though the use of the following generic terms is permitted – burgundy, chablis, champagne, chianti, claret, hock, madeira, malaga, moselle, port, rhine, sauterne, sherry, tokay. Needless to say, wines bearing these descriptions do not often taste like the European originals. The main varietal wines from California are (red) Zinfandel, Carignane, Cabernet Sauvignon, Barbera, Ruby Cabernet, Grenache; (white) French Colombard, Chenin Blanc, Chardonnay, White Riesling, Sauvignon Blanc, Palomino, Gewurztraminer.

Utiel-Requena – a demarcated Spanish wine region.

Valdeorras – a demarcated Spanish wine region.

Valencia – a demarcated Spanish wine region.

Valdepeñas – a demarcated Spanish wine region.

Valpantena – one of the better-known Italian wines.

Valpolicella – well-known light red wine of northern Italy.

Varietal – description of wine by variety of grape that has mainly been used in its production.

VDQS – French; the letters stand for *vin délimité de qualité supérieure*, 'demarcated wine of a superior quality'. These wines are approaching what is taken to be the highest quality of all, *Appellation Controlée*.

Vendanges – French; grape harvest.

Vendemmia – Italian; vintage.

Venegazzù – a classic Italian 'claret'.

Verdicchio – one of the better-known Italian dry white wines, sold in a distinctive amphora-shaped bottle.

Vibrona – a proprietary tonic wine.

Vin – French; wine.

Vin de Corse – wine from the island of Corsica. This description is sometimes followed by a specific name, such as Calvi, Coteaux d'Ajaccio, Coteaux du Cap Corse, Figari, Patrimonio (said to be the best), Porto-Vecchio, Sartene.

Vin de paille – French; straw wine. Dessert wine produced in the Jura region from grapes which have been

brought inside and allowed to ripen on straw during the winter.

Vin de pays – French; regional wine. Of a higher quality than vin de table but below VDQS. Prices should be reasonable.

Vin de table – French; table wine. Everyday wine, making no claims to distinction.

Vin gris – French; grey wine. Of a pale red colour, made from red grapes which are pressed before fermentation sets in.

Vin jaune – French; yellow wine. A sherry-like yellowish wine from the Jura region. Affected by the flor yeast.

Vinho consumo – Portuguese; table wine.

Vinho generoso – Portugese; strong dessert wine.

Vinhos Verdes – Portuguese; (region of) green (new) wines, to be drunk in the spring following their production. The wines can be red or white and are light, slightly sparkling and dry, though sometimes sweetened for foreign markets.

Vino da pasto/tavola – Italian; table wine.

Vino de masa/pasto – Spanish; table wine.

Vin ordinaire – French; ordinary (cheap) wine.

Vino verde – Spanish; green (young) wine.

Volkach – see Franken.

Volnay – see Côte de Beaune.

Voslauer – Austrian red and white wines of good repute.

Vosne-Romanée – see Côte de Nuits.

Vougeot – see Côte de Nuits.

Vouvray – see Loire Valley.

Wachenheim – see Rheinpfalz.

Waldrach – see Mosel-Saar-Ruwer.

Walporzheim – see Ahr.

Wawern – see Mosel-Saar-Ruwer.

Wehlen – see Mosel-Saar-Ruwer.

Weingutesiegel – German; good wine seal. A seal awarded in Austria for wines of superior quality.

Weissherbst – German; rosé QbA wine made from a single variety of grape.

Weisswein – German; white wine.

Wiltingen – see Mosel-Saar-Ruwer.

Wincarnis – a proprietary tonic wine.

Wine-dot – Australian slang for an addict of cheap wine.

Winkel – see Rheingau.

Worms – see Rheinhessen.

Württemberg – one of the 11 German wine regions of designated quality (*Qualitäts-Anbaugebiete*). A name of particular significance within the region (according to wine experts) – Weinsberg.

Würzburg – see Franken.

Yecla – a demarcated Spanish wine region.

Yugoslavia – known mainly for its Laski Riesling, light, fresh and fruity. The history of Dalmatian wine-making stretches back to the 6th century BC. A number of interesting red and white wines are produced.

Zell – see Mosel-Saar-Ruwer.

Zeltingen-Rachtig – see Mosel-Saar-Ruwer.

WINE CONSUMPTION PER HEAD

Litres per head

Country	1970	1975	1980	1984	1985	1986	1987	1988	1989
European Community									
Belgium	14.2	17.8	20.6	22.9	22.7	21.7	23.0	23.8	23.0
Denmark	5.9	11.5	14.0	18.9	20.7	19.6	20.6	21.6	19.2
France	109.1	103.7	91.0	82.0	79.7	76.4	75.1	74.0	74.0
Greece	40.0	38.0	44.9	43.9	42.5	37.0	31.8	32.0	29.9
Ireland, Rep. of	3.3	4.2	3.6	3.3	3.5	3.5	3.5	3.9	4.1
Italy	113.7	103.9	92.9	90.5	84.8	73.3	70.0	65.0	63.0
Netherlands	5.2	10.3	12.9	15.2	15.0	14.9	14.6	14.8	14.8
Portugal	72.5	89.8	68.7	84.2	87.0	70.0	64.3	58.0	53.0
Spain	61.5	76.0	64.7	48.0	48.0	47.0	54.0	40.6	37.6
West Germany	17.2	23.4	25.8	25.7	25.4	23.3	21.1	20.9	21.1
UK	3.7	6.3	8.1	10.4	10.9	11.3	12.0	12.4	12.8
Rest of Europe									
Austria	34.6	35.1	35.8	36.4	34.3	32.8	33.9	34.2	35.2
Bulgaria	20.9	23.5	22.0	23.4	20.2	22.1	22.5	22.5	21.8
Czechoslovakia	14.6	16.3	15.5	15.5	16.0	12.3	13.7	13.0	13.8
East Germany	5.0	7.4	9.6	10.9	10.3	10.9	11.7	12.1	12.1
Finland	3.3	5.1	4.8	4.7	4.5	4.9	5.1	5.5	6.0
Hungary	37.7	34.2	35.0	30.7	24.8	23.2	21.5	22.0	20.0
Iceland	1.8	3.0	6.0	7.9	7.3	6.8	6.8	6.1	5.7
Norway	2.3	3.3	4.4	4.4	5.1	5.2	5.9	6.4	6.6
Poland	5.6	7.5	10.1	8.3	7.9	8.2	8.4	7.7	7.7
Romania	23.1	33.0	28.9	29.0	29.0	28.0	28.0	28.0	17.2
Sweden	6.4	8.3	9.5	11.6	11.7	12.0	11.9	12.0	12.5
Switzerland	41.9	43.9	47.4	49.9	49.6	48.6	49.5	49.9	49.6
USSR	15.2	13.4	14.4	14.5	11.6	5.6	5.7	6.4	6.5
Yugoslavia	28.3	28.2	28.2	29.0	26.5	27.5	27.5	21.1	21.1
Africa									
Nigeria	..	..	..	..	..	..	..	..	..
South Africa	9.2	10.4	8.8	9.1	9.2	8.9	9.3	8.3	9.1
Asia									
China	..	..	..	..	..	..	..	..	..
Japan	0.3	0.5	0.5	0.8	0.8	0.7	0.9	0.9	1.2
Korea, Rep. of	..	..	..	..	..	..	..	0.4	0.4
Philippines	..	..	3.5	3.5	3.5	3.5	..	..	..
Australasia									
Australia	9.0	12.1	17.4	20.4	21.3	21.6	20.6	21.0	19.1
New Zealand	5.9	8.7	13.5	14.0	14.4	16.4	15.3	15.1	15.5
North America									
Canada	4.2	6.2	9.0	9.8	10.2	10.0	10.2	10.3	10.9
USA	5.0	6.4	7.9	8.9	9.0	9.2	9.1	8.5	7.9
Central and South America									
Argentina	91.8	83.7	75.8	66.3	60.1	60.0	58.1	55.5	52.6
Brazil	1.8	2.0	2.6	2.5	2.5	2.5	1.5	1.5	1.8
Chile	40.5	41.9	46.9	39.7	40.0	40.0	35.0	35.0	27.4
Colombia	..	..	..	..	..	..	..	0.6	..
Cuba	0.9	0.2	..	..	..	..	..	..	..
Mexico	0.3	0.2	0.3	0.3	0.5	0.3	0.5	0.4	0.3
Peru	1.1	1.0	1.0	0.6	0.6	0.6	0.6	0.6	0.6
Venezuela	..	0.8	0.7	0.7	0.7	0.7	0.7	0.7	0.7

LIFTING THE SPIRITS

Spirits and liqueurs

THE various beers and wines so far discussed in this book all derive from the simple, natural process of fermentation. For beer it is first necessary to prepare a malt, which is liquefied to become a 'mash'. For wine all that is needed is 'must', grape juice (with or without the skins) obtained by crushing the grapes. Fermented mash is beer, fermented must is wine.

Spirits, which constitute the third great family of alcoholic drinks, require another basic process to be applied to those fermented drinks – distillation. Repeated or fractional distillation of a fermented liquid is known as rectification. Broadly speaking, the distillation of a beer-type liquid leads to a whisky; rectification of such a liquid creates gin or schnapps. The distillation of wine gives rise to brandy. As it happens, the starting liquid used to obtain whisky is referred to as the 'wash' rather than beer.

Distillation refers to heating a liquid until it turns to vapour, then cooling the vapour so that it reverts to liquid form. Water, as we know, turns to steam when it boils at 100°C. Even those of us who are unscientific in the extreme know that it is possible to separate the salt from sea-water by simple distillation.

The alcohol in beer or wine vaporises at 78.5°C. It is clear, then, that heating a liquid which contains alcohol to a temperature above 78.5°C but below 100°C will cause the alcohol to separate from the original liquid in vapour form. The vapour can be gathered and recondensed into a liquid of much greater alcoholic strength. It will not be pure alcohol, since water gives off some vapours at even relatively low temperatures. If it did not, to quote L. W. Marrison in *Wines and Spirits*, 'nothing once wetted would ever dry until it was heated to boiling point'. At the boiling-point of alcohol, then, water already has a very strong tendency to vaporise.

The vapour that is given off during distillation contains more than just alcohol – by which is meant ethyl alcohol – and water. This has to be so, or any distillate of a beer-mash or wine-must would be exactly the same. The individual characteristics that give a distilled liquor its own 'personality' are known as congeners or congenerics. They include (to quote a scientific account) 'higher alcohols, aldehydes, ethers, esters, volatile acids, furfural and other organic compounds'.

These congeners all have boiling points lower than water and are therefore vaporised with the ethyl alcohol. They are present in the distillate in only tiny quantities, but have a dramatic effect on its character, aroma and flavour.

HISTORY OF DISTILLING

It would be interesting to know for certain who first discovered the basic fact about distillation, that different liquids have different boiling (and freezing) points. It would provide a clue as to how long Man has been making distilled alcoholic drinks. Aristotle, born 384 BC, mentions casually that pure water can be obtained from sea-water. He does not say how it is done.

The first distillers were probably perfume-makers, perhaps those of Mesopotamia in 3500 BC. What they were distilling, however, was not necessarily a fermented liquid. Then came the physicians, such as Hippocrates of Cos (469–399 BC). He refers to 'boiled-down wine' in some of his remedies, and other Greek physicians write about wine-concentrates. Unfortunately, there is nowhere an unambiguous reference to distillation: it can only be inferred that it was being used. Nor is it known to what use the wine-concentrates were being put. It may be that they were only applied externally, to cleanse wounds.

KIJAFA

'We must drink to happiness,' he said, and poured Kijafa into two glasses. He handed her one, lifted his own, and looked directly into her eyes. '*Skal!*' he said.

'*Skal!*' she said, returning his look with equal earnestness. Each took a sip of the Kijafa and looked meaningfully at the other again.

James Reid Parker *The Merry Wives of Massachusetts*

It is assumed that Arab physicians learned the art of distillation from the Greeks. In the Arab world, once again, it would seem that the external use of distillates for medical or cosmetic purposes would have been far more likely, for obvious religious reasons, than their use in alcoholic drinks. The Arab contribution to the history of distillation is not in doubt. As we have already seen, the word 'alcohol' itself derives from Arabic. Other words of significance from that language include *al-ixsir* 'elixir', *al-raqa* 'arrack' (literally 'sweat') and *al-anbik* 'alembic', another word for a 'still'. *Al-anbik* is particularly interesting because it adapts Greek *ambix* 'vase for distillation' and thus demonstrates the Greek-Arab connection.

Concrete facts begin to replace speculation once we reach the 11th century. In Italy by that time a brandy-type alcohol was being prepared by the distillation of wine. The making of cognac is recorded in France from the 14th century but must have been occurring long before that date. As for malt-based distillation, a primitive whisky was being made in Ireland by the 12th century. The Irish took their knowledge of the process to Scotland, where 'the first recorded allusion to a spirit distilled from barley', according to David Daiches, in *Scotch Whisky Past and Present*, 'is found in the Scottish Exchequer Rolls for 1494'. The reference there is to malt, 'wherewith to

TO WHISKY

You are the prowler of the night
To the beds of virgins;
O God! what powers you have
To gain kindness from girls.

A Gaelic Toast

make aquavitae'. Gin was first produced in the Netherlands in the 17th century.

COGNAC

Of the distilled spirits, then, which are of widespread importance in modern times, the one that has been produced longest is brandy. 'Brandy' derives from Dutch *brandewijn*, a term that was anglicised in the 17th century as 'brandy wine'. The first part of the Dutch word translates as 'burnt', referring to the heat that is applied to the still. In normal use 'brandy' used on its own refers to a spirit distilled from wine, which in turn is made from grapes. 'Wine', though, sometimes describes the fermented juice of fruits other than the grape. If those wines are distilled the liquor that results may be called cherry brandy, apricot brandy, etc.

A specific kind of brandy is 'Cognac', produced in the Charente and Charente Maritime departments of France, centred on the town of Cognac. The area around the town is divided into six regions, two of which (Grande and Petite Champagne) are thought to produce brandy of an exceptional quality. Some people use Cognac as a synonym of brandy, but in France use of the word within the trade is carefully controlled. Cognac is made in a special way, in a well-defined area, using only certain varieties of grape. By general consent, it is brandy at its best.

Tradition is everything in the making of Cognac. The House of Martell, for example, uses a still, or distilling apparatus, of a type that was already in use in the 16th century. It consists of a copper boiler, known as a Charentais pot, in the shape of an onion. Wine is poured into the pot, which is then gently heated over a naked flame. As the vapour rises it is collected and condensed in a swan-neck pipe at the top, to produce a distilled liquid known at this stage as the *brouillis*.

The *brouillis* is then distilled again to produce the so-called *bonne chauffé*. Slightly impure substances are produced at the start of the second distillation, so these 'heads', as they are called, are removed. Then comes the 'heart' of the *bonne chauffé*, followed by the 'tails', which are again slightly impure and have to be removed. What is left is a raw and fiery brandy. This has to be aged for many years in oak casks before being blended.

Even that last statement considerably oversimplifies the situation. The oak that is used to make the casks for Cognac can only come from the forests of Limousin or Troncais. The staves are left to season for several years before the casks are assembled, a necessary stage if certain tannins and acids in the wood are to be removed. Finally the coopers assemble the casks, using external metal hoops but no glue or nails which might come into contact with the brandy.

THE ANGEL'S SHARE

Once in the cask, Cognac undergoes a slow oxidation which mellows it and gives it a great deal of its character. During this lengthy period, the clear liquid that emerged from the *bonne chauffé* slowly changes to an amber colour. There is also a loss in alcoholic strength, and a loss of the Cognac itself by evaporation. Depending on the age of the brandy, the loss can be as much as 4 per cent per year. That sounds an insignificant figure; it becomes considerably more significant when translated, in Martell's case, into its equivalent of two million bottles a year.

This loss is known philosophically, or poetically, as 'the angel's share'. There is also a saying amongst the brandy-producers that 'the sun is our best customer'. The only outward sign of its occurrence is said to be in the black mould that forms on the walls and roofs of buildings in the Cognac region.

Martell was founded in 1715, making it the oldest of the great Cognac houses. The Irishman

Richard Hennessy founded the company that bears his family name in 1765. He had learned to appreciate Cognac while fighting with the French against the English. Rémy Martin dates from 1724 and now specialises in VSOP Fine Champagne Cognac. 'Champagne', incidentally, does not refer in that context to the sparkling drink. In the name Grande Champagne, a specific area within the Cognac region, 'Champagne' is a French form of Latin *campania* 'open country'. 'Fine Champagne' can only be applied to Cognac if at least 50 per cent of it comes from that area.

I mentioned that Cognac is produced in a traditional pot still; I should add quickly that most commercial distilling makes use of the patent, continuous or Coffey, still. Aeneas Coffey was the name of the Irishman who patented it in 1831, but as Pamela Vandyke Price points out in *The Penguin Book of Spirits and Liqueurs*, his surname happens to be useful in explaining how his still works. 'Its operation is indeed somewhat akin to that of a complex coffee percolator.' Perhaps that is all that needs to be said about it here: those interested in precise details will easily find them in specialised scientific literature.

MARC

Cognac is known throughout the world; the more everyday brandy of France, *marc*, is little-known outside that country. The word was partly adapted into English as 'murk', but *marc* is usually left untranslated. In its French form it sets a trap for English-speakers, since the final -c is not pronounced. It is therefore found in some 17th-century texts as 'marre'. *Marc* itself derives from *marcher* 'to walk, tread' and is a reminder of the time when barefooted peasants used to tread the grapes. It is unkindly rumoured that in order to add to the wine's flavour they did not always wash their feet.

Every wine region used to produce its own *marc*; that of Burgundy has long had the reputation of being the best. It is made from the 'murk' in the English sense – the final pressing of the grapeskins, pips and stems that remain after the season's wine has been made. The juice is fermented in the usual way, then distilled. Until recent times a great deal of small-scale production occurred, using pot stills of the simplest kind. This could produce a lethal drink unless the 'heads', which contain a high proportion of methanol, were scrupulously rejected.

Local production of this kind may continue, but wine-producers know that they can sell the wine from their final pressings to be used as industrial alcohol. Writers of the future, therefore, may not be able to repeat the comment of Gabriel Chevallier in *Clochemerle-Babylon*: 'The local *marc*, as indispensable as vodka to the Russians or schnapps to the Scandinavians, gives them that extra warmth which enables them to face the cold.'

I implied that *marc* had no English translation, but it could be argued that 'grappa' serves that purpose. *Grappa* means 'grape-stalk' in Italian, but is used for the Italian equivalent of *marc*. For most English-speakers the word now means a strong, fairly harsh brandy. California grappa, for instance, is a fiery drink which has none of the mellowness of brandy that has been aged in the wood. In Spain, *marc* becomes *aguardiente* (*de orujo*), in Portugal it is *bagaceira*.

ARMAGNAC

Another brandy which goes by a special name is Armagnac. Written references to it in the 15th century pre-date mentions of Cognac. The name was formerly that of a French province in Gascony, in the south-west of France, now mainly in the department of Gers. Armagnac is made from local grapes at Condom (named after a Gaul called Condus) and other small towns in the region. Its production differs from that of Cognac in that it results from a single distillation; it also ages far more quickly than Cognac.

After that, the differences between Armagnac and Cognac become more subjective. Some say that Armagnac is harsher and drier than Cognac. In other circles, Armagnac is described as a feminine brandy, where Cognac is masculine. Whether this has to do with a difference in strength, or with the marked fragrance of Armagnac, is difficult to say. It is true that women enjoy Armagnac, but so do many men. It is certainly worth trying it at the end of a meal as an alternative to Cognac.

Although it is usual to drink brandy after dinner, the British are renowned for drinking it at

---

FLOWERS OF THE PYRENEES

The waiter recommended a Basque liqueur called Izzarra. He brought in the bottle and poured a liqueur-glass full. He said Izzarra was made of the flowers of the Pyrenees. It looked like hair-oil and smelled like Italian *strega*. I told him to take the flowers of the Pyrenees away and bring me a *vieux marc*. The *marc* was good. I had a second *marc* after the coffee. The waiter seemed a little offended about the flowers of the Pyrenees, so I overtipped him.

Ernest Hemingway *The Sun Also Rises*

---

any time of the day. That seems to have been the case for a long time. Jonathan Swift tells Stella at one point: 'I have never been giddy, dear Stella, since that morning: I have taken a whole box of pills, and kecked at them every night, and drank a pint of brandy at mornings.' Notice not only when Swift drank his brandy, but how much of it.

We must assume that the brandy that was formerly consumed in England was considerably weaker than it is now. How else can we account for the great quantities that were drunk at any time of the day? Dickensian characters are constantly drinking it in half-pint glasses, mixed half-and-half with water. In *The Pickwick Papers* Jingle, a hardened drinker, swallows 'full half a pint of the reeking brandy-and-water' without pausing for breath. Sam Weller does not like it heated to that extent, so orders 'nine-penn'orth o' brandy-and-water luke'.

BRANDY-AND-WATER

Earlier in the novel we are told that 'to keep up their good humour, they stopped at the first roadside tavern they came to, and ordered a glass of brandy and water all round, with a magnum of extra strength for Mr Samuel Weller'. Use of that word 'magnum' suggests that Sam drank not only a bottle of brandy, but one which was about twice the usual size. In fact this is a rare example of Dickens misusing a word. Later, when he was rich and famous, he came to know magnums well. Magnums of sherry, port and claret from his cellar at Gad's Hill were auctioned after his death. In his youth, however, he evidently thought that a magnum was a large glass.

Most of Dickens's references to brandy show that it was usually drunk in the manner indicated by Jingle: 'Glasses round – brandy and water, hot and strong, and sweet, and plenty.' In *Nicholas Nickleby* Mr Squeers treats himself to 'a stiff tumbler of brandy-and-water, made on the liberal half-and-half principle, allowing for the dissolution of the sugar'.

Squeers has just completed a long journey, but men rarely needed an excuse for drinking brandy; ladies could delicately claim to be taking it as medicine. The point is made in *Barnaby Rudge*, where Mrs Varden is helped upstairs by

Miss Miggs. That good lady gives her 'brandy-and-water not over weak, and divers other cordials, also of a stimulating quality, administered at first in teaspoons and afterwards in increasing doses, and of which Miss Miggs herself partook as a preventative measure (for fainting is infectious)'.

Brandy is still commonly drunk with water. The Anglo-Indian expression for the mixture was brandy-pawnee, the second word deriving from Hindi *pani* 'water'. Jos Sedley, in Thackeray's *Vanity Fair*, is said to drink a great deal of it. In France, a normal order in a café is *une fine à l'eau*, or *une fine* (pronounced 'feen') if no water is required. The word is occasionally used in an English context to help create a French atmosphere. In *Stop at Nothing*, for instance, John Welcome writes: 'My idea was to have a few *fines* and see what they could do to help me.'

Another association with brandy is coffee. French children are sometimes given *un canard* 'a duck', which is a lump of sugar soaked in brandy and dipped in black coffee. Lizzie Hexam, in *Our Mutual Friend*, gives some to her father to put in his tea. A more bizarre mixture is mentioned in Nathaniel West's *The Day of the Locust*: 'He shared the great quantity of cheap brandy they mixed with hot water and salt butter and drank out of tin cups.'

BRANDY GLASSES

Tin cups are not really to be recommended for brandy-drinking. The taste of any drink is affected by the container from which it is drunk, but none more so than brandy. Experts suggest using a glass which is 'small enough to nestle in the palm of the hand and thin enough for the warmth of the hand to penetrate it and thus bring out the bouquet. The top of the glass must be narrower than the main body so as to prevent a too rapid evaporation of the aroma, but wide enough to enable the nose to fulfil its role.'

Notice the reference to thin glass. Cut glass, however beautiful, is usually too thick to allow the gentle hand-warming to take place. Nor should huge balloon glasses be used, they merely disperse the precious smell. The only purpose of such glasses is to make it clear to others what is being drunk. That in itself adds to the pleasure of some drinkers, since research in several European countries has shown that Cognac is associated with the well-to-do classes of successful people.

By Cognac, of course, I mean the real thing. Like 'Champagne', 'Cognac' is used in many countries as if it were simply a word. The *Concise Oxford Dictionary* defines it as 'a high-quality brandy, properly that distilled in Cognac in western France'. In France the technical definition goes considerably further than that. The wines used for the distillation must only be produced from certain grape varieties, namely the Folle-blanche, Saint Emilion and Colombard, though up to 10 per cent of the wine can derive from the Sémillon, Sauvignon Blanc-Rame, Jurançon-Blanc and Montils grapes. Distillation of the wine has to be in a Charentais still in two consecutive heatings. Alcoholic volume must be at least 40 per cent, and ageing has to take place, as I have already mentioned, in casks made of oak from Limousin or Troncais forests.

Perhaps it does not matter too much if other brandies are called Cognac, provided no deception is intended and the price reflects the actual product. One might cheerfully be plied with 'Cognac' in the restaurants of Crete, regardless of whether one asked for it: Metaxa is not Cognac, but as countless holiday-makers have discovered, it has its own charms.

Greece and Turkey also have mastic, a brandy flavoured with resin from the mastic shrub. Mastic-gum is traditionally used as a chewing-gum and gave us our word 'masticate'. It serves as a reminder that careful drinkers of good brandy talk about 'chewing' it, just as some Irishmen refer to the eating of their Guinness.

KITRO

Kitro is little known because you have to go to the Greek island of Naxos to get it – the neighbouring island of Ios produces another and slightly less nectarean version. They do not export it even to the Greek mainland; at any rate, I have never found it there after plenty of looking. It is based on the lemon, but seemingly on the rind as well as the juice, hence its peculiar tang.

Kingsley Amis *On Drink*

FRUIT BRANDIES

The Greek and Turkish mastic leads us into the confused world of flavoured and so-called fruit brandies. 'Fruit brandy' is used loosely in English to refer to drinks made in very different ways. Since brandy is distilled from wine – fermented grape juice – the term should perhaps only be used of a drink distilled from the equivalent of wine, a fermented fruit juice. Cider, for example, is fermented apple juice, or apple wine. When it is distilled, it gives a true apple-brandy, though few people would refer to it in that way. In Europe it would be Calvados, named after the department in Normandy which has made it famous. (The French department was in turn named after a Spanish galleon, shipwrecked on its coast in 1588.) In America they would speak of apple-jack or perhaps Jersey Lightning. Mary McCarthy, in *The Group*, writes: 'A tall shaggy man told several

THE RIGHT FATHER-IN-LAW

If ever I marry a wife,
I'll marry a landlord's daughter,
For then I may sit in the bar,
And drink cold brandy and water.

Charles Lamb

stories about Jersey Lightning; he warned the handsome young man that this stuff packed an awful wallop. There was a discussion about apple-jack and how it made people quarrelsome.'

The *Independent* reported during 1990 that apple-brandy production was about to begin in England. A Somerset farmer, Julian Temperley, had bought a second-hand still from the Calvados producers and had begun work. At the time of writing it is too soon to taste the results of his efforts, which are locked in bonded warehouses, slowly maturing.

Mr Temperley argued with simple logic that it makes more sense for the English to distil cider than it does for them to make wine. The raw materials are readily available, grown with far less difficulty than vines. Distilling cider he saw as a natural extension of the cider-making skill, whereas the English wine-making movement 'is basically a lot of retired colonels producing second-class German wine in the wrong climate and on no historical basis'. His judgement of the wine-producers and their product was unduly harsh, and cider-making in England has not perhaps been established as long as he seemed to think (see pp. 115–16). Nevertheless, he was theoretically right – wherever cider is made, cider-brandy should follow.

Many fruit brandies begin not with a fruit wine, but with a separately-distilled neutral spirit which is mixed in some way with a must of the fruit. The infusion that results may be distilled in its turn or sold as it is. In either case it is a drink approaching the strength associated with spirits, tasting of the fruit concerned.

The different production methods are perhaps only of interest to those who want to classify drinks rather than drink them. I mention the matter here only to explain why I deal with 'cherry brandy', 'apricot brandy' and the like in a separate liqueur section (see pp. 196–97) rather than here. A true cherry brandy is kirsch, made from a must of either morello or wild cherries (*merises* not *cerises*) and including some of the kernels. The must ferments in wooden vats for several days and is then twice distilled. Similar methods are used in Yugoslavia, with plums substituted for the cherries, to produce slivovitz.

Most common fruits can be used to produce a brandy in this way. Soft fruits such as plums, peaches, pears and cherries are especially popular. After fermentation of the crushed fruit and its double-distillation, the better products are matured in casks before being sold. Apart from those mentioned, true fruit brandies include the Hungarian Barack Palinka (apricot); Romanian Tuica; French Quetsch, Mirabelle; German Zwetschgenwasser (plum); French Mesclou (greengage), Houx (holly berries); German Himbeergeist; French Framboise (raspberry), Coing (quince), Myrtille (bilberry). There are many others, but none has achieved the worldwide popularity or status of brandy itself. In an alcoholic context, the grape remains the fruit of fruits.

CHRISTIAN VIRTUE

People may say what they like about Christianity; the religious system that produced green Chartreuse can never really die.

Saki (Hector Hugh Munro) *Reginald*

WHISKY

In one sense, whisky has almost as long a history as brandy. It is believed that it was being drunk in Ireland by the 12th century and in Scotland by the 15th century. As a drink of international repute it is very much younger, lagging in that respect behind gin. For some reason it has usually appealed more to male drinkers rather than women, though Mrs Thatcher's fondness for a glass or two of whisky at the end of the day has been well-publicised.

The word 'whisky' derives from the first part of the Gaelic expression *uisgebeatha* 'water of life'. That phrase is found in many languages, such as Latin *aqua vitae*, French *eau-de-vie*, Swedish *acquavit*, and is usually a general term for a distillate. Those expressions are invariable, whisky itself is not. It is frequently found as 'whiskey', the usual explanation being that the 'e' spelling is used for the drink that is not scotch.

It is perhaps truer to say that the provenance of the writer rather than the drink usually decides which spelling is used. American writers instinctively refer to whiskey where British writers use whisky. Justification for the American view of the matter is not hard to find. The Royal Commission that was asked to decide in 1908 whether 'Scotch' could be applied to grain whisky from a patent still as well as malt whisky from a pot still ruled that: 'Whiskey is a spirit obtained by distillation from a mash of cereal grains saccharified by the diastase of malt; "Scotch whiskey" is whiskey, as above defined, distilled in Scotland; and "Irish whiskey" is whiskey, as above defined, distilled in Ireland. . . . We have received no evidence to show that the form of the still has any necessary relationship with the wholesomeness of the spirit produced.'

That judgement cleared the way for the bulk production of grain whisky by patent still in Scotland. Ultimately it made possible the blending of grain and malt whiskies which in turn enabled scotch to become a worldwide product. Clearly the Royal Commissioners thought that 'whiskey' rather than 'whisky' was how that product would be described. 'Saccharified', incidentally, which occurs in the above definition, means 'turned into sugar'. More familiar is 'saccharin', used as a

ATHOLE BROSE

This is a mixture of honey and whisky and sometimes oatmeal, first referred to by Sir Walter Scott in *Heart of Midlothian*. 'Brose' is normally made by pouring boiling water or milk on to oatmeal, then seasoning it with salt and butter. The 'Athole' refers to a legend concerning the Earl of Athole. In the 15th century he is said to have captured the Earl of Ross by putting honey and whisky into a small well from which Ross used to drink.

Thomas Hood made Athole Brose the subject of one of his famous puns:

Charm'd with a drink which
    Highlanders compose,
A German traveller exclaimed with
    glee, –
'Potztausend! sare, if dis is Athole
    Brose,
How goot der Athole Boetry must be!'

sweetener by those on a diet. Both words are derived from Latin *saccharum* 'sugar'. 'Diastase' refers to the enzymes which convert the starch in the malt to sugar.

Whatever form seems most appropriate has been used in this book, apart from quotations, where the original word has been adopted. Pronunciation is the same in either case, and was thought to be familiar enough throughout the world to make 'whisky' represent the letter 'w' in the International Phonetic Alphabet.

WHISKY WORSHIP

That familiarity was brought about by the efforts of some outstanding 19th-century salesmen. They had names like Bell, Buchanan, Dewar, Haig, Walker, Mackie, Sanderson, Teacher, Grant and Mackinlay, most of which remain familiar to whisky-drinkers today. These were the men who took it well beyond Scotland's borders. Whisky-lovers would argue that they were able to do so

To friends at home and abroad, Greetings for
a Happy Christmas and a Good New Year

'BLACK & WHITE'
SCOTCH WHISKY

JAMES BUCHANAN & CO. LTD. GLASGOW AND LONDON

BY APPOINTMENT SCOTCH WHISKY DISTILLERS
TO THE LATE KING GEORGE VI

because the product they were selling had some exceptional qualities. It has certainly been the subject of enthusiastic eulogies. In Holinshed's *Chronicles of England, Scotland and Ireland*, which appeared in 1577, readers were informed of its virtues as follows:

'Beying moderatelie taken, it sloweth age; it strengtheneth youthe; it helpeth digestion; it cutteth fleume [phlegm]; it abandoneth melancholie; it relisheth the harte; it lighteneth the mynde; it quickeneth the spirites; it cureth the hydropsie [dropsy]; it healeth the stranguary [difficulty in discharging urine]; it pounceth [reduces to powder] the stone [gall stone]; it repelleth gravel [gravelly matter collected in the kidneys or bladder]; it puffeth away ventositie [windiness]; it kepyth and preserveth the head from whyrling – the eyes from dazelyng – the tongue from lispyng – the mouth from snafflyng [being restrained, as if by a snaffle] – the teeth from chatteryng – the throte from ratlyng – the wesan [windpipe] from stieflyng – the stomach from wamblyng [quaking] – the harte from swellyng – the bellie from wirthchyng [retching?] – the guts from rumblyng – the hands from shiueryng – the sinowes from shrinkyng – the veynes from crumplyng – the bones from soakyng . . . Trulie it is a soveraigne liquor if it be orderlie taken.'

THE WHISKY STRAINER

Mustachus am po'ful things I speck, tu them what hes the stumick tu wear em. Strains whisky powerful good, what hes dead flies in hit, an' then yu kin comb em off ur let em stay, 'cordin to yer taste.

George Washington Harris *Contempt of Court*

Shakespeare, who took a great deal of information from Holinshed, did not choose to make use of this passage. Whisky would not have been familiar enough to his audiences for it to make much sense. He picked up instead on the general idea of being lengthily lyrical about a particular drink. In the Shakespeare version Sir John Falstaff gives a long speech about the virtues of sherris-sack.

THE NATIONAL SPORT

Whisky remained a regional drink long after Shakespeare's time. Very little is heard of it until the 18th century, by which time it was subject to duty. Since that duty was considered to be an unjust imposition on the Scots by an English government, whisky was also subject to the evasion of tax. One writer has described the illicit distillation and smuggling of whisky as a Scottish national sport throughout the 18th century. The attitude was summed up by Burns: 'Freedom and whisky gang thegither.'

The 19th century brought several changes to the situation. One of the most important was an Act of 1823 which made it legally possible for anyone who purchased a £10 licence to distil whisky. Duty still had to be paid on each gallon produced, but whisky-distilling became a commercially viable proposition. It became even more so with the invention of the continuous Coffey still in 1831. By that time, whiskies made from rye and wheat instead of the traditional barley had also appeared.

Within a relatively short time the cheaper grain whiskies were being blended with the malts, as are most Scotch whiskies today. Early blends had a higher proportion of malt whisky than grain, but the blending process was probably hit or miss. It has since become a subtle art. In his *Century Companion to Whiskies*, Derek Cooper quotes a modern blender: 'Today we're using between thirty and forty whiskies in a blend as opposed to ten or so pre-war. It is like an orchestra. The individual players may be brilliant, so are the best malts, but someone has to make the individual players harmonise and a top blender has the same function as a first-rate conductor. He uses Speyside to give it this lovely phenol charac-

DRAUGHT LIQUOR

Many people collect miniature bottles of liquor. They are alcophialists, according to Alfred Lubran, in *There's A Name For It*. Graham Greene wisely side-steps that term in *Our Man In Havana*, where his character Wormold is said to have a collection of 99 miniature bottles of whisky.

There is a well-known scene in the novel where he and Segura play a game of draughts. The 'men' are 12 miniatures of Scotch and 12 of bourbon. The rules of the game are specially adapted for the occasion: 'When you take a piece you drink it.'

Greene describes the game in loving detail. Segura captures a bottle of Old Taylor, then Old Forester. Wormold gets a bottle of Cairngorm. Segura captures and drinks a Four Roses. A Dimpled Haig falls to Wormold who then captures another Scotch and brings the first game to an end.

They start again, swapping drinks. Segura forces Wormold to take a Hiram Walker, then a Harper's, then a Kentucky Tavern. Segura in his turn has to drink a Red Label and a Dunosdale Cream. Wormold drinks a Lord Calvert, though this is a Canadian rye 'which had got mixed with the bourbons'. Segura then drinks a George IV, a Queen Anne, a Highland Queen, a Vat 69, a Grant's Standfast and an Old Argyll. He is entitled to celebrate a victory, but passes out.

Johnnie Walker's Black Label, Chivas Regal, The Antiquary, Old Parr, Red Hackle De Luxe and Usher's De Luxe. There are some who would say that no blend can reach the heights of a first-class single malt whisky, but it would be difficult for them to prove their case.

To return to the 19th century for a moment, an earlier chapter (see p. 135) discussed the devastating effect on French vineyards of the aphid phylloxera. In the late 1870s this had caused a great falling-off in the amounts of French wine and brandy imported into England. Single malts and blended Scotch whisky were now available in greater quantities than ever before. The situation was perfect for the super-salesmen mentioned earlier. They exploited it to the full.

DIP SWITCH

Farmers are said to be especially fond of Original Oldbury Sheep Dip, a Highland malt whisky bottled in Gloucestershire. Somebody once unkindly suggested that one reason for this is that genuine sheep dip, as used by farmers, is a legitimate expense for tax purposes. By chance it costs roughly the same as the whisky, and both products are distributed by agricultural merchants. Tax inspectors would not look too kindly on the inclusion of whisky in a list of business expenses: 'sheep dip' stands more chance of slipping through unnoticed.

All this was hotly denied when the story was made public. Tax inspectors are not that easily taken in, said one spokesman. Invoices clearly state whether the product is the kind meant for drinking, said another. Farmers are too honest, said a third – though he remembered a customer who asked for household bed sheets to be described on the invoice as galvanised sheets, used for building barns.

ter, Islay to give it strength, Lowland to give it volume, grain to give it a background.'

All blenders seem to be agreed that it is not the relative proportions of malts and grains in a blend that make it successful or not. Everything depends on the art of the blender. The idea that more malt automatically means better quality is as false as the greater-age-equals-greater-quality equation. De luxe blends include Haig's Dimple,

SINGLE MALTS

As we have seen at the beginning of this chapter, whisky could be described as distilled beer. Within a whisky distillery the fermentation of the malt is known as brewing and is much as described on pp. 80–95. The wash that is the result of the fermentation is like a very strong ale. It is fed into a wash still which is then heated. The first vapours are condensed and are known by the extraordinary term 'low wines'. As for the residue, the 'spent wash' is also known, significantly, as 'pot ale' or 'burnt ale'.

The second distillation of the low wines is carried out in the spirit still. When discussing the distillation of Cognac, I mentioned the undesirable 'heads' that had to be removed. In the whisky distillery these are known as the 'foreshots'. The equivalent of the Cognac 'tails' are the whisky 'feints'.

Derek Cooper reports that in Irish distilleries 'three distillations are common'. He also mentions an 'ultimate potion', the result of a quadruple distillation, produced in the 16th century. This was of such a high alcohol content that more than two spoonfuls of it would endanger a man's life.

For modern whiskies, ageing is important, but in this area it would seem that the whisky distillers of Scotland are not as careful as the producers of Cognac. As with Cognac, the ultimate flavour of whisky can be strongly affected by the cask in which it is stored, but the Scottish distilleries do not have convenient forests nearby to supply them with oak. There has been a tradition of recycling sherry-casks imported from Spain or bourbon-casks from the USA, all of which sounds very hit-or-miss.

There are hundreds of Scottish malt whiskies available (and hundreds more which are used only for blending). They vary in quality, or perhaps it would be better to say merely that they vary in taste. Experts sometimes produce their own lists of malts which they consider to be exceptional, but as with experts in all fields, the criteria being applied may not be those of the average person. Nevertheless, it is difficult to ignore names that are constantly mentioned. Derek Cooper, for instance, warmly recommends

Glenmorangie: 'I would suggest it every time as an introduction for anyone who has never tried a single malt before.' Brian Murphy, in a *Punch*

WHISKY PHILOSOPHY

'I'll have mine straight,' Captain Todd said. 'It's the man who puts water in his whisky they say gets to be a chronic drunkard. A man drinks whisky straight and he knows what he's doing. But whisky and water now, that's downright insidious. I never allow myself but so much whisky and water, then I take me a straight one so I can get a grip on the facts of the case. To that, gentlemen, I attribute my success in not becoming a chronic drunkard in a world so liberally strewn, you might say, with temptation.'

Mr Christian took a gulp from his glass. 'Naw,' he declared, 'I say ride it saddle or bareback. No matter if it's a horse or a dog or whisky or a woman, I say a man's got to wear the pants. All alike, they'll all break over if they can. A man's got to do the riding. It's me riding the whisky. Not the whisky riding me.'

'You're right,' the Senator said, 'in a way. Whisky is like a woman. You get the best results if you handle it right. You have to treat it like you loved it. A little coaxing and courting, that gives the best results, every time.' He turned his glass gently in his hand, as though to illustrate his words.

'Whisky,' Mr Christian was saying, 'a great democratic institution. Next to the Declaration of Independence and Bunker Hill, damned if it ain't the greatest. Why, whisky, it makes a rich man pore, like they say, and a pore man rich.'

Robert Penn Warren *Night Rider*

article called 'Pass the Malt', also says: 'Glenmorangie – an exceptionally fine malt in my opinion.'

DOWN IN THE GLENS

All such writers mention The Glenlivet and names such as Macallan, Glen Grant, Dufftown, Longmorn, Glenburgie, Glendronach, Glenfarclas, Glen Keith, Strathisla, Glenrothes, Glen Moray, Aberlour, Tomintoul and Milton Duff that are associated with it. Glenfiddich is another name that constantly recurs, though it has not achieved the distinction of an entry in *Chambers English Dictionary*. That reference source does note that Glenlivet is a 'proprietary name for a noted whisky' as well as the name of a valley in Banffshire.

'Glen' is also listed in the dictionary, of course: 'a narrow valley with a stream, often with trees.' The lexicographers may one day have to extend that definition to include a reference to high-quality whisky. When so many whisky-names include 'glen', the association is almost inevitable. Maurice Leitch, for instance, in his novel *Burning Bridges*, has one of his characters ask another which whisky he should buy. The answer is 'Anything beginning with Glen –.' When I quoted this to a Scotsman his immediate response was that he could think of one or two whiskies to which the advice would not apply, but the Leitch comment is understandable.

Some of the names that do not happen to begin with Glen –, but which have been recommended by *Decanter* magazine experts, include Auchentoshan, Aultmore, Balvenie, Blair Atholl, Bowmore, Bruichladdich, Caol Ila, Convalmore, Deanston Mill, Highland Park, Lagavulin, Laphroaig, Linkwood, Lochnagar, Mortlach, Old Pulteney, Rosebank, Springbank, Tormore. These need not remain merely names on a page. Most of them are listed amongst the 46 malts in a recent Oddbins catalogue and are waiting to be sampled.

Visitors to Scotland can go one better and visit many of the distilleries. They are often in picturesque surroundings, taking advantage of the water that runs through the valleys. The quality of that water is frequently cited as one of the reas-

ons for the uniqueness of Scotch. David Daiches, in *Scotch Whisky, Its Past and Present*, says: 'The Highlands of Scotland teem with the most beautiful clear water from stream and spring, and there are many peat bogs; so that if you need peat smoke in order to dry the barley and turn it into aromatic malt, and clear water for the further process of turning that malt into a fermented liquid before distilling it into spirit, there too Nature has laid everything on your doorstep.'

Lovers of traditional Scotch whisky have much in common with those who value Cognac so highly. They value not only a drink, but a wealth of historical associations. Their palates are also very similar, as was shown when *Decanter* arranged a blind tasting some years ago. The majority of those who took part in the tasting – experts drawn from the whisky and Cognac trades – were unable to distinguish between the two products.

THE PSYCHOLOGY OF DRINKING

When reading such reports one wonders just how much our appreciation of a particular drink is to do with emotional reactions rather than physical taste. A certain amount of pleasure can be derived from a familiar bottle and its label, ready to play their part in a personal drinking ritual. A taste can also be enjoyed merely because it is well-known, with thoughts about comparative

---

THOSE AT RISK

It might be a digression, but an interesting one, to remember the case of Robert Warner, a total abstainer. In the year 1840, he applied to a life insurance company in London for a policy on his life. He was told that being a total abstainer, he would have to pay an extra premium. The company was being guided by medical advice and their doctors believed that the lives of abstainers were shorter than those of regular drinkers.

James Ross *Whisky*

---

quality being suspended. Something similar occurs when we meet a relation or close friend. The simple act of recognition, triggering a subconscious reminder of shared emotional experience, is important. We do not need to make objective judgements, assigning friends to a position in some abstract hierarchy. They are a part of our lives and are accepted as such.

Older drinkers have had time to build up a relationship with one drink rather than another. This creates a useful brand loyalty, but can have a depressing side-effect. If a drink begins to be too closely associated with older drinkers, its social image suffers amongst the young. They turn away to drinks that are perceived as being more fashionable. In Britain, for instance, that is partly why there has been a swing in recent years away from traditional bitter beer to lager and from gin to vodka. As for whisky – to bring us back to the matter in hand – the celebration by connoisseurs of a malt's complex subtleties does not always achieve the intended result. Young Britons seem to be turning in the early 1990s towards the more obvious, easy-going charms of bourbon.

BOURBON

Bourbon takes its name from Bourbon County, Kentucky, which in turn was named in honour of the French royal family (France had provided assistance during the War of Independence). Ultimately Bourbon is a French place name of obscure origin. The drink might equally well have been called Kentucky, since it was first sold as Kentucky Bourbon Whiskey. This may have been in 1789, when the Reverend Elijah Craig, a Baptist minister, opened his distillery in Georgetown, Bourbon County. Pamela Vandyke Price, in *The Penguin Book of Spirits and Liqueurs*, is sure that this is what happened. Michael Jackson remarked in an article in *The Independent*, July 1991, that: 'My own occasional travels in Kentucky have failed to turn up any certain evidence that the whiskey was ever distilled in Bourbon County.'

The name is in any case now fixed, and an unblended 'straight Kentucky bourbon' must be distilled and matured in Kentucky. The maturation takes place in new oak casks with

BRANCHING OUT

He spent an hour drinking the drink that Leiter had told him was fashionable in racing circles – Bourbon and branch water. Bond guessed that in fact the water was from the tap behind the bar, but Leiter had said that real Bourbon drinkers insist upon having their whisky in the traditional style, with water from high up in the branch of the local river where it will be purest.

Ian Fleming *Diamonds are Forever*

charred interiors for at least two years, usually four. Charring the casks is said to allow the whiskey to soak more easily into the wood, thus softening its flavour. To qualify as bourbon, the mash must contain at least 51 per cent maize (or 'corn', as it is called in the USA. If the mash has over 80 per cent corn it can be described as 'corn whiskey').

Names seen on bottles of Kentucky bourbon include Jim Beam, Maker's Mark, Old Crowe, Old Fitzgerald, Old Forester, Old Grand-Dad, Old Taylor and Wild Turkey. Jack Daniels and George Dickel, both of which have a maize-based mash, are not included in the list because they are produced in Tennessee. Both make a point of being 'sour mash' whiskeys: residue from one mash is

AFTER EFFECTS

'Don't give me that Jim Beam. Last time I drank it, I got so damn sick I was afraid I'd die. And then I was afraid I wouldn't.'

Garrison Keillor 'Fall' *Lake Wobegon Days*

added to the next one to ensure continuity. Kentucky bourbons mostly make use of a similar process; the Tennessee whiskeys are different because they are filtered through charcoal made from sugar maple.

To British consumers names like Jack Daniels are vaguely familiar, but devoid of personal associations. They begin to come to life when Americans talk about them. Paul Levy, for instance, grew up with bourbon in his native Kentucky. In *Finger Lickin' Good: A Kentucky Childhood*, he says: 'When I was a child, most grown-ups drank bourbon. This was made locally, though not entirely in Bourbon County, and never, *never*, in Tennessee. (This sentiment was directed against Jack Daniels.) It was drunk with the pre-chlorinated, un-fluoridated 'branch-water' we got from the tap.

'Twice a year we all, even the children, drank bourbon. The first occasion was the Kentucky Derby, always the first Saturday in May. Mint juleps were made by "muddling" fresh mint leaves with sugar in a julep cup, topping it up with an unthinkably large slug of bourbon, leaving it to "marry", and then serving it frosty from being filled to the brim with crushed ice. The children were given a sip; any more would have resulted in tight tots.'

THE GENERATION GAP

It is to bourbon, then, that young British drinkers appear to be turning. That is not without irony, as Joanna Simon pointed out in a perceptive *Sunday Times* article: 'Far from adopting one of America's trendiest products, we have taken one that is so decidedly out-of-fashion that its huge home market is in serious decline. On its native soil bourbon is considered almost embarrassingly passé and elderly by precisely the kind of American consumers whose style-conscious British equivalents are adopting the habit with gusto.

'Whereas the typical US bourbon drinker is somebody's middle-aged father or grandfather, his UK counterpart is male, but young (in his twenties), fashion-conscious, in marketing jargon "aspirational" and therefore prepared to pay the necessary £10 to £16 a bottle.'

If the bourbon fashion continues in Britain, it will be yet another of the astonishing changes in drinking habits that pepper our social history. The British attitude to bourbon until recently – if there was an attitude at all – was probably reflected by a remark in *Room At The Top*, by John Braine: '"Drink?" asked George, going to the cocktail cabinet. "Gin, whisky, brandy, rum, sherry, and various other loathsome liqueurs which I can't really recommend." "Whisky, please." "It's not Scotch, alas. An American customer gave me a crate. Tastes like hair-oil, I warn you."'

Joanna Simon believes that the British bourbon 'fashion' is positive, stemming from a wish to ape American ways. That was fairly commonplace some time ago, in Europe as well as Britain. There is a scene in Len Deighton's *Funeral In Berlin*, for instance, where a young German is sitting in a bar: 'Anyone coming in would take him for an American – one of the Embassy people or one of the businessmen like the one sitting against the wall with the blonde. He called the barman and ordered another bourbon. It was a new barman. "Bourbon," he said. He liked to hear himself saying that. "Plenty of ice this time."'

I would be surprised if imitation of that kind is still a motivating force amongst young people in Europe. What does remain is the determination of each generation to separate itself from the habits and tastes of its elders, whether in clothes, music or drinks. That will continue, and it would not necessarily be a good thing, in the long run, for bourbon to become *too* popular in Britain. If that happened a new generation would one day see it as something associated with the middle-aged.

OTHER WHISKEYS

Apart from bourbon, rye whiskey is the other great American product. In the USA rye whiskey means what it says, since it is made from a mash which is of at least 51 per cent rye. In Canada the term is much vaguer, used of a product which can be derived from corn, wheat and barley as well as rye. That remark, however, partly applies to whiskeys made in many other countries. They may not be described as 'rye', but they are distilled from a number of different grains and are usually blended. Their quality varies greatly, especially in countries where the liquor laws are less rigidly enforced, or where 'whiskey' remains a foreign concept that has never really become acclimatised.

That cannot be said of Japan, where the drink has become part of every Japanese businessman's way of life. Taken to a traditional Japanese pub on my first visit to Tokyo I ordered sake, naïvely expecting my hosts to do the same. They drank whisky to a man, in tumblers packed with ice. I learned later that authentic Scotch is so highly prized in Japan that empty bottles are likely to remain on display at home, though Japanese Suntory whiskey, which makes use of Scottish malts in its blends, is of high quality.

Finally there is Irish whiskey, though 'finally' is hardly the word to use of the whiskey that preceded all others. The Irish have been distilling whiskey for nearly 900 years and have learnt a thing or two. The most famous brands are Old Bushmill and Jameson. Irish whiskey can be superb: what it needs is the outstanding marketing effort applied to it that made Scotch such an international product. Irish writers should then do what the Scots, from Burns onwards, have done so well. Scottish writers always praise their national drink; it is high time the Irish did the same. Meanwhile, for many people outside Ireland, Irish whiskey is mainly associated with coffee, drunk through a thick layer of cream.

In that connection I see that in *The Business of Loving* Godfrey Smith writes: 'Through the great noisy gusts of bonhomie, like cream running over Gaelic coffee, there slid the soft seduction of saxophones playing "Sweet Lorraine".' 'Soft seduction' is a useful phrase which could be applied to Irish whiskey itself. Perhaps the copy-writers should bear it in mind as they begin to plan for the future. The bourbon revolution will not last for ever.

GIN

Whatever happens to bourbon, it is unlikely ever to know the swings of social fortune that have affected gin since the 17th century. 'Gin' is from 'geneva', which has nothing to do with the Swiss city of that name: it is a form of *jenever*, the Dutch

word for the juniper berry. Gin is not a kind of brandy, however, distilled from juniper wine. It begins with a grain such as rye, and is distilled until it is a neutral spirit, lacking in the congenerics which would make it whisky (see p. 179). Juniper and other constituents are then added and redistillation takes place.

The 'discovery' of gin is usually credited to a Dutch Professor of Medicine at Leyden University, Franciscus de la Boe (1614-72). As was common at that time, he used a Latin form of his family name and was known as Sylvius. His work on distillates was, as his title suggests, carried out for medical reasons, but the spirit he produced was of an unpleasant taste. He must have been delighted to discover that using juniper berries as a flavouring solved the problem. It was already known that the oil from the juniper was of medicinal value: combining it with a spirit created a double medicine.

Dutch drinkers no doubt responded very well to gin, being already accustomed to distilled drinks. By the 16th century they had acquired a reputation in England for heavy drinking. English soldiers who had fought alongside the Dutch had learnt what was meant by 'Dutch courage', bringing the disapproval of English commentators. William Camden bemoaned the fact that 'the English, who hitherto had, of all the northern nations, shewn themselves the least addicted to immoderate drinking, first learn'd in these Netherland Wars to swallow a large quantity of intoxicating liquor, and to destroy their own health by drinking that of others'.

The English soldiers of the time would have been well used to heavy drinking, but perhaps

THE TWENTY-YEAR STUPOR

By degrees Rip's awe and apprehension subsided. He even ventured, when no eye was fixed upon him, to taste the beverage, which he found had much of the flavour of excellent Hollands. He was naturally a thirsty soul, and was soon tempted to repeat the draught. One taste provoked another; and he reiterated his visits to the flagon so often, that at length his senses were over-powered, his eyes swam in his head, his head gradually declined, and he fell into a deep sleep.

Washington Irving *Rip Van Winkle*

found themselves exposed to spirits far more than at home. It is not clear what these were, but they were not yet gin: the word 'gin' and its synonyms, 'hollands' and 'geneva', only occur in English at the beginning of the 18th century. By that time English links with the Netherlands were stronger than ever. William of Orange had been invited to England in 1688 and had been proclaimed king a year later. Dutch drinks had become respectable.

THE GIN FLOOD

In retrospect, it is easy to see why England was soon awash in gin. For political reasons, the import of French brandy and other foreign spirits was forbidden in the 1690s. At the same time, restrictions on distilling were all but removed and it became patriotic to distil spirits from English grain. Everything conspired to encourage the production of cheap gin, on which it was possible – according to a notorious slogan of the time – to become drunk for a penny and dead drunk for twopence.

The quality of the drink at the time was probably dreadful. It had been discovered earlier that almost anything could be distilled – including beer dregs and stale wine. The spirit obtained could be mixed with rotten fruit, herbs of various kinds, spices and seeds. Nevertheless, gin was sold everywhere, from houses as well as barrows and stalls in the street. Its effects were to be seen on all sides – vividly displayed, for instance, in Hogarth's famous representation of Gin Lane.

A 'Gin Act' introduced in 1729 imposed a licence costing £20 on gin-retailers. In 1736 the magistrates of Middlesex presented a petition to parliament stating:
'That the drinking of Geneva, and other distilled liquors had for some years greatly increased; that the constant and excessive use thereof had destroyed thousands of His Majesty's subjects; that great numbers of others were by its use rendered unfit for useful labour, debauched in morals, and drawn into all manner of vice and wickedness.'

In September that year a new Act was introduced, raising the retail licence to £50 and imposing a duty of £1 per gallon on the gin that was sold. The Act was extremely unpopular, producing many of the same results as Prohibition in America. Bootlegging and smuggling were common; those who informed on unlicensed retailers were

TURNING THE CORNER

'You turn the corner. What a change! All is light and brilliancy. The hum of many voices issues from that splendid gin-shop . . .'

Charles Dickens 'Gin Shops' in *Sketches by Boz*

'Suddenly a corner was turned, a blaze of light burst upon our sight, and we stood before one of the huge suburban temples of Intemperance – one of the palaces of the fiend, *Gin*.'

Edgar Allan Poe *The Man of the Crowd*

'The Gin Shop' by George Cruikshank.

SAD REVELLERS

Gin-shops, or what the English call spirit-vaults, are numerous in the vicinity of these poor streets, and are set off with the magnificence of gilded doorposts, tarnished by contact with the unclean customers who haunt there. Ragged children come thither with old shaving-mugs, or broken-nosed teapots, or any such makeshift receptacle, to get a little poison or madness for their parents, who deserve no better requital at their hands for having engendered them.

Inconceivably sluttish women enter at noonday and stand at the counter among boon companions of both sexes, stirring up misery and jollity in a bumper together, and quaffing off the mixture with a relish. As for the men, they lounge there continually, drinking till they are drunken – drinking as long as they have a halfpenny left – and then, as it seemed to me, waiting for a sixpenny miracle to be wrought in their pockets so as to enable them to be drunken again.

Most of these establishments have a significant advertisement of 'Beds', doubtless for the accommodation of their customers in the interval between one intoxication and the next. I never could find it in my heart, however, utterly to condemn these sad revellers, and should certainly wait till I had some better consolation to offer before depriving them of their dram of gin, though death itself were in the glass; for methought their poor souls needed such fiery stimulant to lift them a little way out of the smothering squalor of both their outward and interior life, giving them glimpses and suggestions, even if bewildering ones, of a spiritual existence that limited their present misery. The temperance reformers unquestionably derive their commission from the Divine Beneficence, but have never been taken fully into its counsels.

Nathaniel Hawthorne 'Outside Glimpses of English Poverty' *Our Old Home*

dealt with brutally. In seven years only two distillers applied for licences, while some 12 000 were convicted of offences related to the making or selling of illicit spirits.

The Gin Act, obviously unenforceable, was repealed in 1742. Gin consumption was greater than ever, but a new Act now came into force. Licensing fees were reduced, but were controlled by local magistrates. Reasonable revenue duties were imposed on distillers, who now became professionals, able to produce a drink of good quality. Improvements of that kind were badly needed; gin had drifted a long way from its original medicinal beginning.

THE NINETEENTH CENTURY

Pamela Vandyke Price tell us in her *Penguin Book of Spirits and Liqueurs* that 'by the beginning of the 19th century, gin had become a more openly respectable drink'. I find it difficult to agree with her. Miss Price quotes Thomas Hood, saying that he was enthusiastic:

'Gin! Gin! a Drop of Gin!
When, darkly, Adversity's days set in,
And the friends and peers
Of earlier years
Prove warm without, but cold within.'

This section actually comes in the middle of a long poem (published 1843) which begins:

Gin! Gin! a Drop of Gin!
What magnified Monsters circle therein!
Ragged and stained with filth and mud,
Some plague-spotted, and some with blood!
Shapes of misery, Shame, and Sin!
Figures that make us loathe and tremble,
Creatures scarce human that more resemble
Broods of diabolical kin,
Ghoule and Vampyre, Demon and Jin!

Gin! Gin! a Drop of Gin!
The dram of Satan! the liquor of Sin!
Distill'd from the fell
Alembics of Hell,
By Guilt and Death, his own brother and twin!
That man might fall
Still lower than all
The meanest creatures with scale and fin.

Only later does Hood try to explain why so many people take to gin, faced with life's disappointments:

Gin! Gin! a Drop of Gin!
Oh! then its tremendous temptations begin,
To take, alas,
To the fatal glass,
And happy the wretch that it does not win
To change the black hue
Of his ruin to blue –
While Angels sorrow, and Demons grin –
And lose the rheumatic
Chill of his attic
By plunging into the Palace of Gin!

GIN PALACES

The gin palaces were a notable feature of early 19th-century city life. They were gaudily-decorated public-houses, named after the most popular drink they sold. Drunkenness was an appalling problem among the poor: by many it was linked with gin – 'liquid madness' in the words of Thomas Carlyle – more than any other drink.

Dickens, however, saw clearly that gin itself was not the cause of the problem. Something, anything, was needed by ordinary people to enable them to escape from the awfulness of their daily lives. In his essay on 'Gin Shops' he points out that the gin palaces 'are invariably numerous and splendid in precise proportion to the dirt and poverty of the surrounding neighbourhood'. He concludes: 'Gin-drinking is a great vice in England, but wretchedness and dirt are a greater; and until you improve the homes of the poor, or persuade a half-famished wretch not to seek relief in the temporary oblivion of his own misery, gin-shops will increase in number and splendour.'

A rise in living standards, as Dickens had foreseen, slowly made the gin palaces less necessary. Gin slowly began to have other associations than the desperate drunkenness of poverty. With the advent of the Cocktail Era in the 1920s and 30s, gin at last began to acquire a positive image of respectability. It was seemingly on its way to being linked in the England of the 1990s with well-to-do middle-class drinkers.

Yet traces of its less reputable past could still be found. In *Saturday Night and Sunday Morning* Alan Sillitoe describes a scene where a miscarriage is induced by means of excessive gin-drinking. The ritual was part of the working-class lore of my own youth; an ordeal that was likely to await any girl who 'got into trouble'. Perhaps it persists even today, as a gruesome reminder of horrific scenes of the past.

LIFE'S LITTLE ESSENTIALS

'I'll be around in the summer to show you the ropes, depend upon it. You'll want to know a source of Gordon's gin, angostura bitters, streaky bacon. All life's little essentials . . .'

John Mortimer *Summer's Lease*

VODKA

All that, however, is the shadowy hinterland of the gin world, a long way from the refreshing gin and tonic or the cocktail. In that role, gin is now under considerable threat from vodka, which has experienced a huge upsurge in interest in western countries since the 1950s. In Russia and Poland the drink has a history which goes back, according to Polish claims, to the eighth century, though it is more likely to have emerged in its present form in the 16th century. First mention of it in English texts occurs at the beginning of the 19th century, when travellers reported on it as a kind of Russian brandy.

It is more closely related to gin, in that distillation continues until the congenerics present after fermentation are almost completely removed. The process is helped by filtration through charcoal, which recalls what happens in Tennessee to bourbon. Like bourbon – and gin – vodka is usually distilled from a grain, though it is said that everything from potatoes to grapes has been used at one time or another. Since the eventual result of filtration and rectification will be an almost tasteless spirit, it hardly seems to matter what is used at the beginning.

As gin is flavoured with juniper berries and other botanical items, so vodka is sometimes flavoured with spices, such as pepper, or fruits (the rowanberry, cherry or lemon). In its purer form, which is odourless as well as tasteless, it is especially suitable for cocktails. It could probably be used to give an alcoholic kick to almost any other drink, though until recently it was mainly linked with tomato juice in the form of the Bloody Mary.

THE NIGHTCAP

When in Moscow he did like a nice lemon vodka to end his day.

John le Carre *The Russian House*

RUSSIAN RED

The play of light on frosted bottles of red rowanberry vodka caught the eye.

Boris Pasternak *Doctor Zhivago*

The word 'vodka' means roughly 'little water'. It is ultimately from Russian *voda* 'water' in the phrase *zhiznennia voda* 'water of life'. The Russians refer to the drink affectionately as *vodoshka*, adding a diminutive ending just as an English-speaker might add an ending to 'drink' and talk about a 'drinky'.

As with all these drink-words, however, etymology is unimportant in the market-place. What matters is the image a word evokes amongst the members of a social group; the associations it arouses. Earlier this century, as J.B. Priestley pointed out in *Angel Pavement*, vodka's main association was with 'romantic fiction of all kinds'. That is no longer true, but vodka is fortunate in a British context, in having a youthful and still rather novel image.

DRINKING CUSTOMS

While vodka may become common in the west, western drinkers are perhaps unlikely to imitate traditional Polish and Russian drinking customs. A bottle of vodka, once opened, is never put away half-empty. It is prudent to drink when several people are present rather than try to keep pace with one companion, especially when glasses are invariably knocked back in one gulp. That becomes slightly more difficult, incidentally, when drinking-arms are intertwined, but no more friendly way of drinking has ever been devised.

Excessive drinking has reportedly been a problem for some time in the former USSR, where the official attitude to alcoholics and alcoholism is, to say the least, unsympathetic. This is in spite of the fact that a third of all fatal road acci-

SECOND THOUGHTS

The destruction of the vodka still was now regretted and those of the distillers who had been acquitted at the trial as less guilty than the rest were asked to mend it or construct a new one. The manufacture of alcohol was started again, officially, for medical purposes. The news was greeted with nods and winks. Drunkenness broke out again . . .

Boris Pasternak *Doctor Zhivago*

dents, three-quarters of all murders and countless hours of lost production time are known to be alcohol-related. Mr Gorbachev tried to do something about the situation in 1985, cutting the production of vodka and the number of hours it was legally available. On television he told the Russians: 'Just don't take a drink.'

When the full history of vodka comes to be written, its abuse in the USSR during the 20th century may reveal many similarities to the excessive gin-drinking that plagued England during the 18th and 19th centuries. In England the introduction of a form of official Prohibition merely led to wholesale flouting of the law, as it did later in the USA. In the USSR, according to an *Observer* report (September 1991), there was, almost inevitably, a similar result. A determination to find some kind of relief from intolerable social circumstances led to a blackmarket trade in vodka, and to the drinking of vodka substitutes such as window-cleaning liquid, fly-spray and perfume. There was also a massive increase in illicit home-distilling, often with fatal results.

SCHNAPPS

In Scandinavia and countries like Germany, Austria and Switzerland the spirit drink normally served is some kind of schnapps. Schnapps has for some reason become the English form of the word, though it is *Schnaps* in Germany and Denmark, *Snaps* in Sweden. The word links with 'snap' in its dialectal sense of 'a hasty mouthful'. A small glass of schnapps is normally drunk in that way, as a single gulp. The drink has a more official name as *aqvavit* or *aquavit*, a further adaptation of the general Latin phrase *aqua vitae* 'water of life'.

Drinking a glass of schnapps is likely to leave a slight after-taste of caraway, though the drink is distilled from either potatoes or grain, whichever happens to be most readily available at the time of year. Flavouring, as with most of the white spirit drinks, occurs at a late stage and is usually with herbs and spices.

Schnapps is not a 'normal' drink in England. Two years' residence in Sweden, however, made me familiar with both the drink and the appropriate toasting ceremony – an exchange of *skåls* while staring into the eyes of a fellow-drinker with glasses held at chest height.

Swedes, and Scandinavians generally, have the reputation of being heavy drinkers. This is not the 18th-century English gin or the more recent Russian vodka situation all over again. The normally high standard of living in all the Scandinavian countries creates little need to escape the misery of one's lot. It is sometimes said, though, that the Swedes find social relationships rather difficult, which is perhaps why they have created

CEMENT MIXERS

'Formerly, before I had the pleasure of practising the teaching profession, I worked in the cement industry. The cement workers used to drink one or two schnappses before breakfast, though not with a coke for a chaser. They preferred several bottles of Nette beer. The Nette is a little river in the Lower Eifel. It winds picturesquely through Germany's largest pumice-mining region. Pumice makes people thirsty.'

Günter Grass *Local Anaesthetic*

a series of rather elaborate verbal and behavioural rituals. Some people explain the inhibitions by referring to Sweden's rural past, when small communities were isolated from one another through the winter months.

Whatever the reasons for it, I did indeed notice that Swedish friends and colleagues found it quite difficult to unbend when they first met. A colleague once told me that his countrymen were like bottles of sauce: 'nothing comes out'. Downing a few schnapps, he said, had the same effect as shaking the sauce-bottle. Next time you tipped it, everything came gushing out. I observed the truth of this in the 1960s, but modern telecommunications, together with the enormous amount of travelling that Swedes do, must have had a profound effect.

I later lived in Germany, where schnapps was mostly the drink one had in the nearest café at the end of the working day. It was always washed down with beer.

OUZO

It is difficult to avoid this drifting off into biographical reminiscence when drinks are being discussed. Say the word 'ouzo' to anyone who has been on a holiday to Greece, Cyprus, Turkey or the Lebanon and a hundred memories will flood back along with the taste of the aniseed. Anyone who took a particular liking to one of the many versions of this herb-flavoured brandy will probably also recall the father of all hangovers.

Even those holiday-makers who did not like its taste or smell probably sat in a Mediterranean café and saw the little magic trick performed by a local customer: ouzo itself is colourless, but adding to it water that is equally colourless causes it to turn milky white.

Ouzo is a modern Greek word, but no one is certain what it means. John Ayto, who is a reliable investigator of such matters, offers an explanation which he admits is very convoluted. It has to do with the Italian phrase *uso Massalia* 'for the use of Marseilles' on packets of top-quality silkworm cocoons exported from Greece in the 19th century. The theory is that the Italian phrase acquired the general sense 'of high quality'. The first word (pronounced in Greek it could well

have led to *ouzo*) was then transferred to the drink.

ABSINTHE

Ouzo recalls absinthe, a drink that is frequently mentioned in accounts of French literary and artistic life towards the end of the 19th century. Absinthe (for the meaning of the word see p. 149) was invented in Switzerland by a Frenchman in exile, a certain Dr Ordinaire, at the end of the 18th century. It was a mixture of herbs, with wormwood as the principal ingredient, infused with distilled spirit which was far stronger than brandy. After Ordinaire's death the recipe was sold to the Pernod family. They began to produce it at Pontarlier, near the Swiss border, and continued to do so for the next hundred years. At one time there were 22 distilleries in the area, all producing absinthe.

The drink was light green, and was popularly known as *la fée verte* 'the green fairy', though Verlaine was to refer to it as *l'atroce sorcière verte* 'the atrocious green witch'. It came to be considered responsible more than any other drink for the spread of alcoholism in France. Its manufacture and sale were finally banned there in 1915. Switzerland had taken that step in 1907, and imports to the USA were banned in 1912. Yet

ABSINTHE

The club men gathered together for the hour of absinthe.

Robert Louis Stevenson and Lloyd Osbourne *The Wrecker*

The absinthe came, and with due solemnity we dropped water over the melting sugar.

Somerset Maugham *The Moon and Sixpence*

earlier, absinthe had been thought of as an aphrodisiac and as a medicine. At one time it was officially prescribed to French troops in order to control fever. By the time it fell from favour, it was being accused of converting drinkers into maniacs or suicidal melancholics and causing vertigo and epilepsy.

Emile Zola gives us a verbal portrait in *L'Assommoir*, describing the hoarse, guttural voice, glazed eyes and cold, clammy hands of an absinthe drinker. We see those glazed eyes in the famous painting by Degas, usually known as 'L'Absinthe'. It shows a young woman sitting at a café table, a full glass of the cloudy green liquid in front of her. She is looking at a point on the floor in front of her but is obviously unaware of her surroundings. The man who sits beside, smoking his pipe, appears to be taking some interest in what is happening around him. She is totally passive, resigned to her fate.

PASTIS

Like ouzo, absinthe was colourless until water was added. This was often done by putting a sugar lump in a special, perforated spoon and dripping the water through it. The operation can still be seen in France when café customers order a pastis, a modern substitute for absinthe. It is a spirit flavoured with aniseed, licorice and herbs, said to take its name from the fact that it is a *pastiche* or 'imitation' of absinthe.

A pastis would often be ordered by a brand name, such as Ricard or Berger. Ordering a Pernod would bring a similar drink, one to which the Pernod company turned when absinthe was banned. Pernod is known as *anis* in Spain, its main ingredient being the seed of the herb anise, rather than the wormwood which was the basis of absinthe. It is said to be similar in taste to absinthe but of considerably less alcoholic strength.

Another drink in this group is anisette. As its name indicates it is again based on aniseed and includes coriander amongst its other herbs. The main difference between anisette and Pernod, Ricard and the rest seems to lie in alcoholic strength. Anisette is far weaker than the others.

There is a reference to anisette in Mary McCarthy's *The Group*: 'Harald told them about a liqueur called anisette that an Italian had taught him to make, from straight alcohol, water, and oil of anis, which gave it a milky colour. He explained the difference between Pernod, absinthe, arrack and anisette.' Unfortunately, Miss McCarthy does not seem to have thought that her readers would be interested in Harald's explanation and she does not give it. Harald no doubt included arrack in the group because that, too, turns milky when water is added. It is made in both the Far and Middle East from fermented rice and molasses. The fermented sap of the coconut palm is also often added, but there is no connection with aniseed or wormwood.

Absinthe is still produced in Spain, one of the few countries not to have banned it. A demand for it also still exists in France, especially in the

PAGAN PERNOD

A group of puffy-eyed blondes huddled together in a corner, sucking milky-green Pernod through lumps of sugar with the serious air of neophytes preparing themselves for the performance of some pagan rite. This was definitely not the sort of pub that Henry was used to.

Jeremy Brooks *Henry's War*

FRUIT DRINK

Mig brought a jug of tequila from the hut. The liquor smelled like rotten fruit, but he liked the taste.

Nathanael West *The Day of the Locust*

Pontarlier area where it was formerly made. In 1990 the owner of a wine-shop in the town was sent to prison for four years, after 75 litres of illegally distilled absinthe were discovered in his shop. His lawyer claimed that drinking absinthe was 'a way of life for the Pontissaliens', and that his client had merely reacted to their constant demand for the product.

The absinthe family of drinks remain 'foreign' to the average English and American drinker. They are mentioned from time to time by writers, but normally when those writers are reporting on their experiences abroad. Much the same is true of the Mexican tequila and mezcal (mescal), which form a tragic background to Malcolm Lowry's superb novel *Under the Volcano* (see p. 68).

RUM

A distilled spirit that has, by contrast, long been part of the western drinking repertoire, much cited in literature, is rum. The word is first mentioned in 1654 in its modern form, occurring three years earlier as rumbullion. If the latter reference did not exist it would be easy to say that rum was used to describe the drink because it was 'good, excellent'. That was the common slang meaning of 'rum' in the 16th century, used for example in the phrases 'rum booze' – good liquor, 'rum bub' – good tipple.

In this early sense of 'excellent', rum is derived from *rom*, the Romany word for man. This gypsy connection later caused rum to

change its meaning to 'odd, strange'. As for the mysterious rumbullion, there is an English dialectal word that resembles it which means 'uproar', something which was likely to result when English sailors drank rum. Professor Weekley also wonders, in his *Etymological Dictionary of Modern English*, whether there is a connection with French *bouillon*, referring to a drink which is 'boiled' or heated.

That kind of explanation, however, is too learned and complicated. Sailors are far more likely to have named the drink using a slang or

A Dutch gentleman about to drink his morning tot of rum, 1881.

A RUM STORY

We had a lot of whisky at dinner and I happened to have a bottle of Bénédictine, so we had some liqueurs afterwards. And at last he told me why he'd come. It was a rum story.

Somerset Maugham *The End of the Flight*

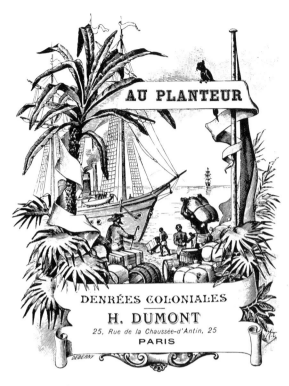

dialectal word that was a part of their everyday language. For that same reason, the suggestion by another writer, that rum derives from the Latin *Saccharum officinarum*, the botanical name for sugar-cane, must also be put aside.

Sugar-cane is not native to the West Indies but had been introduced there by the 16th century. The production of rum was not long in following. Pot stills would have been used at first, to be replaced by continuous stills as they became available. The mash used for fermentation made convenient use of molasses which did not crystallise easily, left over from the sugar-extraction process.

It is easy to think that rum must be a sweet drink because it comes from sugar-cane, but by the time fermentation has changed the sugar into alcohol, and that alcohol has been distilled, the product is no sweeter than a spirit obtained from any other source. A rum which is sweet has been artificially sweetened at a late stage. The colouring in the darker rums also comes later, since any distilled spirit is colourless. Some of the colour, as with brandy and whisky, derives from the casks in which it is aged.

GROG

Rum has proved to be astonishingly adaptable, as much at home in the form of a modern Daiquiri as it was as the sailor's daily tot. Its association with the Royal Navy began at a time when sailors had no modern comforts. A stimulating drink was essential to those who were often in difficult and dangerous circumstances. Over-stimulation caused its own problems, and in 1740 Admiral Sir Edward Vernon was obliged to order that the daily rum ration be diluted with water. The unpopular 'three-water rum' immediately became known as 'grog', a reference to the admiral's nickname. He was known throughout the Navy as Old Grog because his favourite coat was made of grogram (a coarse fabric made of mixed materials, stiffened with gum, from French *gros grain* 'coarse grain').

Grog has gone on to acquire, especially in Australia and New Zealand, the more general sense of alcoholic liquor, including beer. The word groggy, which originally referred to feeling the effects of drinking too much grog, has also taken on a wider meaning. It is now often used of a dazed feeling, not necessarily caused by alcohol. The expression 'grog blossoms' does not seem to have come into general use. At one time it was a naval expression for the heightened colour around the nose, associated with heavy drinking.

The word 'rum' itself almost changed its meaning at one time. Like grog, it was used loosely by

SERGEANT MAJOR'S

At stand-to, rum and tea were served out.

Robert Graves *Goodbye To All That*

'I'd like a drop of tea with some rum in it, good old sergeant-major's.'

J.B. Priestley *The Good Companions*

the Prohibitionists to mean any alcoholic drink. Oliver Wendell Holmes scoffed at such usage in *The Autocrat of the Breakfast Table*: 'Rum I take to be the name which unwashed moralists apply alike to the product distilled from molasses and the noblest juices of the vineyard. Burgundy "in all its sunset glow" is rum. Champagne, "the foaming wine of eastern France", is rum. Hock, which our friend, the poet, speaks of as "The Rhine's breastmilk, gushing cold and bright, Pale as the moon, and maddening as her light", is rum.'

Thomas Pyles, in his *Words and Ways of American English*, says: 'The use of *rum* to refer generically to all alcoholic drinks is an Americanism, confined nowadays pretty much to the Drys; it dates from the early days before whiskey was widely known in this country, when rum was the colonists' favourite strong drink.'

KILL-DEVIL

The Drys, as Mr Pyles calls them, invariably referred not just to rum but to 'the Demon rum'. In *Look Homeward, Angel* Thomas Wolfe describes a campaign mounted by Protestant churches to persuade a town to use its local option and ban alcohol. He quotes a typical temperance song:

> We are some fond mother's treasure,
> Men and women of tomorrow,
> For a moment's empty pleasure
> Would you give us lifelong sorrow?
>
> Think of sisters, wives, and mothers,
> Of helpless babes in some low slum.
> Think not of yourself but others,
> Vote against the Demon Rum.

By an ironic twist, an early name for rum was 'kill-devil'. An anonymous 17th-century writer wrote that 'The chiefe fudling [drink that fuddles] they make in the Island is Rumbullion, alias Kill-Devill, and this is made of suggar canes distilled, a hott, hellish and terrible Liquor.'

Mr Pyles rather gives the impression that the colonists drank neat rum. They had actually discovered at an early stage that it mixed well and they usually drank it as a punch. Nathaniel Hawthorne, in *My Kinsman, Major Molineux*, writes:

'Three or four little groups were draining as many bowls of punch, which the West Indies trade had long since made a familiar drink in the colony. Others preferred the insulated bliss of an unshared potation, and became more taciturn under its influence. Nearly all, in short, evinced a predilection for the Good Creature in some of its various shapes, for this is a vice to which, as Fast Day sermons of a hundred years ago will testify, we have a long hereditary claim.'

RUMMY DICKENSIANS

Rum was a favourite 19th-century drink in England, as Charles Dickens makes clear. His characters drink it in various ways, in punches, diluted with water or mixed with milk. In *Great Expectations*, for instance, Wemmick and Pip meet at eight-thirty in the morning and have a glass of rum-and-milk apiece. Wemmick soon afterwards

---

THE INTERNATIONAL LANGUAGE

'Talking of bars,' said Chelifer, 'has it ever occurred to you to enumerate the English words that have come to have an international currency? It's a somewhat curious selection, and one which seems to me to throw a certain light on the nature and significance of our Anglo-Saxon civilization. The three words from Shakespeare's language that have a completely universal currency are Bar, Sport, and W.C. They're all just as good Finnish now as they are good English. Each of these words possesses what I may call a family. Round the idea 'Bar' group themselves various other international words, such as Bitter, Cocktail, Whisky and the like.'

Aldous Huxley *Those Barren Leaves*

reveals that it is his wedding-day. In *Our Mutual Friend* Riderhood tells Bradley: 'No luck never come yet of a dry acquaintance. Let's wet it in a mouthful of rum and milk.' This is at dawn, and the pub to which they go already has a number of customers.

This same novel has a bizarre reference to another rum-drinker, whose corpse was fished out of the Thames by Gaffer Hexam. We are told that he was a drunken old chap 'wot had suffered – it afterwards came out – to make a hole in the water for a quartern of rum stood aforehand, and had kept to his word for the first and last time in his life'. Equally odd is the passing remark about the king of Borrioboola-Gha, in *Bleak House*. The king frustrates Mrs Jellyby's efforts to help his country by 'wanting to sell everybody – who survived the climate – for Rum'.

Dickens's best-known rum-enthusiast is the appalling hypocrite, the Reverend Mr Stiggins, known as 'The Shepherd'. He is the man who tells Sam Weller that all drinks are vanities: '"Well," said Sam, "I des-say they may be, sir; but which is your partickler wanity? Vich wanity do you like the flavour on best, sir?" "Oh, my dear young friend, I despise them all. If," said Mr Stiggins, "if there is any one of them less odious than another, it is the liquor called rum. Warm, my dear young friend, with three lumps of sugar to the tumbler."'

Stiggins is especially fond of a kind of primitive Pina Colada – pineapple rum and sugar mixed with hot water. He carries around with him a flat bottle which contains about a pint and a half of it.

WIFE-SELLING

The drinking of rum has dramatic consequences in Thomas Hardy's *The Mayor of Casterbridge*. At the beginning of the book, Michael Henchard drinks furmity, described as 'a mixture of corn in the grain, flour, milk, raisins, currants, and whatnot'. In this instance the drink, which was otherwise known as frumenty or furmenty, is laced with rum, and Henchard becomes drunk. As a result he auctions his wife. This curious practice did sometimes occur in former times, though it had no legal validity. If the wife consented to be auctioned, she would subsequently live with her purchaser as his wife.

Rum continues to be mentioned by writers. To bring this chapter to an end, it may be appropriate to quote from a novel called *You Can Call It A Day*. In this, Peter Cheyney has his hard-drinking hero sitting at a bar. The following extraordinary passage speaks for itself: 'He ordered a double Bacardi and when it was served sat looking at it. He realised he didn't want it. Life, he thought, was rather like a Bacardi cocktail. If you wanted one you wanted it like hell; if you didn't want it it was either too weak or too strong. They'd put too much of this or that in it or left it out. But you still drank it. He thought that drinking Bacardi was rather like making love to women. Or wasn't it? He thought he didn't know. He decided he couldn't care less.'

Liqueurs

In English the French word *liqueur* normally refers to a strong alcoholic drink that is usually taken after a meal, theoretically as a *digestif*, something that will help digestion. Some American speakers would still use 'cordial' for 'liqueur', though in Britain that word now tends to suggest a non-alcoholic drink. By implication, a liqueur is of high quality, to be savoured rather than hastily gulped. It is taken in a small quantity, and is meant to put a final seal of excellence on the food and drink that.has gone before.

A liqueur brandy or whisky is one of special quality, for drinking in the manner described above. Most liqueurs, however, are drinks flavoured with herbs, spices, fruit, coffee or chocolate or any of a number of other substances. The precise ingredients and methods of production are usually a well-guarded commercial secret. All one can say for sure is that liqueurs are spirit-based, though whether the spirit was obtained from a grain mash or a fruit must, will probably not be known. The flavouring may be the result of simple infusion or maceration and redistillation.

True fruit brandies are mentioned separately (see pp. 173–74).

Liqueurs can be used as after-dinner drinks, and that is still perhaps their main use. But there is nothing to stop someone drinking cherry brandy, say, at any time of the day or night. Liqueurs are also frequently used as cocktail ingredients. For the moment the word 'liqueur' probably still carries with it the connotations mentioned above, but they may well disappear. In that case a liqueur will become merely a flavoured, spirit-based drink.

The young Graham Greene was reportedly told by Arnold Bennett, when they met at a publisher's party, that 'a serious writer does not drink liqueurs'. The remark was extraordinary: even more so was the effect it had on Greene. By his own admission, he abstained from liqueurs for the rest of his life. Listed below are some of those he might otherwise have sampled. The list is in no way comprehensive, and travellers to different countries will make many local discoveries.

Abricotine – American: apricot.

Advocaat – Dutch: egg yolks, sugar, vanilla, brandy.

Aiguebelle – French: herbs.

Alkermes – French: spirit with cinnamon, cloves, mace, nutmegs, rose water, sugar. Especially famous in the 16th and 17th centuries. Originally the berries from the kermes oak were a principal ingredient. It was later found that the 'berries' were insects.

Amaretto di Saronno – Italian: almond, based on apricot brandy.

Anesone – Italian, American: aniseed.

Anis del Mono – Spanish: aniseed.

Apricot Brandy – various countries: apricot.

Apricot d'Anjou – French: apricot.

Apricot Gin – English: apricot.

Aprikosengeist – German: apricot.

Apry – American: apricot.

Aurum – Italian: pale gold, orange.

Bahia – Brazilian: coffee.

Bailey's Irish Cream – Irish: Irish whiskey, cream, chocolate.

Banadry – French: banana.

B and B – French: Bénédictine mixed with old Cognac. Drier than Bénédictine itself.

Barack Palinka – Hungarian: apricot.

Baska – French: coffee.

Bénédictine – French: herb, brandy-based, amber-coloured; from a recipe said to have been devised by an Italian monk, Bernardo Vincelli. He lived at the Bénédictine Abbey in Fécamp, Normandy. Commercialised in 1863 by Alexandre Le Grand, a French merchant who discovered the formula. He called it Bénédictine in honour of the monk, and added DOM (Latin *Deo Optimo Maximo* 'to God, most good, most great') to the label.

Blackberry Brandy – English. Various countries also produce a Blackberry Liqueur.

Brontë – English: honey, spices, herbs and orange-flavouring. Based on brandy. Sold in Yorkshire in squat pottery jugs.

Calisay – Spanish: herbs and aromatic roots.

Can-y-Delyn – Welsh: whisky-based.

Carmelitano – Spanish: herb, brandy-based.

Casque – English: honey, brandy-based.

Cassis – French: blackcurrant.

Cèdratine – French: citrus, produced in Corsica.

Chartreuse – French: probably the best-known of the French liqueurs, it comes in green and yellow versions, the green being stronger. The yellow variety is sweeter and contains orange and myrtle. At one time there was also a white Chartreuse; an orange Chartreuse has now been introduced. Made from herbs and brandy by the Carthusian monks at Voiron, near

Grenoble, and at Tarragona, Spain. The name 'Chartreuse' was adapted into English in the 16th century as Charterhouse, at first being used for a charitable foundation, later for a famous public school.

Cherry Bestle – Danish: cherry.

Cherry Brandy – various European countries: cherries macerated in spirit.

Cherry Heering – Danish: now known as Peter Heering's Liqueur. Cherry.

Cherry Marnier – French: cherry.

Cherry Whisky – English, French: cherry.

Chocla Menthe – Dutch: peppermint and cacao.

Coffee Bestle – Danish: coffee.

Cointreau – French: orange, made from both bitter and sweet orange peel.

Cordial Campari – Italian: raspberries and brandy.

Cordial Médoc – French: Curaçao, Crème de Cacao and Cognac blended.

Cordial Reby – French: Cognac-based.

Crème d'Amandes – French: almond.

Crème d'Ananas – French: pineapple.

Crème de Banane – French: banana.

Crème de Cacao – French: of chocolate or cocoa flavour and aroma.

Crème de Café – French: coffee.

Crème de Cassis – French: blackcurrant. A speciality of the Burgundy region and used in white wine to make Kir.

Crème de Ciel – Dutch: orange.

Crème de Fraises – French: strawberry.

Crème de Fraise de Bois – French: strawberry. Made from wild strawberries.

Crème de Framboises – French: raspberry.

Crème de Guignolet – French: cherry.

Crème de Kobai – Japanese: plum.

Crème de Mandarine – American: tangerine.

Crème de Menthe – French: peppermint. Clear or green.

Crème de Mokka – French: coffee.

Crème de Myrtilles – French: bilberry.

Crème de Noisette – French: hazelnut.

Crème de Noix – French: walnut.

Crème de Noyau – Dutch: hazelnut.

Crème de Nuits – French: blackcurrant.

Crème de Pecco – Dutch: tea.

Crème de Poire – French: pear.

Crème de Prunelle – French: plum.

Crème de Roses – French: made from the oil of rose petals, vanilla and oils from citrus fruits. Pink-coloured.

Crème des Barbades – French: spices and lemon peel.

Crème de Vanille – American: vanilla.

Crème de Violette – American: made with oil of violets and vanilla.

Crème Yvette – American: violets.

Cremocha – American: coffee.

Cuaranta y Tres – Spanish: a yellow drink also known as Licor 43, a reference to the number of different herbs which are used to produce it.

Curaçao – Dutch: bitter-orange. Curaçoa was formerly a variant spelling. Now available in blue and green as well as orange and colourless.

Danziger Goldwasser – Polish: aniseed and caraway. Fine gold leaf added.

Drambuie – Scottish: whisky, honey and herbs.

Edelweiss – Italian (Fior d'Alpi): extracts from alpine flowers.

Elixir d'Amorique – French: herbs.

Elixir d'Anvers – Belgian: herbs.

Elixir de Garrus – French: vanilla, saffron, maidenhead fern.

Elixir dell'Eremita – Italian: herbs; made by monks.

Elixir de Spa – Belgian: herbs; made by Capuchin monks.

Elixir di China – Italian: aniseed.

Elixir du Mont Ventoux – French: herbs.

Enzian Calisay – Spanish: herbs.

Escarchardo – Portuguese: aniseed.

Filfar – Cypriot: orange.

Fior d'Alpi – Italian: Alpine flowers.

Forbidden Fruit – American: grapefruit, honey, brandy.

Freezamint – French: mint.

Frigola – Spanish: thyme.

Galliano – Italian: spices and herbs. Almost triangular bottle.

Gallweys – Irish: whiskey, honey, herbs, coffee.

Glayva – Scottish: herbs, spices and whisky.

Glen Mist – Scottish: whisky, herbs, spices and honey.

Grand Marnier – French: orange, based on fine Cognac.

Gyokuro Rikyu – Japanese: green-tea. 'Rikyu' represents a Japanese phonetic version of 'liqueur'.

Halb Schimmelgespann – German: half-bitter, half-sweet, herbs.

Halb und Halb – German: Curaçao and orange bitters.

Himbeergeist – German: raspberry.

Irish Cow – Irish: Irish whiskey, double cream, chocolate.

Irish Mist – Irish: Irish whiskey, herbs, honey.

Irish Moss – American: rye whiskey, Irish moss.

Irish Velvet – Irish: Irish whiskey, coffee, sugar.

Isolabella – Italian: herbs.

Izarra – French: also found as Izzarra. Armagnac, fruits, honey, flowers.

Jägermeister – German: herbs.

Kahlua – Danish: coffee.

Kakao mit Nuss – German: white chocolate and hazelnut.

Kamok – French: coffee.

Karpi – Finnish: cranberry.

Kirsch – German: cherry.

Kitron – Greek: lemon.

Kümmel – German, Dutch: uses caraway seeds, orris and fennel.

Lakka – Finnish: cloudberry-based. Also known as Suomuurain.

Liqueur aux Fraises – Belgian: strawberry.

Liqueur d'Angélique – French: Cognac and angelica.

Liqueur de Noix Vertes – French: walnut.

Liqueur de Sapins – French: pine-needle extract.

Liqueur des Moines – French: aromatic plants and Cognac.

Liqueur d'Or – French: lemon with gold flakes in it.

Macvin – French: red wine, marc, cinnamon, coriander.

Mandarine Napoléon – Belgian: tangerine.

Maraschino – originally Yugoslavian: cherry liqueur made from sour Marasca cherries; now produced in Italy.

Marnique – Australian: Australian brandy, quince.

Mentuccia – Italian: about 100 herbs.

Mersin – Turkish: orange.

Mesimarja – Finnish: flavoured with arctic brambles.

Midori – Japanese: melon.

Millefiori – Italian: herbs.

Mirabelle – French: cherry.

Noyau Rosé – French: peach and apricot.

Ocha – Japanese: tea.

Orange Brandy – various countries: orange.

Orange Gin – English: orange.

Oranjebitter – Dutch: orange.

Original Peachtree – Dutch: peach.

Palo – Spanish: thyme.

Parfait Amour – French: Curaçao flavoured with rose petals, vanilla, almonds. The American version of this liqueur is made with citrus fruits, coriander and sugar.

Pasha – Turkish: coffee.

Peach Brandy – various countries: peach.

Peach County Schnapps – Canadian: peach.

Peter Heering's Liqueur – Danish: cherry.

Pimpeltjens – Dutch: orange Curaçao with herbs.

Poire Williams – made in Switzerland and some parts of France: pear. Usually has a pear in the bottle, achieved by tying bottle to buds on the tree.

Pomeranzen – Austrian: orange.

Ponche Soto – Spanish: herbs, sherry and brandy. Sold in a distinctive silver bottle.

Punsch – Swedish: spices, rum-based.

Quetsch – French: plum.

Rock and Rye – American: rye whiskey, rock candy syrup, lemons, oranges, cherries.

Royal Blend – Italian: based on imported Scotch whisky.

Royal Cherry Chocolate – English. Hallgarten produces this and the following liqueurs, all with self-descriptive names: Royal Coconut, Royal Fruit and Nut Chocolate, Royal Ginger Chocolate, Royal Lemon Chocolate, Royal Mint Chocolate, Royal Nut Chocolate, Royal Orange Chocolate, Royal Raspberry Chocolate.

Royal Tara Irish Cream Liqueur – Irish: Irish whiskey and cream.

Royal Triple Sec – Swedish: based on Curaçao.

Sabra – Israeli: orange and Swiss chocolate.

San Michele – Danish: tangerine.

Sapindor – French: herbs. Tree-trunk-shaped bottles.

Senancole – French: herbs.

Sloe Gin – English, Dutch: sloe. The sloe is a wild plum, also known as the blackthorn.

Solbaerrum – Danish: blackcurrant, rum-based.

Southern Comfort – American: orange and peach.

St Hallvard – Norwegian: herb, potato-based spirit.

Stönsdorfer – German: herbs.

Strega – Italian: made from about 70 herbs. The name means 'witch'.

Suomuurain – Finnish: cloudberry. The cloudberry is allied to the raspberry.

Tapio – Finnish: herb and juniper.

Tia Maria – Jamaican: coffee, rum-based.

Trappistine – French: herbs with an Armagnac base.

Tres Castillos – Puerto Rican: aniseed.

Triple Sec – very sweet white Curaçao.

Tuaca – Italian: citrus.

Van der Hum – South African: orange. The name is the Dutch equivalent of 'What's-his-name'.

Vandermint – Dutch: mint-chocolate.

Verveine de Velay – French: herbs. Green and yellow versions.

Vieille Curé – French: herbs, Armagnac, Cognac.

Wisniowka – Polish: cherry.

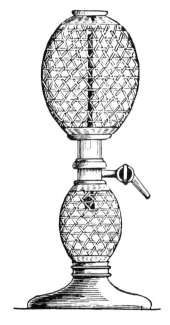

An early soda siphon

Glossary of spirits and mixed drinks

Alembic – a kind of still. (See p. 169.) The French form *alambic* is sometimes used erroneously in English.

Amara – see Bitters.

Amer Picon – see Bitters.

Angostura – well-known bitters used to flavour cocktails, such as the Pink Gin. Named after the town in Venezuela (renamed Ciudad Bolivar in 1846) from which they were originally exported. Once known as Dr Siegert's Aromatic Bitters. The company is now based in Trinidad.

Aqua-vitae – Latin "water-of-life". Used to describe a distilled spirit. Compare Gaelic *usquebeatha* (whisky), French *eau-de-vie*, Swedish *aquavit*, Danish *aqvavit*, Russian *zhiznennia voda* (vodka), all of which mean water of life.

Arquebuse – see Bitters.

Ava – see Kava.

Badminton – a 19th-century term for a mixed drink of claret, sugar and soda water. 'Bring me a tumbler of Badminton.' Benjamin Disraeli *Sybil*. Named after the country seat of the Duke of Beaufort, where it was introduced.

Bathtub gin – term used in America during Prohibition for alcohol mixed with flavouring at home.

Bishop – a popular mixed drink of the 18th and 19th centuries. The chief ingredients were mulled port, oranges or lemons, cloves and sugar. Dr Johnson is said by Boswell to have always been fond of bishop.

Bitters – these are normally spirits blended with roots, spices, fruits, etc., to formulae which are trade secrets. Sometimes drunk as aperitifs, but often used as ingredients in cocktails to give a bitter flavour. The best-known bitters are Angostura, Campari, Fernet Branca and Underberg. Others include Amara (South American), Amer Picon (French), Apricot Bitters, Arquebuse (French), Boonekamp (Dutch), Calisaya (Spanish), Orange Bitters, Peach Bitters, Secrestat (French), Suze (French), Tangerine Bitters, Toni-Kola (French).

Blue ruin – one of the many slang names for gin. Bad gin in the 19th century had a bluish tinge. Ruin may have been meant to rhyme with gin. 'My dear sir, a hair of the dog that bit you is clearly indicated. A touch of Blue Ruin, now?' R.L. Stevenson *St Ives*.

Boonekamp – see Bitters.

Bump – as in '"Lemme buy you a beer! . . . No! Better yet! A beer and a bump!" Wally set up a glass of beer and a shot of whiskey next to Mr Berge's.' Garrison Keillor 'Revival' *Lake Wobegon Days*.

Bushie – a South American term for moonshine.

Busthead – an early slang term for US whiskey.

Calisaya – see Bitters.

Campari – a well-known Italian bitters, made to a secret formula. Used as a cocktail ingredient or drunk with soda.

Chaser – used of a glass of beer or water which 'chases' a glass of spirits, though some people reverse this and speak of the spirits as the chaser. 'It was the chaser, the water. The whisky would certainly be in that other lil sawed-off glass. And it was. With a smirk of self-admiration he sucked in the raw bourbon.' Sinclair Lewis *Elmer Gantry*.

Chota-peg – an Anglo-Indian word for a measure of whisky. 'In the evening, a gentle walk from the Bombay office to the Yacht Club for a chota-peg in a tumbler of soda water was a wonderful pick-me-up after the tiring heat of the day.' Cedric Dickens *Drinking With Dickens*.

Cobbler – iced fortified wine (e.g. sherry), rum or whisky with sugar, garnished with citrus fruit. Probably from cobbler's punch, which 'patched up' the drinker.

Compound – another word for a mixed drink. 'They were soon occupied in discussing an exhilarating compound, formed by mixing together, in a pewter vessel, certain quantities of British Hollands and the fragrant essence of the clove.' Charles Dickens *The Pickwick Papers*.

Cooler – a long drink based on spirits, usually containing lemon or lime juice, iced or topped up with soda water, ginger beer or Coca-Cola.

Cup – used for a mixture of drinks, of smaller quantity than is usual in a punch but greater than a cocktail.

Daisy – applied to cocktails of various kinds, usually served in tall glasses with plenty of ice. 'Daisy' presumably has its slang meaning of 'something excellent'.

Demerara – a dark, highly flavoured kind of rum, considered by some connoisseurs to be even better than Jamaican rum.

Devil's toothbrush – wardroom drink of brandy and gin, in equal measure, taken neat. Wilfred Granville *A Dictionary of Sailors' Slang*.

Eau-de-vie – French 'water of life'. Used of distilled spirit. *Eau-de-vie de grain* is grain spirit, such as whisky and gin. *Eau-de-vie de vin* is brandy. *Eau-de-vie de cidre* is Calvados. *Eau-de-vie de marc* is brandy made from the 'murk' of grapes after they have been pressed to make wine.

Eye-water – a slang term for gin.

Fernet Branca – an Italian bitters, often recommended as a hangover cure.

Fine, une – French 'a brandy'.

Firewater – a 19th-century American term for whiskey, said to have been used by the American Indians.

Fizz – a long drink, often gin-based, with soda-water. Other ingredients can include sugar, lemon-juice, egg white, cream, liqueurs. The best-known is probably Bucks Fizz (see p. 209).

Flap – brandy and soda.

Flip – popular in the 18th and 19th centuries. In Britain it is beer mixed with spirit, sweetened and heated with a hot poker. Americans define it as a sweetened spiced liquor of any kind to which beaten eggs have been added.

Frappé – poured into a glass over crushed ice; used of liqueurs. 'Morley went to a restaurant and ordered a sirloin and a pint of inexpensive

Château Breuille. "And now, green Chartreuse, frappé and a demi-tasse."' O. Henry *The Assessor of Success*.

Garnishing - fruit and vegetables added to cocktails. 'Some of the drinks were more like vases of flowers, stuck with garnishes of cucumber and cress, pineapple slices and cherries.' Len Deighton *Close-up*.

Geneva - a former name for gin, based on the Dutch word for the juniper berry, *genever*, and by some falsely associated with the Swiss city.

Gin-and-Jaguar belt - British criminal slang for parts of the Home Counties, suitable for burglaries.

Gin-mill - US slang for a saloon, bar or tavern. 'I'll be waiting in the little gin-mill across the street.' John Dos Passos *The Great Days*.

Gin-names - 'Ingenuity is exhausted in devising attractive titles for the different descriptions of gin; and the dram-drinking portion of the community are left in a state of pleasing hesitation between "The Cream of the Valley", "The Out and Out", "The No Mistake", "The Good for Mixing", "The Real Knock-me-down", "The Celebrated Butter Gun", "The Regular Flare-up" and a dozen other equally inviting and wholesome *liqueurs*.' Charles Dickens, 'Gin Shops' in *Sketches by Boz*. Other names included cholic water, Tom Row, Make Shift, Ladies' Delight.

Gin-rummy - an alcoholic-sounding card-game, a variation of rummy. Sequences, triplets, etc., are laid on the table. It is not clear why the game was called rummy, but the *Reader's Digest Dictionary* thinks that 'gin' was jokingly used to pick up on the 'rum'.

Gunga Din - Julian Franklyn, in his *Dictionary of Rhyming Slang*, says that Gunga Din and Squatter's Daughter is an Australian expression for gin and water.

Hard liquor - in the USA, any distilled alcoholic spirit.

Hell's brew - a strong mixed drink. 'Jack mixed a hell's brew with a brandy base. I was as high as a kite after the first glass.' Jilly Cooper *Prudence*.

Hollands - Dutch gin made from malted rye. Other terms for it include Geneva and Schiedam.

Jersey lightning - a 19th-century American term for applejack.

Joy water - a 19th-century American term for whiskey.

Julep - see Mint julep, p. 213.

Jungle juice - originally a beverage concocted by servicemen in the tropics, e.g. surgical spirit and fermented coconut milk. Loosely used of any rough and ready concoction.

Kanyak - Turkish 'brandy'. The word 'Cognac' in disguise.

Kava - a Polynesian drink based on the chewed or pounded roots of the pepper shrub. Also known as Ava.

Kentucky horn - rhyming slang for corn (whiskey).

Koumiss - a drink of the Tartars and other nomadic Asiatic tribes, believed to have many medicinal properties. Distilled from fermented mares' milk. Imitations are made from asses' and cows' milk.

Marc - brandy made from the very last pressing of the season's grapes. (See p. 171.)

Moonshine - whiskey made by unlicensed distillers, especially during the Prohibition period in the USA. 'Bad rye and moonshine corn were the prevailing beverages.' Thomas Wolfe *Look Homeward, Angel*. 'I've got a quart of first-rate corn whisky from a moonshiner I've dug up here in the country . . .' Sinclair Lewis *Elmer Gantry*.

Mother's ruin - a slang expression for gin.

Mountain dew - raw, inferior whiskey; moonshine.

Mur - back slang for rum.

Nantz - a former term for brandy; a corruption of the French place-name Nantes, on the Loire, where it was made.

Napoleon - used of brandy to imply that it is of great age.

Neat - with no added water.

Negus - a punch made of sherry or port, boiling water, nutmeg, lemon. Named after a Colonel Francis Negus who made it known in the 18th century. In Dickens's *Our Mutual Friend*, Miss Abbey Potterson usually

has a tumbler of hot port negus at bed-time.

Nelson's blood - Royal Navy slang, rum. From the belief that Lord Nelson's body was brought back to England after Trafalgar pickled in rum.

Nobbler - a glass of spirits and water.

Oh Be Joyful - a term used by soldiers during the American Civil War to describe an alcoholic drink made from whatever ingredients happened to be available.

Old Tom - the gin of this name is constantly referred to in 19th-century texts. Typical is this mention in Thomas Hardy's *A Tragedy of Two Ambitions*: '"As for the victuals at the Cock I can't testify to 'em at all; but for the drink, they've the rarest drop of Old Tom that I've tasted for many a year." Joshua could fully believe his father's testimony to the gin, from the odour of his breath.' It is impossible to be certain about the origin of the name, but a much-told story concerns a Dudley Bradstreet. He is said to have put the sign of a tom-cat in his window in Blue-Anchor Alley. Putting coins into a slot in the cat's mouth produced a trickle of gin that could be drunk immediately or taken away in a bottle.

Old Tomahawk - early type of whiskey in the USA.

Panther piss - US slang for inferior whisky.

Pimple and blotch - Scotch, in rhyming slang.

Poteen - illicit liquor made in Ireland, often from potatoes, using a pot still.

Prescription whiskey - whiskey obtainable by doctor's prescription for medical reasons during Prohibition. 'Harald told her about a drugstore he and Kay knew on West Fifty-ninth Street, where you could get prescription whiskey without a prescription.' Mary McCarthy *The Group*.

Punch houses - taverns where punch was sold.

Red eye - American slang, cheap whiskey.

Red ribbon - 19th-century British slang for brandy.

Rhum - French 'rum', as in *baba au rhum* 'rum baba'.

Rhyming slang - terms for spirits include blue ruin, Brian O'Linn, bung it in, mother's ruin, needle and pin, strong and thin, thick and thin, Vera Lynn, Lincoln's Inn (gin); Highland frisky, gay and frisky, I'm so frisky (whisky); Rosy Loader (whisky and soda); finger and thumb, thimble and thumb, Tom Thumb, torn thumb (rum).

Rickey - a cocktail based on gin, whiskey, rum, applejack, etc., with lime or lemon juice and soda water. Said to be named after a distinguished Washington drinker at the end of the 19th century whose identity is disputed.

Rocks, on the - an undiluted drink served with ice-cubes.

Rotgut - US slang for inferior whiskey.

Rumbo - a name for rum punch in the 18th and 19th centuries. 'He and my good master Hatchway come hither every evening, and drink a couple of cans of Rumbo a-piece.' Tobias Smollett *The Adventures of Peregrine Pickle*.

Rum omelette - eaten by Colonel Blount and Adam Symes in Evelyn Waugh's *Vile Bodies*.

Sangaree - red wine diluted with fruit juice and soda water. Sangaree is an English form of Spanish *sangria* 'bloody'. Sangaree is also used of port or sherry lightly sugared and iced.

Schiedam - an early term for gin, referring to Schiedam near Rotterdam, the Dutch gin-distilling area. 'I'll do my part in the drinkables, and see to the rum and schiedam – maybe a dozen jars will be sufficient?' Thomas Hardy *The Mayor of Casterbridge*.

Scotia's nectar - whisky.

Secrestat - see Bitters.

Shrub - a drink made with a spirit, usually rum, sugar and orange or lemon juice, popular in the 18th and 19th centuries. In 19th-century American usage, shrub came to mean a cordial made from raspberry juice, vinegar and sugar. Both British and American authors sometimes used the spelling srub. The word has nothing to do with the plant, but derives from an Arabic word meaning 'drink, draught'. '"Will you take something? A glass of srub and water, now? I smoke on srub and water myself," said Mr Omer, taking up his glass, "because it's considered softening to the passages, by which this troublesome breath of mine gets into action."' Charles Dickens *David Copperfield*.

Skokian - a South African drink: 'a wicked and dangerous drink, and it is illegal. It is made quickly in one day, and may contain many different substances. On this night it has mealie-meal, sugar, tobacco, methylated spirits, boot polish and yeast. Some skokian queens use magic, such as the limb of a dead person . . .' Doris Lessing *Five*.

Slammer - a drink meant to bring about drunkenness quickly, such as tequila and soda water. The more absurd and dangerous types of slammer include the Blazing Lamborghini – rum, vodka and blue Curaçao, set alight and drunk through a straw before the plastic melts. The 'cocktail' that is composed of tots of whisky, gin, rum, vodka and brandy is known by various names. Kingsley Amis calls it the Tigne Rose and associates it with the Tigne Barracks, Malta. *The Correspondent*'s radio critic calls it The Wild Man of Bonio because he decorates it with a Bonio dog biscuit. Versions of it are drunk at stag parties, occasionally with fatal results.

Sling - defined by *Webster's New Collegiate Dictionary* as 'an alcoholic drink usually made of whiskey, brandy, or especially gin with plain or carbonated water, sugar and sometimes bitters and often garnished with lemon or lime peel if cold or dusted with nutmeg if hot'.

Smash - a kind of junior julep. Spirits such as Bacardi, brandy, gin or whisky are added to a glass containing mint dipped in dissolved sugar. Decorated with orange and lemon peel.

Sol y Sombra - Spanish 'sun and shade'. A mixed drink, equal parts of gin and brandy.

Sour - whiskey, etc., with sugar, lemon or lime juice and chopped ice, strained into a glass. H.L. Mencken says in *The American Language* that 'fancy forms contain liqueurs or even eggs, but are not favoured by connoisseurs'. He adds that sours were once popular 'as a morning pickup to allay gastritis'.

Stone fence - a 19th-century American mixture of whiskey and cider. In modern cocktail-recipe books the cider has usually been replaced with a drop or two of Angostura bitters.

Streak of lightning - 19th-century British slang for a glass of spirits.

Suze - see Bitters.

Swizzles - spirits mixed with sugar and soda-water. 'Calmed by rum swizzles, those tart and commanding aperitifs which are made in their deadly perfection only by the twirling swizzle-sticks of the darkies at the Ice-house bar, the exiles become peaceful, and have another swizzle.' Sinclair Lewis *Martin Arrowsmith*.

Tarantula juice - early American slang term for crude whiskey.

Toddy - this varies considerably in different parts of the world. In Britain it is whisky, sugar and hot water. In the USA often iced and spiced but not sugared. In India it can refer to a drink made from tree sap.

Toni-Kola - see Bitters.

Underberg - a well-known German herb-based bitters, often recommended as a hangover cure.

VSO - on Cognac bottles: 'Very Superior Old'.

VSOP - on Cognac bottles: 'Very Superior Old Pale.'

Whiskers - whisky. 'Have some more whiskers, Brad, it'll do you good.' Iris Murdoch *The Black Prince*.

Whisky Insurrection - riots protesting against excise duties which occurred in Western Pennsylvania in 1794.

Whisky Mac - whisky with ginger wine.

White lightning - US slang for inferior whiskey.

White mule - US bootleg whiskey. '"We can get some white mule. Come on." Martin led him into the lunch-room where they had raw whisky in granite-like coffee cups.' Sinclair Lewis *Martin Arrowsmith*.

White satin - also white tape, white wine. Early slang terms for gin.

SPIRITS CONSUMPTION PER HEAD

Litres per head of 100% alcohol

Country	1970	1975	1980	1984	1985	1986	1987	1988	1989
European Community									
Belgium	1.3	2.0	2.4	1.9	2.1	2.0	2.2	1.5	1.2
Denmark	1.3	1.7	1.5	1.5	1.7	1.6	1.5	1.4	1.4
France	2.3	2.4	2.5	2.2	2.3	2.3	2.3	2.5	2.4
Greece	..	..	..	..	..	..	..	1.5	1.5
Ireland, Rep. of	1.5	2.0	2.0	1.5	1.8	1.7	1.6	1.7	1.7
Italy	1.8	1.8	1.9	1.2	1.2	1.2	1.0	1.0	1.1
Netherlands	2.0	3.4	2.7	2.4	2.2	2.2	2.1	2.1	1.9
Portugal	0.5	0.9	0.9	0.8	0.8	0.8	0.8	0.8	0.8
Spain	2.8	2.6	3.2	2.8	3.0	3.0	3.0	3.3	2.9
West Germany	3.0	3.0	3.1	2.3	2.4	2.3	2.2	2.3	2.5
UK	0.9	1.5	1.8	1.6	1.7	1.7	1.7	1.8	1.8
Rest of Europe									
Austria	1.4	1.7	1.6	1.5	1.5	1.5	1.6	1.6	1.5
Bulgaria	2.4	2.9	3.2	3.2	3.2	3.4	2.8	2.8	3.2
Czechoslovakia	2.4	2.9	3.5	3.3	3.4	3.4	3.3	3.3	3.4
East Germany	2.6	3.5	4.7	4.6	4.8	4.9	5.1	5.2	5.0
Finland	1.8	2.8	2.8	2.9	2.8	2.9	3.0	2.5	3.2
Hungary	2.7	3.6	4.8	5.1	5.5	5.3	4.7	4.5	4.7
Iceland	2.2	2.4	2.3	2.2	2.3	2.4	2.4	2.6	2.2
Norway	1.6	1.8	1.9	1.3	1.4	1.3	1.3	1.2	1.1
Poland	3.2	4.6	6.0	4.6	4.6	4.7	4.7	4.6	4.5
Romania	2.2	1.9	2.3	2.0	2.0	2.0	2.0	2.0	2.5
Sweden	2.6	3.0	2.7	2.1	2.1	2.1	2.0	1.9	1.9
Switzerland	2.0	1.9	2.0	2.1	2.2	2.1	2.0	2.1	1.9
USSR	3.8	3.9	5.7	5.2	4.5	2.7	1.6	1.8	2.0
Yugoslavia	3.1	2.8	2.2	2.1	2.1	2.2	2.0	1.9	1.6
Africa									
Nigeria	..	..	..	..	..	..	..	..	..
South Africa	1.3	1.4	1.3	1.2	1.1	1.0	1.1	1.0	1.0
Asia									
China	..	..	..	..	..	..	..	..	..
Japan	1.1	1.3	1.8	2.3	2.4	2.3	2.3	2.6	2.1
Korea, Rep. of	..	..	..	..	..	..	..	..	..
Philippines	..	..	2.9	2.7	2.7	2.7	..	..	..
Australasia									
Australia	1.0	1.2	1.0	1.1	1.2	1.3	1.2	1.3	1.3
New Zealand	1.1	1.6	1.9	1.8	1.7	1.4	1.6	1.5	1.4
North America									
Canada	2.2	3.2	3.3	2.7	2.6	2.5	2.5	2.5	2.5
USA	3.1	3.2	3.1	2.8	2.7	2.6	2.5	2.3	2.3
Central and South America									
Argentina	..	..	2.0	1.0	1.0	1.0	1.0	0.6	0.4
Brazil	..	..	..	..	..	..	..	..	..
Chile	..	..	..	..	..	..	..	..	..
Colombia	..	..	..	..	..	..	..	..	..
Cuba	0.8	0.7	..	..	..	..	..	..	..
Mexico	0.7	0.7	0.9	0.9	1.0	0.8	1.1	0.9	0.8
Peru	1.4	2.0	3.0	3.0	3.0	3.0	..	..	..
Venezuela	..	..	..	..	..	..	..	..	..

MIXING IT

Cocktails, punches and other mixed drinks

A GREAT deal of mixing and blending goes on in the world of drinks. A mixture of various grains goes into the mash which leads to beers, whiskies and gins. Wines are blends of different varieties of grapes and may be fortified (mixed) with spirits. Liqueurs, as we have seen, mix spirits with any number of other ingredients. The results of all this mixing within the trade are then offered as finished products to the consumers. They then proceed to do some mixing of their own.

The tradition of mixing drinks goes back to at least the 14th century. Ale and mead were two distinctive drinks of the time; we know that they were being mixed together as bragget (see p. 110). By the 17th century wines, spirits, spices and fruits were being mixed together and served in punch or wassail bowls. Rum shrubs (rum with orange or lemon juice), flips and purls (mixtures of beer and spirits), sangarees (wine with spices) and toddies (spirits with water and sugar) were a feature of the 18th century. The beginning of the 19th century saw the rise of the cocktail, cobbler, cooler, julep, sling and swizzle, though they were at their most fashionable in the 1920s. Some of the more successful remain with us today.

PUNCH

The word 'punch' is often explained as being derived from the word for 'five' in several Indian languages. The place-name Punjab, for instance, means 'five waters (rivers)'. The *Oxford English Dictionary* long ago pointed out that this derivation was unlikely on phonetic grounds. There is also no evidence that punch was originally made from five ingredients. The word is more likely to be an abbreviation of 'puncheon', a kind of large cask.

ON LENDING A PUNCH BOWL

This ancient silver bowl of mine, – it tells
   of good old times,
Of joyous days, and jolly nights, and
   merry Christmas chimes;
They were a free and jovial race, but
   honest, brave, and true,
That dipped their ladle in the punch
   when this old bowl was new.

A Spanish galleon brought the bar; so
   runs the ancient tale;
'Twas hammered by an Antwerp smith,
   whose arm was like a flail;
And now and then between the strokes,
   for fear his strength should fail,
He wiped his brow, and quaffed a cup
   of good old Flemish ale.

'Twas purchased by an English squire to
   please his loving dame,
Who saw the cherubs, and conceived a
   longing for the same;
And oft, as on the ancient stock another
   twig was found,
'Twas filled with caudle spiced and hot,
   and handed smoking round.

But, changing hands, it reached at
   length a Puritan divine,
Who used to follow Timothy, and take
   a little wine,
But hated punch and prelacy; and so it
   was, perhaps,
He went to Leyden, where he found
   conventicles and schnapps.

And then, of course, you know what's rest,
   – it left the Dutchman's shore

With those that in the *Mayflower* came,
  – a hundred souls and more, –
Along with all the furniture, to fill their
  new abodes, –
To judge by what is still on hand, at
  least a hundred loads.

'Twas on a dreary winter's eve, the
  night was closing dim,
When brave Miles Standish took the
  bowl, and filled it to the brim;
The little Captain stood and stirred the
  posset with his sword,
And all his sturdy men-at-arms were
  ranged about the board.

He poured the fiery Hollands in, – the
  man that never feared, –
He took a long and solemn draught,
  and wiped his yellow beard:
And one by one the musketeers – the
  men that fought and prayed –
All drank as 'twere their mother's milk,
  and not a man afraid.

Then fill a fair and honest cup, and
  bear it straight to me;
The goblet hallows all it holds, whate'er
  the liquid be;
And may the cherubs on its face protect
  me from the sin,
That dooms to me those dreadful words,
  – 'My dear, where *have* you been?'

Oliver Wendell Holmes (abridged)

(Right) A party, 18th century. After Hogarth.

These days a punch can certainly be made with as many ingredients as desired, though beer is never one of them. Punch-like mixes which are based on beer tend to have individual names, such as Lamb's Wool (see p. 111) or Huckle-my-butt. The latter consists of beer, brandy, sugar, eggs and spices and inspired an anonymous 19th-century poet:

Huckle-my-butt, Huckle-my-butt,
It is welcome alike both in palace and hut,
Should I have fifty children, each rogue and
  each slut,
All shall be christened Huckle-my-butt.

Huckle-my-butt, Huckle-my-butt,
If there ever was nectar, 'tis Huckle-my-
  butt;
The haughty may sneer, and the swaggerer
  strut,
Let them keep their Tokay, give me Huckle-
  my-butt.

Punches, sometimes called 'cups', normally mix wine and a spirit with fruit juices, sugar and water or milk. In the 18th and 19th centuries, rum was normally the spirit used and the water or milk was always hot if it was being drunk in winter.

RUM PUNCH

A typical rum punch might be made with rum, sweet vermouth, orange juice, spices and sugar. The spices, such as peppercorns, cinnamon, root ginger and cloves, would be simmered in the orange juice before the rum and vermouth were added. Individual drinkers would then add sugar to their own glasses according to taste. Stanley Belgrave, in his *Caribbean Cocktail Guide*, suggests that a summer punch could be made with sugar, claret, sparkling water, rum, brandy, white wine and Italian vermouth, mixed in a large punch bowl with a block of ice.

A lot of the pleasure associated with punches lies in the idea of sharing and group identity. In the past, a punch might well have been served in a loving-cup, a wassail-bowl from which everyone

MICAWBER AMONGST THE LEMONS

I informed Mr Micawber that I relied upon him for a bowl of punch, and led him to the lemons . . . I never saw a man so thoroughly enjoy himself amid the fragrance of lemon-peel and sugar, the odour of burning rum, and the steam of boiling water, as Mr Micawber did that afternoon.

Charles Dickens *David Copperfield*

drank as it was passed round the table. These days it is more likely to be ladled out into individual glasses, along with the bits of fruit and vegetables that add to the fun, but a punch still seems especially suitable for a family gathering.

Dickensian characters are often to be found mixing punches, exercising great skill in that art. Mr Micawber's delight in that occupation is well known, but he is not alone. In *Martin Chuzzlewit*, a novel which features a wide range of drinks, we learn that the undertaker Mr Mould is an adept: 'The room was fragrant with the smell of punch, a tumbler of which grateful compound stood upon a small round table, convenient to the hand of Mr Mould; so deftly mixed that, as his eye looked down into the cool transparent drink, another eye, peering brightly from behind the crisp lemon peel, looked up at him, and twinkled like a star.'

Time and again Dickens mentions the odour of punch, which is clearly a boyhood memory. It is there again in *Our Mutual Friend*. The odour of rum, says Dickens, 'with the fostering aid of boiling water and lemon-peel, diffused itself throughout the room, and became so highly concentrated round the warm fireside, that the wind passing over the house-roof must have rushed off charged with a delicious whiff of it, after buzzing like a great bee at that particular chimney-pot'.

Dickens does not provide us with recipes; in *The Group* Mary McCarthy is more obliging: 'A punch was being served, over which the guests were exclaiming: "What is it?" "Perfectly delicious." "How did you ever think of it?" and so on. To each one Kay gave the recipe. The base was one third Jersey applejack, one third maple syrup, and one third lemon juice, to which White Rock had been added. The punch was adapted from a cocktail called Applejack Rabbit.'

COCKTAILS

As that quotation partly suggests, cocktails are like punches in miniature, made in smaller quantities. They are spirit-based and mixed with something other than water. I think we also expect them to be individually named, which is why I do not think of drinks like gin and tonic, rum and Coke, whisky and soda, as cocktails. With these we specify the ingredients as we order them: once we ask for a Bloody Mary or a Whisky Mac or a Dry Martini we are using a kind of shorthand which someone else needs to be able to interpret.

It is sometimes disconcerting not to be able to make such an interpretation in a social situation or when reading a novel. There is no problem with an author like Arthur Conan Doyle, who

FAMILY CHRISTMAS

'I can offer you port, brandy, Madeira or Tia Maria.'

'Hmm, sounds nice. How about a cocktail of all four? Let's live dangerously.'

Addy took a swig of her drink and pronounced it sensational. 'We'll have to think of a name for it,' said Kay. 'How about *Family Christmas*, strained and shaken but not stirred?'

Addy laughed. 'God, you're a fork-tongued bitch, but I know what you mean.'

Imogen Winn *Coming to Terms*

Club Cocktails

A SPLENDID APPETIZER.

A good Cocktail is a capital thing to start the dinner with, but it must be carefully blended. You should always keep some Club Cocktails on hand, as they are scientifically blended from the choicest old liquors and are the original and standard American Cocktails —the only ones listed by the best American houses.

Martini (Gin Base) and Manhattan (Whisky Base) are the two most popular varieties. If you have any difficulty in getting the Club Cocktails, write to J. L. DENMAN & CO., 20, Piccadilly, W., or MOREL BROS., COBBETT & SON, 210, Piccadilly, W.

G. F. HEUBLEIN & BRO., Sole Proprietors, HARTFORD, CONN., & NEW YORK, U.S.A.

An early attempt to launch Heublein ready-made cocktails in Britain.

remarks in *The Red-headed League*: '"You see, Watson," he explained in the early hours of the morning, as we sat over a glass of whisky-and-soda in Baker Street . . .' He leaves one in no doubt what Sherlock Holmes is drinking. So it is with Dickens, when he describes in his essay on 'Gin Shops' old women asking for their gin and peppermint, or with Vladimir Nabokov in *Lolita*, when he tells us: 'Gin and pineapple juice, my favourite mixture, always doubles my energy.' Notice how Nabokov, always meticulous with his choice of words, refers to a mixture rather than a cocktail.

More irritating may be a passage like this, in Robert Daley's *Only A Game*: 'She orders a negroni. "What's a negroni?" Craig asks. She tells him, and for a moment they discuss drinks.' At that point, one may interrupt one's reading to consult a reference book. A negroni consists of gin, sweet vermouth and Campari. Even that explanation is, in its way, a kind of shorthand. It assumes that everyone knows that Campari is an Italian orange bitters, and that bitters are spirits flavoured with roots, herbs or fruits which have a bitter taste. (See also p. 199.)

Sometimes the novelists themselves comment on the problem. 'Try not to hold this against me,' says a character in *Thirteen Days*, by Ian Jefferies, 'but I don't know what a whisky sour is. Is there a book here I can look it up in?' Here the reader

might expect an explanation of a whisky sour to follow. Instead we get: '"Let me," she said. She poured her whisky, and soured it.' No mention by the author of lemon juice or sugar.

BARTENDER PROBLEMS

Bartenders can obviously be faced with special problems when it comes to cocktails. In *Sauce for the Goose*, Peter de Vries hilariously sympathises with a man faced with a large party of women 'whose cocktail order was as follows: "Three Martinis, one on the rocks, two up, with twist, olive and onion respectively, two Manhattans, two bloody Marys . . . Three sidecars, a pink lady, two grasshoppers, an angel's kiss, two Margaritas, *one not too much salt*, a gimlet, a between the sheets, a Mamie Taylor, two Alexanders, a bee's knees, Lord give me strength – " "That's a drink?" "No, no, that's me crying out . . . A Gertie's garter, a blood and sand, a King Alphonse, and two Rob Roys . . . See that guy going out the door putting on his hat and coat? That's the bartender."'

THE PERFICK BOOK

Pop stood by the cocktail cabinet consulting a book, *A Guide to Better Drinking*, given him by Montgomery for Christmas. It was the only book he had ever read.

'Here's one we never tried,' Pop said. 'Rolls-Royce.'

'That sounds nice,' Ma said.

'Half vermouth, quarter whisky, quarter gin, dash of orange bitters.'

'Dash you will too,' Ma said, 'with that lot. It'll blow our heads off.'

[Later] 'How about a Chauffeur? Dammit, the Rolls has to have a Chauffeur.' He stood earnestly consulting the *Guide to Better Drinking*. 'One third vermouth, one third whisky, one third gin, dash of angostura. Sounds perfick.'

H.E. Bates *The Darling Buds of May*

THE CONSPIRACY

'Will some bright young physician kindly undertake an investigation as to the exact function of the olive in the Martini? Mind you, I warn you beforehand – I have my suspicions. But what do you think, doctor?'

'Why – ' Andrew stammered. 'I – I hardly know – .'

'My theory!' Challis took pity on him. 'A conspiracy of bar-tenders and inhospitable fellows like our friend Vaughan. An exploitation of the law of Archimedes. By the simple action of displacement they hope to save the gin!'

A. J. Cronin *The Citadel*

A SELECTION OF COCKTAILS AND MIXED DRINKS

Recipes for cocktails and punches, as well as the suggested proportions of their ingredients, vary greatly in books devoted to the subject.

Alexander – 1 part gin, 1 part Crème de Cacao, sweet cream. Shake with ice and strain into glass. Sprinkle with nutmeg. Equally popular is the version where brandy replaces the gin. There is an Alexander's Sister cocktail: 1 part gin, 1 part Crème de Menthe, 1 part cream.

Americano – equal parts of Campari and sweet vermouth are poured into a tall glass over ice cubes. Topped up with soda water and decorated with lemon peel.

Black Russian – 2 oz vodka, 1 oz Kahlua or any coffee-flavoured brandy. 'I'd love a Black Russian.' 'Uh – what goes into it?'

THE AMERICANO

The American Colony is divided into three parts: those who have their cocktails at Leland's or Doney's, a small sect who have them at home, and the third part, a tiny and suspect group, which does not have cocktails. Hayden himself – he had daily only an Americano, that mixture of vermouth and kindness of which no American ever hears till he comes to Italy.

Sinclair Lewis *World So Wide*

'Vodka and – ?' 'Kahlua.' 'As I feared. We don't have any Kahlua.' 'How about a Grasshopper, then?' 'And *its* ingredients are – ?'

John Updike *Roger's Version*

Black Velvet – a fifty-fifty mixture of Guinness and Champagne. The drink is said to have been invented in 1861 at Brooks's Club in London. Prince Albert had died and everyone was in mourning. The club steward decided that even the Champagne should be in mourning and therefore mixed it with Guinness.

In *Stop at Nothing* John Welcome writes: 'Roddy was busy at a table on which were cans of stout and two bottles of Champagne. A large delph jug was also on the table and in this he was expertly mixing the stout and the wine. "It's a bit early for that, isn't it?" I said. "It's never too early for morning magic," was his cheerful reply as he handed me a tall glass. The stout, faintly touched with a golden bloom, frothed and bubbled. I took a sip from the glass. He knew how to mix it, all right. And he was right, too, when he said that there was no drink to touch it in the morning.'

Other mixed drinks which use Guinness include Arthur Narf (half bottled, half draught), Black 'n' Black (with blackcurrant), Black 'n' Tan (with bitter), Blacksmith (with barley wine), Calcutta Cup (with tonic water), Guinness and Lime, Guinness and Mild, Guinness Shandy (with lemonade), Light 'n' Dark (with light ale), Longship (with lager), Midnight (with a dash of port), Red Head (with tomato juice), Top Hat

THE DIFFERENCE

To please Kay, they had started having cocktails every night in the aluminium cocktailshaker. The difference between them was that what she liked was the little formality and what Harald liked was the liquor.

Mary McCarthy *The Group*

(with ginger beer), Trojan Horse (with cola), Two-lane Blacktop (with American dry ginger), Wasp Sting (with orange juice).

Blood and Thunder – a mixture of port and brandy, according to Charles Hindley, in his *Tavern Anecdotes and Sayings*. He adds: 'Formerly much drunk by "swell coachmen", guards and Oxonians, at Hatchet's, and the Gloucester Coffee-house, Piccadilly.'

Bloody Mary – vodka and tomato juice, usually with a dash of Worcestershire sauce added. Garnished with lemon and ice added if required. Said to be a good drink for the morning, especially after heavy drinking the night before. Bloody Mary was the nickname of Queen Mary Tudor (1516–58). She was the daughter of Henry VIII and Catherine of Aragon. Became Queen of England in 1553, married Philip II of Spain 1554. She was firmly Catholic and revived anti-Protestant laws, causing at least 200 Protestants, including Archbishop Cranmer, to be burnt at the stake in the space of four years.

Bronx – this is basically a gin and mixed vermouths, 2 parts dry gin to 1 part dry vermouth, 1 part sweet vermouth. Add a dash of orange juice, shake with ice, strain and serve with a slice of orange. Mentioned in print for the first time in 1919. Bronx derives from the name of a Dutch farmer, Bronck.

Bucks Fizz – orange juice mixed with Champagne. Just as effective with various sparkling wines, or even still white wine. The name comes from Buck's Club in London, where the drink was popular in the 1920s. It is said to have been drunk in France before that date.

Chambre d'Amour – vodka, green Izarra, banana nectar and orange juice.

Champagne Cocktail – 1 lump of sugar soaked in Angostura bitters is put into a Champagne glass. Topped with chilled Champagne, decorated with lemon peel.

Corpse Reviver – a name applied to a number of different cocktail recipes, all of which are claimed to bring one back from the dead after a heavy drinking session. The Savoy Corpse Reviver consists of equal parts of brandy, Fernet Branca and white Crème de Menthe. Non-alcoholic drinks are perhaps to be preferred in these circumstances. The Prairie Oyster is the best known: 2 dashes vinegar, (unbroken) yolk of 1 egg, 1 teaspoon Worcestershire sauce, 1 teaspoonful tomato ketchup, a dash of pepper.

Cuba Libre – the juice of half a lime, with the rind, is put into a tall glass. A measure of rum is added and the glass topped up with cola and ice cubes.

Daiquiri – of the various recipes the simplest is a teaspoonful of sugar, 3 parts Bacardi or other white rum to 1 part lime juice. Shake with ice and strain. In Barbados frozen daiquiris are served in chilled, saucer-type Champagne glasses. Daiquiri is the name of the town in Cuba where the drink was invented. President

John F. Kennedy was especially fond of a daiquiri.

'"Make us all a daiquiri," Stevie said. Angus went on stirring and eventually poured the cloudy opal into a glass, which she sipped from several times. "Mmmm. Bit too sour. Anyway, I think it's better if you make it in the blender. Just a touch of sugar," she said, and waited while Angus did it and poured her another glass. "That's nearer," she said.'

Sumner Locke Elliott *Edens Lost*

Dry Martini – see Martini.

French 65 – 'I ordered up three French 65s. This drink, served in a tall highball glass, is a blend of Champagne, gin, a spot of sugar, a squirt of lemon juice, the whole topped off with a brandy float. Consumed in quantity they can flatten a longshoreman. I drained all three, then weaved to my feet and announced: "As of now I'm on the wagon!"'

Tallulah Bankhead *Tallulah*

'The Cocktail King'. From Punch, *1922.*

Gibson – see Martini.

Gimlet – equal parts of gin (or vodka) and lime juice, stirred with ice. Some people add a small amount of sugar. 'In ten minutes and two gimlets apiece we liked each other exuberantly. Her beauty grew on me, aided by the gin I had drunk.' Han Suyin *A Many Splendoured Thing*. ' "What do you want to drink?" he said. "A gimlet, please," I said, thinking that would fox him. But he reached straight for the vodka. "I'm sorry I haven't any fresh limes," he said. "Will lime juice do?" '

Jilly Cooper *Prudence*

Gin and French – traditional name in Britain for a Martini.

Gin and Italian – traditional name in Britain for gin and sweet vermouth in equal proportions. Often abbreviated to Gin and It.

Gin and tonic –one of the most common mixed drinks. The tonic water contains a small amount of quinine, originally of medicinal value to the British expatriates who began to drink it in the 1930s. Commonly referred to as G and T. Now associated in Britain with an older, middle-class social group.

Gin sling – the formulae for slings vary considerably. One way of making this drink is to dissolve 1 teaspoon sugar in 1

A REASON FOR DRINKING

Jess learned to drink a cocktail in order to get the cherry.

O. Henry *The Rubaiyat of a Scotch Highball*

teaspoon water and add juice of half a lemon. Add 2 oz dry gin. Pour into tall glass over ice-cubes and stir. Add twist of orange peel.

Grasshopper – 1 oz green Crème de Menthe, 1 oz Crème de Cacao, 1 oz cream. Shake with ice. See Black Russian.

Highball – originally a measure of whiskey served over ice-cubes in a tall glass, topped up with soda water and stirred. A twist of lemon added if desired. The practice of substituting ginger ale for soda water, especially with rye whiskey, began during Prohibition. Purists reject it. 'Highball' is also generally used of a drink based on any kind of liquor if served in a tall glass over ice with soda water, ginger ale or other carbonated liquid.

The origin of the term is fully discussed by Thomas Pyles in his *Words and Ways of American English*. He quotes an article in *American Speech* for February 1944. There Professor I. Willis Russell pointed out that *highball* was a term used by railroaders to denote a signal to go ahead, or to go full speed. The use of the term to denote the drink was probably related to this use in railroading. He compared French *rapide* 'express train', an argot term for *vin qui saoule rapidement* 'wine which gets you drunk quickly'. At one time *train direct* 'non-stop train' in slang applied both to a litre of wine and a glass of absinthe. Others have suggested that highball is from a raised glass, resembling a train conductor's raised fist as a signal to depart.

Because highballs are served in high glasses, some have said that 'ball' must have been a slang term for a drink. No documentary evidence to support this assertion has ever been found. The 'highness' is sometimes commented on, as in remarks like: ' "It's terribly cold. Don't you think a small highball would be nice?" "Now, by golly, there's a woman with savvy! I think we could more or less stand a highball if it wasn't too long a one – not over a foot tall!"'

Sinclair Lewis *Babbitt*

'The highballs, gold in the glasses, tasted, as her own never did, the way they looked in the White Rock advertisements.'

Mary McCarthy *The Man in the Brooks Brothers Shirt*

Jack Rose – apple jack (or Calvados), grenadine, lime or lemon.

John Collins – traditionally this is a Tom Collins using Hollands gin instead of dry gin. Some reference sources equate it with the Whiskey Collins (see below).

In and Out – see Martini.

Kir – a mixture of dry white wine and Crème de Cassis. Its popularity in Britain has led to its being made available in ready mixed forms, still and sparkling. Named after Canon Felix Kir, resistance hero and mayor of Dijon, who died at the age of 92. Originally a speciality of Burgundy, where the local rather sharp white wine is ideal for the mix. Elizabeth Jane Howard, in her novel *Getting It Right*, has: '"Now, you can have whisky, or my little concoction. Winthrop and I got rather attached to it when we were in the South of France. It's called Kir." He poured a faintly pink liquid from a jug. It was cool, a bit fruity and rather nice. "It's just white wine with a spot of blackcurrant cordial."' John Ayto would not agree that this is 'getting it right'. He stresses, in *The Glutton's Glossary*, that: 'Crème de Cassis should on no account be replaced by blackcurrant cordial or other inauthentic substitutes.'

Manhattan – whiskey with vermouth. Sweet vermouth is usual, but a dry vermouth version is possible. One part

LUNATIC'S BROTH

About once a month he used to get drunk on Red Lisbon – a deadly and incalculable wine concocted of the squeezed-out scrapings of rotted port casks and laced with methylated spirits – a terrible drink which smites the higher centres as with a sandbag. It is otherwise known as Lunatic's Broth or Red Lizzie.

Gerald Kersh *I Got References*

vermouth to 2 parts whiskey. Stir with ice and strain into glass. Sweet Manhattan is served with a cherry, dry with an olive. First recorded in 1890.

Martini – also called the Dry Martini. A mixture of gin and dry vermouth, the proportions according to individual taste. Pour gin over cracked ice, add vermouth and stir. Serve in chilled glasses. An alternative is to serve the Martini on the rocks, with the ice-cubes in the glass.

The drink began as equal parts of the two basic components. Since the 1950s it has been fashionable in the USA to favour the gin at the expense of the vermouth. At least 4 parts of gin to 1 of vermouth is now normal. An extra-dry Martini is 7 or more parts of gin to 1 of vermouth. Legendary dry Martinis are made by waving the bottle of vermouth at the gin, or merely whispering the word vermouth near the rim of the glass. For drinking at home Bob Burton, bartender at the Ritz Hotel in London, recommends opening a bottle of gin, topping it up with dry vermouth and recapping it. It should then be kept in the fridge and shaken when needed.

Individual drinkers also have their own preferences about the inclusion or not of a cocktail olive. (An extra-dry Martini with a cocktail onion becomes a Gibson.) A Martini drunk between two glasses of beer is known as a Martini sandwich. ' "Make it a double Martini, almost no vermouth." "That's about as pale as they come isn't it? That's what they call an 'in and out'." '

John P. Marquand *Women and Thomas Harrow*

Mint julep – Frederick Marryat (1792–1848), captain in the Royal Navy and novelist, kept a diary of his travels in the USA. He wrote: 'I must descant a little upon the mint julep, as it is, with the thermometer at 100 degrees, one of the most delightful and insinuating potations that ever was invented, and may be drunk with equal satisfaction when the thermometer is as low as 70 degrees.

'There are many varieties such as those composed of Claret, Madeira, etc., but the ingredients of the real mint julep are as follows. Put into a tumbler about a dozen sprigs of the tender shoots of mint, upon them put a spoonful of white sugar, and equal proportions of Peach and Common Brandy, so as to fill it up one-third, or perhaps a little less. Then take rasped or pounded ice, and fill up the tumbler. Epicures rub the lips of the tumbler with a piece of fresh pineapple. As the ice melts, you drink.'

A footnote in H.L. Mencken's *The American Language* says: 'The old and extremely bitter controversy over the spirituous content of the julep need not be gone into here. In Kentucky and its spiritual dependencies bourbon is always used, but in the Maryland Free State it would be an indecorum verging upon indecency to use anything save rye whiskey. There is every reason to believe that in the first juleps the motive power was supplied by brandy.'

The mint julep is certainly an American invention, but the word 'julep', which is ultimately from Persian and means 'rose water', was used in English from the 15th century for a syrupy drink used to disguise the bad taste of a medicine. The American mint juleps are first mentioned at the beginning of the 19th century.

Negroni – gin, sweet vermouth and Campari. See p. 207.

Old-Fashioned – muddle a cube of sugar, dash of Angostura bitters and teaspoonful of water. Add 2 oz blended whiskey (or any other spirits instead) and stir. Add twist of lemon peel and ice-cubes. Decorate with a cherry and slices of orange and lemon. Serve with a swizzle stick. One of the earliest definitions of 'cocktail' ever found in print (1806) gives the formula 'spirits of any kind, sugar, water and bitters', which is almost an Old-Fashioned. It seems to deserve its name. 'She insisted on a real public house with atmosphere, and then was aggrieved to find, in the private bar

THE COCKTAIL HABIT

He had never had the cocktail habit until he knew her. 'Your class rite,' he called it, and she was not sure whether he meant Class of '33 or social class; back in Salt Lake City, her parents never dreamed of having liquor even when they entertained, despite the fact that Dads could get prescription whisky. But in the East it was the social thing to do.

Mary McCarthy *The Group*

of the "Black Swan", that the landlord had never heard of an Old-Fashioned.'
Monica Dickens *Mariana*

Orange Blossom – American version of the gin and orange; equal parts of dry gin and orange juice. Small amout of sugar can be added. Shaken with ice, strained into glass.

Piña Colada – 3 tots Malibu liqueur, dash of lemon juice, top up with pineapple juice. Mix in blender, serve with straw. Decorate with pineapple chunks. An alternative is to use Goya cream of coconut, white rum and pineapple juice. Spanish *piña colada* means 'strained pineapple'.

Pink Gin – a drop or two of Angostura bitters is put into a glass and swirled round. Surplus bitters are then thrown away and a measure of gin is added. Iced water to taste. Plymouth gin is recommended by some Royal Navy drinkers. The drink must only be a very pale pink.

Planter's Punch – traditionally made with 'one of sour, two of sweet, three of strong and four of weak'. In other words, 1 part lime juice, 2 parts sugar syrup, 3 parts rum, 4 parts crushed ice. The lime juice may be replaced by lemon juice. Bitters and grenadine may also be used. A popular Caribbean tourist drink.

Ramos Gin Fizz – juice of half a lemon, egg white, 1 teaspoon sugar, 2 oz dry gin, 1 tablespoon cream. Shake with ice and strain into a tall glass. Top up with soda water and stir. ' "You need a drink," he said with the air of a diagnostician. "A drink," she answered bitterly. "I'm sick of the drinks we've been having. Gin, whisky, rum, what else is there?" He took her into a bar, and she cried, but he bought her a fancy mixed drink, something called a Ramos gin fizz, and she was a little appeased because she had never had one before.'
Mary McCarthy, 'Cruel and Barbarous Treatment' in *The Company She Keeps*

Sazerac – 1 lump of sugar, 1 dash of Angostura bitters, 2 oz rye whiskey. Stir and drain into a cooled glass. Add a dash of Pernod and a twist of lemon. This drink is associated especially with New Orleans, and is said to have been made originally with brandy supplied by Sazerac du Forge et Fils, of Limoges. (Sazerac is a French surname/placename.) The rye whiskey later replaced the brandy. 'Late every afternoon Peony was at Winifred Homeward's office, mixing Sazerac cocktails . . .'
Sinclair Lewis *Gideon Planish*

Sherry Cobbler – half fill a glass with ice-cubes, add a teaspoon of sugar, top up with sherry, garnish with orange or pineapple. Drink through a straw.

Sidecar – 1 part lemon juice, 1 part Cointreau, 2 parts brandy. Shake with ice. Liqueurs other than Cointreau can be

---

THE ROUND HEELER

He started to mix two highballs at the bar. He knew what the build-up called for: a few suavely administered doses of the special drink called the Round Heeler . . . drinks loaded with three or four jiggers but never mixed, so the first sips would taste real harmless and by the time they were down to the bottom their taste buds were slugged.

Bernard Wolfe *The Late Risers*

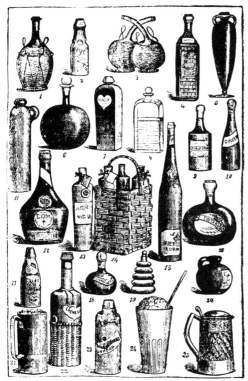

An illustration from Mrs. Beeton's famous book on household management.

bartender. 'She and old Marty were drinking Tom Collinses – in the middle of December, for God's sake. They didn't know any better.'

J.D. Salinger *The Catcher in the Rye*

Vodkatini – a Martini with vodka substituted for gin.

Whiskey Collins – 5–6 dashes of Gomme Syrup, juice of a small lemon, 2 oz whiskey, ice. Shake well and strain into glass.

White Lady – white of 1 egg, 1 teaspoon of sugar, 1 teaspoon sweet cream, measure of dry gin. Shake with ice and strain into glass.

Zombie – 1 oz pineapple juice, juice of 1 lime, juice of 1 small orange, 1 teaspoon sugar, half oz apricot brandy, 4 oz rum (white and dark), crushed ice. Blend at low speed, strain into frosted glass. Decorate with pineapple and cherries. 'He didn't actually order champagne but a couple of innocent-tasting drinks called "Zombies".'

Sinclair Lewis *Gideon Planish*

used. Proportions vary in different reference sources.

Stinger – 1 part white Crème de Menthe, 3 parts brandy. Shake with ice and strain into glasses. 'Tiffany ordered a Stinger made with white *Crème de Menthe* and Bond ordered the same.'

Ian Fleming *Diamonds Are Forever*

Tequini – a Martini substituting tequila for the gin.

Tom Collins – juice of half a lemon, teaspoon of powdered sugar, 2 oz dry gin. Shake with ice and strain into glass. Add ice-cube and soda-water, stir gently. Decorate with lemon, orange and a cherry. Serve with a straw. Said to be named after its inventor, a distinguished

Joseph Wambaugh, in *The Choir Boys*, has the following exchange between a policeman and a black barman: '"A Bombay martini straight up, very dry, with a twist, please." The bartender said: "I been workin' hard all night, chief. Can't you just make it easy on me?" "J and B and water?" offered Harold Bloomguard, rightly

assuming from the number of black bandits who asked for J & B Scotch before sticking up a liquor store that the bartender would have no problem filling that order.'

There are other ways of dealing with the problem. In his novel *Sybil*, Benjamin Disraeli has 'two American gentlemen singing out for Sherry Cobbler' in an English inn. 'Don't know what it is,' says the landlord, to one of his staff. 'Give them our bar-mixture; if they complain, say it is the Mowbray Slap-bang, and no mistake.' He adds, shrewdly: 'Must have a name, Mr Morley; name's everything.'

Modern real-life bartenders, or mixologists, presumably have by them a copy of *The Savoy Cocktail Book* or *Mr Boston's Official Bartender's Guide*. My copy of the latter book was published in 1981, and even then had reached its 61st edition, with eight million copies sold since 1935. It deals with about a thousand cocktails, but over 7000 cocktails have been registered with the American Bartenders' Association. Some of them are available commercially in ready-made form. Pimms is well-known in Britain, Heublein in the USA.

Both books also give general advice about the

THE SHERRY COBBLER

Tapley produced a very large tumbler, piled up to the brim with little blocks of clear transparent ice, through which one or two thin slices of lemon, and a golden liquid of delicious appearance, appealed from the still depths below to the loving eye of the spectator.

'What do you call this?' said Martin.

But Mr Tapley made no answer, merely plunging a reed into the mixture – which caused a pleasant commotion among the pieces of ice – and signifying by an expressive gesture that it was to be pumped up through that agency by the enraptured drinker. Martin took the glass, with an astonished look; applied his lips to the reed; and cast up his eyes once in ecstasy. He paused no more until the goblet was drained to the last drop.

'There, sir!' said Mark, taking it from him with a triumphant face; 'if ever you should happen to be dead beat again, when I ain't in the way, all you've got to do is to ask the nearest man to go and fetch a cobbler.'

'To go and fetch a cobbler!' repeated Martin.

'This wonderful invention, sir,' said Mark, tenderly patting the empty glass, 'is called a cobbler. Sherry-cobbler when you name it long; cobbler, when you name it short.'

Charles Dickens *Martin Chuzzlewit*

ALL SHOOK UP

Sometimes the ship pitched and sometimes she rolled and sometimes she stood quite still and shivered all over, poised above an abyss of dark water; then she would go swooping down like a scenic railway train into a windless hollow and up again with a rush into the gale; sometimes she would burrow her path, with convulsive nosings and scramblings like a terrier in a rabbit hole; and sometimes she would drop dead like a lift.

'It's just exactly like being inside a cocktail shaker,' said Miles Malpractice.

Evelyn Waugh *Vile Bodies*

art of mixing cocktails. Ian Fleming would presumably have been interested in this note: 'Since the *Savoy Cocktail Book* first appeared in 1930, there has been a change in the preparation of cocktails. At that time it was considered correct to shake most cocktails: now it is regarded as wrong to do this unless in the ingredients there is a fruit juice. There are exceptions to this rule, but briefly it is safe to stir a clear mixture and shake a cloudy one. In the case of clear mixtures to be served cold, the liquid should be poured into a cocktail shaker and then strained into the glasses, but not shaken.'

James Bond, it will be remembered, thought otherwise. 'The waiter brought the Martinis, shaken and not stirred, as Bond had stipulated.' (Ian Fleming *Diamonds Are Forever*.)

THE WORD 'COCKTAIL'

Before one gets to individually-named cocktails, there is the problem of where 'cocktail' itself came from. The earliest occurrence of the expression in print was in an American periodical in 1806: 'Cock tail, then, is a stimulating liquor, composed of spirits of any kind, sugar, water and bitters. It is vulgarly called bittered sling.' This and other early references suggest that cocktail was originally the name of a particular drink, not a generic term.

The other meaning of 'cocktail' at the beginning of the 19th century was a horse which had had its tail shortened, usually a hunter or coachhorse, not a thoroughbred. In slang, the word was also used of a harlot, and of a person attempting to be a gentleman whose family background was deficient.

Many guesses have been made, all of them unconvincing, as to how cocktail came to be applied to a mixed drink. They range from a connection with French *coquetier* 'egg cup' and *coquetel* (supposedly a French dialect word for a mixed drink, but no one has been able to trace it), to links with cock-ale and an Aztec princess Xochitl. The last-named is supposed to have given a mixed drink to a king with romantic results.

Until documentary evidence is found from the beginning of the 19th century which settles the matter, the origin of cocktail remains a mystery. This conveniently allows everyone to have his own pet theory. Dickens makes a remark in his *American Notes*: 'The bar is a large room with a stone floor, and there people stand and smoke, and lounge about, all the evening, dropping in and out as the humour takes them. There, too, the stranger is initiated into the mysteries of gin-sling, cock-tail, sangaree, mint-julep, sherry-cobbler, timber-doodle, and other rare drinks.'

Dickens is referring to Boston in 1842, and it is the 'timber-doodle' which strikes me as significant. It is another name for the American *woodcock*, a game bird, and at the time was clearly being used as the name for a mixed drink. Is it the tail of the woodcock that is referred to in cocktail, and if so, why?

Meanwhile we can say that the word has been highly productive, giving rise to variants such as 'mocktail' – a non-alcoholic cocktail – and verbal compounds which range from the cocktail dress for wearing at the cocktail party (or by barmaids, according to Doris Lessing, in *Landlocked*) to the cocktail sausages which may be eaten there. We have fruit cocktails and prawn cocktails and even Molotov cocktails. The word is now metaphorically used of almost any kind of mixture.

INVENTING COCKTAILS

Trying to invent a new cocktail was something of a national sport in the 1920s and 30s. Eric Linklater made it a sub-theme of his novel *Poet's Pub*. The barman, Holly, invents two blue cocktails: 'One glass shone with a liquid palely blue as April skies, the other more nobly glowed with a darker hue, the colour of darkest blue-bells in a wood. "Blue cocktails," said the little man. "Nobody's ever made one before, not proper blue, like these. Mr Keith, I'm an inventor!" "They're like butterflies," said Joan. "Can I taste them?" "A cocktail after dinner? Certainly not." Professor Benbow was indignant at the suggestion.'

There follows the all-important question of naming. Heaven is suggested for the light blue version, though the inventor himself has Butterfly and Bluebell in mind. Another suggestion, inevitably, is that they be named Oxford and Cambridge.

WITCH'S COUGH MIXTURE

He arrived in the kitchen carrying two small glasses filled with dark, reddish-brown liquid. 'I made us a drink,' he said. She sipped it. It tasted like cough mixture for a witch, she thought: very nasty, *and* burning. 'What is it?' she gasped.

'I don't know. I just used what bottles you had to hand.'

She tried to visualize the bottles in the sitting-room – some very old cooking rum, a lot of French vermouth, and the dregs of some pure Polish spirit that Cressy had given.

'I put a spot of cherry linctus in for the colour,' he said complacently.

Elizabeth Jane Howard *After Julius*

Beverly Nichols also commented on the cocktail-invention phenomenon in *Self*: 'Nancy proceeded to pour various liquids into the silver flask. "This is a very special one," she said, "quite my own invention. The great thing about it is that there's absolutely no vermouth in it. You haven't any vodka, have you? Just a very tiny drop." "The hand that makes the cocktail rules the world." "Or at any rate the better part of it," added Nancy. "I think they're horrid things myself," said Helen.'

That last remark is a useful reminder that there are many who consider cocktails to be absurd. Their argument runs that drinks such as whisky and brandy, champagne and hock have been prepared with great care and skill, and that mixing them makes a mockery of all that effort. There is something in this, but drinks such as bitters, or the highly rectified spirits such as gin and vodka, can improve considerably when mixed with something suitable.

There are recipes for some of the better-known mixed drinks on pp. 208–15. Some of them are well enough known to warrant entries in general dictionaries. The *Concise Oxford Dictionary*, for example, deals with a pink gin, a Bloody Mary, a manhattan, a daiquiri, a black velvet, a sherry cobbler. (It also mentions certain trade names, treating them as meaningful words. Martini is deemed to have acquired this status, but there are dozens of others in everyday use which are not recognised.)

Included in the selection above are those drinks which one might reasonably be expected to have heard of and perhaps tried. Others are there because they are mentioned in literature or are interesting for one reason or another. But recipes, as dedicated mixologists will tell you, are only part of the story. Here is that great punch-enthusiast, Charles Dickens, making the point in *Our Mutual Friend*: He is describing cobblers' punch, but by chance his remark might equally well apply to the mixture of fact and fiction, statistics and anecdotes, poems and pictures, which have gone into the making of this book. 'It's difficult to impart the receipt for it because, however particular you may be in allotting your materials, so much will depend upon the individual gifts, and there being a feeling thrown into it.'

OPAL HUSH

'Who is for opal hush?' she asked, and all, except the American girl and the picture dealer, who preferred whisky, declared that their throats were dry for nothing else. Wondering what the strange-named drink might be, I too asked for opal, and she read the puzzlement in my face. 'You make it like this,' she said, and squirted lemonade from a siphon into a glass of red claret, so that a beautiful amethystine foam rose shimmering to the brim. 'The Irish poets over in Dublin called it so . . .'

Arthur Ransome *Bohemia In London*

INDEX